S0-GQF-330

Ethics and Remembrance

Ethics and Remembrance in the Post-Holocaust Poetry of Nelly Sachs and Rose Ausländer is the first comparative study in English of two German-Jewish women poets who survived the Nazi genocide but did not escape its effects. The study begins with a reading of Sachs's and Ausländer's poetry in the context of the wider scope of Holocaust literature. Focusing on the poet as a witness who bears the double burden of survival and remembrance, Kathrin Bower argues that the "work of memory" achieved by Ausländer and Sachs exemplifies the complexity of poetic reflection on trauma and history. A commonality in the lives of both poets was the strength of their bond to their mothers, a connection which had an enormous impact on their perceptions, relationships, and survival.

In addition to aesthetic considerations, the book concentrates on the implications of Sachs's and Ausländer's poetic engagement for an "ethics of remembrance." The poetic dialogue with memory exemplified in these poets' works offers a model for working through the trauma of the past that has significance not only for Holocaust studies, but also for investigations of memory and trauma. Sachs's and Ausländer's poems are conscientious yet troubled efforts at representing the diversity of individual and collective suffering that embrace both Jewish experience and the human condition. They can be read as subjective and at the same time universal injunctions to an awareness of the connections, divisions, and tensions that memory brings to bear on social relations.

Kathrin M. Bower is assistant professor of German at the University of Richmond (Virginia). She has previously published on Ausländer, Sachs, Holocaust poetry, and contemporary German film.

Studies in German Literature, Linguistics, and Culture

Edited by James Hardin
(*South Carolina*)

43552453

Kathrin M. Bower

ETHICS AND REMEMBRANCE

IN THE POETRY OF NELLY SACHS AND ROSE AUSLÄNDER

PT
2637
A4184
Z593
2000

CAMDEN HOUSE

OHIO UNIVERSITY
LIBRARY

88 2/13/01

Copyright © 2000 Kathrin M. Bower

All Rights Reserved. Except as permitted under current legislation,
no part of this work may be photocopied, stored in a retrieval system,
published, performed in public, adapted, broadcast, transmitted,
recorded, or reproduced in any form or by any means,
without the prior permission of the copyright owner.

First published 2000
by Camden House

Camden House is an imprint of Boydell & Brewer Inc.
PO Box 41026, Rochester, NY 14604–4126 USA
and of Boydell & Brewer Limited
PO Box 9, Woodbridge, Suffolk IP12 3DF, UK

ISBN: 1–57113–191–4

Library of Congress Cataloging-in-Publication Data

Bower, Kathrin M., 1963–
    Ethics and remembrance in the poetry of Nelly Sachs and Rose Ausländer /
Kathrin M. Bower.
        p. cm. – (Studies in German literature, linguistics, and culture)
Includes bibliographical references and index.
ISBN 1–57113–191–4 (alk. paper)
1. Sachs, Nelly, 1891–1970—Criticism and interpretation. 2. Ausländer, Rose,
1901–1988—Criticism and interpretation. 3. Holocaust, Jewish (1939–1945),
in literature. I. Title. II. Studies in German literature, linguistics, and culture
(Unnumbered)

PT2637.A4184 Z593 2000
831'.91409358—dc21

                                                    00–026514

A catalogue record for this title is available from the British Library.

This publication is printed on acid-free paper.
Printed in the United States of America

WITHDRAWN

To my parents,
whose biographies instilled in me
a deep appreciation for both
remembrance and ethics

Contents

Acknowledgments

A S I LOOK BACK over the years I spent thinking, reading, and writing about the ideas presented in this book, I realize that it would never have achieved the form it has today without the many encounters and relationships with other scholars, readers, works, and institutions that occurred during that interval of time. The book has matured and grown through this diversity of experiences and in the process has become an archive of memory in its own right. In that spirit, I would like to take the opportunity here to remember and thank those who helped further my work and my thinking along the way. I am grateful to the Leo Baeck Institute and DAAD for a summer grant that enabled me to examine archival materials on both Rose Ausländer and Nelly Sachs; the congenial and knowledgeable staff at the Stadtsbibliothek Dortmund; the Heinrich-Heine Institut in Düsseldorf; and the Bibliothek Germania Judaica in Cologne. Helmut Braun was an inspiration, for his unflagging dedication to the promotion of Rose Ausländer's work, his expansive contributions of time and information in numerous conversations, and for unprecedented access to materials in the Rose-Ausländer-Dokumentationszentrum. Nancy Kaiser, Klaus Berghahn, and Marc Silberman provided many thoughtful comments and criticisms on an earlier version of this manuscript. The Franz Rosenzweig Center for German-Jewish Studies at the Hebrew University in Jerusalem sponsored me as a post-doctoral fellow, an experience that greatly enriched the present study. The generous support of the University of Richmond encouraged the transformation of so many electronic files into a bound volume. Finally, I would like to thank the readers and editors at Camden House, whose informed and attentive engagement with my manuscript inspired further refinements of the text.

The poems of Rose Ausländer are reprinted with the permission of S.Fischer Verlag and Pfaffenweiler Presse. Nelly Sachs's poems and the excerpts from her letters are reprinted with the permission of Suhrkamp Verlag. Else Lasker-Schüler's "Mein Volk" is also quoted with the permission of Suhrkamp Verlag.

Abbreviations

Works by Rose Ausländer:

Gesammelte Werke in acht Bänden. Edited by Helmut Braun. Frankfurt am Main: Fischer, 1984–1990. [I–VIII = Abbreviated as volume and page number]

Works by Nelly Sachs:

Fahrt ins Staublose. 1961. Frankfurt am Main: Suhrkamp, 1988. [*FS*]

Suche nach Lebenden. Edited by Margaretha and Bengt Holmqvist. Frankfurt am Main: Suhrkamp, 1971. [*SL*]

Introduction

Every being cries out silently to be read differently.
— Simone Weil[1]

Ire zikhroynes
her memories
will become monuments
ire zikhroynes
will cast shadows.

— Irena Klepfisz[2]

Through remembrance comes redemption; by going back one
also moves toward the future. . . .

— Susan Handelman[3]

WHILE RECOGNITION OF THE ACHIEVEMENTS of poets Nelly Sachs
(1891–1970) and Rose Ausländer (1901–1988) is certainly not
lacking in German poetry anthologies and critical reviews of their work,
there have been few extensive analyses of the body of their writings, and
none in English exploring the themes, impulses, and resonance that their
lives and poems clearly share. My purpose in this study is to present
readings of Nelly Sachs's and Rose Ausländer's poetry in the context of
the events, philosophies, and traditions that impinged upon them, not
in order to fix their writings as topical artifacts, but rather to reveal
their continued significance in the pursuit of what Saul Friedländer has
called "probing the limits of representation."[4] The Holocaust for some,
perhaps most famously Theodor Adorno, represents a limit to representation, a boundary in both a literary and an ethical sense that cannot
and even should not be crossed. Adorno's oft-quoted and frequently
misapplied dictum against writing poetry after Auschwitz can be seen as

---

[1] Simone Weil, *Gravity and Grace*, trans. Arthur Wills (1952; Lincoln: U of Nebraska P, 1997), 188.

[2] From the poem "*Di rayze aheym* / The journey home," Irena Klepfisz, *A Few
Words in the Mother Tongue* (Portland, OR: Eighth Mountain Press, 1990), 224.

[3] Susan Handelman, *Fragments of Redemption: Jewish Thought and Literary Theory in Benjamin, Scholem, and Levinas* (Bloomington/Indianapolis: Indiana UP,
1991), 171.

[4] See Saul Friedländer, ed. *Probing the Limits of Representation: Nazism and the
"Final Solution"* (Cambridge, MA: Harvard UP, 1992).

evidence of a perceived radical disruption between aesthetics and ethics, most dramatically concentrated in the corpus of the lyric poem.[5] While Adorno was to later modify and modulate his interdiction,[6] the tone of his original statement still lingers.

Although the aesthetic and ethical power evident in the poems of Nelly Sachs and Rose Ausländer speaks for itself, it is prudent to consider the impact of Adorno's legacy on the reception of their poetry as well as that of other writers who have sought to give voice to the catastrophe in the medium of poetic language.[7] In an understanding of representation as a wedding of aesthetics and ethics or what Adrienne Rich refers to as "a long dialogue between art and justice,"[8] poetry has a special place. While poetry cannot redeem or repair loss, Rich argues quoting John Berger that "it defies the space which separates ... by its continual labour of reassembling what has been scattered."[9] What has been scattered are the memories of those whose lives were prematurely extinguished, and the communities and cultures that cannot be reconstructed but that have nevertheless left their traces in the collective memories of a dispersed people.

For Nelly Sachs and Rose Ausländer, writing itself became an act of recuperation and reflection, not only in relation to memories of the past, but also in pursuit of the integrity and continuity of the self in a morally disrupted world. As acts of remembrance, their poems are constituted by the relationship between the poetic voice and the poem. In

---

[5] See Theodor Adorno, "Kulturkritik und Gesellschaft," in *Prismen. Kulturkritik und Gesellschaft* (Frankfurt am Main: Suhrkamp, 1955) 31: ". . . nach Auschwitz ein Gedicht zu schreiben, ist barbarisch. . . ."

[6] See Adorno, "Engagement," in *Noten zur Literatur III* (Frankfurt am Main: Suhrkamp, 1965) 125–26: "Den Satz, nach Auschwitz noch Lyrik zu schreiben, sei barbarisch, möchte ich nicht mildern: negativ ist darin der Impuls ausgesprochen, der die engagierte Dichtung beseelt. (. . .) Aber wahr bleibt auch Enzensbergers Entgegnung, die Dichtung müsse eben diesem Verdikt standhalten, so also sein, daß sie nicht durch ihre bloße Existenz nach Auschwitz dem Zynismus sich überantwortete. Ihre eigene Situation ist paradox, nicht erst, wie man zu ihr sich verhält. Das Übermaß an realem Leiden duldet kein Vergessen. . . ." Here Adorno ultimately comes out on the side of remembrance, although he desires this an a form that does not rob the victims of the ethical integrity that he adamantly insists is their due.

[7] As the editor of the volume *Lyrik nach Auschwitz? Adorno und die Dichter* (Stuttgart: Reclam, 1995), Petra Kiedaisch has done a great service to scholars of Holocaust poetry. This collection of essays and excerpts brings together both Adorno's various statements on the subject and the responses to his proclamations from writers and critics beginning in the 1950s and continuing into the early 1990s.

[8] Adrienne Rich, "Defy the Space That Separates," *The Nation*, October 7, 1996, 34.

[9] Ibid., 31.

this relationship, the poetic voice assumes the role of witness, while the poem mediates between the testimony and its recipient, the implied reader. In his discussion of the interplay between testimony and witnessing, Dori Laub argues that it is in the act of testifying, of giving voice to the event, that real witnessing occurs.[10] Further, the relationship between the testifier and the listener is marked by a shared responsibility for the narrative that results from their encounter. In the absence of a listener, the testifier may resort to the construction of an "internal witness" with whom the dialogue of remembrance takes place.[11] In one form, this constructed Other or internal witness parallels the role that the poem assumes for the poet in the absence of an interlocutor with whom to share the responsibility for the poet's testimony.

My approach to the poetry discussed in the present study is not only one of interpretation; I also attempt to locate within and beyond the poems a theory of ethics that grows out of the dialogical impulses that animate them. In my use of the term "ethics" I am distinguishing it from another term that often seems to share the same semantic space but deserves a separate category.[12] In contrast to "morality," which I define as a fixed set of standards or norms determining and distinguishing "good" and "bad," ethics is a process, both interactive and negotiable, but always aimed at what a social consensus has determined to be "right" behavior. The allusion to the combination of social consensus and "right" behavior in the preceding statement is of extreme importance in distinguishing ethics and morality, for as Peter Haas points out in his provocative study *Morality after Auschwitz: The Radical Challenge of the Nazi Ethic*, it is the system of behaviors that constitutes an ethics, not a universal standard of good and evil.[13] The ethics that emerge out

---

[10] See Shoshana Felman and Dori Laub, *Testimony: Crises of Witnessing in Literature, Psychoanalysis, and History* (New York: Routledge, 1992), 85–86.

[11] Felman and Laub, 87.

[12] In my distinction between "ethics" and "morality," I am following in somewhat modified form the definitions Paul Ricoeur outlines in the seventh study contained in the collection *Oneself as Another* (trans. Kathleen Blamey. Chicago/London: U of Chicago P, 1992), 170: ". . . I reserve the term 'ethics' for the *aim* of an accomplished life and the term 'morality' for the articulation of this aim in *norms* characterized at once by the claim to universality and by an effect of constraint. . . ."

[13] Thus in Haas's analysis, the Nazis too were operating under an ethics in that they had constructed a coherent system of behavior in which the concepts of "good" and "bad" had been redefined according to the precepts of Nazi ideology. Haas's *Morality after Auschwitz* (Philadelphia: Fortress Press, 1988) is a daring and ambitious attempt at analyzing the Holocaust from a perspective outside of any appeal to universal standards of "good" and "evil," as he himself suggests in his opening

of Sachs's and Ausländer's writings represent a very different phenomena from what Haas observes in his study. The "ethics of remembrance" that evolve out of their works focus on the role of the poet as
witness and on the fashioning of the poem not only as metaphorical
testimony, but also as a kind of linguistic witness to the poet's act of
transformational remembrance. This doubling of the witness role
through the poet and the poem reveals a level of meta-awareness in the
poetic process, whereby the act of witnessing is simultaneously filtered
through the activity of self-reflection.

The necessity of dialogue in the unfolding and realization of this
ethics of remembrance points to a condition of mutuality or responsibility between the I and the Thou, the Self and the Other of this discourse. In encountering this relationship in Sachs's and Ausländer's
poetry, it is incumbent upon the reader to assume the role of the Thou.
Lyric poetry, by virtue of its form and formulation, demands the active
involvement and commitment of the reader if there is to be a production of meaning or an achievement of understanding. This condition of
shared obligation further enables a shift in interpretations of the Holocaust away from the focus on morality in terms of culpability and guilt
to an engagement with ethics in terms of responsibility and "right" action. In the area of post-Holocaust moral theory, the philosopher Emmanuel Levinas has done much to demonstrate the connections
between ethical behavior and the responsibility to the "other."[14] It is
part of my project here to apply aspects of his thought on the relationship between the self and the other to the interactive and ongoing process of remembrance and the processing of memory evident both in the
biographies and the poetry of Nelly Sachs and Rose Ausländer.

---

chapter (13–14): "The thesis I am developing and testing here is that any ethic, even
one as brutal as the Nazis', can become dominant if it is internally consistent and can
be made persuasive to a sufficiently large population. That it is the formal characteristic of an ethic that makes it viable, not its particular content, seems to be the overarching lesson of the Holocaust in Europe."

[14] In *Time and the Other*, trans. Richard Cohen (Pittsburgh: Duquesne UP,
1987), Levinas presents his concept of responsibility in relation to the other as a
condition of identity that is in a sense both answerable to and independent of historical time (111–12): "In the ethical anteriority of responsibility, for-the-other, in its
priority over deliberation, there is a past irreducible to a presence that it must have
been. This past is without reference to an identity naively — or naturally — assured
of its right to presence, where everything must have begun. In this responsibility I
am thrown back toward what has never been my fault or my deed, toward what has
never been my presence, and has never come into memory. (. . .) It is the significance of a past that concerns me . . . and is 'my business' outside of all reminiscence,
re-tention, re-presentation [*sic*], or reference to a remembered present."

Although they were born in different countries, Nelly Sachs in Germany and Rose Ausländer in Austria-Hungary, the two women shared a common upbringing in the German cultural tradition. As children in enlightened, bourgeois households, both Sachs and Ausländer were educated and avid readers of the classics of German literature, particularly German Romanticism, as well as of a variety of Jewish and Christian texts. Both initially attended public schools, but then received instruction from private tutors. In Sachs's case her protective and doting parents found her too fragile for public school and, after a period of home tutoring, placed her in an exclusive private school for girls. Rose Ausländer's education was largely directed by her mother, who played a significant role in inculcating her daughter with a respect and an appreciation for the German literary classics. This carefully directed yet enlightened education, particularly the early exposure to works of German Romanticism, was to have a lasting impact on both poets' views of the world.

Nelly Sachs, born in 1891 in Berlin as the only child of William and Margarete Sachs, was raised in a comfortable, bourgeois household where she intently pursued her interests in music, dance, and Romantic literature. Her earliest writings testify to her familiarity and fascination with Romanticism as well as her affinity with mysticism.[15] Her parents belonged to the Berlin Jewish community in name only, contributing financially but not attending synagogue or celebrating traditional Jewish holidays. In this home environment, Sachs developed a sense of self that was defined neither by racial nor by religious categories, so that when she was once referred to as a Jewess in her school, she was confused as to what it meant.[16] It was not until the Nazis assumed control of Germany's ideological destiny that Nelly Sachs was forced to confront her Jewish heritage and reassess her relationship to Germany and her identity as a German and a Jew. The disparity and conflict between these simultaneous identities would trouble her for the rest of her life, further complicated by her unshakeable self-understanding as a German-speaking poet.[17] Partly in response to the forced attribution of a

---

[15] See *Legenden und Erzählungen* (Berlin: F. W. Mayer, 1921).

[16] See Bengt Holmqvist, "Die Sprache der Sehnsucht," *Das Buch der Nelly Sachs* (1968; Frankfurt am Main: Suhrkamp, 1977), 25.

[17] In contrast to Paul Celan, Nelly Sachs did not experience a conflict of loyalties as an exile writing in German. Her affinity with the German language transcended the post-Holocaust perception shared by writers such as Celan that it was a language forever tainted by Nazism. Michael Braun goes so far as to argue that for Sachs there were no "disappeared" words in the German language, she continued to use and call upon the entire spectrum of vocabulary at her disposal. See Birgit Lermen and Mi-

Jewish identity in Nazi Germany, Sachs became fascinated with Hasidic
mysticism, seeing in it affinities to the mysticism of Jakob Böhme and
Christian mystics she had admired before the Nazis came to power.[18]
This fascination with mysticism and the mystical belief in transcendence
would play a central role in her subsequent writings and survival during
and after the Holocaust. Through the assistance of German friends and
the support of Prince Eugen among others, Nelly Sachs was able to flee
to Sweden together with her aging mother in 1940. She settled in
Stockholm and managed to eke out a modest existence by translating
and writing poetry. Although she applied for and was granted Swedish
citizenship in 1952 and remained there until her death in 1970, she
never truly felt at home in Sweden or in the Swedish language and remained loyal to her mother tongue as the medium for her poetry.

Ten years Nelly Sachs's junior, Rose Ausländer was born Rosalie
Scherzer in 1901 to Sigmund and Etie Scherzer and grew up in a traditional Jewish household. Unlike Nelly Sachs, Rosalie was not an only
child, and in 1906 her younger brother, Maximilian was born. She
would remain close to her brother all her life, despite the hardships that
pulled them apart and the geographical distances that often separated
them. In the cultural melting pot of Czernowitz, the Scherzer family
practiced Jewish customs and rituals but without religious dogmatism.
As a girl, Rosalie was instructed in both Hebrew and Yiddish, languages
that remained foreign to Nelly Sachs. Because of Sigmund Scherzer's
background as a rabbinical student in Sadagora, renowned as a center for
Jewish learning both orthodox and mystical, readings from the Torah as
well as from the Kabbalah were a regular occurrence in the Scherzer
household.[19] As a student at the university in Czernowitz, Rosalie became interested in the philosophy and teachings of Benedict Spinoza and
the work of Constantin Brunner. Ethical philosophy interested her more
than mysticism and her faith was one tempered with philosophical re-

---

chael Braun, *Nelly Sachs "an letzter Atemspitze des Lebens"* (Bonn: Bouvier Verlag,
1998), 56.

[18] Gisela Dischner argues that Sachs's early fascination with the Christian mystical
quality of German Romanticism evidenced in the writings of Novalis predisposed her
toward the teachings of the Kabbalah. See Dischner's introductory essay to the volume *apropos Nelly Sachs* (Frankfurt am Main: Verlag Neue Kritik, 1997), 27–28.

[19] In her biography of Rose Ausländer, Cilly Helfrich notes that Sadagora was a
center of Hasidic mysticism since 1769. Ausländer's father was born in 1872 and
studied there with the so-called "Wunderrabbi" until age seventeen, at which point
he was accorded the status of a rabbi in his own right. See Helfrich, *Rose Ausländer.
Biographie* (Zürich: Pendo Verlag, 1998), 34, 46–48. See also Ausländer's poem
"Der Vater" (II 318).

flection rather than spiritual fervor. She saw religion as a synthesis of ideas, rather than one program for salvation within rigid bounds, and her sense of identity as a Jew was in line with this concept of synthesis. Despite her closer connections to Judaism since childhood, Rose Ausländer shared with Nelly Sachs a view of faith as a blend of different beliefs and philosophies taken from German culture, Christianity, and Judaism.

Following Sigmund Scherzer's death in 1920, young Rosalie emigrated to the United States in 1921 to take some of the financial strain off of her mother. After her emigration, Rose Ausländer began publishing poetry in German. In 1931 she returned to Czernowitz where she continued with her publication activities. Her first book-length collection of poetry, *Der Regenbogen*, was, however, also to be her last in the Czernowitz literary market. Published in a small edition of four hundred copies in 1939, *Der Regenbogen* received positive reviews in the Bukovina, Rumania, and in Switzerland, but had little hope of success in Nazi Germany. Aware of the Nazi threat that was sweeping eastward, Ausländer returned to the safe haven of New York in 1939. Deeply concerned for her mother's welfare, Ausländer was too anxious to enjoy her own safety for long and returned to Czernowitz at the end of 1939. Shortly after her return it became clear that neither she nor her mother would be able to leave Czernowitz, and after the SS occupied the city in 1941, Rose Ausländer and her mother went into hiding in the Jewish ghetto. From the uncertain refuge of the cellar that served as their hiding place, Ausländer continued to compose poetry, turning to writing as a means of coping with the extremity of her situation.[20] The poems that arose out of this experience were later grouped together in the cycle *Gettomotive* (I 151–84). It was during this period of occupation, persecution, and surreptitious literary production that Ausländer met Paul Celan, also a resident of Czernowitz and a kindred poetic spirit.[21]

Sachs and Ausländer were not alone in their openness to a variety of traditions, and the synthesis of religious and existential perspectives evident in their writings can also be found in works of other German-Jewish writers of the period. Most notable of these is perhaps Else Lasker-Schüler, who responded to the pressures of assimilation by fashioning her own brand of belief out of the elements of her Jewish

---

[20] For a discussion of Ausländer's ghetto experiences see Cilly Helfrich, *Rose Ausländer. Biographie,* 164–84.

[21] One of Celan's most famous images, the celebrated metaphor of the "black milk" in "Todesfuge" (~1945) can be found in a much earlier poem by Rose Ausländer, "Ins Leben" (~1938), published in *Der Regenbogen* (I 66).

and Christian heritage that appealed to her.[22] While Lasker-Schüler figured her Jewishness as one of several personæ of the other and outsider in her poetry already well before the implementation of the racial laws in 1935, the Nuremberg citizenship regulations served as a caesura in the self-understanding of many German-Jews. In her study of German-Jewish women writers, Dagmar Lorenz argues that the alleged success of Jewish assimilation in Western Europe at the turn of the century must be viewed with some skepticism. On the one hand, widespread assimilation diminished the presence of Jewish religion and culture; on the other, resurgent anti-Semitism indicated that assimilation was not achieving integration.[23]

For assimilated Jews who had generated a worldview and a moral system grounded in the tenets of European humanism and Christianity, the sudden confrontation with the Jewishness they had denied or forgotten catalyzed a crisis of identity. Some continued to stubbornly adhere to the humanistic legacy of the Enlightenment despite the obvious refutation of its ideals in the reality they confronted.[24] Under the influence of National Socialism and its policies of segregation and persecution, others, like Nelly Sachs and Rose Ausländer, turned more and more to Jewish traditions and teachings, in Sachs's and Ausländer's cases particularly Kabbalistic mysticism and the works of Martin Buber and other Jewish philosophers and theologians.[25]

---

[22] In her discussion of Else Lasker-Schüler's position as a German-Jewish writer, Dagmar Lorenz holds her up as a model of emancipation, not only as a woman, but more specifically as a German-Jewish woman. Lorenz's admiration for the poet is obvious in her portrayal of Lasker-Schüler as successful both in defying patriarchal law and in creating an intercultural space for her writing. See Dagmar Lorenz, *Keepers of the Motherland: German Texts by Jewish Women Writers* (Lincoln/London: U of Nebraska P, 1997), 69–78.

[23] See Lorenz, *Keepers of the Motherland*, 95–96.

[24] See Rachel Feldhay Brenner, *Writing as Resistance: Four Women Confronting the Holocaust* (University Park, PA: Pennsylvania State UP, 1997), here esp. 8–9, 19.

[25] Sachs read widely in Gershom Scholem's writings on Jewish mysticism and his translation of the *Zohar*. She was also familiar with Franz Rosenzweig's *Stern der Erlösung* and felt a strong connection to the writings of Simone Weil. Rose Ausländer, as a student of philosophy at the University in Czernowitz, became involved with the work of Constantin Brunner and through his investigations also with that of Benedict de Spinoza. For a detailed discussion of the philosophical influences and foundations in Ausländer's work, see Gerhard Reiter, "Das Eine und das Einzelne. Zur philosophischen Struktur der Lyrik Rose Ausländers," *Rose Ausländer: Materialien zu Leben und Werk*, ed. Helmut Braun (Frankfurt am Main: Fischer, 1991), 154–97.

It would be misleading, however, to imply that Sachs and Ausländer came to acknowledge their Jewish identity as a result of Nazi racial policies, or to indicate that they came to be poets only in response to the Holocaust. Like Rose Ausländer, Nelly Sachs was writing and publishing poetry well before the Nazis began to dictate the identity and fate of European Jewry. Nelly Sachs's first published poem appeared in an October 1929 issue of the *Vossische Zeitung*, and her last in Germany before her flight to safety in Sweden was in the April 1939 newsletter of the Jüdischer Kulturbund. After her father died in 1930, Nelly Sachs became actively involved with the Jüdischer Kulturbund in Berlin, where she participated in the literary life of the organization. In the company of such as Gertrud Kolmar, a German-Jewish poet whom Sachs greatly admired at the time, Nelly Sachs's poetry readings at the Kulturbund indicate that she too enjoyed a degree of recognition as a voice in the Jewish literary and cultural life of pre-war Berlin.[26]

In the atmosphere of crisis surrounding the Holocaust, Sachs and Ausländer felt compelled as poets and witnesses to search for alternative and transformed perspectives of faith in order to come to grips with the moral and psychological anomie and chaos that followed in the wake of catastrophe. In their respective quests for new or revised models of belief and representation, they looked back to their memories of a time before their worlds had forever been disrupted, to childhood remembrances where the mother was both the locus of origin and the embodiment of refuge. The act of reflection back to a time of security represented by genuine and imaginary re-collections of childhood is one strategy for working through the past, reconstructing the stability of the familiar as a perspective from which to engage the destabilizing experiences and negativity of history. The mother in these reflections is a multivalent trope: alternately and at once the finite, human mother grounded in historical time; the Shekhinah, the female aspect of God in Jewish mysticism; and the archetypal mother of cosmic time, the Great Mother whose vastness encompasses both good and evil, creation and destruction, nurturance and violence.

The Mother, however, does not become a substitute for the Father in a one-for-the-other exchange of transcendental subjects. Instead, the appeal to the maternal both suggests and enacts a synthesis of beliefs and perspectives that offer an alternative to the destabilized belief in a

---

[26] See Birgit Lermen and Michael Braun, *Nelly Sachs*, 25. See also *Briefe der Nelly Sachs*, ed. Ruth Dinesen and Helmut Müssener (Frankfurt am Main: Suhrkamp, 1985), 31, 95 where Nelly Sachs expresses her admiration for Gertrud Kolmar (Chodziesner).

supreme and benevolent Godhead. While figurations of the mother, both biographical and metaphorical, recur in a myriad of variations in the writings of the two poets, the father himself rarely appears.[27] Sachs's and Ausländer's figurations of the paternal imago center on a Divine Father whose omnipotence and role as a benevolent protector have been called into question. Yet even as they decry this Father for His lack of intervention in the catastrophe of the Holocaust, they do not renounce their faith in the Divine. Nevertheless, the form of this Divine was dramatically molded and altered by the historical events that confronted them. In their poetic representations of the Cosmic Mother, Sachs and Ausländer, whether willfully or unconsciously, undermine the primacy of monotheism. In contrast to a monotheism based upon an exclusionary concept of belonging and redemption in which some are blessed at the expense of others,[28] Sachs and Ausländer offer a complex, pantheistic faith in a Divine power that is at once diffuse and all-encompassing. This conception of the Divine is at once inside and outside of history, beyond good and evil.

The turn to a figuration of the Cosmic Mother in bitter disappointment at the Divine Father has a parallel in the poets' turn to the mother during and after the Holocaust. Deprived of the "home" that had been destroyed forever by the events and aftermath of disaster, Sachs and Ausländer literally and figuratively turned to their mothers. Situated in spiritual as well as geographical exile, they sought refuge not only in the close familiarity of the mother/daughter relationship but also in language as an extension of the maternal realm. In the absence of the motherland, the mother tongue became a surrogate home. Tending their mothers,[29] biological and linguistic, provided a center and a purpose in their lives that had otherwise been completely disrupted. For Nelly Sachs writing in exile in Stockholm, the German lan-

---

[27] One isolated example is Rose Ausländer's idealizing tribute to her father and his Sadagora origins in the poem "Der Vater" (II 318) which begins with the strophe: "Am Hof des Wunderrabbi von Sadagora / lernte der Vater die schwierigen Geheimnisse / Seine Ohrlocken läuteten Legenden / in den Händen hielt er den hebräischen Wald"

[28] Cf. Regina Schwartz's discussion of the story of Cain and Abel as the originary narrative of monotheism because it is the first demonstration that the God of the Bible neither accepts nor confers multiple allegiances. *The Curse of Cain: The Violent Legacy of Monotheism* (Chicago/London: U of Chicago P, 1997), esp. 3, 16.

[29] Both Sachs and Ausländer tended their mothers through extended periods of ill health. That this loyalty did not shy away from risk is clear from Ausländer's decision to leave her safe haven in the United States in 1939 against the protests of her friends in order to return to Czernowitz to care for her sick mother.

guage was all she had left after her forced departure from a home she would never return to and which could never be recovered. For Rose Ausländer, language became a realm in which she could shape her world according to her ideals and fantasies while simultaneously fashioning an image of herself as an agent of transformation and change.[30]

Although Sachs and Ausländer survived the persecution and psychological trauma of the Third Reich in different ways, they are connected by their suffering and their tenacious faith that redemption could be found not only in the transcendent realm of the beyond, but also within or via language as a medium for communicating memory and formulating an ethical connection between past and present. Spirituality and language were composites of the traditions that situated them. The poetic word echoed the power of the Divine Word and shared in its regenerative, transformative polyvalence. The trauma of their experiences drove both Sachs and Ausländer into an intensive dialogue or concern with the Word and its divine and poetic possibilities. For a time, they were able to mediate their trauma in and through their poetic creations while proceeding in their search for communication and dialogue with the world outside the word. Strikingly, both poets experienced a resurgence of the trauma and withdrawal that had marked their survival — the years of exile and hiding, the reclusiveness that was necessary in order to be able to live — in their latter years and both retreated more and more into a world of language, confined yet not contained by the written page.

While there are many similarities in the attitudes the two poets exhibit toward poetic language, it is important to point out the differences in their allegiance to and faith in the word. Here I am in agreement with Claudia Beil, the first scholar to engage in an extensive comparative study of Nelly Sachs and Rose Ausländer in German. Beil emphasizes that while both poets share a strong faith in the creative capacity of the word, this faith in language, particularly poetic language, is differently motivated. According to Beil, language and writing for Nelly Sachs are momentary manifestations of Divine Presence in the world and indicate a path to transcendence. For Ausländer, the poet is able to realize the Divine or Divine immanence via the written word — the goal and the way converge (or the means is congruent with the end).[31]

---

[30] For a detailed treatment of the representation of language as home and refuge in Nelly Sachs's and Rose Ausländer's works see Claudia Beil, *Sprache als Heimat: Jüdische Tradition und Exilerfahrung in der Lyrik von Nelly Sachs und Rose Ausländer* (Munich: tuduv, 1991).

[31] See Beil, *Sprache als Heimat*, esp. 412.

In their comparative analysis of Hilde Domin and Rose Ausländer, Harald Vogel and Michael Gans discuss Rose Ausländer's retreat from the world during the last decade of her life, which she spent in self-imposed seclusion as a bedridden invalid, living out her present and her past through her writings and maintaining only minimum, and strictly regulated, contact with friends and acquaintances.[32] Nelly Sachs spent her last years in emotional and psychological decline, withdrawing ever further into the melancholy wilderness of her mind, suffering from chronic depression that led to a series of institutionalizations and radical measures (including electro-shock therapy) to exorcise her anxieties. While Rose Ausländer's poetry came more and more to resemble a clipped and fragmented dialogue with the memories of a past that held more plasticity for her in the sanctuary of her bed than did the contemporary world she had shut out of her life, Nelly Sachs turned to spare and stark lyrical lines where the boundaries between perception and transcendence became increasingly blurred.

Despite the extensive parallels between Sachs's and Ausländer's biographies and works, their relationship remains largely unexplored in contemporary critical scholarship.[33] Claudia Beil's *Sprache als Heimat: Jüdische Tradition und Exilerfahrung in der Lyrik von Nelly Sachs und Rose Ausländer* mentioned above, was published in 1991 as the first book-length comparative study of the two poets. In her book, Beil examines the syntheses of German and Jewish cultural traditions in Sachs's and Ausländer's poetry. Her main focus is on the interplay of mysticism and German Romanticism evident in their writings. In addressing this aspect of their poetry, Beil bridges a gap left by earlier studies that had emphasized the primacy of Jewish mysticism as the fundamental influence on their works.

Beil's analysis privileges language as a medium of culture and as a surrogate home for both poets, although her broader project is concerned with examining Nelly Sach's and Rose Ausländer's lives and works as representative of contemporary German-Jewish identity. The outcome of her study, particularly in light of her emphasis on the influence German Romanticism had on the works of both writers, is that the articulation of German-Jewish identity in their poetry demonstrates a successful synthe-

---

[32] Vogel and Gans, *Rose Ausländer/Hilde Domin: Gedichtinterpretationen* (Baltmannsweiler: Verlag Schneider, 1997), 43.

[33] Annette Jael Lehmann's comparative study *Im Zeichen der Shoah: Aspekte der Dichtungs- und Sprachkrise bei Rose Ausländer und Nelly Sachs* (Tübingen: Stauffenberg, 1999) is the most recent addition to Sachs and Ausländer scholarship, but appeared too late to be addressed in any detail here.

sis of German and Jewish traditions. What is left out of this conclusion, however, is a nuanced investigation of the socio-historical and ethical implications of their biographies and writings beyond the topicality of the time during which they worked and lived.

Nelly Sachs's and Rose Ausländer's poetic testimonies must be read both in the context of the historical situation in which they arose and for their continued relevance in the present, especially in light of the ongoing conflicts and the many persistent, exclusionary practices that continue to divide the world. The victims they speak for in these poems should not, however, be viewed exclusively as representations of the Jews as absolute Others, or generally as signifiers for an unspecified collective of oppressed and persecuted peoples. The victim as a term here shares the simultaneous specificity, plurality, and relativity characterizing the Other. The ethics of remembrance I am developing out of this encounter with the Other takes place at the intersection of temporal understanding and historical positioning of the Self, in this case signified by both the poet and the poetic I, and the Other, here understood as both the poem and the implied reader.

The Other in this relationship is both the "face of the other" outside oneself, a concept central to the work of Emmanuel Levinas,[34] and the "others" contained and sustained within the Self. An ethics of remembrance requires a recognition and acknowledgment of the Other as well as a sensitivity to the context of the encounter encompassing not only the moment, but also the multiplicity of events, interpretations, and identifications that stretch back into the past and forward into the future. The dialogue that must take place with the past necessitates an openness similar to the encounter with the Other. In order to be conducive to understanding, the relationship must be both compositional and particularlistic, permeable and distinctive, conscious of the past of the other as discrete from that of the self, but also aware that in discursive form as remembrance these separate histories become simultaneous.

As may already be apparent, Nelly Sachs and Rose Ausländer as poets and as representatives of German-Jewish responses to the Holocaust are being treated here as sisters in a common project. A degree of fusion and confusion of their independent identities as writers and social subjects is the paradoxical yet inevitable outcome of an analysis grounded in the-

---

[34] Levinas's concept of the "face of the other" signifies the moment of recognition of the other's existence as well as the realization of the responsibility to the other. In his choice of the term "face," Levinas is likely appealing to the Jewish tradition of referring to the "face of God" as that which is present and thus commands obligation, but which is also absent because it cannot be seen. For a discussion of Levinas's concept of the other and the relationship between the other and God see *Time and the Other*.

matic parallels and biographical similarities. While the two poets are certainly distinctive in terms of their life and work, I have consciously chosen to organize my analysis so that their resemblances are highlighted,
interweaving readings of poems by both writers, rather than segregating
them into discrete chapters in which the writings of each are addressed
independently. In a sense, the intention of this approach is to mirror the
investigation of the Self/Other relations and the dialogics and the ethics
of that encounter that are the focus of my study.

In their complex poetic figurations of the Self/Other relation, Nelly
Sachs and Rose Ausländer present conceptions of social interaction and
subjectivity extending beyond the specificity of the Holocaust toward a
figuration of universal humanity cognizant of the differences between
and among its members. By examining Sachs's and Ausländer's works
both in relation to the body of writing broadly referred to as the literature of the Holocaust and in connection to philosophical and social
theories of Self/Other relations and community, I explore the implications of their writings within and beyond the Holocaust context. My
approach incorporates and conjoins studies on memory and the Holocaust with an examination of the influence of Jewish mysticism and addresses issues of subject formation and social relations. Because of the
consciously thematic focus of my analysis, formal aspects of the poems
are specifically addressed only where they are relevant to the theme or
image under discussion.[35]

Sachs's and Ausländer's poetic treatments of subjectivity and relation are localized in the context of memory. Memory in the sense I am
using it refers both to real and imagined events, further distinguished as
personal or collective, reflecting the experience of an individual and/or
that of a group. The imagined aspect of memory refers not only to the
idealization of the past in nostalgic representations of childhood as an
idyll, but also reflects the cultural legacy inherited by each subject and
how that subject perceives herself in relation to this heritage. In Sachs's
and Ausländer's writings, the realm of inherited memory connects them
with the history of the Jewish people as a cultural and spiritual entity
diversely figured as primordial Israel, country, tribe, bride of God, and

---

[35] For a detailed formal analysis of Sachs's poetry, see Gisela Dischner, *Poetik des
modernen Gedichts: Zur Lyrik von Nelly Sachs* (Bad Homburg: Gehlen, 1970), which
addresses both lexical and grammatical aspects of Sachs's work. On Rose Ausländer,
see Gabriele Köhl, *Die Bedeutung der Sprache in der Lyrik Rose Ausländers* (Pfaffenweiler: Centaurus, 1993), which focusses on techniques and structures in Ausländer's
writings. Köhl's method of comparing published and unpublished versions of specific
poems, however, is more descriptive than analytical and offers little insight into the
thematic aspects compelling Ausländer's work.

wandering exile. As poets in exile, Sachs and Ausländer demonstrate an allegiance to a past that is not bound to place. Like the covenant with God alluded to in Jeremiah (31:33),[36] their sense of obligation to their faith and their people is written into their hearts and thus mobile because it is internal.

In their transformations of memory into poetry, Sachs and Ausländer appealed to a Thou representing those whom they had lost forever as well as those they still hoped to reach through their words. The address to the Thou also served to reinforce the construction of an imagined Other within the context of the poem whose existence was necessary for the realization of a dialogue taking place in the absence of a concrete Other. The Thou appealed to in this dialogue is akin to the Thou in Martin Buber's conception of the I/Thou relation presented in *Ich und Du*[37] in which the Thou is necessary for the I to realize itself as a Self in relation to an Other.[38] Buber's Thou, like the Other of social theory, has both concrete and abstract aspects. Concretely, the Thou in Buber's configuration is the human other encountered in social interactions. Abstractly, it is the transcendent, absolute Other of belief, the Divine Other. These concrete and abstract aspects of the Thou cannot, however, be regarded as independent of each other. The relation of the I to the human Other, the human Thou, reflects the relation to the Divine Thou, a connection intended to promote respect and responsibility in human interactions as these influence the self not only socially and morally, but also spiritually in relation to God.[39]

The dialogical character of the I/Thou relation is inextricably connected to both being and subject formation. The I comes into subjectivity through the relationship to the Thou in an encounter that has both discursive and extra-linguistic aspects. Extra-linguistic here refers to those elements that influence and affect the encounter between the Self and the Other that are not at the level of words. These could be

---

[36] "But this shall be the covenant that I will make with the house of Israel; After those days, saith the LORD, I will put my law in their inward parts, and write it in their hearts; and will be their God, and they shall be my people."

[37] Martin Buber, *WERKE I* (Munich: Kösel, 1962).

[38] Buber, *WERKE I*, 97: "Der Mensch wird am Du zum Ich."

[39] In *Standing Again at Sinai* (San Francisco: Harper & Row, 1990), Judith Plaskow adopts and adapts this view of the self-in-relation to God directly connected with the relationship to a human community in her conceptualization of a Jewish feminism which takes the relation between the spiritual and the everyday as its basis (xix): "Relationship with God is mediated through community and expresses itself in community."

emotions, gestures, facial expressions, but also the unspoken histories and memories of each individual interlocutor that position them in relation to each other. The complexity of this I/Thou relation is anticipated but not addressed by Buber's spiritual ethics of dialogue. The ethics of remembrance that I see evolving in Sachs's and Ausländer's poems moves beyond the spiritual specificity characterizing Buber's perspective towards an attitude of acceptance and an openness to the difference of the Other that has both a spiritual and a concrete socio-historical component.

In ideologies founded upon a homogeneous construct of group identity, the otherness of the Other is perceived as a threat to the artificial and precarious uniformity of the group. In the "othering" of the Jews in the ideology of Nazism, it was the "Jew" as a category who was targeted for systematic persecution and eradication. In this process of "othering," characteristics of the Other are rendered absolute. The singularity, particularity, and diversity between and among individuals are thereby consciously denied in favor of a homogenized view of the Other as enemy in a radicalization of the "Us versus Them" dichotomy that not only levels the differences inherent in "Them" and denies "Them" a shared humanity, but also reifies the ostensible differences separating "Us" from "Them."

Psycho-social theories of subject formation and the ethics of relation have variously emphasized linguistic and positional aspects of the Self/Other relation within a given social context, but often overlook the confluence of temporal levels inherent in that relationship and its implications for Self/Other interaction. The reality of social relations requires an examination of the psychological and temporal quality of the Self's encounter with the Other in order to assess ethical behavior. A viable theory of ethical social practice therefore must not only consider factors of gender, race, ethnicity, and social class, but must also address the historical and cultural inheritance that necessarily informs and positions every social subject.

Conceptualizations of ethics put forth by contemporary philosophers and social theorists have relied on differing foundational premises and emphases ranging from adherence to the Enlightenment legacy of universal reason and justice to presuppositions that human behavior is motivated by self-interest and desire for power. Lawrence Kohlberg's pioneering work on morality and his stage theory of moral development are based on a concept of universal justice that presupposes universal reason and privileges a definition of moral consciousness as governed by principles of impartiality and "rightness."[40] Kohlberg's theory ultimately places the right and the just life ahead of the good life, or presupposes that the former will beget the latter. Carol Gilligan was one of the first theorists to criticize Kohlberg's model for its failure to include the factor of gender, and her revised moral theory emphasized what she termed an ethic of care which she claimed characterized women's social interactions.[41] Gilligan's gender critique of Kohlberg, however, is offset by the gender bias of her own study, and her neglect of other factors such as race, ethnicity, social class, and power limits the applicability of her ethical theory.[42] Jürgen Habermas, Anthony Cortese, Iris Marion Young, Seyla Benhabib, and Joan Tronto have all offered various revisions to Kohlberg's and Gilligan's ethical theories, constructing models of moral social practice that not only include the components of justice and care, but also take into account the communicative aspects inherent in social relations as well as the hierarchies of power that differentially position social subjects.[43]

These modifications and syntheses in themselves, however, are insufficient if they continue to neglect history and memory as aspects of social relations even as they strive to do justice to situational factors. The field upon which the Self/Other encounter occurs is multi-levelled: discursive, psychological, political, situational, and transtemporal. In order to be adequate to the complexities of socio-historical reality, moral theory must go beyond restrictive emphases on abstract principles (justice, care, responsibility, consensus) to an examination of concrete practice, including the practice of remembrance and the preservation and transformation of memory.[44]

---

[40] See Lawrence Kohlberg, *The Psychology of Moral Development*. Vol. 2. *Essays on Moral Development* (New York: Harper & Row, 1984). Kohlberg has been widely and variously criticized for his privileging of justice and reason in a theory that claims to address universal morality.

[41] See Gilligan, *In a Different Voice: Psychological Theory and Women's Development* (Cambridge, MA: Harvard UP, 1982).

[42] Cf. Anthony Cortese's critique of Gilligan's moral theory in *Ethnic Ethics: The Restructuring of Moral Theory* (Albany: State U of New York P, 1990).

[43] See Jürgen Habermas, *Moralbewußtsein und kommunikatives Handeln* (Frankfurt am Main: Suhrkamp, 1983); Cortese, *Ethnic Ethics: The Restructuring of Moral Theory*, Young, *Justice and the Politics of Difference* (Princeton: Princeton UP, 1990); Benhabib, *Situating the Self: Gender, Community and Postmodernism in Contemporary Ethics* (New York: Routledge, 1992); and Tronto, *Moral Boundaries: A Political Argument for an Ethic of Care* (New York/London: Routledge, 1993).

[44] Here I am taking these principal categories from ethical theories postulated by Lawrence Kohlberg (justice); Carol Gilligan (care); Emmanuel Levinas (responsibil-

Because of their multiple positions as German, Jewish, women, poets, survivors, and exiles, Nelly Sachs and Rose Ausländer were constantly confronted with the boundaries and borders that separate and
divide identities. The plurality of subject positions they held are inscribed in their lyrical concerns with memory, identity, faith, and history, while the search for the Other in their writings resonates with
their efforts to give voice to the multiplicity of their identifications, loyalties, and experiences. As conscientious efforts at representing the diversity of individual and collective suffering that goes beyond the
specificity of "Jewish" experience to that of humanity as a whole,
Sachs's and Ausländer's poems evidence a dialogue of remembrance
and mourning at once historical and redemptive, subjective and ethical,
conscious of the connections and divisions informing the social relations in which memory is enacted, preserved, and transformed.

In her essay on the metaphorical power of memory, Aleida Assmann
distinguishes memory from remembrance using architectonic metaphors. She compares memory with a library preserving knowledge of
the past, while remembrance is likened to a temple for the future.[45] In a
striking parallel to the image Irene Klepfisz chooses in the poem that
serves as an epigraph for this Introduction, Assmann expands her architectonic metaphor for remembrance to include its figuration as a
commemorative monument for coming generations.[46] In a sense, the
study before you represents my affirmation that both Sachs's and
Ausländer's testimonials to the dead and to the living not only merit
reading and re-reading, but that preserved in the compelling language
of their poetry, their remembrances have also become monuments.

---

ity); and Jürgen Habermas (consensus).

[45] See Aleida Assmann, "Zur Metaphorik der Erinnerung," in *Mnemosyne: Formen und Funktionen der kulturellen Erinnerung*, ed. Aleida Assmann and Dietrich
Harth (Frankfurt am Main: Fischer, 1991), 14–18. The terms in German that Assmann distinguishes here are Gedächtnis (memory) and Erinnerung (remembrance).

[46] See Assmann, 18: "Den einen Modus der Erinnerung assoziieren wir mit dem
Denkmal, den anderen mit dem Archiv."

1: Mourning Death / Bearing Witness

And if a soul sin and hear the voice of swearing and is a witness, whether he hath seen or known of it; if he do not utter it, then he shall bear his iniquity.

— Leviticus 5:1

But every survivor of the Hitlerian massacres — whether or not a Jew — is Other in relation to the martyrs. *He is consequently responsible and unable to remain silent. (. . .) It is impossible to remain silent. There is an obligation to speak.*

— Emmanuel Levinas[1]

On the one hand, the creative imagination is compelled by its ethical-judicial involvement in historical time to bear witness against that time; on the other hand, it is conscious of its impotence to do so. The witness role is not the role of the judge; it is the role of limited vision and power.

— Hamida Bosmajian[2]

T HE EXPECTATION THAT THE SURVIVORS writing of the Holocaust, especially if Jewish, assume the role of witness and guardian of the sacred memories of the dead is pervasive in an ever-growing number of works seeking to give structure to the diverse literatures that arose in response to that devastating event. This witness role is one fraught with complexities and conflicts and cannot be viewed as a homogeneous po-sition based on clear-cut boundaries between good and evil or right and wrong. As the statements above suggest, the writer who is at once reporter and witness is pulled and torn by opposing forces. The ethical sense of responsibility to preserve the legacy of the victims is under-mined by a deep feeling of inadequacy to the task compounded by guilt at being in the position to even attempt to do so. Nelly Sachs and Rose Ausländer both felt compelled to bear witness in their poetry, and the texts in which they sought to transform mourning and memory into language are etched with the scars of their own internal conflicts as sur-vivors. Their poetic testimonials to the victims evidence recurring themes

---

[1] Emmanuel Levinas, "Poetry and the Impossible," *Difficult Freedom: Essays on Judaism*, trans. Seán Hand (Baltimore: The Johns Hopkins UP, 1990), 132.

[2] Hamida Bosmajian, *Metaphors of Evil: Contemporary German Literature and the Shadow of Nazism* (Iowa City: U of Iowa P, 1979), 16.

of guilt and complicity, bereavement and loss, language and silence, confrontations between Self and/as Other, questions of faith, and a tenacious belief in spirituality and writing as strategies for survival and resistance.

In this chapter, I examine poems that address the complexity inherent in the act of bearing witness, question the position of the poet-survivor as an agent of memory, and offer hypotheses about the reading and reception of these poems in a context both geographically and temporally removed from the historical event that engendered them. For the sake of coherence, I have grouped poems into thematic categories, beginning with those works that address the question of the poet-witness's guilt and complicity in the destruction and the credibility of the survivor's testimony. This grouping of poems is intimately related to the one following, which examines the poet's relationship to language and her alleged access to truth. The poet as a wielder of language is also implicated in the violence in which language played a signal role, and as a writer becomes caught in a double bind between communicating and resisting the suffering of the past in a medium contaminated by dehumanization.[3] The third and final category of poems addressed in this chapter includes those that deal with questions of faith, poems that are bitter with disappointment in a God who has seemingly abandoned His Chosen People and sharp with longing for succor and sanctuary in a brutal, chaotic world. Some of these poems mimic the tone and form of biblical verse, as hymns and psalms to the memory of the dead, at times reading like parodic commentaries on the omnipotent and terrible God of the Hebrew Bible.

---

[3] In her open letter to Nelly Sachs, Hilde Domin describes the unique linguistic dilemma of the persecuted exile poet who is simultaneously dependent upon and in flight from the language that shapes her/his world. See *Nelly Sachs zu Ehren: Zum 75. Geburtstag am 10. Dezember 1966* (Frankfurt am Main: Suhrkamp Verlag, 1966), 195: "Und während er noch flieht und verfolgt wird, vielleicht sogar umgebracht, rüstet sich sein Wort schon für den Rückweg, um einzuziehen in das Lebenszentrum der Verfolger, ihre Sprache. (. . .) Und er kann nicht anders als die Sprache lieben, durch die er lebt und die ihm Leben gibt. In der ihm doch sein Leben beschädigt wurde."

Survival and Guilt

But can the call of the land silence the cries of Auschwitz which will echo until the end of time? Can any human wash his hands of all that flesh turned to smoke?

— Emmanuel Levinas[4]

The denunciation of widespread bystander apathy in the face of victimization is a recurring moment in Holocaust testimonial poems expressed in tones ranging from bald accusation to more subtle innuendo. Nelly Sachs's and Rose Ausländer's post-Holocaust poems indicate that temporal distance from the event mitigates the bitterness of the accusation, whereas poems written in the immediate aftermath of the Holocaust are still sharp with pain and trauma. In a letter to Carl Seelig shortly after the end of the war Nelly Sachs describes the inescapable necessity of giving expression to the sufferings the event has caused. In this letter she identifies the catalyst for her relentless poetic memorials to the dead, but she denies that her personal identity as the writer of these poems is of any significance.[5] She wished to subordinate herself as an individual survivor to the collective mass of victims with whom she so strongly empathized. It is not *her* voice that needs to be heard, but any voice that will guard and preserve the legacy of the murdered:

> . . . es ist auch gänzlich gleichgültig, ob ich sie schrieb oder irgend jemandes Stimme erklang. Aber es *muß* doch eine Stimme erklingen und einer muß doch die blutigen Fußspuren Israels aus dem Sande sammeln und sie der Menschheit aufweisen können. Nicht nur in Protokollform![6]

The passionate and forceful outcry of accusation in this letter from October 1946 is representative of the accusatory tone untempered by

---

[4] Levinas, *Difficult Freedom*, 131.

[5] In the Introduction to *Jewish Writers, German Literature: The Uneasy Examples of Nelly Sachs and Walter Benjamin* (Ann Arbor: U of Michigan P, 1995), Timothy Bahti and Marilyn Sibley Fries note that this subordination of the poet to the poetic message in Nelly Sachs's self-understanding is in the tradition of mystics, martyrs, and saints (5). While this latter group could be seen as vessels for the Voice, Sachs as a poet-witness saw the source of her inspiration both in the Word and in the dead. Despite the tone of self-effacement in Sachs's description of her role as a poet, she regarded herself as a representative of the victims' suffering.

[6] *Briefe der Nelly Sachs* [hereafter cited simply as *Briefe*], 67–68.

reconciliation characterizing Sachs's early testimonial poems in the 1947 collection *In den Wohnungen des Todes*. The following poem from that collection, "IHR ZUSCHAUENDEN" (*FS* 20), illustrates how the poet transformed her pain and outrage into lyrical indictment:

> IHR ZUSCHAUENDEN
>
> UNTER DEREN BLICKEN getötet wurde.
> Wie man auch einen Blick im Rücken fühlt,
> So fühlt ihr an euerm Leibe
> Die Blicke der Toten.
>
> Wieviel brechende Augen werden euch ansehn
> Wenn ihr aus den Verstecken ein Veilchen pflückt?
> Wieviel flehend erhobene Hände
> In dem märtyrerhaft geschlungenen Gezweige
> Der alten Eichen?
> Wieviel Erinnerung wächst im Blute
> Der Abendsonne?
>
> O die ungesungenen Wiegenlieder
> In der Turteltaube Nachtruf —
> Manch einer hätte Sterne herunterholen können,
> Nun muß es der alte Brunnen für ihn tun!
>
> Ihr Zuschauenden,
> Die ihr keine Mörderhand erhobt,
> Aber die ihr den Staub nicht von eurer Sehnsucht
> Schütteltet,
> Die ihr stehenbleibt, dort wo er zu Licht
> Verwandelt wird.

The poetic voice here addresses the bystanders, who by their very apathy are to be judged as complicitous in the murder of the victims. By referring to these silently acquiescent others as You (ihr), the poetic voice is establishing a pronomial distinction that separates her from this second-person collective, thereby placing herself in a space outside or apart that provides her with privileged insight. From this position, privileged both morally and perspectively, the poetic voice seeks to inculcate in the plural other, the You, a sense of conscience and guilt for their ("Your") shared responsibility in the wanton killings of innocent people.

The opening strophe has the tone of a curse upon those who stood by and watched. In the second strophe, nature is figured as a witness in the absence of survivors, instrumentalized as a potential source of evidence and testimonial to the perpetrators' unpunished actions. The following strophe shifts from the implicit warning of a latent possibility of natural retribution and the admonishment that the eyes of justice have seen and recorded the evil to a lament of the loss of innocence, moral consciousness, and idealism in a world where such horrors have apparently become commonplace. Here the poetic voice moves from accusation to mourning for the prematurely terminated lives that could have reached for the stars. The poem ends with a reiteration of the accusation of complicity and an ironic reference to the biblical declaration of human mortality (Genesis 3:19: "for dust thou art and unto dust shalt thou return"). The bystanders are equivalent to accomplices because of their dust-covered inertia (they make no move to shake it off), and the dust that characterizes their weakness is simultaneously symbolic of the humanity and mortality they share with the victims.

Nelly Sachs's second volume of poetry, *Sternverdunkelung*, was published in 1949 in Amsterdam. The poems in this collection reflect a greater distancing from the immediacy of the Holocaust experience presented with such starkness in *In den Wohnungen des Todes*, but they still continue to reflect the poet's compulsion to bear witness to the fate of the Jewish people. In the poem "WENN IM VORSOMMER" (*FS* 153) from *Sternverdunkelung*, Sachs again presents the poetic voice as a witness in relation to nature, but in contrast to "Ihr Zuschauenden," the image of nature here is one allied not with the forces of justice, but rather with indifference.

> WENN IM VORSOMMER der Mond geheime Zeichen aussendet,
> die Kelche der Lilien Dufthimmel verströmen,
> öffnet sich manches Ohr unter Grillengezirp
> dem Kreisen der Erde und der Sprache
> der entschränkten Geister zu lauschen.
>
> In den Träumen aber fliegen die Fische in der Luft
> und ein Wald wurzelt sich im Zimmerfußboden fest.
>
> Aber mitten in der Verzauberung spricht eine Stimme klar und
> verwundert:
> Welt, wie kannst du deine Spiele weiter spielen
> und die Zeit betrügen —
> Welt, man hat die kleinen Kinder wie Schmetterlinge,
> flügelschlagend in die Flamme geworfen —
>
> und deine Erde ist nicht wie ein fauler Apfel
> in den schreckaufgejagten Abgrund geworfen worden —
>
> Und Sonne und Mond sind weiter spazierengegangen —
> zwei schieläugige Zeugen, die nichts gesehen haben.

The figuration of nature in the opening strophe is a conflation of mysticism, Romanticism and kitsch, recalling nineteenth-century German Romantic paintings more than the cold and calculated savagery of the genocide the poem is denouncing. Sachs has been repeatedly pilloried for this poem, which many critics regard as one of her weakest although better known works. The focus of the criticism is on the perceived sentimentalization of the victims in the use of the butterfly image, which several readers have argued is a potentially dangerous deflection of attention away from the real victims of the genocide.[7] The comparison of the child victims to butterflies thrown into the flames lifts the reader out of a position of confrontation with the horror of mass murder by diminutizing it through allegory. In a sense, Sachs is here giving voice to her own physical distance from the events themselves, her retreat into allegory is not an escape from the trauma of lived experience but rather a substitution for it.

Although Sachs herself was dissatisfied with the imagery and formulation of this poem,[8] it nevertheless brings together the many tasks and conflicts that weigh upon the poet-as-witness: the burden of memory, the protest against injustice, the sense of personal and collective guilt, and the feeling of helplessness in the face of the monumental indifference or denial expressed so vividly in the closing lines. Life goes on unquestioned like the continuous presence of the sun and the moon which shine upon the earth as usual as if nothing had happened. The idyll of nature depicted in the first two strophes is disrupted by the accusatory voice of memory that cries out against apathy, forgetting, and injustice. The poet's already Sisyphean task of guarding memory in the face of monumental impassivity is compounded by her inability to fully accept the fact of her own survival.

Rose Ausländer's poem "Wo waren" (IV 92), written at a distance of some thirty years from the historical event of the Holocaust, affords a contrast to the tone of bald accusation apparent in the preceding poems by Nelly Sachs and reflects the transformation of the experience

---

[7] Ehrhard Bahr devotes a large part of his discussion of Sachs's poetry to an analysis of this particular poem in his article, "'My Metaphors Are My Wounds': Nelly Sachs and the Limits of Poetic Metaphor," *Jewish Writers, German Literature: The Uneasy Examples of Nelly Sachs and Walter Benjamin*, ed. Timothy Bahti and Marilyn Sibley Fries, esp. 50–54. Bahr's criticism of this poem is echoed by Michael Braun who uses "Wenn im Vorsommer" as a point of comparison in his discussion of "Völker der Erde". Braun is dismissive of Sachs's choice of imagery, particularly the parallel she draws between butterflies and children, a parallel he regards as not only sentimentalizing, but also dehumanizing. See Lermen and Braun, *Nelly Sachs 'an letzter Atemspitze des Lebens'*, 49.

[8] Bahr alludes to Sachs's reservations toward the poem in his discussion, "'My Metaphors. . . '," 50.

and its representation over time. The force of the impact may have weakened with age, but the bitterness remains against a world that consciously participated in the catastrophe through its indifference.

> WO WAREN
>
> Wo
> waren die Freundesländer
> als wir versanken
> in sumpfige Nacht
>
> Wo waren
> die laut schweigenden
> Menschen[9]

The poetic voice inquires where the saviors and rescuers were in the darkness of destruction, a question that was rendered almost absurd by the sudden wave of good Samaritan claims that washed over Germany in the post-war period. If all those who later claimed to have lent aid to the Jews had in fact done so, countless numbers of victims who were deported and murdered with no apparent resistance from the general population would have been saved. Yet neither supposed allied countries nor human neighbors came to the aid of the persecuted We with whom the voice identifies itself. What echoes even after thirty years is the loudness of the bystanders' silence, a silence that is not one of resistance and disapproval, but rather one of acquiescence. And it is this recognition of the silent acquiescence of the bystanders that continued to weigh heavily on the tongues and minds of post-Holocaust writers attempting to represent the genocide without trivialization or aestheticization.

In Rose Ausländer's poem "Anklage" (IV 182), the poetic persona takes a position doubly outside herself, addressing herself as You and assuming a hypothetical character with access to the perspective of the cruelly murdered victims while she herself is privileged to be alive:

> Tote Freunde
> klagen dich an
> du hast sie überlebt
>
> Du weinst um sie
> und lachst schon wieder
> mit andern Freunden

---

[9] In a letter to Hugo Bergmann during a period of severe unrest in Palestine in 1948, Nelly Sachs is asking a similar question when she notes the attention the conflict in Palestine is getting and implies that this international interest stands in stark contrast to the apathy and apparent indifference to the Jewish fate several years earlier (*Briefe*, 89): "Aber wie leicht wäre auch damals die kleine Judenheit zu retten gewesen, wenn, ja wenn die Lauheit aus der Welt wäre."

> Deine Blumen
> auf ihren Gräbern
> versöhnen sie nicht
>
> Du trauerst um ihren Tod
> und machst Gedichte
> aufs Leben

The poetic perspective reveals the conflict between a devotion to the remembrance of the victims and a desire to begin anew and continue life.[10] The poem bears the imprint of the survivor's loss, but also offers hope for the possibilities and pleasures of continued living, even if in the shadow of violent death. The lyrical voice expresses a wish to be able to fulfill her obligation both to the memory of the dead and to the existence of the living. The poet cannot accept a poetry that is always and only black with mourning; she recognizes that the dead can never be vindicated, whether with flowers or with words. In contrast to Nelly Sachs's death-saturated imagery that looks forward only through lenses that have been stained and forever blurred by tears of mourning, Ausländer's perspective here looks toward the possibility of life. This image of life should not be read as a return to a lost past or a celebration made possible only through denial, but rather as the mature consciousness of a survivor seeking to mediate existence and experience.

The longing for a normal life despite the haunting memories of the Holocaust achieves at best temporary fulfillment; indeed the work of both poets is informed to the end by the pain of their identification with the victims. Rose Ausländer's "Erwachen I" (III 124) from the 1974 cycle *Ohne Visum* shows the poetic subject plagued by dreams of mass destruction in which she is fated to join her people in death:

ERWACHEN I

> Aus zerrütteten Träumen
> erwachend
> im Nessellager

---

[10] The poet Czeslaw Milosz expressed this distinction between the duty and desire that informs the writing of Holocaust survivors in a letter to *The New York Review of Books* [quoted in Norma Rosen, *Accidents of Influence: Writing as a Woman and a Jew in America* (Albany: State U of New York P, 1992), 106]: ". . . we should distinguish between our duty to preserve memory and our natural desire to move forward with our affairs of the living. People should not freeze, magnetized by the sight of evil perpetrated in our lifetime."

> ich beobachte
> den Bau
> gigantischer Galgen
>
> für mich
> und
> mein Volk

The poetic I awakens from a dream that confronts her with her passivity and complicity in the literal death of her people and in her own figurative demise. Stung by the nettles of conscience, she is nevertheless capable of assuming the role of meta-observer: in her dream she watches herself watching the construction of gigantic gallows intended for herself and her people. Yet despite her clairvoyance and insight into what manner of execution awaits her people, she is reduced to the role of witness: there is no discursive or real space available to enable or encourage her resistance.

The traumatic situation of the witness-survivor pursued by a constant fear of death is powerfully illustrated in Nelly Sachs's "CHOR DER GERETTETEN" (*FS* 50–51), which utilizes an image similar to the gallows in Ausländer's "Erwachen I" as a metaphor for death.

CHOR DER GERETTETEN

WIR GERETTETEN,
Aus deren hohlem Gebein der Tod schon seine Flöten schnitt,
An deren Sehnen der Tod schon seinen Bogen strich —
Unsere Leiber klagen noch nach
mit ihrer verstümmelten Musik.
Wir Geretteten,
Immer noch hängen die Schlingen für unsere Hälse gedreht
Vor uns in der blauen Luft —
Immer noch füllen sich die Stundenuhren mit unserem
tropfenden Blut.

Wir Geretteten,
Immer noch essen an uns die Würmer der Angst.
Unser Gestirn ist vergraben im Staub.
Wir Geretteten
Bitten euch:
Zeigt uns langsam eure Sonne.
Führt uns von Stern zu Stern im Schritt.
Laßt uns das Leben leise wieder lernen.
Es könnte sonst eines Vogels Lied,
Das Füllen des Eimers am Brunnen
Unseren schlecht versiegelten Schmerz aufbrechen lassen
Und uns wegschäumen —

Wir bitten euch:
Zeigt uns noch nicht einen beißenden Hund —
Es könnte sein, es könnte sein
Daß wir zu Staub zerfallen —
Vor euren Augen zerfallen in Staub.

The survivors in "CHOR DER GERETTETEN" are haunted by the specter of death and painfully aware of the fragility of their precariously balanced lives, which could be destroyed by something as commonplace as a birdsong, a water bucket, or a vicious dog. The poetic voice speaks from the perspective of one who has been brought back from the brink of death, speaking thus also for the dead whose bodies have already been transformed into dust. The perspective of the We sets up a dichotomy of survival between the persecuted and those who were not victims. In contrast to William West, who discusses the last three lines of this poem in his article "The Poetics of Inadequacy: Nelly Sachs and the Resurrection of the Dead," I read the voice of the We as not addressing the dead, but rather the living.[11] West's reading hinges on his discussion of the poem as epitaph, and he takes this passage from Sachs as evidence of an inversion of the traditional epitaph structure, which is conceived as an address to the living. While a reading of the poem as a transformation of the epitaph is certainly plausible, Sachs does not engage here in a simple reversal, but instead presents an alliance of the saved and the dead against the living, i.e. she disrupts the binary that is traditionally associated with the epitaph through the addition of a third term, the saved.

Similarly to the pronominal gesture employed in "IHR ZUSCHAUENDEN," the poetic persona in "CHOR DER GERETTETEN" allies and identifies herself with the victims in opposition to the victimizers. The We designates the victims, who in their demoralized, traumatized state ask the You, the others (bystanders, accomplices, and fellow travelers), to help them reintegrate themselves, reacclimate themselves to "normal" life. This appeal to the non-victims of the catastrophe demonstrates the lack of vengeance and hatred toward both bystanders and perpetrators that is characteristic of Nelly Sachs's testimonial poems. Despite the extreme cruelties the victims suffered at the hands of their compatriots, the We recognize the common humanity they share. The closing lines of the poem, however, indicate that there can be no true reconciliation, that the bond of humanity connecting victim and tormentor, like the indifference of dust in "IHR ZUSCHAUENDEN," is only one of shared mortality.

---

[11] Cf. *Jewish Writers, German Literature*, 79.

Wir Geretteten,
Wir drücken eure Hand,
Wir erkennen euer Auge —
Aber zusammen hält uns nur noch der Abschied,
Der Abschied im Staub
Hält uns mit euch zusammen.

The act of leave-taking is the tie that binds the living, the saved, and
the dead and that in its contiguity with the image of dust implies both
shared mortality and a recognition of (at least the potential for) a common fate. The knowledge of the inevitable return to dust figured as a
leave-taking from the living and hence the world is also the tie that enables the survivors to acknowledge the dead. Their own eventual part-
nership in the community of dust is both a lament to the passing of
those before them and a means to rationalize the fears and guilt that
haunt them in their present condition among the living.

The victims' exculpation from guilt and complicity in the murder of
their brethren implied in Nelly Sachs's "CHOR DER GERETTETEN"
is further complicated in Rose Ausländer's "Die Angeklagten" (VI
236), written some thirty-five years after the end of the war. Influenced
by developments in German social and historical conscience after re-
construction, Ausländer's poem engages with the past in an awareness
of its manipulation and modification in the present, reminding the living of their responsibility. "Die Angeklagten" presents guilt as a universal condition connecting all survivors regardless of their positions as
either victims or oppressors. The undeniable common denominator of
mortality in Sachs's poem has become a psychological one of mutually
experienced or perhaps mutually repressed feelings of guilt.

Die Angeklagten
am Ufer
des uferlosen Wassers
waschen eifrig

Von Millionen Menschen
angeklagt
waschen eifrig
am Ufer
des uferlosen Wassers
die Angeklagten
ihre Hände
in Unschuld

Although this poem bears witness to the guilt of the perpetrators, it
simultaneously raises the question of who is innocent in the aftermath of
such a catastrophe. Can the survivors be said to be free of the stain of

complicity, or is to be alive tantamount to being guilty?[12] The technique
of repetition formally mirrors and emphasizes the semantic message. The
process of denunciation and absolution is cyclical and repetitive and the
poetic voice remarks with bitter irony the diligence with which the accused scrub their hands in response to the testimony of countless witnesses. An extreme travesty of justice seems to be implied here, yet the
tone of the poem is ambivalent. The testimonials of the victims can either be washed away, or they are waterproof and stubbornly persist as
indelible marks signaling wrongdoing. We are given no indication as to
what form these accusations take, but are left with the simple yet powerful image of the accused obsessively washing their hands.

The effects of the witnessing experience seem equally ineradicable, a
condition that is given powerful expression in one of Nelly Sachs's most
famous poems "LANDSCHAFT AUS SCHREIEN" (*FS* 221–23) from
the 1957 collection, *Und niemand weiß weiter*. The recognition of the
immensity and recurrence of horrible suffering has an extreme impact
on the eye-witness, whose insight into the pain of the world is likened
to a physical mutilation.

> LANDSCHAFT AUS SCHREIEN
>
> IN DER NACHT, wo Sterben Genähtes zu trennen beginnt,
> reißt die Landschaft aus Schreien
> den schwarzen Verband auf,
>
> Über Moria, dem Klippenabsturz zu Gott,
> schwebt des Opfermessers Fahne
> Abrahams Herz-Sohn-Schrei,
> am großen Ohr der Bibel liegt er bewahrt.
>
> O die Hieroglyphen aus Schreien,
> an die Tod-Eingangstür gezeichnet.
>
> Wundkorallen aus zerbrochenen Kehlenflöten.
>
> O, o Hände mit Angstpflanzenfinger,
> eingegraben in wildbäumende Mähnen Opferblutes —

---

[12] This contention of the universal guilt of survival is a central point in André
Neher's analysis in *The Exile of the Word: From the Silence of the Bible to the Silence of
Auschwitz*, trans. David Maisel (Philadelphia: The Jewish Publication Society of
America, 1981), of Holocaust survivor Elie Wiesel's portrayal of the position of the
survivor after Auschwitz. Neher asks the provocative and probing question (219):
"How, ultimately, can any survival be anything else than a cowardly betrayal?" And
indeed, this is the question that disrupts the testimonials of the survivor-witnesses.

Schreie, mit zerfetzten Kiefern der Fische verschlossen,
Weheranke der kleinsten Kinder
und der schluckenden Atemschleppe der Greise,

eingerissen in versengtes Azur mit brennenden Schweifen.
Zellen der Gefangenen, der Heiligen,
mit Albtraummuster der Kehlen tapezierte,

fiebernde Hölle in der Hundehütte des Wahnsinns
aus gefesselten Sprüngen —

Dies ist die Landschaft aus Schreien!
Himmelfahrt aus Schreien,
empor aus des Leibes Knochengittern,

Pfeile aus Schreien, erlöste
aus blutigen Köchern.

Hiobs Vier-Winde-Schrei[13]
und der Schrei verborgen im Ölberg
wie ein von Ohnmacht übermanntes Insekt im Kristall.

O Messer aus Abendrot, in die Kehlen geworfen,
wo die Schlafbäume blutleckend aus der Erde fahren,
wo die Zeit wegfällt
an den Gerippen in Maidenek und Hiroshima.

Ascheschrei aus blindgequältem Seherauge —

O du blutendes Auge
in der zerfetzten Sonnenfinsternis
zum Gott-Trocknen aufgehängt
im Weltall —

"LANDSCHAFT AUS SCHREIEN" can be read as a recurring
nightmare that is rooted in the sacrifice and suffering demanded of
Jewish experience that goes back to God's test of Abraham on Mount
Moriah. The connection between biblical agony and historical agony is
achieved through the medium of the dream as a nexus of imagination,
experience, and memory. The poem opens with the image of the black
band that evokes both sleep and blindness being torn asunder by the
vision of an intangible landscape constituted by screams. The poetic
persona, blinded by the pain that serves as the connective thread of experience through the ages, is simultaneously rendered clairvoyant
through her suffering such that she "sees" the screams of the victims
transformed into indecipherable signs ("die Hieroglyphen aus Schrei-

---

[13] This is an allusion to the passage in the Book of Job where Job seeks God in all
four directions but is unable to locate him (Job 23:8–9).

en") inscribed into the gates of death. To her senses in the traumatic aftermath of catastrophe, everything is composed of screams: screams have become the basic building block of her existential world.

The ubiquitous screams connect with the cries of suffering expressed by Abraham about to sacrifice his only son as a tribute to his exacting God ("Abrahams Herz-Sohn-Schrei") as well as with those of the biblical martyrs Job and Christ pushed to the limits of their belief ("Hiobs Vier-Winde-Schrei / und der Schrei verborgen im Ölberg"). In all three of these instances there is a recognition of the strength of devotion to God even in the face of the most arduous travails,[14] but also an implied protest against the extremity of God's tests of faith. This implied protest against the biblical tests of faith instantiated by God's demand for absolute loyalty and obedience carries over into a historically concrete reference to extremity of pain and destruction. In the eleventh strophe, the sacrificial knife referred to in the allusion to Abraham in the second strophe has been horrifically transformed into the technological weapons of death evoked by the names Maidanek and Hiroshima. Where is the God who can give meaning to this annihilation?

The escalation of violence and destruction from the biblical instances to the extremes of twentieth-century horror is mirrored in a rising tone of pain and madness. Driven mad by the overwhelming recognition of an unbroken legacy of increasing suffering, it is as if the witness is struck blind, overcome by visions too horrible to contemplate. The eye of the seer in the single line preceding the final strophe is not only representative of the witness, but also of the victims, whose ashes cry out synesthetically *from* the eye, which is both tortured and blinded by what it has seen. The final strophe underscores the tone of anguish and protest in the face of an apparently absent or unseeing God. Here the eclipse of the sun offers a divine or heavenly parallel to the witness's blindness, while the activity "Gott-Trocknen" implies a passivity or indifference of the heavens to the fate of the world.

The association of the eye with suffering that is at once spiritual and real recurs in Sachs's writings, where the eye itself has the capacity to become visionary on the brink of death. Ursula Rudnick discusses this quality of "seeing" as a threshold to union with the Divine in her analysis of the epigraph to an earlier poem, "Deine Augen, o du mein

---

[14] Job makes the claim that even if his skin and bones are consumed by worms, his faith will be rewarded by the sight of God. Job 19:26–27. It is significant that Nelly Sachs chooses this passage from Job as the epigraph for the opening poem of her 1947 collection *In den Wohnungen des Todes.*

Geliebter" (*FS* 32).[15] This epigraph, which reads "Ich sah, daß er sah," is attributed to Rabbi Yehuda Zvi and Rudnick traces it to Buber's *Tales of the Hasidim* where Rabbi Yehuda speaks those words in order to explain how he knew that his mentor was on the edge of death.[16] The recognition of the moment of death expressed in vision goes back to Exodus 33:20: ". . . for no man shall see me, and live." Notably, Rabbi Yehuda as the witness to the witnessing, as a spectator to the vision, becomes by virtue of his secondary position and the fact of his testimony in this context implicitly also a survivor.

Unlike Rabbi Yehuda, the witness in "Landschaft aus Schreien" survives only as a bloody eye, not in this instance to record Divine presence, but rather Divine absence in the destruction visited by humanity upon itself. The eye-witness is mutilated by the violence of what she has seen: deprived of her organ of sight, she nevertheless achieves a level of cosmic insight. This portrayal of clairvoyant blindness recalls the mythological blind prophet Teiresias, whose power of prophecy was acquired at a heavy price. The ripped-out eye of the seer in the closing lines of the poem serves as a disturbingly vivid metaphor for the destruction of the poetic persona's formerly intact and unified worldview. The seer's resulting blindness, however, is imbued with a divine wisdom that paradoxically echoes in her mute speech. Struck blind and dumb by a horror that defies representation, the poetic voice trails off into the resonant silence of the inexpressible.

But does the mutilation of the witness provide the necessary insight into the truth of the catastrophe, does it precede the silencing of the poetic persona, or is it rather punishment for the witness's keeping mum? George Steiner, an early theorist on the representability of the Holocaust and its impact on Jewish identity, saw the obligation of the Jewish witness to history in drastically physical terms. In keeping with the tradition of Leviticus (5:1) that those who remain silent in the face of injustice are themselves guilty, he writes: "For a Jew to be silent about any determining part of his [*sic*] own history is self-mutilation."[17] The conflict between testimony and silence informs not only the poetic text, but also the physicality of the poet's own self-understanding.

---

[15] Ursula Rudnick, *Post-Shoa Religious Metaphors: The Image of God in the Poetry of Nelly Sachs* (Frankfurt am Main: Peter Lang, 1995), 113.

[16] Ibid.

[17] George Steiner, "The Long Life of the Metaphor: An Approach to the 'Shoah'," in *Writing and the Holocaust*, ed. Berel Lang (New York/London: Holmes & Meier, 1988), 155.

Speech and Silence / Memory and Forgetting

Wie macht man dem Menschen-Thiere ein Gedächtnis? ... Man brennt etwas ein, damit es im Gedächtnis bleibt: nur was nicht aufhört, weh zu tun, bleibt im Gedächtnis.

— Friedrich Nietzsche[18]

It is better for the poet to mutilate his own tongue than to dignify the in-human either with his gift or his uncaring. (. . .) Silence is an alterna-tive.

— George Steiner[19]

Silence is the dried blood of the wound.

— Edmond Jabès[20]

The poet as witness and survivor is also the guardian of memory, charged with maintaining a truthful account of the fate of her people. The aim of authenticity in the recording of history and experience is subject to the limitations of language and the poet's ambivalence toward a medium that both constrains her and challenges her to express that which is beyond conventional words and understanding. The recognition of the inade-quacy of existing language to represent incomprehensible experience is evidenced in the poets' experimentation with form and image.

How does one portray the dilemma of the survivor caught between speech and silence? This is the central concern of studies that question the representability of the Holocaust, address the limitations of lan-guage in expressing experience, and explore the possibilities for writing in the aftermath of such an apocalyptic historical event. In an essay en-titled "The Long Life of Metaphor: An Approach to the 'Shoah'," George Steiner offers an extreme view on the problem of language after the Holocaust. As a society of human beings, we have reached a nadir in our history that has eradicated humanity from our speech, perhaps forever. Because of this, we are now confronted with what he terms a "post-human" language with which we cannot hope to do justice to

---

[18] Friedrich Nietzsche, *Zur Genealogie der Moral*, in *Sämtliche Werke. Kritische Studienausgabe*, vol. 5 (Munich: Deutsche Taschenbuch Verlag; Berlin/New York: Walter de Gruyter, 1980), 295.

[19] George Steiner, "Silence and the Poet," *Language and Silence* (New York: Atheneum, 1967), 55.

[20] Edmond Jabès, *The Book of Margins*, trans. Rosmarie Waldrop (Chicago/London: U of Chicago P, 1993), 67.

memory. In fact, Steiner makes the radical contention "that to try to speak or write intelligibly, interpretatively, about Auschwitz is to misconceive totally the nature of that event and to misconstrue totally the necessary constraints of humanity within language."[21] He follows this unequivocal assertion, however, with the surprising position that if it is at all possible to represent or address the event in any language, then that language is German:

> . . . if there is to be a rehumanization of language after the Shoah, a restoration to language of its lost capacities to speak to and about God, to speak to and about man in any answerable (*verantwortlich*) sense, such reparation and restoration can come only from within the death-idiom itself.[22]

This "death-idiom" German is the tainted idiom within which Sachs and Ausländer confronted their experiences of persecution and suffering as victims and survivors, and their poems reflect a continuous struggle with the oppressor's language that was also undeniably their mother tongue.[23] In their writing, both poets sought, with fluctuating confidence and conviction in the means at their disposal, to construct spaces of unalienated speech as sanctuaries for and against suffering. In the haven they made for themselves in their poetry they endeavored to counter the atmosphere of fragmentation and irretrievable loss characterizing the historical reality from which they desired to escape. While

---

[21] Steiner, "The Long Life of the Metaphor," 156. Cf. Sander Gilman's discussion of the function and perception of silence in post-Holocaust writing by German-speaking Jews in *Jewish Self-Hatred* (Baltimore: The Johns Hopkins UP, 1986) where he argues that silence has become the new language of the Jews, but is also characteristic of poetic discourse after Auschwitz in general (322): "the silence ascribed to the Jews is turned about and made the universal of poetic discourse."

[22] Steiner, "The Long Life of the Metaphor," 157.

[23] Hilde Domin describes the unique position of the German-Jewish survivor poet in her open letter to Nelly Sachs referred to above, in which she expresses gratitude to Sachs for her dedication to the memory of the dead. Nelly Sachs, as a representative of the persecuted writing in exile, has a privileged relationship to the idiom that is both her mother tongue and that of the oppressors whereby she is able to achieve a renewal of language. See *Nelly Sachs zu Ehren: Zum 75. Geburtstag am 10. Dezember 1966*, 195: "Da wird einer verstoßen und verfolgt, ausgeschlossen von einer Gemeinschaft, und in der Verzweiflung ergreift er das Wort und erneuert es, macht das Wort lebendig, das Wort, das zugleich das Seine ist und das der Verfolger. (. . . .) Und während er noch flieht und verfolgt wird, vielleicht sogar umgebracht, rüstet sich sein Wort schon für den Rückweg, um einzuziehen in das Lebenszentrum der Verfolger, ihre Sprache. (. . .) Und er kann nicht anders als die Sprache lieben, durch die er lebt und die ihm Leben gibt."

this may have been the ideal, it was difficult if not impossible to achieve in the language they had at their disposal. The tensions between the longing for release through language and the recognition of language's limitations generated a condition of frustration and anguish that was more disturbing to Sachs than to Ausländer. In a letter of November 1947 to Hugo Bergmann, Nelly Sachs offers a vivid portrayal of the unbridgeable gap between language and experience: "Es reicht ja doch kein Wort zu nichts mehr hin, von gestern auf morgen ist eine Kluft wie eine Wunde, die noch nicht heilen darf."[24] This comparison of memory to an unhealed wound is one that Sachs had taken up several years earlier as the pivotal image in "CHOR DER TRÖSTER" (*FS* 65–66), a poem from the 1946 cycle *Chöre der Mitternacht*.

> GÄRTNER SIND WIR, blumenlos gewordene
> Kein Heilkraut läßt sich pflanzen
> Von Gestern nach Morgen.
> Der Salbei hat abgeblüht in den Wiegen —
> Rosmarin seinen Duft im Angesicht der neuen Toten verloren —
> Selbst der Wermut war bitter nur für gestern.
> Die Blüten des Trostes sind zu kurz entsprossen
> Reichen nicht für die Qual einer Kinderträne.
>
> Neuer Same wird vielleicht
> Im Herzen eines nächtlichen Sängers gezogen.
> Wer von uns darf trösten?
> In der Tiefe des Hohlwegs
> Zwischen Gestern und Morgen
> Steht der Cherub
> Mahlt mit seinen Flügeln die Blitze der Trauer
> Seine Hände aber halten die Felsen auseinander
> Von Gestern und Morgen
> Wie die Ränder einer Wunde
> Die offenbleiben soll
> Die noch nicht heilen darf.
>
> Nicht einschlafen lassen die Blitze der Trauer
> Das Feld des Vergessens.
>
> Wer von uns darf trösten?
>
> Gärtner sind wir, blumenlos gewordene
> Und stehen auf einem Stern, der strahlt
> Und weinen.

---

[24] *Briefe*, 85.

Although the survivors are here likened to gardeners, they are faced with the impossible task of sowing viable memory between the past and the future, battling against the inevitable transience of experience and remembrance. The finite, fleeting endurance of blossoms, scents, and tastes serves as a metaphor for the ephemeral nature of memory and the terminal insufficiency of consolation. Consolation itself is not only fated to insufficiency, it is also a privilege that ironically cannot be presumed. The repetition of the question "Wer von uns darf trösten?" echoes both the survivors' guilt and their despair of atoning for the trauma, suffering, and death of the victims.

The appearance of the cherub grinding sorrow to bits with his wings in the second strophe poses yet another threat to the dual task of mourning and remembrance. The cherub is a polyvalent symbol in Christian iconography, featured cavorting carefree in the heavens, but also shedding bitter tears at the tombs of saints. The cherub figure in "Chor der Tröster" is marked by a similar ambivalence. By not allowing yesterday to meet tomorrow, the cherub is not only responsible for the destruction of grief, but also for the obstruction of memory, creating a rupture in time and experience that gapes like a wound. This choice of imagery seems misplaced if we accept the cherub as the new mascot of amnesia and narcotized presentness, the unreflected oblivion of a here and now in which memory has been erased or suppressed. The wound image undercuts this vision of an existence unperturbed by past suffering and heralds the command in the strophe that follows.

A comparison with Nelly Sachs's use of this figuration of the wound as both a sign of separation and a condition of suspension between temporal levels occurs in a later poem, "Jakob," which deepens and widens the incision of suffering and pain evoked by the image of the wound by referring to it as a dwelling place: "o die Wunde zwischen Nacht und Tag / die unser Wohnort ist!" (*FS* 90). In "Jakob," which takes the biblical tale of Jacob's battle with the angel (Genesis 32:23–32) as an allegory for the tenacity of Israel's faith in the face of both Divinity and adversity, the wound is representative of suffering as the mark of Divine grace, a mark that inflicts rather than grants a privileged relationship to God. Just as the privilege of grace is achieved only through pain and struggle, the task of remembrance is arduous, yet part of a dual responsibility to the victims of the past and to faith in and for the future.[25] The immediacy of remembered suffering may pass, but the

---

[25] In her discussion of the biblical figure of Jacob in Sachs's poetry, Birgit Lermen argues that this poem connects the tradition of Jewish remembrance with a tes-

wound remains. Nevertheless, the poetic voice continues to be tormented by the obstacles to engaged mourning and the seductions of forgetting, a torment that cannot be resolved but which instead adds another dimension to the survivors' dilemma.

The refusal of transcendence in this poem appears and reappears across the breadth of Nelly Sachs's works and reflects both the all too human desire for peace of mind, and the harsh and bitter obligation to remember. Lawrence Langer praises Nelly Sachs as unique among Holocaust writers for just this refusal to retreat into a "terminology of transcendence,"[26] a tendency he notes and criticizes in the Holocaust writings of Viktor Frankl and Bruno Bettelheim. In contrast to Frankl and Bettelheim, Langer maintains, Nelly Sachs continually exposes "the inadequacy of our verbal and spiritual resources to express and transcend the wound of atrocity."[27]

The difficulty, impossibility, or even danger of figuratively representing the Holocaust is further compounded by the contaminated nature of the medium available to the poet.[28] In *Writing and Rewriting the Holocaust*, James E. Young posits the disturbing connection between metaphor and reality in the reification of Nazi propaganda during the Third Reich. Regarding the extent to which the dehumanization of language was translated into the dehumanization and extermination of human beings, Young asks whether the literalization of metaphor under the Nazis has forever destroyed the possibility of "innocent figuration."[29] The

---

tament to the contemporary situation of Jewish survivors returning to the recovered fatherland. See *Nelly Sachs "an letzter Atemspitze des Lebens,"* 169.

[26] Lawrence Langer, *Versions of Survival: The Holocaust and the Human Spirit* (Albany: State U of New York P, 1982), 38.

[27] Ibid., 219.

[28] George Steiner dwells on the damaged nature of the German language after Nazism in a 1959 essay "The Hollow Miracle" in which he takes an acerbic position on the magnitude of evil that permeates post-Holocaust German (*Language and Silence*, 101): "Use a language to conceive, organize, and justify Belsen; use it to make out specifications for gas ovens; use it to dehumanize man during twelve years of calculated bestiality. Something will happen to it. (. . .) Something will happen to the words. Something of the lies and sadism will settle in the marrow of the language." The prognosis he offers for this infected patient later in the essay is not promising (108): "Everything forgets. But not a language. When it has been injected with falsehood, only the most drastic truth can cleanse it." Although he did move away from the extreme pessimism expressed here in later writings, he continued his self-appointed role as a critical and watchful conscience for the developments in post-war German literature.

[29] James E. Young, *Writing and Rewriting the Holocaust* (Bloomington/ Indianapolis: Indiana UP, 1988), 93. Here Young questions the relationship between fig-

poet is both witness to and victim of the oppressor's language, yet cannot escape from it into a new autonomous and viable idiom. The screams of the victims that echo in the protest of the witness are silenced by the deafness of those who control language. This is the poignant theme of Rose Ausländer's "Überhört" (VIII 117), a poem written late in her life and one that powerfully demonstrates the enduring concern with memory and historical experience that informs her entire œuvre.

ÜBERHÖRT

Ich habe ihre Schreie
gehört

Ich schrie auf
als ich sie hörte

Wir wurden

von den Wortführern
stillschweigend
überhört

The lyrical voice identifies with the victims whose screams still ring in her ears. She was witness to their martyred cries and tried in vain to transmit their pain to the world ("Ich schrie auf / als ich sie hörte"); but none of these screams are acknowledged by the governors of speech. Because they are either unable or unwilling to speak in the language of their tormentors, the victims' cries are literally rendered mute. By allying herself with the victims, the poetic persona portrays herself too as one of those intentionally ignored in the oppressors' monopoly on recognized, audible expression. Her voice, like the tortured and dead she is desperate to speak for, falls on deaf ears, silenced by the impassivity and indifference of the ruling majority.[30]

---

uration and literalization, and the possibility of metaphorical expression after the Holocaust: "After the Holocaust, we might ask whether by making something imaginable through metaphor we have also made it possible in the world. That is, to what extent does 'imaginative precedent' — the kind we effect in metaphor — prepare human sensibility for its worldly reification? This is not to say that metaphor makes its own reification likely, but one might still ask to what extent, for example, the repeated figurative abuses of the Jews in Nazi Germany prepared both killers and victims for the Jews' literal destruction."

[30] The deafness of the oppressors implied in Ausländer's poem indicates the poetic persona's inability to communicate in their idiom of dominance, a phenomenon of linguistic power relations that recalls Hélène Cixous's portrayal of the dilemma of the woman speaker in "The Laugh of the Medusa," trans. Keith Cohen and Paula Cohen, *Signs* 1.4 (1976), 880–81:". . . how great a transgression it is for a woman to speak . . . in public. A double distress, for even if she transgresses, her words fall al-

The theme of the silencing of the poetic witness is a paradoxical am-
plification of the brutality with which the perpetrators sought to eradicate their victims. The poetic persona struggles with the barbed wire of
words that confine and cut her tongue in her attempts to speak in an
other voice. The words she seeks to verbalize her horror flee like refugees
in search of a sanctuary that does not exist. In Nelly Sachs's "Als der
große Schrecken kam" (*SL* 50), the poetic persona as a silenced witness
to history expresses a longing for a "not-yet" condition, a wish for an
unsullied realm of language beyond time and space.

> Als der große Schrecken kam
> wurde ich stumm —
> Fisch mit der Totenseite
> nach oben gekehrt
> Luftblasen bezahlten den kämpfenden Atem
>
> Alle Worte Flüchtlinge
> in ihre unsterblichen Verstecke
> wo die Zeugungskraft ihre Sterngeburten
> buchstabieren muß
> und die Zeit ihr Wissen verliert
> in die Rätsel des Lichts —

The dumbstruck condition of the poetic persona portrayed in this
poem inspires associations to an actual event in Sachs's biography.
While still in Germany, Nelly Sachs suffered a temporary paralysis of the
larynx after being interrogated by the Gestapo and was unable to speak
for a week thereafter.[31] This experience made a lasting impression on
her. It comes up in the only prose text Sachs ever published during her
lifetime, "Leben unter Bedrohung,"[32] which depicts the psychological
distress of life under Nazi occupation:

---

most always upon the deaf male ear, which hears in language only that which speaks
in the masculine."

[31] See Olof Lagercrantz, *Versuch über die Lyrik der Nelly Sachs*, trans. Helene
Ritzerfeld (Frankfurt am Main: Suhrkamp, 1967), 16; and Gisela Dischner, "Noch
feiert der Tod das Leben. . . ," *apropos Nelly Sachs*, 19–20. In her essay, Dischner
adds a further nuance to the story. After Sachs was released by the Gestapo and sent
home, a group of SA men and their wives came and plundered Sachs's and her
mother's apartment before their very eyes. It was the combined shock of these two
extreme events that rendered Sachs mute for days afterward.

[32] Originally published in 1956 in the literary journal *Ariel*, which had a tiny,
private subscribership of two hundred, the text has since been reprinted in Walter
Berendsohn's *Nelly Sachs. Einführung in das Werk der Dichterin jüdischen Schicksals*
(Darmstadt: Agora, 1974) and most recently in *apropos Nelly Sachs*, 76–80.

Fünf Tage lebte ich ohne Sprache unter einem Hexenprozeß. Meine Stimme war zu den Fischen geflohen. Geflohen ohne sich um die übrigen Glieder zu kümmern, die im Salz des Schreckens standen. Die Stimme floh, da sie keine Antwort mehr wußte und "sagen" verboten war.[33]

Sachs also regarded this incident as a symbolic moment in her development as a poet, an association evident in the parallel she draws in a letter to Margit Abenius in 1958 between the inexpressible power that catalyzed her momentary muteness and the silent, pulsing force that inspires her writing: "Puls und Atem haben diese Dinge geschaffen, genau wie ich damals unter den nazistischen Drohungen die Sprache für eine Woche verlor — hatte keine Atemhilfe mehr."[34] In the poem "Als der große Schrecken kam," it is the fish as the embodiment of silent suffering which struggles for breath in a hostile environment.

The helpless and vulnerable fish as a symbol of martyrdom recurs in Sachs's poetry and serves a similar symbolic function in Ausländer's work. In a poem entitled "Ruinen" (I 184) from the cycle *Gettomotive* written in immediate response to the persecution and destruction of the Rumanian Jews, Rose Ausländer is more specific in her fish iconography than Sachs. In place of Sachs's generic reference to "fish," Ausländer deliberately chooses the carp as the representative of mass suffering, all the more powerful and moving because of the carp's symbolic association with persistence, endurance, and courage in the face of extreme adversity.[35] Although the two poems originate in different creative periods, they both bear witness to the poets' struggles with representation as well as their ambivalent attitudes toward the language that both defined and confined their art.

RUINEN

Karpfen liegen auf dem Rücken
im Teich aus Lauge und Chlor.
Vermummte, die Bahren tragen
begleitet ein Nebelhornchor.

Kein Rauch steigt aus den Ruinen.
Im Saal ist die Braut.
Was frommt deine Frage, da niemand
der Lippe die Antwort vertraut?

---

[33] Quoted in *apropos Nelly Sachs*, 77.

[34] *Briefe*, 190.

[35] Cf. *Wörterbuch der Symbolik*, ed. Manfred Lurker (Stuttgart: Kröner, 1988), 360.

The dead carp lying on their backs in a pool of chemicals introduce the image of devastation in a landscape inscribed with death. The pallbearers who clear the wasteland of bodies wear masks to hide their identity and, perhaps, to save their breath; and, like the accomplices and indifferent bystanders who witnessed and participated in the final solution, these "Vermummte" retreat behind a veil of anonymity and a relative safety in numbers. The second strophe moves from a macroview of destruction to an interior perspective: "Kein Rauch steigt aus den Ruinen. / Im Saal ist die Braut." This is an image dredged in bitter irony, for who would still anticipate the prospect of love and procreation in an atmosphere of such absolute barrenness? The pathetic ludicrousness of this solitary bride echoes in the hopeless and frustrated tone of the poem's closing lines: belief and trust have no place in this world in which language has become the vehicle of deception and death, a corrupted idiom in which questions are futile: "Was frommt deine Frage, da niemand / der Lippe die Antwort vertraut?"

The frustrated and anguished quest for truth in a polluted environment is the poet's thankless mission, one that holds little hope for reward. In Nelly Sachs's "Nur Sterben lockt ihnen des Jammers Wahrheit heraus" (*SL* 16), the poetic voice tersely proclaims the irreconcilable rift between truth and life. Only on the brink of death is it possible to entice the truth out of "Them", a collective plural designating all survivors who would rather forget than confront the blackness of their history.

> Nur Sterben lockt ihnen des Jammers Wahrheit heraus
> diese Kehrreime aus Nachtschwärze geschnitten
> diese Zungenübungen
> am Ende der Tonorgel —

Yet just as Ausländer's poetic persona questions the capacity of existing language to authentically convey experience in "Ruinen," the tone characterizing the poetic voice in Sach's poem is imbued with disillusionment and disbelief that truth can be achieved or adequately represented through speech. The confessions wrested from the survivors, regardless of their status as victims or perpetrators, are all cut from the same cloth of darkness ("diese Kehrreime aus Nachtschwärze geschnitten"). Even on the threshold that separates life and death, the survivors cannot break through the barrier of the language that prevents them from speaking in a voice equal to truth and multiplicity. Instead they are consigned to engage in compensatory, mechanical tongue exercises at the extremity of sound ("diese Zungenübungen / am Ende der Tonorgel"). This poem, akin to those in the preceding discussion, thematizes and concretizes the boundary between language and silence, with the accompanying implication that the truth that would speak the reality of human experience lies beyond the reach of our present possibilities for vocalization.

Quests and Questions: Faith and Restitution

> *Hear, O Israel: The LORD our God is one*
> *LORD: And thou shalt love the LORD thy*
> *God with all thine heart, and with all thy*
> *soul, and with all thy might.*
>
> — Deuteronomy 6: 4–5

The silence that appears to be the culmination of the conflict between experience and representation in poetic language echoes in the vastness of the cosmos as an appeal to a God who has seemingly abandoned His People. The message implied by or inherent in this multivalent silence can be variously understood, but here it can in part be "read" as a wordless deference to the unspeakable greatness of either Nothingness or a sublime Divine Being in a mystical expression of belief.[36] While Rose Ausländer was well versed in Jewish culture and tradition, Nelly Sachs had been raised in a secular bourgeois environment in Berlin. Immersed as a young woman in the Christianized aura of assimilated Berlin Jewry, Sachs developed strong interests in Christian lore and legend as well as in German Romanticism. And it was to the tales of Christian mystics and martyrs that she would later turn for solace during the doomed love affair[37] that would haunt her poetry for years after, culminating in a final testament to her lover after news of his death in a concentration camp in the poem cycle "Gebete für den toten Bräutigam" (*FS* 22–32).

---

[36] Claudia Beil reads silence in Nelly Sachs's poetry as the gap with which the poet seeks to represent experience in the language available, rather than as a symbolization of the inexpressibility of experience. See *Sprache als Heimat: jüdische Tradition und Exilerfahrung in der Lyrik von Nelly Sachs und Rose Ausländer* (Munich: tuduv, 1991), 203: "Schweigen . . . ist nicht mit Verstummen gleichzusetzen, mit dem Verzicht auf oder der Verweigerung von Aussage und Äußerung. Ganz im Gegenteil wird hier der Versuch unternommen, das eigentlich Unsagbare doch in Worte zu kleiden und so auch für diese Welt mitteilbar und wirkmächtig werden zu lassen."

[37] Ruth Dinesen, in her essay on Nelly Sachs's Jewishness, discusses an early group of poems in which Sachs attempts to come to terms with the enforced separation from her lover. In these poems, dating back to ca. 1920, Sachs figures the Madonna as the sister of her suffering and death as her brother. See Dinesen, "The Search for Identity: Nelly Sachs's Jewishness," in *Jewish Writers, German Literature*, ed. Bahti and Fries, 25–26.

With the advent of anti-Semitic discrimination and the exclusionary politics promoted by Nazi Germany, Sachs did not relinquish her affinities with the traditions she found so compelling before Hitler came to power. Instead she set about combining her interest in Romanticism and mysticism with those features of a — for her — newly recovered Judaic tradition that appealed to her.[38] Under Nazism, Jewishness took on a much more concrete and insistent aspect as both an obligation and a stigma. Secular Jews lost the power to choose their own cultural identity as they were labeled and segregated according to a rigid code based on blood and not belief. In Sachs's case, both this coerced identification under Nazism and her later sense of rootlessness in exile led her to explore the system of traditions and beliefs with which she had never fully identified.[39]

For both Ausländer and Sachs, however, the engagement with religious tradition was not exclusive to their Jewish heritage, but combined the religious narratives and beliefs that grew out of Christian and Jewish biblical interpretations. Confronted with the oppression and atrocities visited upon their people regardless of whether they had elected to be among the Chosen inspired both a spiritual search for meaning and a crisis of faith, a questioning of the credibility of any concept of the Divine in the aftermath of such calculated brutality.

The crisis of faith intersects the crisis of language, gravitating both toward a void of silence resonating with prayer, accusation, and despair and toward a poetic calling to give voice to this troubling and complex state of crisis. In an interconnection of language, faith, and self-understanding, the poetic persona attempts to confront the Other whom she wishes to provoke into reflection and reaction through the destabilized medium of language.[40] The Other serving as the object of the po-

---

[38] Claudia Beil engages in a thorough examination of both Sachs's and Ausländer's dual affinities with Romanticism and mysticism, Christianity and Judaism, in her comparative study of the two poets. In an earlier study, Ruth Dinesen addresses Nelly Sachs's affinities with literary Romanticism, not just in the German tradition: *"Und Leben hat immer wie Abschied geschmeckt": Frühe Gedichte und Prosa der Nelly Sachs* (Stuttgart: Hans-Dieter Heinz, 1987), 11–20.

[39] David Roskies refers to the widespread resurgence of interest in Judaism among assimilated Jews in Western Europe in the 1930's, a phenomenon which he interprets as a direct response to the growing atmosphere of anti-Semitism and persecution. See Roskies, *Against the Apocalypse: Responses to Catastrophe in Modern Jewish Culture* (Cambridge, MA/London: Harvard UP, 1984), 11. See also Ruth Dinesen, "The Search for Identity" 33–34 for a discussion of Sachs's engagement with the writings of Jewish mysticism after her mother's death in 1950.

[40] Cf. Hamida Bosmajian's discussion of Nelly Sachs's and Paul Celan's relation-

etic persona's provocation is none other than the God who has deliberately spared the witness-survivor as the guardian of the word, and, like the biblical prophets, the poet ultimately cannot refuse to be a messenger.[41] In contrast to the power of the Divine Word that lends the prophet irrefutable credibility, the poet in her act of bearing witness is confronted with a situation in which both the form and the content of the message have been so diminished and weakened that the lyrical voice swells and fades in and out of the static of wavering conviction. Yet the poet must take the existing language, assume responsibility for it,[42] and place it into the crucible of poetic creation in order to transform it into meaning. The challenge of meaningfulness is bound up with the assumption of responsibility for the word, and the messenger must confront the obstacles that accompany the pursuit of meaningfulness and the task of responsibility: inarticulable experience and self-doubt. In the poems by Sachs and Ausländer that reflect the conflict between witness-bearing and faith, the message is at times one of accusation and anguish towards the divine lack of intervention in the catastrophe; at others it is a hymn of hope inspired with a belief in restitution.

Rose Ausländer's "Der alles weiß" (I 151) from the cycle *Gettomotive* appears at first to be a poem of the first type, but concludes with an ambiguous declaration of faith.

    DER ALLES WEIß

    Du weißt, wie diese Tage mir begegnen:
    mit Schatten, die sich kreuzen auf der Brust.
    Der Priester kam, mich mit dem Kreuz zu segnen
    und fluchte meiner letzten Lebenslust.

---

ship to language and its significance for their self-assigned roles as witness-bearers in *Metaphors of Evil*, 184: "Alienated in its consciousness of historical evil and urged by the ethical necessity to bear witness for the landscape of the dead, the lyrical self has only the impotent power of the word with which to address, aggressively challenge, and provoke 'the quite other'."

[41] Cf. André Neher, *The Exile of the Word* where Neher discusses the inescapable responsibility of the chosen prophet (164): "The prophet who refused to transmit the message for which he had been chosen would have utterly falsified the very purpose of his election. The election had not been entrusted to man so that he might enjoy a private disclosure, but in order that he could transform it into an active element in history. And for that transformation the prophet is responsible."

[42] Nelly Sachs described her sense of responsibility toward language in a letter to Walter Berendsohn in 1949 (*Briefe*, 104): ". . . ich fühle die Verantwortlichkeit, die jedes Wort mir auferlegt, so stark, daß ich oft etwas zu leicht Gefundenes fallen lasse und mir lieber, wenn auch noch ungeschickt, das Felsgestein an unbebauter Stelle lockere."

Die Spinnen lauern schon in ihren Ecken,
und draußen sind die Schwerter blank gezückt.
Die alten Träume lassen sich nicht wecken,
die neuen stehen noch zu tief gebückt.

Und du, der alles weiß, läßt es geschehen,
und sendest nicht ein Heer von Engeln her?
Wer wird nach mir dich so wie ich verstehen,
und wer wird dich so tief erleiden, wer?

The poetic persona begins with the presupposition that the You whom she addresses is omniscient and therefore aware of the ominous, threatening atmosphere that surrounds her ("Du weißt, wie diese Tage mir begegnen"). Yet the next lines already put her faith in this You as the implied divinity of organized religion into question. The equivocal if not bitter quality of her belief is conveyed in the first strophe in her reception of the priest's last blessing, which she regards not as a blessing but as a curse. The negativity of this sanctioned blessing parallels the dubious honor of the Chosen People whose covenant with God not only granted them a privileged relationship to Divine Grace but also singled them out for special trials, tests, and punishments. While the fact that this blessing is bestowed by a priest and represents the sign of Christian faith renders the religious affiliation of the poetic I ambiguous, the connection of the "blessing" with suffering can be read as the association between belief and torment apparent both in the crucifixion of Christ and the history of religious persecution of the Jews as Christ-killers. The second strophe conveys the pervasiveness of the hostility in the poetic persona's environment: whether interior or exterior, there is no escape from dread and even past and future dreams are powerless to offer solace or refuge. The third strophe begins with a question that is both reproach and appeal to an all-knowing Divine being who has demonstrated such apparent indifference towards the suffering of the faithful.

The reproachful tone of the third strophe is immediately softened by the poetic persona's submission to the fate meted out to her by her God. In fact, she implies that she has a privileged relationship to this Divine Thou, or at least she constructs a position of uniqueness for herself in order to justify her suffering. The poetic persona here expresses an attitude that has a long tradition in the religious history of the Jews: as God's Chosen People, they must withstand extreme tests of faith and constantly prove their worthiness through suffering and pain. Although there is an implication of collective identity in the poem's closing question, the plea for salvation that echoes in it is ultimately one for individual redemption.

After the fact, both we as readers and Ausländer as author and survivor are aware that the biographical parallels between poet and poetic persona indeed led to an auspicious outcome that could not have been predicted by Ausländer when she first composed this poem in the Czernowitz ghetto under the threat of deportation and death. In the extremity of the moment where danger was constant and death imminent, the poet formulates her questions of faith through a poetic Other. It is telling, however, that her anguish and doubt do not cause her to abandon the belief that despite her shaken faith she needs and retains as a coping strategy in an atmosphere of total devastation and chaos.

In the aftermath of catastrophe and horror, language and the possibility of prayer are called into question and so, by extension, is the validity of the Divine Word. The credibility of the Father, the power of His Word, and the legitimacy of His Name are the subject of Ausländer's critique in "Vater unser," a conscious parody of the Christian prayer that provokes reflection on the degree to which Judaism and Christianity, as well as the crisis of belief and the crisis of expression, are interrelated. The tone of hope and trusting in a Divine power that informs the closing lines of "Der alles weiß," in part influenced by the proximity of annihilation, changes dramatically in Ausländer's "Vater unser" (VI 274), a much later poem that can be read as an ironic revocation of the prayer of faith invoked in its title.

VATER UNSER

Vater unser
nimm zurück deinen Namen
wir wagen nicht
Kinder zu sein

Wie mit erstickter Stimme
Vater unser sagen

Zitronenstern
an die Stirn genagelt

Lachte irr der Mond
Trabant unserer Träume
lachte der tote Clown
der uns einen Salto versprach

Vater unser
wir geben dir zurück
deinen Namen
Spiel weiter den Vater
im kinderlosen
luftleeren Himmel

While the title and form of the poem parody a traditional Christian prayer of faith, the rejection of a belief in the grace and power of a Divine Father expressed here can be read as without a specific denomination. By virtue of His exaltedness and His distance from His followers, God as the Heavenly Father has sacrificed both credibility and loyalty. Rose Ausländer characterizes the We of the once faithful as anxious children, abandoned by the father they had trusted in to protect them.

The demand that this false Father take back His Name reflects both disappointment and bitterness at the Father's failings, reactions among the We that have a stifling effect in the second strophe. The demand that the Name be taken back is made after the fact, however, and is preceded by an inability to pray. In the third strophe, the synthesis of Christian and Jewish traditions becomes obvious in the use of the yellow star image. Unlike the Star of David that the Nazis required all Jews to wear, this one is not merely fastened to clothing as an external designation of regulation "otheredness," but brutally nailed into the forehead, an image that implies the permanence of the marking and recalls the martyrdom of Christ. As the symbol of Jewish oppression, not only during the Holocaust but also much earlier in the long history of anti-Semitism, the yellow star here becomes a hybrid of the Nazi-assigned "racial" tag, the mark of Cain, and the crown of thorns in Christ's martyrdom. The Jews are the Chosen People, but this Chosenness exacts stigmatization as its price, the association of difference and privilege that inspires maltreatment and hate from the other peoples, nations or *goyim* of the world. In the denunciation of the Name of the Father there is a mixing of Jewish and Christian conceptions of deity, the God of the covenant and the merciful Father of the New Testament, but neither one has proved deserving of unquestioned devotion or childlike faith.

The depiction of the faith of the survivor-witness as one that terminates in nothingness is not unique to post-Holocaust poetic theodicy. The credibility of an omniscient and omnipotent God called into question by such an immense outbreak of evil presented a difficulty that troubled all believers, whether poets, theologians, or laity. Some stubbornly looked for some ultimate redemptive meaning in the Holocaust, while others jettisoned a belief in an all-powerful God, rendered untenable for them by the extremity of the circumstances, in favor of an existentialist creed grounded in a principle of Divine Absence. Richard Rubenstein, a noted American Jewish theologian, represents the latter attitude in his 1966 volume *After Auschwitz*. The book is a compilation of essays in which he progressively develops a Jewish theology based on the death of God as an agent in human history and proclaims instead

the supremacy of an inscrutable yet Holy Nothingness.[43] More conse-
quent in his imagery than Ausländer in "Vater unser," Rubenstein sees
only the void, albeit a void still imbued with a divinity that he respects
despite its formlessness. In contrast, Ausländer populates her vacuum
with a mockery of the paternal deity, represented as a pathetically impotent puppet God deserving of contempt and unworthy of prayers.

A comparison between an early and a later poem by Nelly Sachs reveals a parallel crisis of belief, where the poetic persona vacillates between defiant loyalty to a disturbingly invisible divine force and
disillusioned rejection of an absent God. In both of the following poems the poet takes her office as guardian of memory and mouthpiece of
her people seriously. Her responsibility as a witness-survivor is never
questioned, only the manner and meaning of the victims' deaths and
the subsequent implications for the future of Jewish religious faith. In
"CHOR DER TOTEN" (*FS 56*), a poem from the cycle *Chöre der
Mitternacht* published immediately after the war, the poetic persona
speaks for the victims still persecuted by fear as well as for the martyrs
who claim an ultimate triumph over their tormentors in death.

CHOR DER TOTEN

WIR von der schwarzen Sonne der Angst
Wie Siebe Zerstochenen —
Abgeronnene sind wir vom Schweiß der Todesminute.
Abgewelkt an unserem Leibe sind die uns angetanen Tode
Wie Feldblumen abgewelkt an einem Hügel Sand.
O ihr, die ihr noch den Staub grüßt als einen Freund
Die ihr, redender Sand zum Staube sprecht:
Ich liebe dich.

Wir sagen euch:
Zerrissen sind die Mäntel der Staubgeheimnisse
Die Lüfte, die man in uns erstickte,
Die Feuer, darin man uns brannte,
Die Erde, darin man unseren Abhub warf.
Das Wasser, das mit unserem Angstschweiß dahinperlte
Ist mit uns aufgebrochen und beginnt zu glänzen.
Wir Toten Israels sagen euch:
Wir reichen schon einen Stern weiter
In unseren verborgenen Gott hinein.

The omniscient poetic voice assumes the role of mouthpiece for the
dead who confront the living in an attitude of hard-won wisdom and

[43] Richard Rubenstein, *After Auschwitz: Radical Theology and Contemporary Judaism* (Indianapolis: The Bobbs-Merrill Company, 1966), 153–54.

grace. The We of dead voices admonish the You of the survivors for the hubris inherent in their naive and self-aggrandizing belief that they have an existence independent of the dust that constitutes all being. The transitory pleasures of mortal existence cannot compare to the sublime and astral heights that the perished victims have achieved. They are recompensed for the cruel and violent manner of their deaths on earth by their privileged proximity to God in the next world ("Wir reichen schon einen Stern weiter / In unseren verborgenen Gott hinein").

The implication that the victims' tortured deaths can be justified because of their ostensible transcendence to a higher, more exalted plane of being indicates the poet's attempt to give meaning to an otherwise senseless massacre, a gesture toward rationalization and coherence that is both practiced and criticized by theorists and writers of the Holocaust. During the concluding roundtable discussion at a colloquium on literature of the Holocaust, Cynthia Ozick, a survivor and renowned author in her own right, summarized an attitude shared by many critics when she took issue with efforts to extract redeeming meaning from the historical event of the Holocaust:

> Of course, we do not want to conclude our enterprise with an absence of meaning, without at least a touch of the veil of redemption. We cannot endure it; our moral sense, the yearning for healing, for mending, does not allow us to endure it. We want to escape from the idea of closure, of an absolute dead end. (. . .) Regretfully, sorrowfully, I find this view unacceptable. (. . .) . . . this premise of a moral aura — this search for spots of goodness, for redemptive meaning — seems to me a retroactive impulse, an anachronism.[44]

In her uncompromising view of representing and writing the Holocaust, Ozick here expresses a critical commitment to preserving the memory in all its starkness and pain, unrelieved by the balm of redemption.

In a poem published nearly twenty years after "CHOR DER TOTEN," Nelly Sachs distanced herself from a longing for transcendent meaning and offers instead an unflinching portrayal of post-Holocaust human existence in which individuals must take responsibility for their history without a reliance on a beneficent and powerful God. In "Der hervorstürzende" (SL 95), the poetic persona once again plays a dual role as the guardian and mouthpiece of memory of the dead, but this time does not attempt to justify their murder through an appeal to religious doctrine.

---

[44] Cynthia Ozick's remarks during a roundtable discussion, printed in *Writing and the Holocaust*, ed. Berel Lang, 278.

Der hervorstürzende
Fackelzug der Ahnen
in den Ysopgärten schimmerten ihre Köpfe
in den Verstecken des Blutes landsflüchtig den Gott
Auf den Küsten der Mitternacht
auf den verbannten Inseln
getauft mit den Wetterfahnen des Blitzes
Agonie in brennenden Tempeln
eure Heimat in meine Adern verlegt —

Reich bin ich wie das Meer
aus Vergangenheit und Zukunft
und ganz aus Sterbestoff
singe ich euer Lied —

The poetic I acknowledges her affiliation with the legacy of agony
that marks her forebears and feels the kinship with them in her veins.
The vision of a torchlit parade of dead ancestors winding through their
bloody history of catastrophe and exile reveals a continuity haunted by
the charge of their God. The visual contiguity of the words
"landsflüchtig" and "Gott" in the elusive and obscure fourth line suggests, however, that this God has abandoned His people like the countries that had turned them away or that they had been forced to leave.
The absence of God as mentor and protector necessarily implies the
impossibility of spiritual redemption, but in spite of this revelation hov-
ering between consciousness and denial, the poetic voice accepts the
arduous task of remembering and mourning her people in full recognition of her own human finitude: "und ganz aus Sterbestoff / singe ich
euer Lied." This represents a more grounded, human response to the
catastrophe than the earlier appeal to divine salvation, yet the absence
of God does not ultimately culminate in resignation and despair. On
the contrary, the lyrical voice expresses an unswerving confidence in her
ability to preserve the memory of the dead and thereby in some way
atone for the violent manner in which they perished.

Beyond the Witness

Es ist nicht wahr, daß die Opfer mahnen, bezeugen, Zeugenschaft für et-
was ablegen, das ist eine der furchtbarsten und gedankenlosesten,
schwächsten Poetisierungen.

— Ingeborg Bachmann[45]

In *Erinnerungsarbeit*, Margarete Mitscherlich's 1987 follow-up volume
to the collaborative study *Die Unfähigkeit zu trauern* that she published
together with Alexander Mitscherlich in 1967, Margarete Mitscherlich
claims that the diagnosis of a German collective repression of memories
associated with the Third Reich that she and her husband had analyzed
in the earlier study is still valid. In her independent analysis twenty
years later, she finds that only very few of her German contemporaries
took a genuine, critical interest in confronting their tarnished past,
while most were fully occupied with creating a comfortable situation
for themselves in the present.[46] She observes with apprehension a tendency among generations born after the Holocaust: their stubborn attempt to claim their own innocence by virtue of birth and thereby
proclaim their concomitant exculpation from any need to come to
terms with Germany's Nazi past.[47] In fact, the only groups in contemporary German society to make consistent and conscientious efforts to
come to terms with the horrors of the Hitler era, based on her observations, were the victims and the children of victims.[48] Although Margarete Mitscherlich may here be setting up an overly simplistic "Us
versus Them" dichotomy, the sentiment expressed in the foregoing
statement is one that informs several of the poems I have addressed in
this chapter, perhaps most palpably Rose Ausländer's "Überhört" (VIII
117). In this poem, Ausländer portrays the indifference of those who
are not victims to the cries of anguish emitted by those who are or
were:

---

[45] Ingeborg Bachmann, *Werke IV* (Munich/Zürich: Piper, 1984), 335.

[46] Margarete Mitscherlich, *Erinnerungsarbeit: Zur Psychoanalyse der Unfähigkeit*
zu trauern (Frankfurt am Main: Fischer, 1987), 7.

[47] M. Mitscherlich, *Erinnerungsarbeit*, 14: "Die sogenannten 'weißen' und
nachfolgenden Generationen pochen auf ihre Unschuld: Was wir nicht begangen haben, müssen wir auch nicht tragen und nicht bedenken. Psychologisch und historisch
ist das eine für Gegenwart und Zukunft gefährliche Haltung."

[48] Ibid., 28: "Nur die Opfer der NS-Zeit und deren Kinder kümmern sich noch
intensiv um die Vergangenheit und die Vergangenheit in der Gegenwart."

Wir wurden
von den Wortführern
stillschweigend
überhört[49]

Yet does this mean that the testimonial poetry of witness-survivors is appreciated only by a select readership united by their common experience or collective memory of persecution? Moments in the reception of the work of Nelly Sachs and Rose Ausländer both affirm and belie this assumption. Hilde Domin, in an open letter to Nelly Sachs published in 1966, expressed her gratitude to this poet whose complex and multi-layered identity as a persecuted Jew, exiled German, woman, outcast, and orphan gave her the right to speak as the conscience for both survivors and victims:

> Du hast diesen Toten die Stimme gegeben. Mit Deinen Worten sind sie — klagend aber doch — gegangen, den Weg, den die Toten gehen. Das konnte nur einer tun, der ein Opfer und ein Ausgestoßener war und zugleich ein deutscher Dichter. Einer, dem die deutsche Sprache zu eigen ist und der also ganz ein Deutscher ist. Und der zugleich ganz zu den Opfern gehört. (. . .) In einem äußersten, in einem extremen Sinne bist Du daher die Stimme des Menschen. Und Deine Stimme spricht deutsch. Zu Deutschen.[50]

In the immediate aftermath of the war, however, Nelly Sachs had difficulty finding a German publisher for *In den Wohnungen des Todes*, her first volume of poems in which her painful visions of the Holocaust were conveyed with unrelieved starkness. Her perceived status as what William Rey termed "die berufene Sprecherin der Opfer"[51] inspired both reverence and rejection. The poignant account of the catastrophe conveyed without hatred or vengeance in her poetry was too much for many Germans to bear, and those poems today retain a painful intensity that is disturbing in its clarity and at times overwhelming in its articulation.

---

[49] Cf. Alexander Mitscherlich's and Margarete Mitscherlich's pessimistic view proffered in *Die Unfähigkeit zu trauern* on the impact writers conscientiously striving to work through the Nazi past have on contemporary German audiences of writers (Munich: Piper, 1988), 56: "Die Gruppe derer, die eine aktive Auseinandersetzung mit unserer Vergangenheit leisten, ist klein, ihrerseits ziemlich isoliert und einflußlos auf den Gang der Dinge."

[50] Domin, *Nelly Sachs zu Ehren. Zum 75. Geburtstag am 10. Dezember 1966*, 192–93.

[51] William Rey, *Poesie der Antipoesie: Moderne deutsche Lyrik* (Heidelberg: Lothar Stiehm Verlag, 1978), 179.

The current focus on the Holocaust and the seemingly unending production of books and studies on the subject, ranging from the fictional to the scholarly and encompassing a large mass of speculation and generalization in between, throws those periods (particularly during the 1950s and 1960s when it was not such an object of obsessive interest) into the shadows. But it is part of the work of contextualized and historicized reception and reading to acknowledge the effects of time and the telescoping impact of its passage on the writings we inherit from a past that can only be grasped as a multiplicity of diverse representations where meanings are mutable and conclusions hypothetical. Michael Bernstein comments on the heterogeneity and persistence of questions regarding the Shoah in his book *Foregone Conclusions*, where he warns against attempts to regulate the way the Shoah can or should be represented:

> There is only a series of specific works . . . each of whose seemliness needs to be considered on its own terms without recourse to any overarching formulae. Instead of a single problem, there are the constantly changing questions raised by each new work that addresses the Shoah, and instead of a set of criteria determined in advance, only a kind of extreme localism of attention can come to terms with the variety of ways the Shoah is figured in our historical and moral imaginations.[52]

The position of the poet as a witness to a retreating event blurred by the lengthening shadows of time offers an aesthetic perspective, one in which choices have been made where a concern with language and image both marks and limits the message conveyed. One of the guiding principles of the present study is to read both backwards and forwards, with an eye to the poets' representations as at once backward-looking and forward-directed, in order to sidestep the kind of backshadowing Bernstein renounces as the substitution of a superiority gained by hindsight for a sensitivity to the past as an unstructured array of lived moments.[53] There is a temptation to read history and its manifold textualizations as an intricate but decipherable tale of inevitability, but to give in to this hermeneutic seduction is to disable the open potential of the present as a series of possibilities, and more pertinently, choices. Here I profoundly agree with the thesis presented by Gary Saul Morson in his book, *Narrative and Freedom: The Shadows of Time*. Morson argues that there can be no ethics if we operate with closed concepts of

---

[52] Michael André Bernstein, *Foregone Conclusions: Against Apocalyptic History* (Berkeley/Los Angeles/London: U of California P, 1994), 52.

[53] Ibid., 16.

time, i.e. those inextricably linked with determinism and inevitability. By precluding the possibility of choice, such closed concepts of time deny the individual the opportunity to decide and judge her/his actions as valid in the moment.[54]

The task of memory must be an ongoing process, as the Mitscherlichs argued in their oft-cited study, *Die Unfähigkeit zu trauern*, in order to combat the human tendency to deny, project, and sublimate events that threaten to disrupt the deception of a stable psychological equilibrium.[55] It is the calling of the poet-as-witness to keep these memories in the public consciousness, to focus on the representation of the past in texts that are unflinching in their confrontations with human history. The messages contained in Sachs's and Ausländer's poetry are not intended for a select audience of insiders, but address all readers willing to open themselves to an encounter with the traumatic traces of the Holocaust without the bolster of self-congratulatory outrage. The disturbing continuity in the present of attitudes that thrived under Hitler have made philosopher Emil Fackenheim's injunction to the survivors and future generations all the more pressing and compelling: "The truth is that to grasp the Holocaust whole-of-horror is not to comprehend or transcend it, but rather *to say no to it, or resist it.*"[56] Sachs's and Ausländer's writings represent examples of such resistance,

[54] See Gary Saul Morson, *Narrative and Freedom: The Shadows of Time* (New Haven/London: Yale UP, 1994), 21.

[55] Alexander Mitscherlich and Margarete Mitscherlich, 24: "Der Inhalt einmaligen Erinnerns, auch wenn es von heftigen Gefühlen begleitet ist, verblaßt rasch wieder. Deshalb sind Wiederholung innerer Auseinandersetzungen und kritisches Durchdenken notwendig, um die instinktiv und unbewußt arbeitenden Kräfte des Selbstschutzes im Vergessen, Verleugnen, Projizieren und ähnlichen Abwehrmechanismen zu überwinden."

[56] Emil Fackenheim, *To Mend the World* (New York: Schocken Books, 1982), 239.

but unless their works continue to be read and re-read for their relevance to the present time, the not insignificant gains they achieved through their *Trauerarbeit* will be lost, and their efforts to represent memory and generate an ethical dialogue of remembrance will gradually fade into the willed amnesia that accompanies concentration on a future in disregard of the lessons of the past.

2: Searching for the Mother

Woman will be the great German mother, the stricken motherland, the resuscitated motherland, the motherland at war. She is Mother and Death at the same time.

— Maria-Antonietta Macciocchi[1]

Earth is a Mother, but Earth is a cannibal Mother. (. . .) Both the Jews and the Greeks attributed masculine traits to God in order to dull the sense of terror and wonder men feel before Earth's demonic facticity.

— Richard Rubenstein[2]

Every God, even including the God of the Word, relies on a mother Goddess.

— Julia Kristeva[3]

AS SURVIVORS OF THE HOLOCAUST, Nelly Sachs and Rose Ausländer shared a commitment to preserving the memories of that catastrophe and the suffering that accompanied it. Faced with events that defied understanding, both sought after new means of figuring the disjunctive relationship between faith and history, for metaphors and language reflective of the dissonances between experience and belief. Comparing the poetry they wrote after the Holocaust reveals how both poets begin to shift away from conventional lyrical structures and the security of mellifluous rhyme toward equivocation, fragmentation, and condensation, qualities that have come to be associated with much of the lyric "after Auschwitz." In Nelly Sachs's poems, the destabilization of form and familiarity is evident in abruptly truncated lines and synthe-

---

[1] Maria-Antonietta Macciocchi, "Female Sexuality in Fascist Ideology," *Feminist Review* 1 (1979): 73.

[2] Richard Rubenstein, *After Auschwitz*, 125–26. Rubenstein argues that the dichotomy between masculine-centered and feminine-centered religions is irrelevant in a conception of God as unrepresentable nothingness, as ungendered divinity: "God in His holiness is beyond both the masculinity of the Judaeo-Christian tradition and the femininity of the pagan goddesses. The old problem of patriarchal and matriarchal religions evaporates in this final reality. (. . .) The holiness of God knows neither masculinity nor femininity; it knows only life, fecundity, death, mystery, and wonder." (125–27)

[3] Julia Kristeva, "Stabat Mater," *The Kristeva Reader*, ed. Toril Moi (New York: Columbia UP, 1986), 176.

sized images that seem to aspire to the mystical realm while still trailing roots in the reality of human suffering. Rose Ausländer's lyric becomes increasingly more spare and condensed, yet the paucity of words and the brevity of the lines concentrates rather than diminishes the multiplicity and elasticity of meaning.

The facticity of the Holocaust catalyzed a crisis of belief and raised questions about the nature of God as well as the capacity to keep the faith in the face of extremity. In their responses to this crisis, both Sachs and Ausländer came to question the supremacy of a monotheistic God whose apparent indifference to the fate of His People was shattering and inexplicable in the face of conventional representations of a benevolent and omnipotent Divinity. As shaken as their faith was by the mass murder and destruction of their people, the voice of protest that echoes in their poems retains a tone of reluctance to unequivocally renounce or completely relinquish the faith of their fathers. Instead, their questions and explorations led them in search of heterogeneous spiritual imagery capable of expressing the simultaneity of good and evil. This search resurrected older configurations of the life cycle as an alternation of destruction and regeneration: the cycle of existence as portrayed in Hasidic mysticism and traditional Jewish theology and as embodied in the even more archaic figure of the Cosmic Mother, the maternal goddess conjoining life and death, creation and destruction.[4]

Although the rabbinical conception of God included a belief in an oscillation between catastrophe and redemption as a continuous testing and rewarding the people of Israel, it presumed a more or less regular alternation of these based on a justificatory principle of discipline and reward. This system was developed as a means of giving religious significance to Jewish history and is especially apparent in the teachings of the Kabbalah that began to gain a following in the thirteenth century.[5]

---

[4] The point has often been made, especially in feminist criticism and theory, that the cult of mother goddess as earth goddess predates worship of a paternal god. See Robbie Pfeufer Kahn, "Women and Time in childbirth and During Lactation" in *Taking Our Time: Feminist Perspectives on Temporality*, ed. Frieda Forman and Caoran Sowton (Oxford/New York: Pergamon Press, 1989), 24: "Female earth goddesses antedate male gods . . . and were associated with the organic cycle of life;" and Rachel Blau Du Plessis, *Writing beyond the Ending* (Bloomington: Indiana UP, 1985), 119.

[5] As Harold Bloom describes it in *Kabbalah and Criticism* (New York: The Seabury Press, 1975), 51, Kabbalah is an interpretive approach that strives to read events in reality according to their alleged parallels in the Scripture: "Kabbalah proposes to give suffering a meaning, by way of an interpretation of Scripture that depends overtly upon an audacious figuration, the *Sefirot*." See also Seymour Cain's

Suffering and devastation were seen in causal relation to the sinful actions of the Chosen People and God's punishments for their transgressions against the covenant were severe but never meted out without the possibility of restitution. If Israel again proved itself worthy of God's grace through demonstrations of piety, what had been lost would be restored.[6] Destruction and catastrophe would eventually engender revitalization and redemption in accordance with the eternal covenant; but what if the experience of catastrophe went unredeemed? The traditional belief system did not make provision for such a scenario and it was this painful failure to account for the immensity of guiltless massacre that culminated in the widespread crisis of faith after the Holocaust and the quest for alternative mythologies expansive enough for the explosive dimensions of this modern outbreak of evil and destruction.[7]

Sachs's and Ausländer's longing for a focus and an outlet for their need for belief was an understandable response to the collapse of values and the sense of isolation they experienced as exiles and survivors in post-Holocaust Europe. Their lyrical confrontations with the genocide and the devastating revelations that followed it attest to their efforts to creatively synthesize historical, spiritual, and biographical themes often intersecting with maternal imagery in their writing. Both maternal and paternal images function in their poetry as polysemous tropes spanning cosmic, terrestrial, and temporal realms, and they serve as compensatory representations through which the poets strove to recover a sense of spiritual and personal equilibrium.[8]

Both Nelly Sachs and Rose Ausländer lost their fathers long before World War II. Sachs's father died in 1930 after a protracted battle with cancer, a disease Nelly Sachs would painfully succumb to in 1970. The

---

review of Jewish responses to questions of faith following the Holocaust in "The Questions and the Answers after Auschwitz," *Judaism* 20.3 (1971): 263–78.

[6] For a more in-depth analysis of this belief in an alternation between destruction and redemption see Yosef Yerushalmi, *Zakhor: Jewish History and Jewish Memory* (1982; New York: Schocken, 1989), esp. 21–25, and David Roskies, *Against the Apocalypse: Responses to Catastrophe in Modern Jewish Culture*, esp. 26–27.

[7] Yerushalmi even goes so far as to assert that nothing has developed to replace the strength of faith that guided and sustained Jewish religion before the Holocaust (*Zakhor*, 95).

[8] Alicia Ostriker offers the thesis that women poets' revisionist approaches to biblical belief fall into three categories: a hermeneutics of suspicion, a hermeneutics of desire and a hermeneutics of undecidability. The three levels she describes in *Feminist Revision and the Bible* (57–59, 66) in conjunction with her analysis of Emily Dickinson and H. D. are also relevant to the shifting revisionary processes I see evinced in the lyric of Nelly Sachs and Rose Ausländer.

death of Ausländer's father in 1920 catalyzed the first major rupture in her life, forcing her to leave both mother and motherland and venture forth on her own. The poetic depictions of paternal figures in Sachs's and Ausländer's works after the Holocaust indicate a kind of delayed response to their fathers' early deaths, offering a contradictory combination of reverence and disappointment: a nostalgic reverence for the deceased, biological father, and a disappointment mixed with lingering expectations in the Divine Father.[9] The Father becomes an uneasy conflation of divinity, myth, and memory.

The loss of the father effectively intensified and enhanced the maternal bond, which in Nelly Sachs's case had been especially close even before her father's death. Once they had settled in Stockholm, Nelly Sachs's bond to her mother grew even stronger. Margarete Sachs was all that she had left of the home and family she had known, and Nelly Sachs looked to her mother as an anchoring force, the connection to the reality and home they once had shared, treating her mother as both patient and muse, confidante and child.[10] Rose Ausländer's relationship to her mother, Etie Scherzer, was made both more complicated and intense due to the circumstances of her birth. Born after her parents' first child, a son, had died in infancy, Rose's early years were marked by parental overprotection and disappointment. Even after her younger brother, Maximilian was born in 1906, Rose continued to feel the pressure to serve as a substitute for her dead first sibling.[11] After her father's death, Rose's relationship to her mother transformed into a strong and complex one, and many of her poems reflect her attempts to come to terms with her conflicting desires for a reunion with the maternal force even as she remained aware of its destructive potential. While her mother was the cultural power in her life and inculcated in her a strong bond with the German language and literary tradition,[12] she was also the impetus for

---

[9] Ruth Dinesen discusses Nelly Sachs's relationship to her father and her pride in and reverence for him in *Nelly Sachs: Eine Biographie*, trans. Gabriele Gerecke (Frankfurt am Main: Suhrkamp, 1992), 30–33. Rose Ausländer's respect and awe for her father was attested to by Helmut Braun, editor of Ausländer's collected works and a close friend to the poet during the last twelve years of her life, in a personal communication in August 1993, and has since been chronicled in Cilly Helfrich's biography, *Rose Ausländer*, esp. 51–52.

[10] Gabriele Fritsch-Vivié, *Nelly Sachs* (Reinbek bei Hamburg: Rowohlt, 1993), 94.

[11] Cilly Helfrich offers a thorough, if somewhat speculative, discussion of Rose Ausländer's childhood and the evolution of her relationship to her mother in *Rose Ausländer. Biographie*, esp. 45–46, 56–58.

[12] See Helfrich, 60.

young Rose's emigration from her beloved city of Czernowitz to the U.S. in 1921. Although Rose must have understood the necessity of this move for the sake of the family's welfare, she nevertheless felt cast away by her mother. Despite these biographical differences, common to both Sachs and Ausländer is the poetic turn to the maternal image as a means of negotiating a destabilized relationship to reality.

Mysticism and doubt, belief and rejection, maternal metaphors and paternal images coexist in Sachs's and Ausländer's struggles to mediate history, tradition, and experience. Neither poet ultimately rejected the figure of a paternal God in favor of an originary maternal power, yet their experimentation with maternal images in poems after the Holocaust reflected efforts to represent the contradictions and dilemmas of historical experience both in despair and in hope of conceiving a means of moral existence in the world. In this sense, neither poet goes as far with the maternal image as the originary Great Mother implies. They are unable to relinquish their belief in morality even while they decry its absence.[13]

The play with figurations of the maternal as an approach to history is not unproblematic[14] and could be read as a mere substitution of one reductive trope with one less reductive, but I would argue that their use of the maternal metaphor is revisionary and reflects an effort to reconcile morality with reality, memory with continuity, subjective autonomy with community.[15] This revisioning is an effort at literary appropriation of the maternal imago to counter or subvert traditional representations of the mother, or, here especially in the light of National Socialist ideological manipulations of maternity, an attempt to recuperate the maternal trope as a polyvalent figuration resistant to conflation with fascism.[16]

---

[13] In contrast, Karen Elias-Button describes the goddess figure of Neolithic times as beyond good and evil in her essay "The Muse as Medusa," in *The Lost Tradition: Mothers and Daughters in Literature*, ed. Cathy Davidson and E. M. Broner (New York: Frederick Ungar, 1980), 205: "the fact that the goddess figure of the Neolithic Age represents the forces of death and decay as well as those of birth and renewal reflects the wisdom of prehistory: the knowledge that every creative act is firmly rooted in the dark."

[14] Note the connections to the cultification of motherhood that was so central to Nazi racial and martial ideology. See Weyrather's thorough study of this aspect of Nazi politics in Irmgard Weyrather, *Muttertag und Mutterkreuz: Der Kult um die "deutsche" Mutter im Nationalsozialismus* (Frankfurt am Main: Fischer, 1993).

[15] Cf. Alicia Ostriker's discussion of the revisionary reappropriations of myth and metaphor in women's poetry in *Stealing the Language* (Boston: Beacon Press, 1986), 211–15.

[16] Cf. Macciocchi, "Female Sexuality in Fascist Ideology": 70. Macciocchi argues that the genius of fascism, i.e. as evidenced in the cultification of motherhood and its

In the discussion to follow, I examine the contrasting figurations of the paternal and the maternal in poems after the Holocaust and explore how myth, archetype, and Jewish and Christian theology intersect in these representations. The cosmic figurations of Father and Mother stand in contrast to more terrestrial and domestic images of the mother in poems addressing the mother/daughter relationship that was so profoundly influential for both Nelly Sachs and Rose Ausländer. The poetic persona both encounters and perceives the world through her relationship to the maternal as divinity, cosmos, logos, homeland, mother, and originary other. It is this matrix of maternity that serves as the ground for the poetic persona's self-understanding as well as the inspirational model requisite for the creation of poetry. The presence of the biographical mother was a stabilizing force in an atmosphere of chaos, but it was the subsequent loss of this maternal presence that engendered an intensified relationship to poetic language. [17] Language came to represent the one remaining maternal connection for both writers and their literary efforts were not only confrontations with their identity vis-à-vis the past but also attempts to wrest some control over the configuration of history through their own reproductions of memory.

---

implicit valorization of reproduction for the purpose of war, was "to challenge women on their own ground: they make women both the reproducers and the guardians of death, without the two terms being contradictory."

[17] See Margaret Homans' reception of Lacan in *Bearing the Word* (Chicago/London: U of Chicago P, 1986) and her reiteration of the view that the child's entry into the symbolic order, i.e. language, is contingent upon separation from the mother (3). In other words, language acquisition is in some sense a response to maternal absence. This view is also offered by Julia Kristeva in her work on subjectivity and language as a dynamic of symbolic and semiotic processes. For Kristeva, the semiotic/maternal must be repressed in order for the symbolic/paternal to function, as she describes in "From One Identity to an Other": "Language as symbolic function constitutes itself at the cost of repressing instinctual drive and continuous relation to the mother." *Desire in Language* (New York: Columbia UP, 1980), 136.

Crises of Faith: Father God / Mother Goddess?

Yea, for thy sake are we killed all the day long; we are counted as sheep for the slaughter. Awake, why sleepest thou, O Lord? Arise, cast us not off for ever. Wherefore hidest thou thy face and forgettest our affliction and our oppression?

— Psalm 44: 22–4

In dieser Rauchzeit
ist der Glaube erstickt
Zünde eine Gedenkkerze an
  im Tränenglas.

— Rose Ausländer (VIII 160)

Thus the Woman-Mother has a face of shadows: she is the chaos whence all have come and whither all must one day return; she is Nothingness.
— Simone de Beauvoir[18]

The conflict between paternal and maternal conceptions of origin and cosmic power is one battled in the arenas of mysticism and psychoanalysis. Mysticism, in its Jewish and Christian variants, continually shifts between images of male and female manifestations of God in oscillations that prevent the establishment of a clear hierarchy.[19] Psychoanalysis, it could be said, is also grounded in a contest of supremacy between Father and Mother, the phallus and the womb, although in this case Freudian tradition would have it that there is a clear winner. Alice Jardine, in her examination of woman and modernity, brings together the seemingly disparate realms of mysticism and psychoanalysis in an attempt to reach the roots of contemporary views of maternity and alterity. The foundational elements of mysticism that she names: "Mother, Death and the Unknown," are central both to psychoanalysis and to the struggle Nelly Sachs and Rose Ausländer engaged in as German-Jewish women poets in a post-Holocaust atmosphere resonant with

---

[18] Simone de Beauvoir, *The Second Sex* (New York: Vintage, 1974), 166.

[19] It is interesting to note that the controversy concerning a hierarchy of precedence favoring either an originary mother or father is not definitively resolved even in clearly paternal-centered religions such as Christianity. The cult of the Virgin Mother as the Mother of God has led to an emphasis on maternal origins, occasionally with strikingly concrete representations in early reliquaries, such as the 15th-century French piece "Vierge Ouvrante" in which the Virgin's body is fashioned as a case that opens up to reveal the Father-Son dyad of Christianity. Illustrated in Erich Neumann, *Die Große Mutter* (1956; Zürich: Rhein-Verlag; Olten/Freiburg i. B.: Walter, 1989) Plates 176 & 177.

questions, despondency, and suffering.[20] The connections that Jardine draws between mysticism, psychoanalysis, and feminism enable a new dimension for understanding the works of these poets, encouraging re-readings that explore the intersections of religion, identity formation, and historical experience. Mysticism was a powerful influence for both Nelly Sachs[21] and Rose Ausländer, and Jardine's assertion that mysticism "as experience, is about saving the *Mother* from and instead of the Father"[22] offers a provocative perspective on the conflict inherent in these poets' crises and their search for alternative figurations of faith.

In Nelly Sachs's 1947 collection *In den Wohnungen des Todes*, God is an abstraction, a Name spoken with reverence but whose Divine presence is absent from the events of the world. This God is an entity apart, hidden, and inexplicable, an essence mediated only in and through dreams. The image of the mother, in contrast, appears repeatedly in many manifestations: as a nurturing force that ensures peace and love, as the vessel and guardian of memory and suffering, as maternal animal and protectress, but also as a barrier to the child's painful acquisition of autonomy. Still there are moments when the lyric persona feels bereft of all images of hope and faith and identifies with a collective of orphans, poignantly voiced by the We in the poem "Chor der Waisen" from the 1946 cycle "Chöre nach der Mitternacht" (*FS* 54–55):

> CHOR DER WAISEN
>
> WIR WAISEN
> Wir klagen der Welt:
> Herabgehauen hat man unseren Ast
> Und ins Feuer geworfen —
> Brennholz hat man aus unseren Beschützern gemacht —
> Wir Waisen liegen auf den Feldern der Einsamkeit.
> (. . .)

---

[20]   Alice Jardine, *Gynesis: Configurations of Woman and Modernity* (Ithaca/London: Cornell UP, 1985), 142.

[21]   Gisela Dischner, in her lead essay in the volume *apropros Nelly Sachs*, argues that Sachs's strong identification with mysticism is revealed in the personal style of her poetry, where her own experiences are raised through mystical ecstasy to a level of cosmic meaning. For Dischner, this approach is not a symptom of hubris, but rather a coping strategy through which Sachs was able to come to terms with the horrors of history. Dischner, "Noch feiert der Tod das Leben. . . ," *apropos Nelly Sachs*, 26.

[22]   Jardine, 143.

Wir Waisen
Wir klagen der Welt:
Steine sind unser Spielzeug geworden,
Steine haben Gesichter, Vater- und Muttergesichter
Sie verwelken nicht wie Blumen, sie beißen nicht wie Tiere —
Und sie brennen nicht wie Dürrholz, wenn man sie in den Ofen
   wirft —
Wir Waisen wir klagen der Welt:
Welt warum hast du uns die weichen Mütter genommen
Und die Väter, die sagen: Mein Kind du gleichst mir!
Wir Waisen gleichen niemand mehr auf der Welt!
O Welt
Wir klagen dich an!

This poem uses the form of a lament together with images of sever-
ance and destruction to convey the injustice that was done while the
"world" stood by and did nothing. Yet the accusation is directed at a
disturbingly anonymous object. "One" has done these things and the
"world" stands accused, but who exactly is to be blamed? The depersonalization of the perpetrator, represented as "*man*" (one), in effect
heightens the sense of frustration and loneliness expressed by the orphans. Bereft of mother and father (although not of their memories)
and of the opportunity to exact retribution from their oppressors, the
orphans can only impotently cry out their denunciations to the world.
Their only solace is in the durability of stone that now holds the
memories and legacies of the annihilated parents and the lost past. It is
interesting to note here the echoes of the figurative power of stones
from the Holy Scriptures as well as from Jewish memorial customs. In
Genesis 28:11–12, Jacob stops to rest at Bethel and takes a stone as his
pillow. It is here that he has his dream of angels coming down a ladder
from heaven. When he awakens he realizes that the stone forms the
threshold to heaven and makes it into a sacred monument to his dream
and to God (Genesis 28:17–22). In Jewish commemorative practice, it
is customary for visitors to bring a small stone from a familiar place and
place it on the grave of the deceased, again underscoring the symbolism
of the stone as a substantiation of remembrance and loss.

The tone of lament and denunciation in Sachs's "Chor der Waisen"
underscores the sense of bereavement and betrayal felt by the survivors,
but addresses the accusation to the world. In Rose Ausländer's "Vater
unser" (VI 274) discussed in the previous chapter, the accusation is
levelled directly at the Divine Father, who is held responsible for the
abandonment of His children. The divine claim both to paternity and
omnipotence is derisively refuted. In the aftermath of catastrophe and

horror, language, the possibility of prayer, and by extension also the validity of the Divine Word are called into question.

The bitterness and disappointment toward an absent God and the lack of divine intervention do not, however, lead to the rejection of the Jewish religious world view per se, but rather to a selective appropriation of those elements, especially those drawn from Hasidic mysticism, that seem to address the poet's specific situation. For both Sachs and Ausländer, one of the aspects of the mystical theology of the Kabbalah that appealed to them most powerfully was the Shekhinah. In the hierarchy of divine emanations outlined in the Kabbalah,[23] the tenth and lowest *sefirah* is the female-gendered figure of the Shekhinah, who because of her position among the *sefirot* was closest to Israel and shared in its suffering and exile. The Shekhinah, as the emanation of God-in-the-World, is simultaneously part of and apart from God and serves as the mediator between divine and human realms. As the representation of exile, as Divine Presence in an atmosphere of Divine Absence, the Shekhinah embodies the Diaspora, shame, mourning, and remembrance, and wanders the Earth in dark garments.[24]

Despite her apparent benevolence, however, the Shekhinah, like the ancient mother that serves as her model, is a conglomeration of both good and terrible aspects: she is both "the merciful mother of Israel" and the "Tree of Death."[25] Her attribution as the mother of Israel[26] associates her with the condition of exile defining the historical situation of the Jews and the fundamental ambivalence that informs the portrayal of the Shekhinah reflects this connection to the Diaspora. The moon and the ocean also represent the Shekhinah, illustrating by their very nature the cyclical condition of redemption and exile, with the implication that this alternation is as regular and natural as the waxing and waning of the moon or the ebb and flow of the tide.[27]

---

[23] See Gershom Scholem's excellent and concise discussion of Talmudic treatments of the Shekhinah in *On the Kabbalah and Its Symbolism*, trans. Ralph Manheim (1965; New York: Schocken Books, 1969), 104–5. Scholem further explains that the feminine quality of the Shekhinah is interpreted as akin to that of mother, wife, and daughter simultaneously. (105)

[24] Scholem, *The Messianic Idea in Judaism* (New York: Schocken Books, 1971), 74.

[25] Scholem, *On the Kabbalah*, 107.

[26] See also Scholem, *Major Trends in Jewish Mysticism* (New York: Schocken Books, 1954), 230: "She [= Shekhinah] is not only Queen, daughter and bride of God, but also the mother of every individual in Israel."

[27] See Scholem, *On the Kabbalah*, 151–52; and Scholem, *Major Trends in Jewish*

The Shekhinah, undecidable, hopeful, subject to the vicissitudes of the people's faith, symbolic of their redemption as well as their guilt,[28] serves as a dualistic mediator between human and divine. She is imaged in alternating and overlapping figurations of mother and other and invested with the potential for both good and evil, presence and absence. The Kabbalistic conception of the Shekhinah explicitly indicates that her relative distance to and from the Chosen People is determined by their faith and actions. If they doubt and commit evil acts, she retreats further into a state of exile. Conversely, she is drawn closer if the people adhere to the principles of their faith and commit themselves to good works and the study of Scripture.[29] Exile and shame, mourning and remembrance — these are the conditions evoked by the Shekhinah, but in addition to these is her acknowledged affiliation with the Divine, an affiliation that lends her a proximity to redemption despite her wandering distance from it in the present. The figure of the Shekhinah, as a construct that contains opposition and conflict without reconciling them, offers a possibility of negotiating a religious understanding after the Holocaust grounded neither in divine omnipotence and exclusionary monotheism[30] nor in an acceptance of the ultimate triumph of evil.

In Nelly Sachs's "Immer hinter den Rändern der Welt (*FS* 194–95), the poetic subject allies herself with a series of archetypal female representations of marginalization: the sixth-century Christian saint Genoveva, unjustly banished with her newborn child; the Shekhinah, who also represents the state of Israel in exile; and finally the mythical figure of Melusine,[31] the embodiment of otherness as half-woman/half-

---

Mysticism, 220.

[28] Scholem, *On the Kabbalah*, 108.

[29] Alan Unterman, *Dictionary of Jewish Lore and Legend* (London: Thames and Hudson, 1991), 181.

[30] In his discussion of Nelly Sachs's lyrical drama "Abram im Salz", Peter Michel interprets the battle between Abram and Nimrod as a contest between monotheism (represented by Abram) and polytheism (represented by Nimrod). Cf. Michel, *Mystische und literarische Quellen in der Dichtung von Nelly Sachs* (Unpublished Doctoral thesis, Albert-Ludwigs-Universität, Freiburg i. Br., 1981), 32.

[31] Gisela Brinker-Gabler, in accordance with Paul Kersten, *Die Metaphorik in der Lyrik von Nelly Sachs* (Hamburg: Hartmut Lüdke Verlag, 1970), esp. 178, makes this associative connection in her article on Nelly Sachs's poem "Bin in der Fremde." See Brinker-Gabler, "Mit wechselndem Schlüssel: Annäherungen an Nelly Sachs' Gedicht 'Bin in der Fremde'," *The German Quarterly* 65.1 (1992): 37. This interpretation is contested in Anke Bennholdt-Thomsen's and Alfredo Guzzoni's article, "Melusine: Herkunft und Bedeutung bei Nelly Sachs," *Euphorion* 81.2 (1987): esp. 160, which Brinker-Gabler does not refer to in her analysis. Claudia Beil associates the figure of

animal. By linking herself to these diverse representations of excluded otherness, the lyric persona conjoins the Jewish mystical tradition with Christian legend and folk mythology.

> IMMER HINTER den Rändern der Welt
> die ausgesetzte Seele Genoveva wartet
> mit dem Kinde Schmerzensreich
> im Heimwehgestrahl.
> Auch *Schechina* kannst du sagen,
> die Staubgekrönte,
> die durch Israel Schluchzende
>
> Und die heilige Tierfrau
> mit den sehenden Wunden im Kopf,
> die heilen nicht
> aus Gotteserinnerung.
>
> In ihren Regenbogenpupillen
> alle Jäger haben
> die gelben Scheiterhaufen der Angst entzündet.
>
> Auch mein Fuß
> hier auf der Straße
> stößt an den Aschenhorizont —
> ein Granatsplitter,
> nachtbehaustes Fragezeichen,
>
> liegt in der Fahrtrichtung.
>
> Aus der Kriegerpyramide,
> blitzverkleidet,
> erschießt wehrlose Sehnsucht
> die Liebe
> im letzten Schwanenschrei —

The banished maternal figure of Genoveva pining away with home-sickness at the edges of the world parallels the image of the Shekhinah, the feminization of Israel. In fact, the two figures are presented as equivalents: "Auch *Schechina* kannst du sagen." True to Buber's depiction of the Shekhinah in *Die Legende des Baalschem* with which Sachs was familiar, she is portrayed here in the second strophe as the suffering woman who weeps and wanders.[32] With the addition of the figure of the "Tierfrau" and her prescient wounds, the maternal figural chain be-

---

Melusine with Romanticism and argues that the use of this image in Sachs's poem is evidence of the degree to which Sachs was influenced by the Romantic tradition (Beil 226).

[32] Buber, *Die Legende des Baalschem* (Zürich: Manesse Verlag, 1955), 27.

comes associated with memory, a connection significant for the poet's own perceived duty as the guardian and vessel of the historical, collective, and individual memories of her people. This animal-woman holds the pain, suffering, and fear of the victims in her eyes, which reflect the fires set by the perpetrators. The heterogeneity of the victims and their experiences is expressed in the fourth strophe in the spectrum of colors refracted in these human/animal eyes, a colorful multiplicity that is contrasted by the monochromatic and single-minded destructiveness of the oppressors. The yellow of the bonfires recalls the stigmatic yellow star used to identify the Jews in Nazi Germany, but like fire, it has an almost elemental, mythic quality, and a history that can be traced back to before the thirteenth century as the classic color used to stigmatize the Jewish Other.

In the fifth strophe the lyric persona joins the succession of archetypal female figures of exile, suffering, and memory, thereby connecting the mythic past with the literal present. Her figurative foot stubs against the horizon of ashes left by the bonfires that had been burned into the eyes of the "Tierfrau." Her path leads through a wasteland, a war-ravaged landscape represented *pars pro toto* by a piece of shrapnel: "ein Granatsplitter, / nachtbehaustes Fragezeichen, / liegt in der Fahrtrichtung." The shell splinter is not only a synecdoche for the destruction wrought by the war, but in its physical shape as a question mark lying in the path, also symbolizes the questioning and doubt that causes the lyric subject to ponder how, why, and where to continue her wandering journey.

The entrance of the lyric persona in this strophe signals her participation in the process of mourning and memory. Yet the mission to carry on the legacy that has been passed down to her is one fraught with longing and despair, and the final lines of the poem leave the outcome open. The dangers to the continuity of memory addressed semantically in the text are formally reinforced by the brutal dash at the end of the last line, where both form and content emphasize the tone of dramatic undecidability. The ambiguity of the poem's end is deepened by the apparent contradiction between the hope for a better world implied in the appearance of love and the portrayal of this appearance as a swan song, a last outcry that is cut off or interrupted by the final dash that signals both silence and unspokenness.

In the first poem in the 1966 cycle "Die Suchende," Nelly Sachs transforms the mythological figure of the Shekhinah into a trope for sorrow, loss, and the lyrical search for home (*SL* 100):

Sie sucht sie sucht
brennt die Luft mit Schmerz an
die Wände der Wüste wissen von Liebe
die jung in den Abend steigt
diese Vorfeier auf den Tod —

Sie sucht den Geliebten
findet ihn nicht
muß die Welt neu herstellen
ruft den Engel
eine Rippe aus ihrem Körper zu schneiden
bläst sie mit göttlichem Atem an
weißes Palmenblatt im Schlaf
und die Adam träumend gezogen
Die Suchende in ihrer Armut
nimmt zum Abschied die Krume Erde in den Mund
aufersteht weiter —

The female seeker in this poem is in mourning, but her mourning is neither passive nor accepting. On the contrary, she assumes the role traditionally associated with Adam, establishing an alternative tradition of female precedence and transformation by fashioning an object out of her own rib to compensate her love and pain. The seeker, unlike Adam who was the passive recipient of God's gifts, has an interactive relationship with divinity and creation. The reference to godly breath is a further allusion to Genesis (2:7) with its portrayal of the (re)generative power of Divine exhalation: "And the Lord God formed man of the dust of the ground and breathed into his nostrils the breath of life; and man became a living soul." The seeker's aspirations to imitate the divine creation of man remain unrealized, fixed at the level of a dream, and in her disappointment she ingests the clod of earth that she had sought to imbue with life. This act can also be read as a symbolic critique of God's failure to protect and preserve His creation.[33] As an imitation of Divine creation followed immediately by its destruction, the seeker's actions resemble earlier myths of origin characterized by competitive violence, evoking, for example, associations to Cronus, who out fear of threats to his power, swallows each of his children as soon as they are born. In Sachs's poem, the clod of earth that was to be the

---

[33] Cf. Ursula Rudnick's interpretation of the seeker's actions as not only an attempt to re-create the moment of Divine creation, but also as a critique of a God who would make the world and then allow it to be destroyed (*Post-Shoa Religious Metaphors*, 107).

seeker's self-created Other becomes instead a part of her, incorporated as substitute gratification for both her desire and her loss.

In the sixth poem in this cycle, the seeker not only represents the condition of exile, but also embodies a line of demarcation, a border between the familiar, terrestrial realm and the "horror vacui"[34] of the unknown (*SL* 102):

> Wo sie steht
> ist das Ende der Welt
> das Unbekannte zieht ein wo eine Wunde ist
> aber Träume und Visionen
> Wahnsinn und Schrift der Blitze
> diese Flüchtlinge von anderswo her
> warten bis Sterben ist geboren
> dann reden sie —

The seeker as the poetic figuration of the Shekhinah here is missing something that would provide her with a sense of wholeness and harmony, a masculinized Other whose loss she mourns. In Kabbalistic mysticism, the Shekhinah is portrayed as joining with God in His male aspect in an act of erotic mystical union, the *hieros gamos*, which was viewed as the symbolic marriage of God and Israel and a celebration of the covenant.[35] In Sachs's "Die Suchende" cycle, the female seeker is described as the source of longing in the world, the embodiment of a plea for reunion, incomplete without her Other, figured in the closing poem as a strange hybrid of maternal and paternal qualities (*SL* 102):

> Was für eine Himmelsrichtung hast du eingenommen
> gen Norden ist der Grabstein grün
> wächst da die Zukunft
> dein Leib ist eine Bitte im Weltall: komm
> die Quelle sucht ihr feuchtes Vaterland
>
> Gebogen ohne Richtung ist das Opfer —

This image is paradoxical in its associative conflation of moistness and paternity. The adjective "feucht" inspires associations to swamps, oceans, and fecundity, which are more often connected with the maternal than with either paternity or fatherland. This play on the concept of wetness and its liquid, oceanic associations in anticipation of a return to origins occurs frequently in Nelly Sachs's poetry, where elemental

---

[34] In *Kabbalah and Criticism*, Harold Bloom uses this term to designate fear of a godless world, a condition of spiritual anxiety inspired by the anchorless state of exile (83).

[35] Scholem, *On the Kabbalah*, 138.

images of water and air recur as multivalent metaphors for maternity, memory, mystical union, and female creative and destructive power. The final line, broken off like an open question, recalls both the form and meaning of the question mark-shaped piece of shrapnel in "Immer hinter den Rändern der Welt" (FS 194–95). Here, however, the victim has become the physical manifestation of that unanswered question, bent with the weight of inquiry and uncertainty that seemingly has neither direction nor resolution.

The ambiguity surrounding the figurations of the cosmic and spiritual maternal demonstrates that neither Ausländer nor Sachs engaged in simple substitution, rejecting the untenable faith in an omnipotent Father in favor of an unequivocal belief in a maternal power. The absence of the father does not result in an unwavering belief in the mother as a protective force and eternal presence. The figuration of the mother is fraught with conflict and contradiction, compounded by fear of loss, desire for power, and longing for peace. The maternal metaphor that best demonstrates the ambivalent interconnections of desire and resistance, the longing for dissolution and autonomy, is the recurring association of the mother with the sea that permeates both Nelly Sachs's and Rose Ausländer's poetry. The oceanic maternal metaphor represents the fluctuation of opposing forces as well as the oscillation between fear and desire that characterizes the lyrical mother/daughter relationship. The use of oceanic imagery ranges from allusions to the sea as a simultaneously creative and destructive originary force, to anthropomorphic representations of the ocean as a wild and passionate female entity.

The desire for union with the maternal ocean is simultaneously escapist, emancipatory, and erotic: a combination of attraction and repulsion that marks the daughter poet's relationship to her mother muse. In the poems "Pupillen" (II 89) and "Meer II" (II 306–7), Rose Ausländer plays with the multivalence of the sea as a trope, combining its various associations as a primal originary source and as the fluid commotion of life and death, passion and submersion. "Pupillen" opens with a question that presumes an affirmative answer, a question intended to provoke the reader into reflecting on the commonality of all origin represented by the maternal sea:

> War nicht das Meer das wellengestufte unsere Mutter
> mit Brüsten voll salziger Milch
> War nicht der Fisch der silbergezackte unser Bruder
> brüderlich herzlich im Schweigen
> Wohnten wir nicht Äonen im kühlen Brand der Wogen
> Waren die strahlenden Sterne uns nicht gewogen

Sie leugnen es nicht sie schweigen beredt
Nachkommen sind wir nicht erste nicht letzte
Urrunde Muscheln sind wir wo die Mutter noch träumt
noch seufzt noch das Wiegenlied singt
noch die Perlen weint ihre Tränen

Sieh die Pupille die Perle im Glanz unsres Blicks
Perlmutterrund ist die Welt in ihr die sternende Erde
grün ist der Grund des Meers wie das Eden der Erde
wie der erstaunte Wald im See der Pupille

The opening question appears to the poetic voice to be more rhe-
torical than real since she seems already convinced of the answer. In
"Pupillen" the sea is figured as maternal infinitude, forever bringing
forth new life and reabsorbing the lost and the mourned. But despite
its encompassing capacity for both life and death, the sea in the opening strophe represents a utopian potential, albeit a remembered and not
a present one, for harmonious co-existence. This utopian condition is
not denied in the shift from the past to the present tense in the second
strophe, but it is represented as a lost condition, or at best the residue
of dreams. Afloat in the expansive generosity of the ocean, the eye of
the poetic persona reflects on the implications such a condition has for
the world. The reflection of the originary ocean in the eye of every be-
holder implied in the poem's last lines is both a signal and a reminder
of those common origins that should encourage harmonious coexistence. With the comparison of the elemental ocean to the fluid lake of
the human eye, the poetic voice connects the self with infinity, collapsing the boundaries between the self and the world as well as between
terrestrial and celestial, between mortality and eternity. This parallel
between the eye (as synecdoche for the I) and the sea is an empowering
and hopeful gesture strengthened by the references to paradise and the
implied desire to celebrate the positive potential for life in this world.

This all-encompassing, oceanic, self-regenerating environment is not
taken for granted but is rather noted with some perplexity in
Ausländer's "Meer II" (II 306) — a perplexity that is accompanied by
the shift from the collective We of "Pupillen" to the solitary I in relation to the sea.

MEER II

Ich weiß nicht wie es kam
daß alles was ich sehe und höre
zu Meer wird
der Fremde der Nachbar der Freund
Wellen
die Stadt
            brüllende Brandung
Worte
            Bewegung Schimmer und Schaum
Ich
eine ungenaue Gestalt aus Tropfen
deine authentische Tochter
            Meer

zusammengeballt
und wieder in deine
Wasserschaft gesogen
flüssiger Staub

Wir atmen dich ein
du atmest uns aus
mich und meine Quecksilberschwestern
die Fische
unser Wald aus
Korallen Seemoos Sirenen
hat viele Funktionen
den Tauchern vertraut

Here the poetic persona speaks directly in the first person singular, admitting her filial relationship to the ocean that formed her and addressing it as her mother. This admission of daughterhood, however, does not grant the poetic voice a privileged relationship to the life force. She is aware that her appearance in the cycle is momentary, that she too will be reabsorbed in the continual fluid process of appearance and disappearance that is echoed in the visual structure of the poem, especially in the weaving and undulating lines of the first strophes. The daughter-persona feels a sense of community and solidarity in this amniotic atmosphere, where the symbiosis between the maternal ocean and her "children" is as natural and regular as breathing. But the oceanic mother also embodies a vast wildness and a violent playfulness that the poetic persona at once envies, suffers, and desires:

Den Delphin auf dem Rücken
reitest du nachts
durch Sternsteppen
dein saftiges Fleisch
von Haien und Walen massiert
der heilige Monster Leviathan
wacht über deine Seele

Dich begleiten darf ich nicht
nur meine Nerven folgen dir
aber auch das ist ein Übergriff
und ich leide die Strafe der
Steine Scherben gemarterten Muscheln
Ich trink mich satt an Salz
Schlamm und den Schickanen der Wetter

Du spülst mich von
Golf zu Golf
von Klippe zu Klippe
in deinem Spiegel seh ich mich
einen vermuschelten Körper voll Rillen

The poetic persona's narcissistic desire to join with the watery mirror that reflects her own image ("in deinem Spiegel seh ich mich") is a wish to be reunited with her origins, to combat the fragmentation resulting from separation from the maternal by dissolving into an ocean that is both the Other and the self-same. The poetic persona is simultaneously reflected (in the mirror) and inscribed (with ridges) by the sea of her desire. As a reflection she is outside and separated, but as a mussel-like body etched with traces of her origins, she is physically marked as an insider. The surface of the sea becomes the permeable boundary between the Self and/as Other, and the desire for dissolution is concurrently a desire to disrupt this state of suspension in favor of an erotic union that is at once expansive and explosive.[36] Despite the tensions in their relationship, the poetic persona is able to harness her longing for the oceanic mother as a means to represent her self.[37] This self, how-

---

[36] The profoundly erotic nature of this image of union with an oceanic fluidity exemplifies Alicia Ostriker's thesis on the nature of women's eroticism in *Stealing the Language*, 174: ". . . this breaking down of boundaries, this fluidity whereby microcosm and macrocosm exchange places and we reenter the natural world from which we have been exiled, lies at the core of women's eroticism. Strikingly often, the key metaphors themselves involve water."

[37] My interpretation of the ocean as maternal mirror here is influenced by Julia Kristeva's discussion of narcissism as "a defense against the emptiness of separation" and her hypothetical image of Narcissus leaning "over that emptiness to seek in the maternal

ever, is diffuse, pluralistic, unbounded like the sea it seeks to emulate and converge with in an act of desire that can be read as both destructive (in that the boundaries of the Self as a separate entity are dissolved) and emancipatory (in that the Self has become permeable and inclusive rather than closed off to otherness and difference).[38]

While the daughter-persona recognizes that a joining with this maternal element is taboo, that even her desire to imagine such a union is subject to punishment, she persists in her fantasy of incestuous fulfillment with the maternal substance that both identifies and excludes her. This fantasy escalates from an enjoyment of being tossed about by the waves to the wish to be impregnated by the phallic oceanic mother, who in her infinitude displays both male and female characteristics:

> Auf einer Schäre
> unter Ravello
> möchte ich deinen letzten Anprall erfahren
> deinen kühlen Kuß ohne Kontur
> Eine Perle wächst mir ins Fleisch
> eine harte Träne
> du wächst in mir Meer
> du wächst in mir
> flüssig und hart

The choice of the pearl image in the concluding strophe of "Meer II" remarkably parallels the imagery Nelly Sachs uses to portray the encapsulation of sorrow in "Verzeiht ihr meine Schwestern" from the *Glühende Rätsel* cycle (*SL* 27):

> Verzeiht ihr meine Schwestern
> ich habe euer Schweigen in mein Herz genommen
> Dort wohnt es und leidet die Perlen eures Leides
> (. . .)
> Es reitet eine Löwin auf den Wogen Oceanas
> eine Löwin der Schmerzen
> die ihre Tränen längst dem Meer gab

In contrast to the raucous eroticism of Ausländer's imagery, Sachs here uses the oceanic trope as a representation of suffering. The sisterly

---

watery element the possibility of representing the self or the other — some one to love" in *Tales of Love*, trans. Leon Roudiez (New York: Columbia UP, 1987), 42.

[38] This again ties in with Ostriker's theorization of female eroticism as an implicitly transgressive impulse towards a unity that encourages plurality (*Stealing the Language*, 178): "The female erotic vision, then, amounts to a subversion of the identification of self with ego as bounded form committed to preserving its boundaries, and begins to propose an alternative scheme of larger units wherein the self is plural, a spinning array of multiple selves."

identification with the silent oppressed is internalized like a pearl, an impregnation with sorrow that does not climax in a dissolution of a sensual, celebratory *jouissance*, but rather reflects the hardened pain of the tormented that can only join with but not be washed away by the salt waters of the sea.

In Ausländer's "Meer II," the daughter's narcissism reflects a desire to be reunited with a prior version of herself, to overcome the separation from the maternal and return to the unobstructed mingling of that lost union by dissolving into an ocean that is at once the other and the self-same. The depiction of the ocean as a kind of mirror for a plurality of selves occurs elsewhere in Ausländer's work. In the poem "Treue I" (VIII 139), the sea is portrayed as the loyal servant to the lyric persona who, in contrast to the poetic daughter in "Meer II," here seems to be in control of oceanic power. In "Treue I," the otherwise omnipotent ocean is figured as merely a lady-in-waiting, attending the narcissistic musings of the poetic subject with multiple mirrors. The infinitude of the ocean has here become a quality claimed by and embodied in the now unabashedly multiple poetic self.

> Mein Meer
> bewahrt mir die Treue
> in seinen Spiegeln
> find ich mich wieder
> vielfältig
>
> Es singt mich
> zur Ruh zur Unruh
> aufgelöst
> in endlose Rhythmen
> singt es
> meinen wässrigen Leib
> in den Sand

The multiplicity nurtured in the maternal mirror and the specular affirmation of the first strophe is offset by the tonal shifts in the concluding strophe. The ocean's aspect has undergone a sea change from visual to aural, where the self-affirmation echoed in the multitude of mirrors in the first strophe becomes destabilized through the tonal variation of the second strophe. The melody brings both harmony and discord, a sense of peace but also disquiet accompanying the fear that the submission to the oceanic maternal lullaby will ultimately lead to the dissolution of the self.

The oceanic imaging of the mother in these poems represents the dualism inherent in the maternal trope and the poets' attitudes towards it. The ocean as mother offers the possibility of a return to an originary state of communion with nature and the world as well as the danger of dissolution and engulfment. The latent dangers in the maternal-filial relationship inspire oppositional fears in the daughter-poet: a fear of separation as well as a fear of destruction. The oceanic maternal metaphor serves as a point at which the figurations of the Great Mother of myth and the Terrible Mother of ego psychology meet and converge. The poetic attitude of simultaneous longing for union and fear of dissolution evidenced in both Sachs's and Ausländer's oceanic images connects with the ambivalent figuration of the preoedipal mother in ego psychology: "all-giving and all-punishing, an all-powerful being who contains within her the means of satisfying every desire."[39] The ocean as mother offers the possibility of a return to an originary state of communion with nature and the world as well as the danger of dissolution and engulfment. The tension within this polarity is parallel to the tensions that define and inform the mother/daughter relationship suspended in ambivalent oscillation between longing and resentment, mourning and bitterness, desire and language.

Nelly Sachs's "Rufst du nun den einen Namen verzweifelt" (*SL* 18) demonstrates the intersection of desire, disappointment, and dissolution in the sea image.

> Rufst du nun den einen Namen verzweifelt
> aus dem Dunkel —
>
> Warte einen Augenblick noch —
> und du wandelst auf dem Meer
> Das Element durchdringt schon deine Poren
> du wirst mit ihm gesenkt und gehoben
> und bald im Sand wiedergefunden
> und bei den Sternen anfliegender erwarteter Gast
> und im Feuer des Wiedersehens verzehrt
> still — still —

The poem begins with a desperate call to the One, the incantation of the Name that should bring forth life and light. But the use of the word "verzweifelt" already predisposes a sense of doubt about the outcome, a doubt reinforced by the abrupt break at the end of the second line that leaves both a visual and a semantic space in which the cry of the lyric persona echoes. The poem is structured to reflect a contiguity and continuity of form and message: the gap between the first and second strophes concretizes the sense of emptiness and anxiety in the act

---

[39] Patricia Waugh, *Feminine Fictions: Revisiting the Postmodern* (London/New York: Routledge, 1989), 65. This mother is simultaneously terrible and benevolent and inspires conflicting feelings in the child, both fear of destruction and fear of separation.

of waiting for a response. The first line of the second strophe underscores this anticipatory attitude and the hopefulness that inspires the lyric persona to wait just a bit longer, her state of expectancy signaled by a dash into nothingness. The moment of anticipation passes and the You (du), designating both the Other and the lyric persona in monologic dialogue, returns to an elemental state of union with the sea.

The absence of the Father is evidenced in the lack of response to the once-sanctified Name without which the lyric persona cannot become an agent of language. At the end of the poem the lyric voice leaves the realm of language and is engulfed by the stillness of the cosmos. The final dash can be read as symbolic of the plunge into a reunion with inexpressible, maternal silence,[40] or as a cathartic absolution preceding potential rebirth. This silence is the infinitude of the void, the threat of engulfment by the Cosmic Mother as well as the anticipation of union with Nothingness. By confronting this danger, however, the lyric persona opens herself up to unknown possibilities. What here could be read as a silence on the verge of a rebirth of language, as Gisela Dischner interprets silence in Sachs's poetry,[41] can also be seen as the threshold to a new, self-aware stage of being.[42]

The significance of the sea as a trope for mystical figurations of infinitude also plays a role here, especially in view of Nelly Sachs's self-definition as a mystic whose belief was not grounded in orthodox religion but in something "other" — vast, amorphous, and elusive — that could best be described as a kind of faith without fixity.[43] That Sachs was ultimately unsuccessful in resisting categorization became all too apparent when she was awarded the Nobel prize together with the Israeli poet Samuel Josef Agnon in 1966. The splitting of this distin-

[40] In *Tales of Love* Julia Kristeva posits the view that silence is a representation of the unnameable mother and serves as a maternal substitute (311): "Silence as an artificial mother."

[41] Gisela Dischner, "Zu den Gedichten von Nelly Sachs," *Das Buch der Nelly Sachs*, ed. Bengt Holmqvist, 330: "Vor dem Hintergrund von tödlichem Schweigen vollzieht sich die Geburt des neuen Wortes, die die Wiedergeburt des alten Wortes ist."

[42] Cf. Karen Elias-Button's discussion of mother/daughter relationships in literature in "The Muse as Medusa," *The Lost Tradition*, 205: "By confronting the Terrible Mother in order to move beyond the entanglements of the mother/daughter relationship, and by claiming her as metaphor for the sources of our own creative powers, women are creating new self-configurations in which the mother is no longer the necessary comfort but the seed of a new being. . . ."

[43] In the opening essay to *apropos Nelly Sachs*, Gisela Dischner alludes to Sachs's vehement resistance to being pigeonholed according to religious or ethnic categories. See *apropos Nelly Sachs*, 29.

guished prize was justified by the judges because it was being shared by two outstanding *Jewish* writers, who each in their own way were seen as messengers for Israel.

In Sachs's imagining, the ideal mystic was an individual filled with desire for experience on a grand scale and the images she used to contrast the mystic with a conventional believer parallel the oceanic longing expressed in her poems. In her critical commentary on Walter Berendsohn's draft of an essay about her work, Sachs rejected as overly simplistic his description of her spiritual belief. She countered his portrayal with her own view of herself as a mystic, who by her definition is a transgressor of the boundaries defining traditional, orthodox faith and who "aus dem hiesigen ausbricht um am Meer zu trinken und nicht an Wasserleitungen."[44] The oceanic trope not only serves as a polysemous signifier for spirituality, origin, and memory but also represents the source for the creative and destructive forces that inspired the poet's writing, distinguished her belief, and shaped her understanding of human history. Her faith was one that demanded a readiness to open herself to a sublime and potentially destructive infinitude approximated in the image of the sea:

> da wo das Meer beginnt, wo nichts mehr sicher ist, wo es beginnt, das große Geheimnis, dem man sich überlassen muß, auch wenn es kommt, das Furchtbare, Ertrinken, das aber doch nur scheinbar ist, denn ich *glaube* —.[45]

The loss of faith in a Divine Father and the ambivalent relationship to the maternal confound and disturb the poetic persona's relationship to the world and to language, inspiring figurations of the mother as presence in an atmosphere of paternal absence. In "Der Dom" (II

---

[44] From Sachs's remarks to Berendsohn's draft of the text "Ekstatischer Aufstieg der Dichterin jüdischen Schicksals Nelly Sachs," Nelly-Sachs-Archiv, Arch. 366, Stadts- und Landesbibliothek Dortmund. This contrast between "true" spiritual sources and their diminution through technology is one that recurs in Sachs's writings, both in her letters and in her poetry. In a poem from her first collection, *In den Wohnungen des Todes*, Sachs admonishes her readers to be on their guard against the alienating effects of civilization and commerce and to remain true to their faith and their God, a spiritual commitment she figures as a kind of "listening" : "Wenn wir auch Geschäfte haben, / Die weit fort führen / Von Seinem Licht, / Wenn wir auch das Wasser aus Röhren trinken, / (. . .) / Verkaufen dürfen wir nicht unser Ohr, / O, nicht unser Ohr dürfen wir verkaufen." (*FS* 18) She returns to this same image in a letter to Peter Huchel in March 1950 in which she praises the power of the work in *Sinn und Form* (*Briefe*, 114): "Hier läuft kein Wasser durch Röhren, hier ahnt man immer das Meer!"

[45] *Briefe*, 130.

214), Rose Ausländer combines different levels of speech and silence with the multivalence of the maternal and paternal tropes. In contrast to the poem "Vater unser" (VI 274) discussed above and in Chapter One, the paternal is not explicitly represented here, but is rather evoked through the image of the cathedral, in its Christian association as the "Father's house."

DER DOM

Ich habe einen Dom geerbt
Ich kann nicht beten
Ich stammle Blume Waldruh Wolkenstern
ich stammle Mutter Meermund du und du

Meine Gebete sind mir nicht geglückt

As in "Vater unser," the poetic I here is unable to pray. Although she has inherited the father's house, she is unable to speak the father's language. Despite her lack of proficiency in the father's tongue, the I nevertheless ventures speech, bringing forth utterances that seem to have no relation to each other, stuttered phrases, word-syntheses and neologisms that attest to the creative potential of the mother tongue, demonstrating that its failure as a medium of prayer is not an obstacle to its realization as a medium of poetic expression. In the staccato of words the I gives voice to a pattern emerges, a pattern of associations to nature as well as to the author's name. The reference to the flower in the third line evokes the rose that is both the poet's name and the symbol for Israel in the Song of Salomon; the neologism "Waldruh" recalls the idealized world of the Bukovina conjured up elsewhere in Ausländer's poetry; and finally the image of "Wolkenstern" can be read as an allusion to the destruction of the Jews, combining the symbol of their stigmatization with the fate this stigmatization consigned to them. The last line of the first strophe reveals the desire for a restoration of relationship with an absent You, a return to the source of origin, figured as both maternal and oceanic ("Mutter Meermund du und du"). This desire is not the regressive wish to return to the security and intimacy of the womb, but rather the longing for a condition of intimacy and communication with the other (the You), and the possibility of dialogue rather than (just) prayer. Prayer, the poem implies, is an expressive form that has failed as a means of communication.

Significantly then, while her presence in the cathedral reflects her exploration of her paternal legacy in the house of God, the poetic I has no connection to His language. In the Father's house she speaks the Mother's name, an other with whom she shares a bond that is beyond or outside the language sanctioned by paternal law. The stuttering disruption of speech ("Ich stammle Mutter Meermund du und du") can be read as a conflict between symbolic (linguistic, conscious) and semiotic (pre-linguistic, unconscious) processes representing an oscillation between paternal and maternal allegiance at the level of language. I am taking the terms symbolic and semiotic here in all their associative plurality from Julia Kristeva's distinctive brand of psychoanalytic semiotics.[46] Kristeva contrasts the situation of the subject within symbolic language, who has repressed the desire for the maternal semiotic, with the more unsettled and dangerous situation of the "questionable subject of poetic language" who "maintains itself at the cost of reactivating this repressed, maternal element."[47]

In the closing line of Ausländer's "Der Dom," the poetic I bitterly notes the gap between her words and an absent God who does not or will not hear them, implying that a reconciliation or reunion is impossible: "Meine Gebete sind mir nicht geglückt." The self-contradictory nature of the poetic persona's own admissions, however, in which she claims on the one hand to be unable to pray, and on the other insists that her prayers were unsuccessful, indicates the tenacious ambivalence that the poetic persona feels toward God. It is a relationship shadowed with doubts and disappointments and governed by paradox, yet also one that the poetic persona can never fully reject or abandon.[48] Nevertheless, the tension remains between the language that is recognized as prayer and the words that the poetic persona is able to stammer.

In the poem "Bekenntnis" (III 263), Rose Ausländer connects associative images of Mother, beginning with the Earth and Nature and then retracts from the archetypal into the domestic, moving from the nurturing, sustaining presence of home to the maternal creative power she associates with language:

> Ich bekenne mich
>
> zur Erde und ihren
> gefährlichen Geheimnissen

---

[46] See Julia Kristeva, *Revolution in Poetic Language* (New York: Columbia UP, 1984) and *Desire in Language*.

[47] Kristeva, *Desire in Language*, 136.

[48] Cf. Judith Butler's discussion in *Gender Trouble: Feminism and the Subversion of Identity* (New York/London: Routledge, 1990) of the temporary rebellion inherent in poetic language, a resistance to paternal law that ultimately submits to it (88): "poetic language and the pleasures of maternity constitute local displacements of the paternal law, temporary subversions which finally submit to that against which they initially rebel."

zu Regen Schnee
Baum und Berg

zur mütterlichen mörderischen
Sonne zum Wasser und
seiner Flucht

zu Milch und Brot

zur Poesie
die das Märchen vom Menschen
spinnt

zur.ı Menschen

bekenne ich mich
mit allen Worten
die mich erschaffen

This poem, presented like a litany of vows, offers a foil to the poetic persona's stumbling inability to "pray" in "Der Dom." Here she admits her relationship to the natural forces of the earth, to good and evil, but also to humankind and poetry as the means she has adopted to influence and transform her world, trusting in the creative capacity of the (maternal) language that brought her into being. The interstices of biography, self-formation, and poetic language in the relationship between the daughter-poet and a multivalent maternal muse are the focus of the next section.

Mother Muse / Daughter-Poet

"Vaterland?" Ich will lieber von Mutterland reden, dem Land meiner Herkunft, dem Land meiner Sprache. (. . .) Das Land der Geburt. Muttersprache. (. . .) Muttersprache ist die Sprache der Kindheit.
— Hilde Domin[49]

Language becomes the substitution for the forbidden mother . . . The desire to be the subject of meaning is the desire to have the other, the mother.

— Janet Todd[50]

---

[49] Domin, *Aber die Hoffnung: Autobiographisches aus und über Deutschland* (Munich: Piper, 1982), 12.

[50] Janet Todd, *Feminist Literary History: A Defense* (Cambridge: Polity Press, 1988), 52.

The primary relationship between women is the relationship of mother and daughter. This relationship is the birthplace of a woman's ego identity, her sense of security in the world, her feelings about her self, her body and other women.

— Kathie Carlson[51]

The play of presence and absence that influenced the poets' figurations of deity and history has parallels in each poet's biography. After her father's death in 1930, Nelly Sachs and her mother suffered the years of increasing hardship and terror that followed. In 1938 the apartment the two shared in the Lessingstrasse in Berlin was plundered by Nazi thugs and Nelly was briefly arrested and interrogated. Forced to sell their residence in 1939, Sachs and her mother moved into several furnished rooms in Charlottenburg where they lived in constant fear of deportation until they were able to escape to Sweden in May 1940. In exile in Stockholm, Sachs mentioned repeatedly in letters to friends that her mother was not only her most trusted companion but also her one incentive to continue living.[52] While her mother was alive, Margarete Sachs was Nelly Sachs's consolation, her most intimate confidante, her patient, her beloved, her child: a projected extension of herself.[53] Their

---

[51] Kathie Carlson, *In Her Image: The Unhealed Daughter's Search for Her Mother* (Boston: Shambhala, 1989), xi.

[52] Nelly Sachs frequently referred to the connection between her mother and her writing as reasons for her survival in her letters both before and after her mother's death. In a letter to Kurt Pinthus in February 1950 still overwhelmed by her mother's loss she wrote (*Briefe*, 112): "Aber ich bin bis in meine letzten Grenzen getroffen, durchgeschnitten. Dieses letzte, teuerste Erdengut hatte mich zusammengehalten, alles, was schon längst auseinander wollte, brauchte ich in letzter Glut, um dieses so oft vor meinen Augen schon Sterbende wieder zum Leben zu rufen. Nun ist nur noch Sehnsucht übrig." In another letter of the same period, to Manfred George, she summarized the significance her mother had had for her even more explicitly and succinctly: "*Meine Mutter ist gestorben. Mein Glück, meine Heimat, mein Alles.*" (Quoted in Fritsch-Vivié, 92).

[53] In her monograph on Nelly Sachs, Fritsch-Vivié describes Sachs's relationship to her mother during the Stockholm years as follows (94): "In Wechselwirkung hat sie die Mutter zum Objekt ihrer eigenen Projektionen gemacht. Sie hat sie vereinnahmt als die ungefragte Teilhaberin an ihrer metaphysischen Gedankenwelt und auch als die Bewahrerin all dessen, was sie anderen Menschen gegenüber verschweigt — beides bindet sie *im Geheimnis* noch stärker aneinander. Sie nimmt sie als ihre Zuflucht, *Mutterseele, Eiland und ständiges "Zurück"* [*Briefe aus der Nacht*]. Aber auch als die, die sie ihrerseits mit all ihren Liebes- und Schutzkräften überhäufen kann, wodurch sie sich selbst verwirklicht und bestätigt." [italics in original].

relationship was characterized by constantly shifting roles and expectations, so that the boundaries between mother and child became blurred, even indistinguishable, as if the two had indeed melded into the kind of mother/child symbiosis ("Wir sind Eines geworden durch die Inbrunst")[54] that has been referred to in Freudian psychoanalytic studies as the negative and deleterious outcome of an unresolved, dependent mother/child bond.[55] Such studies, however, do not account for situational factors that could encourage the intensity and longevity of this bond, nor do they address the positive aspects, such as the supportiveness of enduring love and mutual understanding, that are also implied in continued mother/child intimacy.

In Sachs's case, the situational factors of persecution and isolation that dominated her last years in Berlin and later the extreme isolation and alienation that characterized her life as an exile in a country with which she shared neither language nor nationality (and which only grudgingly granted her citizenship after repeated applications[56]), her relationship to her mother assumed focal importance as a point of interpersonal mediation and as a refuge of identification.[57] An "over-

[54] Unpublished manuscript of *Briefe aus der Nacht*, Nelly-Sachs-Archiv, Arch. 238: 19.

[55] Klaus Angel, a psychologist Chodorow makes reference to in her discussion of the preoedipal mother-daughter bond, defines symbiosis as a condition in which "merging fantasies are a true reflection of the state of the ego; the self and object representations are merged." Cf. Angel, "On Symbiosis and Pseudosymbiosis," *Journal of the APA*, 15.2 (1967): 315. Chodorow's comment on Angel's concept of what she terms "real" symbiosis is that it is accompanied by a psychological ambivalence, "an extreme fear of merging as well as a wish to merge, because there is no firm sense of individuation in the first place." Cf. Chodorow, *The Reproduction of Mothering* (Berkeley: U of California P, 1978), 102.

[56] Franz-Josef Bartmann quotes passages from Sachs's correspondence in the early 1950s when her efforts to obtain Swedish citizenship seemed doomed to failure. Sachs's hunch was that the Swedish government's delaying tactics were prompted by suspicions of her past connections with East Germany and communism: her first two books were published at the recommendation of Johannes R. Becher and Curt Trepte, active and high-placed members of the East German Communist party. Although this supposition on Sachs's part may seem to border on paranoia from today's perspective, it is difficult to reconstruct the political environment in Sweden at that time and determine whether there may have been some basis for her line of reasoning. Sachs was finally granted Swedish citizenship on April 24, 1952. See Bartmann, *". . . denn nicht dürfen Freigelassene mit Schlingen der Sehnsucht eingefangen werden . . ." Nelly Sachs (1891–1970) — eine deutsche Dichterin* (Dortmund: Zimmermann-Engelke, 1991), 99.

[57] Cf. Ruth Dinesen's discussion of Nelly Sachs's situation in Sweden and her subsequent dependence and reliance on the relationship to her mother as the outlet

identification" between mother and daughter from a psychoanalytic perspective can be an indication of emotional immaturity,[58] and it could be argued, based on Nelly Sachs's own admissions as well as the observations made by acquaintances, that Nelly Sachs's relationship to her mother did indeed fall under that category. In a letter to Walter Berendsohn in 1944, Sachs makes a reference to her first published book, the *Legenden und Erzählungen*, which appeared in 1921 and which she dedicated to Selma Lagerlöf. Sachs remarks on the response her "Märchenbuch" received from her revered literary idol. In Sachs's recollection of the event, Lagerlöf wrote back and thanked the "still very young girl" with high praise for her book.[59] At the time the book appeared, however, Sachs was already almost thirty years old and hardly qualified for the label "very young girl" she appropriated for herself. In her biography of Nelly Sachs, Ruth Dinesen attributes Sachs's sense of living out a prolonged childhood both to her unmarried status and to her continued devotion to her parents, whose protracted illnesses kept her at home and which fostered a relationship of mutual dependency.[60] Johannes Edfelt, a friend of Sachs and her mother in Stockholm, recalled the quality of Sachs's connection to her mother in a memoir after the poet's death:

> Ich habe niemals eine vollkommenere Symbiose zwischen Mutter und Tochter gesehen wie die zwischen Nelly Sachs und ihrer Mutter. In ihrer Untröstlichkeit geradezu erschütternd war ihre Trauer, als die Mutter gestorben war.[61]

The relationship of mutual dependence described by Edfelt had both positive and negative aspects, and the degree to which Sachs had relied

---

for her emotional needs in Dinesen, *Nelly Sachs*, 186: "Umgeben von lauter fremden Menschen, von einer Sprache, die ihr lange verschlossen bleiben sollte, hatte Nelly Sachs keinen anderen Menschen, mit dem sie alle Erinnerung und alles Gefühl hätte teilen können."

[58] I am borrowing the term "overidentification" from Christine Olden's study on empathy, "Notes on the Development of Empathy," *Psychoanalytic Study of the Child*, 13 (1958): 505, in which she defines it as extremely intimate and close mutual attachment between mother and child stemming from the emotional immaturity of the mother. The immaturity of the mother results in a narcissistic relationship to the child precluding the child's individual emotional needs and desires.

[59] See *Briefe*, 40. Here Sachs reminisces about that experience and refers to herself at the time as "das noch ganz junge Mädchen."

[60] Cf. *Briefe*, 8, and Dinesen, *Nelly Sachs*, 80.

[61] Johannes Edfelt, "Nelly Sachs von nahem," *Svenska Dagbladet* (1974), quoted in Dinesen, *Nelly Sachs*, 184.

on and identified with her mother became dramatically apparent in her intense emotional reaction to her mother's death in 1950. The physical loss of her mother became the impetus for compensatory moves to re-create the intimacy they had shared. The mother's physical absence did not erase the daughter's spiritual affinity with her, and Nelly Sachs's need and desire for her mother's emotional companionship lingered on. Through a process of textual mourning immediately following her mother's death, she sublimated her longing for her mother as companion, kindred spirit, muse, and substitute child into language. When her mother died, Nelly Sachs wrote a series of hitherto unpublished prose fragments articulating her feelings of despair and loss. These texts, grouped under the title *Briefe aus der Nacht*, are structured like a dialogue with an absent, silent mother who serves as the locus of identification and difference for the poet's voice. Language as the mother tongue assumes the qualities and fulfills the function of the maternal refuge she sought while simultaneously serving as an outlet for her own creative desires as a daughter-poet. Although there was an extended period in which she was publicly "silent" — from the date of her mother's death in 1950[62] until the publication of her next volume of poetry, *Und niemand weiß weiter*, in 1957[63] — her repeated references to work-in-progress (especially the lyrical dramas *Das Haar* and *Abram im Salz*) in *Briefe aus der Nacht*[64] indicate a continued intense, private preoccupation with writing. As in the period of acute crisis preceding and following her escape from Nazi Germany, her reflections on language in the unpublished *Briefe aus der Nacht* once again illustrate that writing served her as a means with which to combat the specter of mental instability[65] and thus as the battleground of her own psychological survival even if her words on paper were destined only for the kitchen cabinet.[66]

---

[62] Margarete Sachs died in Stockholm on February 7, 1950.

[63] Unpublished letter to Walter Berendsohn, dated September 7, 1959, Nelly-Sachs-Archiv, Arch. 176.

[64] Unpublished manuscript, written between 1950 and 1953, Nelly-Sachs-Archiv, Arch. 238.

[65] After her mother's death, Sachs feared that she would suffer a nervous breakdown and wrote of this well-founded anxiety in her *Briefe aus der Nacht*: "Mein Kopf ist krank. Die gleiche Krankheit wie du, meine Mutter. Es beginnt mit Vergessen." (Quoted in Fritsch-Vivié, 110).

[66] Nelly Sachs never had a place set apart purely for writing and literary pursuits in her tiny apartment in Stockholm and she stored her manuscripts in a kitchen cupboard. Cf. Sachs's denial that she would qualify as a "writer" in a letter of 17 March 1958 to the Swedish literary critic Margit Abenius (*Briefe*, 189): "Liebste Margit

In these acts of writing as self-therapy, Sachs also mused with uncritical nostalgia upon her relationship to her father before his death, as
if looking for points of anchor for her unfocussed need for emotional
support and stability. Although Sachs recalled her bond with her father
as one rooted in their mutual love and appreciation for music, she acknowledged a stronger sense of intimacy and closeness with her
mother. While she enjoyed the sensual musicality of those moments
when her father played piano and she accompanied him through spon-
taneously improvised dance movements, their connections seemed to
be attempts to bridge a distance that could not be negotiated in words.
Sachs's recollections of her relationship to her father, particularly after
the death of her mother, are colored by a longing for the lost magic of
childhood fantasy. Writing to Margit Abenius on March 17, 1958,
Sachs reminisced:

> Als Kind tanzte ich Selbsterdachtes, wenn mein Vater am Klavier
> phantasierte. Wir sprachen so wenig miteinander, jeder hatte eine
> Scheu, aber wir waren fortgezaubert zusammen von diesem Stern.[67]

Despite the wordless intimacy of their musical connection, the daughter's awe of the father attests to the distance that otherwise separates
them, an aspect of their relationship that Sachs describes in a 1959 letter to Walter Berendsohn:

> Aber ich kann nicht sagen, daß ich in meiner Jugend, außer einer
> grenzenlosen Bewunderung, ein nahes Verhältnis zu meinem Vater
> gewann. Es war eine tiefe Scheu, fast mit Furcht gemischt, und er ließ
> auch keinen zu sich. (. . .) So war es ganz natürlich, daß meine Mut-
> ter der heißgeliebte Stern meiner Jugend war und bis in die letzte Mi-
> nute ihres Hierseins verblieb.[68]

In her *Briefe aus der Nacht*, written between 1950 and 1953 in reaction
to the death of her mother, Sachs referred to the father of her memory as
a near divinity with whom she communicated through music.[69] Ruth
Dinesen, in her biography of Nelly Sachs, describes this father-daughter

---

Abenius — bin ja niemals eine Dichterin gewesen, was man vielleicht als solche dar-
unter versteht. Habe nie einen Schreibtisch bis zum Augenblick besessen — meine
Manuskripte liegen hier im Küchenschrank."

[67] *Briefe*, 189.

[68] *Briefe*, 198–9.

[69] Nelly Sachs-Archiv, Arch. 238: 7: "In der Zwischenzeit lebte der geliebte Vater und wurde so begrüsst [*sic*], fast heilig er, in der Musik. . . ."

bond as a complex of intimacy, possessiveness, intensity, and shyness,[70] while Gisela Dischner portrays the relationship as symbiotic.[71]

For both Sachs and Ausländer, the mother of their life experiences was more emotive and down-to-earth than the father, who was viewed as a distant figure, almost like a being from another realm, or a near deity commanding fear, respect, and devotion. Rose Ausländer lost her father to illness at an even younger age than Nelly Sachs. While Sachs enjoyed the company of both her parents until she was well into adulthood, Ausländer was only nineteen when her father, a learned Jew from Sadagora, died in 1920.[72] Because of his early death, Ausländer's father was temporally disassociated from the horrors of the Nazi occupation, a disassociation that lent him a purity that enabled Rose Ausländer to connect her memory of him with an image of an intact deity. He was the unquestioned paternal God of her childhood.[73] With the loss of her father, she, like Sachs, developed a strong bond with her mother, one that was characterized, however, by a mixture of guilt, dependency, sorrow, and resentment. The significance of the father's death and the compensatory turn to the mother as the last outpost of familial identification and sanctuary parallel the shifts in paternal and maternal figurations found in Sachs's and Ausländer's post-Holocaust poems. The dominance of the maternal metaphor in the post-1945 works of these poetic daughters would seem to verify the re-valuation of the mother-daughter bond that Marianne Hirsch claims comes "to replace the rupture between self and world implied in the destructiveness of war."[74]

[70] Dinesen, *Nelly Sachs*, 41–42. Dinesen discusses the special nature of the father and daughter's relationship to music and that their communication through music and dance illustrate the complexity of their bond: "Gerade aufgrund der Scheu, die zwischen Vater und Tochter herrschte, mußte das Kind versuchen, den Abstand mit Hilfe von Phantasievorstellungen zu überwinden. Es schafft sich eine andere Welt, in der es ihm erlaubt ist, seiner hingebungsvollen Liebe im Tanz zur Musik des Vaters Ausdruck zu verleihen. Die Tochter gestattet es niemandem sonst, sich in dieses Verhältnis zu drängen, und der Vater will seine Tochter für sich allein haben. Auch für ihn soll sie Vaters Tochter sein."

[71] See Dischner's introductory essay to *apropos Nelly Sachs*, 8.

[72] Helmut Braun, "'Es bleibt noch viel zu sagen'," *Rose Ausländer: Materialien zu Leben und Werk*, ed. Helmut Braun (Frankfurt am Main: Fischer, 1991), 11–12.

[73] See Ausländer's nostalgic remembrance of her relationship to her father in a prose text written in 1967 entitled "Warum?" (III 278–83) here esp. 279: "Papa, das war natürlich mein Vater, aber er war auch: der liebe Gott. Als mir einmal der liebe Gott im Traum erschien, mit langem weißen Bart natürlich, hatte er Papas Gesicht und seine blauschwarzen Augen."

[74] Marianne Hirsch, *The Mother/Daughter Plot* (Bloomington/ Indianapolis: In-

After Sigmund Scherzer's death, Ausländer's mother, Etie Scherzer, was left with insufficient means to care for her family. The family's economic straits served as the catalyst for young Rosalie's[75] emigration to the United States in 1921 to ease the financial burden on her mother.[76] She experienced both pain and anger at this separation from her mother, one she perceived as a kind of banishment.[77] The move away from her mother and her motherland also threatened to explode the idyllic image Rosalie had created of her childhood and her parents. Cilly Helfrich argues that it was to strengthen this threatened image that Rose Ausländer developed an exaggerated reverence for her mother, raising her up from the plane of mortals to a level of saintliness: "Ihr zukünftiges Mutterbild gleicht einer Heiligenverehrung, einer Glorifizierung, die ihr hilft, die wirklich erfahrene menschliche Schwäche der Mutter ertragbar zu machen ...."[78]

Even after her emigration to the U.S., Rose maintained a strong sense of loyalty and devotion to her mother, so strong that she returned to Czernowitz to care for her in 1939 despite the dangers obviously developing in central Europe.[79] Rose Ausländer's choice to return to her mother in Czernowitz at the end of 1939 effectively prevented her from returning the U.S. and she was trapped in Rumania, anxiously anticipating a fate similar to that which befell so many of her fellow Jews. During the years of persecution and suffering she spent with her mother in the Czernowitz ghetto, Ausländer's rejection or denunciation of an impotent, unjust or uncaring God added a new dimension to an already ambivalent mother/daughter relationship. Wolfgang Wenzel describes Ausländer's reaction to the atmosphere of extremity of the ghetto years as a turning away from God in favor of a mother figure that was physically present.[80] This compensatory move was not without

---

diana UP, 1989), 135.

[75] Rose Ausländer's maiden name was Rosalie Scherzer.

[76] Cf. Helmut Braun's biographical essay on Rose Ausländer in *Rose Ausländer: Materialien zu Leben und Werk*, esp. 13.

[77] Personal communication with Helmut Braun, editor of Rose Ausländer's collected poems and a close friend of the poet during the last twelve years of her life.

[78] Helfrich, 92.

[79] Cilly Helfrich reads Rose Ausländer's rash move back to Czernowitz in 1939 as evidence of the bond of sorrow and suffering that connected Rose to her mother, a residue of her sense of being inadequate already as a young child, unable to compensate her parents for the loss of their first-born son. See Helfrich, 160–61.

[80] Wolfgang Wenzel, "Jüdische Tradition in Rose Ausländers lyrischem Werk" (Abschlussarbeit für das Lehramt, Universität des Saarlandes, 1986: Rose-Ausländer-

its problems, not only because of the underlying attraction/repulsion of the mother/daughter relationship, but also because of the associations it inspired with the cult of motherhood propagated by the Nazis. The Nazi cult of motherhood, central to their ideology of racial superiority and their policy of "racial hygiene," was conceived as a pseudoreligion designed to seduce the masses and coopt women's loyalties.[81]

The mothers of Nazi propaganda were perceived as false and evil surrogate mothers whose existence is evoked in Nelly Sachs's poem "O der weinenden Kinder Nacht!" (*FS* 10) from the 1947 collection, *In den Wohnungen des Todes*:

> O DER WEINENDEN KINDER Nacht!
> Der zum Tode gezeichneten Kinder Nacht!
> Der Schlaf hat keinen Eingang mehr.
> Schreckliche Wärterinnen
> Sind an die Stelle der Mütter getreten,
> Haben den falschen Tod in ihre Handmuskeln gespannt,
> Säen ihn in die Wände und ins Gebälk —
> Überall brütet es in den Nestern des Grauens.
> Angst säugt die Kleinen statt der Muttermilch.
>
> Zog die Mutter noch gestern
> Wie ein weißer Mond den Schlaf heran,
> Kam die Puppe mit dem fortgeküßten Wangenrot
> In den einen Arm,
> Kam das ausgestopfte Tier, lebendig
> In der Liebe schon geworden,
> In den andern Arm, —
> Weht nun der Wind des Sterbens,
> Bläst die Hemden über die Haare fort,
> Die niemand mehr kämmen wird.

In the absence of the genuine mother, or the loving mother as foil to the terrible nannies who only strike fear into the mouths of babes, the world has become the plaything for unmitigated powers of horror and destruction. The world of yesterday depicted in the first lines of the second strophe is the world of a protected and beloved childhood guarded by a nurturing mother whose presence had made the poetic persona feel safe and secure. This is clearly a time past, swept away by the winds of change that bring death and destruction to the present.

Dokumentationszentrum, Cologne), 4: "In der Zeit der schlimmsten Bedrohung wandte sich die Tochter eher hilfesuchend an ihre Mutter als an Gott. . . ."

[81] The substitute-religion quality of the Nazi cult of motherhood is discussed at length in Irmgard Weyrather's study, *Muttertag und Mutterkreuz*.

Without the mother of yesterday, there is no one to care for the child
and the world has become a cold, loveless place of neglect and death.

The depiction of the loss of the maternal force as engendering an
environment of devastation and death is transformed into a self-
conscious nostalgia for the lost comfort and security of childhood in
Rose Ausländer's poem "Ruhe" (V 218).

> RUHE
>
> Ich habe dich
> immer gesucht
>
> Zuweilen
> lag ich einen Augenblick
> in deinem Arm
> Kind an der Mutterbrust
> von deiner Wärme gewiegt
> von deinem Schatten beschützt
>
> Du schöne Legende
> aus tausendundeinem Traum

Here the poetic persona openly expresses her desire to re-discover the
lost peace and comfort of childhood, embodied in the figure of the
mother, and to experience again the pleasure of being held, suckled,
rocked, and protected, even if only for a moment in a fantasized reunion so powerful with longing that she remembers it as if it had really
occurred. Yet in the end, the thrust of her desire is disarmed by the
clarity of her waking vision and she regretfully disassociates herself from
her seductive but unrealizable dream in the poem's final lines. The legend of the good mother as all-powerful, protective, and nurturing is at
best a temporarily soothing fantasy. At worst, the apotheosis of maternity could be twisted into a vehicle of ideology and propaganda, culminating in the Nazi cult of motherhood that figured the good German
mother as the pillar of purity, stability, virtue, and fortitude upon which
the future of the master race rested.[82]

---

[82] In contrast to arguments and evidence brought forth by Irmgard Weyrather,
Gisela Bock suggests that the cult of motherhood under Nazism was not as pre-
dominant as the propaganda suggests. The crux of her argument rests on the historical evidence that racist policies took precedence over gender politics. See Gisela
Bock, "Ordinary Women in Nazi Germany: Perpetrators, Victims, Followers, and Bystanders," in *Women in the Holocaust*, ed. Dalia Ofer and Lenore J. Weitzman (New
Haven/London: Yale UP, 1998), 85–100. My point in the above discussion is to
highlight the propagandistic appropriation of the mother figure in the service of racial privilege and not to affirm or refute historical evidence of the Aryan cult of
motherhood during the Third Reich.

Nelly Sachs's depictions of maternal suffering and loss counter the figurations of the "false" mothers populating National Socialist propaganda. In the poem "Trauernde Mutter" (*FS* 122–23), Sachs portrays the situation of the bereaved mother as a condition of desolate and unheroic sorrow. The poem begins with the mother's dream vision of her dead son as a bitter reminder of all of the wishes and desires she had invested in his existence:

> NACH DER WÜSTE des Tages,
> in der Oase des Abends,
> über die Brücke welche
> die Liebe sich über zwei Welten weinte,
> kam dein toter Knabe.
> Alle deine versunkenen Luftschlösser
> die Scherben deiner flammenversehrten Paläste,
> Gesänge und Segnungen
> untergegangen in deiner Trauer,
> umfunkeln ihn wie eine Feste,
> die der Tod nicht eingenommen hat.
>
> Sein milchbetauter Mund,
> seine Hand, die deine überholt hat,
> sein Schatten an der Zimmerwand
> ein Flügel der Nacht,
> mit der gelöschten Lampe heimwärtssinkend —
> am Strande zu Gott
> hingestreut wie Vogelbrocken in ein Meer
> des Kindesgebetes Echolaut
> und übern Rand des Schlafs gefallener Kuß —
> O Mutter, Erinnernde,
> nichts ist mehr dein
> und alles —
> denn die stürzenden Sterne suchen
> durch die Mohnfelder der Vergessenheit
> auf ihrem Heimweg dein Herz,
> denn alle deine Empfängnis
> ist hilfloses Leid.

The voice of the poetic persona is the voice of memory, of the pain, loss, and despair the mourning mother feels in confronting the senseless death of her child. The emptiness of the void that faces the child upon its separation from the mother is a mirror of the emptiness and silence the mother experiences in the second strophe after the loss of her child. The mother is left with nothing, for even those memories of her son's childlike innocence ("Sein milchbetauter Mund") are destined to fade gradually into a numbed realm of the forgotten, repressed by an overwhelming and unrelievable sense of suffering. Further, the atmosphere of intimacy and love that once marked the mother's relationship to her child is called into question, not only by the act of remembrance which crosses the threshold into forgetting and the realm of fantasy, but also by the realization that by giving birth to life, the mother always gives birth to the possibility of suffering, pain, and death. In the poem's closing lines, the mother is portrayed as the antithesis of the cosmic, all-powerful Goddess or maternalized infinitude that elsewhere served as the site of the poetic persona's desire; instead she is painfully and palpably mortal, a victim of the forces of history that have taken from her what was most precious. This alternation between cosmic and human figurations of the mother points to the polyvalence of the maternal imago and encourages a more expansive understanding of maternity in its spiritual and its social aspects. Sachs's suffering mother is a dramatic and poignant rebuttal to the Nazi propaganda images of stoic maternal patriots selflessly procreating in service of the Fatherland.[83]

The mother is frequently figured in Rose Ausländer's poetry as a trope for love, peace, and justice in contrast to the self-annihilating tendencies of a world complicit in its own destruction. "Betrübnis" (V 241) depicts a disturbed and disconsolate existence in a motherless world, where the absence of the mother signals the world's liaison with the forces of war:

> Betrübnis
> weil unsre Welt
> die Mutter verlor
>
> Diese schöne
> abstoßende Welt
>
> die sich mit Bäumen
> und Blumen schmückt
>
> die sich hingibt
> dem Krieger
>
> die deine Liebe und
> deinen Haß
> ignoriert

The poetic voice notes and recognizes the absence of moral justification in the process of history yet cannot resist a despairing wish for a

---

[83] This recalls the intent behind the artist Käthe Kollwitz's stark charcoal drawings of mothers in wartime. Her images were similarly powerful as dissenting portrayals of the consequences and implications of war.

benevolent power she could appeal to that would not be deaf to her feelings and needs. Ultimately, however, she must confront the reality of her situation. The world, both a feminine noun and a frequently feminized construct, is not a nurturing, all-giving source of refuge and gratification, but is rather completely indifferent to the poetic persona's affective projections. Just as it is illusory to project an underlying moral cognition onto the events of history, so too is it fallacious to imply that the world has made a pact with evil, that the world figuratively as female imago has been seduced by the warrior. In effect, the world and the universe exhibit only indifference to human fate, but the poetic voice cannot bring herself to relinquish a nostalgia that clings to the security of a time before wartime, when she herself was unconscious of evil and still enjoyed an intact bond with the lost mother. Losing the mother is here equivalent to gaining consciousness and sacrificing innocence, and the implication is that there can never be a return to that childlike state of peace. There is no place like home, but simultaneously no chance of going home again.

The poetic sorrow in Ausländer's "Betrübnis" is the informed sadness of maturity that imbues her nostalgic sense of loss with bitterness. The indifferent world she depicts as complicit with the forces of destruction symbolized by the warrior stands in contrast to the earth depicted in Nelly Sachs's poem "WER" (*FS* 331–32), where the earth itself is portrayed paradoxically as anchorless, adrift, homeless. The concluding strophe intimates that the condition of homelessness and longing for home is indigenous to the earth which itself can offer neither salvation nor a stable place of refuge for the wanderer and the seeker.

. . .

Überall die Erde
baut an ihren Heimwehkolonien.
Nicht zu landen
auf den Ozeanen des süchtigen Blutes
nur zu wiegen sich
in Lichtmusik aus Ebbe und Flut
nur zu wiegen sich
im Rhythmus des unverwundeten
Ewigkeitszeichen:
                Leben — Tod —

The only consolation left to us comes in the form of a rhythmical lullaby that serves as the melodic accompaniment to the cyclical movement of the cosmos. The eternal cosmic cycle is figured in oceanic terms as the ebb and flow of the tides, the rise and fall of the waves that rock the poetic persona's consciousness into a realization of the relentless yet somehow reassuring continuity of existence. Yet the lyrical voice here, like the voice in Ausländer's "Betrübnis," has not entirely transcended her longing for refuge, for a grounding in a geographically localizable space that she can call home. The break at the end of the final line, the dash that pierces through life and death by connecting and resisting them, is both a visual signal that the cycle could be continued indefinitely and a vivid representation of the poetic persona's longing cast like a line out into the oceanic void of the inexpressible.

The blurring and merging of parental identities is another manifestation of the poet's longing for security and her ambivalence toward the implied dependency of her desire.[84] This attitude comes across clearly in Rose Ausländer's conflation of mother and father in the poem "Beichten" (VI 211) which begins with a playful twist on the distinction between maternal and paternal roles:

> Meine Mutter ist
> mein Beichtvater
>
> Ich beichte ihr
> meine Glücksminuten
> meine Unglücksjahre
>
> meine Liebe zu
> dem Menschen den
> ich haßte
>
> meine Reise
> zu den Zwergen
> zu den Riesen
>
> Ich beichte ihr
> meine Zukunft

After the opening moment of convergence, the poetic voice shifts solely to an examination of the role her mother plays or has played in her memory. Every pair of lines is a paradox, each negating what comes before and highlighting the equivocal tone of the poetic voice. This paradoxical stance culminates in a willful refutation of linear concepts of time: the poetic persona and her mother are present in a discursive simultaneity of past, present, and future ("Ich beichte ihr / meine Zukunft"), a condition of mythic time that eludes fixity and bespeaks

---

[84] See Marianne Hirsch's discussion of the "double consciousness" characterizing much of women's writing, namely a combination of androgyny and male identification and an attitude of "thinking back through our mothers" that she regards as a positive approach toward creating different conceptions of femininity and writing. Cf. *The Mother/Daughter Plot*, 95.

continual presence.[85] The maternal imago is that which remains suspended between opposing conditions of happiness and sorrow, love and hate, while sustaining signifying power as the oracle and the vessel for the poetic persona's unextinguished hopes for a livable future.

The longing to preserve the connection to the mother in a timeless condition of reassuring presence reflects the poet's need for sanctuary in a world where she finds herself orphaned and alone. The fear of separation from the mother in the face of the facticity and finality of her absence becomes conflated with a kind of homesickness for a motherland whose loss precedes that of the mother.[86] In "Ein totes Kind spricht" (FS 13), Nelly Sachs portrays the pain of mother/child separation through the voice of a dead child, illustrating through an inversion of roles (the mother has suffered the loss of the child, yet it is the child who speaks) how the suffering of maternal loss persists beyond death. In the child's recollection, the bond with the mother was one of unity and security that was suddenly, abruptly, and brutally severed by an unseen force:

> DIE MUTTER hielt mich an der Hand.
> Dann hob Jemand das Abschiedsmesser:
> Die Mutter löste ihre Hand aus der meinen,
> Damit es mich nicht träfe.
> Sie aber berührte noch einmal leise meine Hüfte —
> Und da blutete ihre Hand —

The knife raised to divide mother and child separates them by virtue of the threat it implies: the mother disengages her hand from the child's in anticipation of the cut. In a maternal reconfiguration of the sacrifice scenario between Abraham and Isaac, the mother offers herself as the target for the knife's (and by association God's) demand for blood. But while Abraham's hand is stayed, the mother's hand in Sachs's poem bleeds; yet the structuring of the lines, themselves severed by dashes, obfuscate the cause of her wound. Was it the knife of separation or the

---

[85] Cf. Mary O'Brien's discussion of maternity and time in "Periods," *Taking Our Time: Feminist Perspectives on Temporality*, ed. Frieda Forman and Caoran Sowton, 15–16, where she describes the maternal as a condition in which linear and cyclical time are linked.

[86] See Michaela Kessner's discussion of the conflation of mother and "Heimat" in Rose Ausländer's poetry in "Die Lyrik Rose Ausländers" (master's thesis, Ludwig-Maximilian-Universität München, 1990), 60: "Heimat, in der Bedeutung von Sicherheit und Geborgenheit, findet ihr Äquivalent im Bild der Mutter. Mutterbild und Heimatvorstellung werden identifiziert. (. . .) In der Mutter findet das Ich einen Zugang zur Vergangenheit . . . . Die Mutter repräsentiert die verlorene Einheit des ursprünglichen Welterlebens und wird zum Symbol überhöht. In ihr kann das Ich zu seinem Ursprung zurückkehren."

child-become-knife, whose sharp blade-like hip is visually accentuated by the dash protruding from the word "Hüfte—" at the end of the line? The mother's wounded, bleeding hand, reaching to touch the child in a gesture of farewell, is similarly marked with a visual signal. The line breaks off with a dash that illustrates both the cut and the suddenness of the separation. The empty space that then divides this line from the next strophe intensifies the atmosphere of loss and the silence that follows. The strophe breaking this silence describes a condition already far removed from the moment of separation in the poem's opening lines and transforms the image of the child-become-knife to one in which the knife has become an internalized part of the child:

> Von da ab schnitt mir das Abschiedsmesser
> Den Bissen in der Kehle entzwei —
> Es fuhr in der Morgendämmerung mit der Sonne hervor
> Und begann, sich in meinen Augen zu schärfen —
> In meinem Ohr schliffen sich Winde und Wasser,
> Und jede Trostesstimme stach in mein Herz —
>
> Als man mich zum Tode führte,
> Fühlte ich im letzten Augenblick noch
> Das Herausziehen des großen Abschiedsmessers.

This representation of the child separated from the mother as effectively divided within itself illustrates what David Patterson observed as the symbiotic vitality of the mother/child bond in Holocaust literature: "This distance that isolates the child from the mother is a wound that cuts through the self."[87] The internalized knife of leave-taking ("das Abschiedsmesser") symbolically cuts the child's self and voice in two: every bite the child takes, i.e. every effort she makes to flourish and survive, is a reminder and a reenactment of the initial severing that caused her painful independence, to the point that the knife's edge cuts through and into all she sees and hears in her surrounding environment.[88]

The release from this hallucinatory condition of fragmentation comes with death and the removal of the knife. Death, for the child as a subject deprived of a livable present, becomes the ultimate substitute for the lost connection to maternal infinitude. The voice of the dead child is a disembodied voice that speaks through the poetic persona. The lingering of this voice after the childhood symbiosis with the

---

[87] David Patterson, *The Shriek of Silence* (Lexington: UP of Kentucky, 1992), 78.

[88] This depiction of the child's voice severed by a blade of separation recalls Nelly Sachs's description of her own sensation in response to her mother's death in a letter to Kurt Pinthus in February 1950 (*Briefe*, 112): "ich bin bis in meine letzten Grenzen getroffen, durchgeschnitten."

mother has been violently and viciously severed symbolically represents the end of a pre-linguistic unity with the maternal and the resultant entrance into language.[89] Yet the memories of this childhood state of communion haunt the poetic voice and fill it with a desire for restoration of that lost unity. The recurring themes of bereavement and loss in Sachs's poetry are often represented through the figures of either a solitary mother or an orphaned child.

Childhood as a time of peace and supportive unity becomes conflated with the lost "Heimat" imbued with a mixture of nostalgic memory and utopian anticipation. The nostalgia for the bygone and never-to-be-regained days of childhood innocence reflects a wish for parental protection and authority that is associated with the memory of a peaceful and harmonious homeland. This idealized memory of home is a homogenized construct that blends out the conflicts inherent in any childhood past. The fiction of harmony, however, is not left entirely unreflected or unquestioned in Sachs's and Ausländer's works, although each demonstrates a strong nostalgic tendency in the representation of childhood. Despite moments of critical self-reflection, the ideal of home from the past serves more as a foil to the crisis-ridden, nomadic nature of the present rather than as a means of questioning the viability or validity of the concept of home in general.[90]

The valorization of a childhood state of security culminates in a utopian ideal of home that is at once grounded in the past and projected into the future, a wishful vision of the future rooted in an idealized memory of the pre-war past. In Rose Ausländer's "Luftschlösser" (IV 56), the poetic persona portrays herself as a child despite her age and the acknowledged loss of her childhood environment:

> Die Schwalben
> sind ausgewandert
> aus dem Kinderland

[89] Margaret Homans critiques Lacan's view of language for its implication that a violent separation from the maternal is a prerequisite for entrance into the symbolic; in fact, she goes as far as to assert that: "The symbolic order is founded, not merely on the regrettable loss of the mother, but rather on her active and overt murder." See *Bearing the Word*, 11.

[90] For a discussion of the tension between the desire for a unified place of being in the world and the exclusionary aspects that such a home construct implies, see Biddy Martin and Chandra Mohanty, "Feminist Politics: What's Home Got to Do with It?," *Feminist Studies/Critical Studies*, ed. Teresa de Lauretis (Bloomington: Indiana UP, 1986), 191–212, here esp. 206.

> Ausgewandert
> das Kinderland
>
> Die Kinder
> alt geworden
>
> Ich
> im Niemandsland
> baue Luftschlösser
> aus Papier

In the absence of a "Kinderland," she constructs paper substitutes, fully conscious of their insubstantiality. These paper reconstructions of a bygone past also signify her attempt to compensate for losses in the present, sublimating sorrow into language and creating substitute bodies through the regenerative power of the word. The exercise of building and re-creating cannot ultimately serve its compensatory purpose because the poetic persona remains realistic in her acknowledgment that her constructions are mere illusions ("Luftschlösser").

The turn to language as a means of coming to terms with bereavement and loss recurs in both Sachs's and Ausländer's poetological writings, serving as a consciously manipulated and implemented defense and survival mechanism. Sachs mentioned repeatedly in letters after the war that writing was what enabled her to continue living.[91] Ausländer most explicitly addressed the role poetry played for her during the extremity of her ghetto experiences and the homelessness that followed in an autobiographical text written in 1971 entitled "Alles kann Motiv sein" (III 286):

> während wir den Tod erwarteten, wohnten manche von uns in Traumworten — unser traumatisches Heim in der Heimatlosigkeit. Schreiben war Leben. Überleben.

The practice of coming to terms with crisis and loss through poetic language also characterizes the manner in which Sachs and Ausländer wrote as a response to mourning. They experienced the death of their real mothers as traumatic events, and the psychological shock of their loss culminated in nervous collapse — a striking biographical parallel. For Nelly Sachs caring for her dying mother in exile in Stockholm, the anticipation of what this loss would mean to her catalyzed an increase of poetic activity and creativity. Poetry became an outlet for her fears

---

[91] Cf. esp. *Briefe*, 130 ("Und so ist alles, was ich schreiben muß, wie Atmen. Ich müßte ersticken, täte ich es nicht."); and *Briefe*, 199 ("Alles was vielleicht in meiner Dichtung aufgespeichert liegt, ist ja entstanden immer nur aus äußerster Not und nur aus dem Bedürfnis, Hilfe zum Weiterleben zu bekommen.")

and anxieties, and writing a coping strategy to deal with the imminent loss of the mother who had become a necessary foil to herself. She described this condition of anticipation and sublimation during the last years of her mother's life in a letter to Margit Abenius in 1958:

> Aber dieses Leben in den Nächten viele Jahre ohne Schlaf und immer wieder hineingeworfen in ein "Außerhalb," eigentlich jede Nacht den Tod neu gelernt, da ich das letzte mir gebliebene geliebte Wesen so weit fort umfangen sah, zwang mir immer im Angesicht der Leidenden die Worte auf, die dann später meine Gedichte und dramatischen Versuche hießen.[92]

The aftershocks of maternal loss were devastating and long-lasting. Nelly Sachs had herself admitted for institutional treatment and gave expression to her suffering and emptiness in an imagined textual dialogue with her recently deceased parent: "Wir haben soviel geredet im Schweigen. Trafen uns. Jetzt singt mein Gebein. Eine Muschel, die verrauschte Meere hielt."[93] Here Nelly Sachs as a daughter-poet expresses a sensation akin to that of the poetic persona in Rose Ausländer's "Meer II" — she is the silent vessel for the sea's music, a mussel shell that sings its communion with a vast primal element. In the prose fragments that comprise the *Briefe aus der Nacht*, Sachs seeks to recreate her mother's influence and presence through language. By constructing her mother as the fictive Other of her imagined dialogue, she is simultaneously giving expression to her loss and attempting to refute it. This process of coming to terms with the facticity of the mother's permanent absence through literary dialogue lasted for three years, after which she had incorporated the lost body of the mother into the materiality of the poetic word. Her reliance on her writing as a means of survival was deepened by the sublimation of her desires for intimacy and communication with an Other into language. This act of sublimation is simultaneously an act of re-creation, in that the lost mother's body is re-produced in the body of the poem.[94]

---

[92] *Briefe*, 189.

[93] *Briefe aus der Nacht* , Nelly-Sachs-Archiv, Arch. 238: 30.

[94] This act of maternal re-creation stands in contrast to the Kristevan and Lacanian views of language that Deborah Kloepfer reiterates in her study *The Unspeakable Mother* (Ithaca, NY/ London: Cornell UP, 1989). In her rendering of their views, the constitution of text is based on maternal absence and/or the repression of desire for the mother. Kloepfer furthers this linguistic perspective on absent, unspeakable maternity by inserting an erotic component in her own understanding of the maternal within language (2): "I further suggest not only a linguistic but an erotic component to the relation with the mother: she is *unspoken* both because rep-

The assumption and assertion of maternal, creative power in its literary transformation as the creation of poetry and the insistence on controlling memory is expressed most clearly in Nelly Sachs's poem "Was stieg aus deines Leibes weißen Blättern"(*FS* 227–8) from the 1957 collection *Und niemand weiß weiter*. In this poem, as in *Briefe aus der Nacht*, the poetic persona addresses the absent mother as if she were present through a dialogue that intimates a denial of separation — or an effort to convert absence into presence by giving voice to memory. The poetic persona acknowledges the loss of the mother, or the loss of that being whom she had once called mother; but her focus here is more on the legacy that this mother has left behind. The expiration of the "Mutter" has a residual quality, both as substance and as remembrance.

WAS STIEG aus deines Leibes weißen Blättern
die ich dich vor dem letzten Atemzug
noch Mutter nannte?

Was liegt auf dem Leinen für Sehnsuchtsverlassenes?

Welche Wunde schließt die durchschmerzte Zeit
die rann aus deinem Puls
mit Sternmusik?

Wohin der Kranz deiner warmen Umarmung?
In welchen Azur dein geflüsterter Segen?

Welches Lächeln gebar sich
an deines Fingers
luftiger Zeichensprache?

Auf welchen Spuren
soll ich deines Blutes Dichtung suchen?
Wo deine Seligkeit anfragen?

Wie unter meinen Füßen
die saugende Kugel fortstoßen
um die Todestreppe hinaufzustürmen?

Oft waren wir
geladen
zu überzeitlichen Empfängen
versteinerte Rinden
Meer- und Feuer-Vorhänge zurückschlagend —

---

resentation requires her repression and because releasing her, in the economy of desire, is illicit (incestuous) and therefore *unspeakable*."

Aber nun:
die Entlassene der Liebe hier
gebeugt über das Leid — Steine — Trauerspiel
dem Haar der Trennung nachsinnend

und eine Herzenszeit schaffend
wo Tod sich atmend füllt
und wieder abnimmt —

The mother's last breath is not the last of the mother. Her presence lingers as memory and image for the poetic persona, who apparently experiences these memories as palpable and painful sensations, as if in her identification and empathy with the suffering that preceded her mother's death she had incorporated her mother's pain and consciousness. Yet the poetic persona's articulation of the mother's undeniable death is colored with despair, expressed in the relentless series of questions that follow the initial question of how the wound of separation is to be healed. There is ultimately no substitute for maternal presence, and in recognition of this fact, the poetic persona in the seventh strophe fervently wishes to deny the hold life has on her in order to join her mother in death. The tone of the poem then turns to nostalgic reminiscence of the degree of intimacy that the poetic persona had once shared with the irrevocably lost one. The eighth strophe depicts a time before time, a kind of timeless, mythic condition of unity,[95] where the poetic persona reflects on the primal power of shared experience where she as We had wielded control over the elements.

But this mythical vision of a united and powerful We is almost immediately recognized as a wishful dream. In the succeeding strophe, the poetic subject must admit to the immediacy and reality of her loss and portrays herself as bereft of love. Enigmatically, the poetic persona attempts to alleviate her sorrow at the death of the mother by recreating the memory of the initial separation from her mother's body at birth ("dem Haar der Trennung nachsinnend"). The hair of separation she imagines symbolizes her growth outside of her mother's body and implies the severing of the organic umbilical connection she once experienced in her mother's womb.[96] This reflection on separations from the

---

[95] Cf. the collapse of linear demarcations of time that results in a condition of continual presence in Rose Ausländer's poem "Beichten" (VI 211) discussed above.

[96] Birgit Lermen offers a different reading of "hair" in Sachs's poetry, suggesting that in Sachs's mystical understanding, hair signifies the border or point of tangency between the skin and the Divine, "die Hautgrenze, an der der Mensch vom Göttlichen berührt wird." See *Nelly Sachs "an letzter Atemspitze des Lebens"*, 194. This reading is not incompatible with the interpretation I offer above. As an allegory for

mother both because of the daughter's birth and because of her mother's death conjoins birth and death in a cyclical continuum that enables the daughter-poet to relate to her grief.

In the final strophe, the motherless poet assumes the role of omnipotent creator, fashioning for herself a temporal state of being guided by feelings and emotions ("eine Herzenszeit schaffend") in which death and life are in a state of symbiosis. Through the medium of the poem, the daughter has achieved a sense of equilibrium regarding her loss. Using her access to poetic language as an expression of agency, she is able to regulate the cycle of life and death, in effect here reversing the irrevocable loss of the beloved by inspiring the image of death with the attributes of the living. In the poem's last lines, death is invested with lungs inhaling and exhaling air. This paradoxical image of a living, breathing, anthropomorphized death reflects the daughter-poet's attempt to gratify her own desire for recuperation of the lost through a language that itself has served as the vehicle for death.

In the act of writing, the poet links herself to the continuum of life and death by asserting the transformative power of poetic expression. Already in the poem's first line, "Was stieg aus deines Leibes weißen Blättern," the mother's expiring body is likened to white leaves or pages, a comparison that not only evokes associations to the passage of the seasons and the subsequent gradual disappearance of color from fall to winter; but also figures the mother's body as the surface for the daughter's inscriptions. This image of the maternal body as white, hence unwritten, blank pages connects the pallor of death to the initial confrontation with emptiness that precedes the act of creating a physical text. The mother's body, then, serves as a multivalent trope: concretely physical in her mortality and maternity, yet provocatively inspirational beyond death, she bequeaths her procreative powers to her daughter in transmuted form. The connection between body and text flows fluidly through the poem, appearing in the ethereal musical pulse that reverberates in the mother's suffering ("die durchschmerzte Zeit / die rann aus deinem Puls / mit Sternmusik"); in the airy configurations the mother's finger describes ("deines Fingers / luftiger Zeichensprache"): and in the mother's blood, which is portrayed as a liquid source of poetry ("deines Blutes Dichtung"). In writing this poem in homage to her mother's memory, Sachs both inscribes and recreates the maternal body in and as poetic text. The poetic persona becomes the symbolic mother to her own mother (as memory) and the

---

the mystical union with the One, the relationship between the child and the mother in the womb can be seen as symbolic of this brush with the Divine.

literary mother of the poem child. This effectively constitutes an incorporation of the other into the self, or as David Patterson describes the processual interrelationship between discourse and identity in Holocaust narratives: "the one-for-the-other of signification becomes the other-in-the-one of subjectivity."[97]

The reversal of roles played out in the context of this poem reflects the real situation of Sachs's relationship to her mother during her ailing parent's declining years in Stockholm, when she required constant care and attention like a helpless and dependent child.[98] In this relationship, the use of conventional labels to distinguish the roles of mother and child no longer reflect the actual roles each assumed, but instead highlight the emptiness of signifiers that serve as placeholders for fictitious distinctions. Ruth Dinesen describes Margarete Sachs's increasing childishness and naiveté during the Stockholm years and the gradual inversion of the mother-daughter relationship in her biography of Nelly Sachs.[99] The feeling of responsibility and caretaking that accompanied this role reversal haunted Nelly Sachs after her mother's death. Despite her dedication to her ailing mother, her memories of this difficult time were tinged with guilt. In a poignant dream after her mother's death described in *Briefe aus der Nacht*, Sachs sees herself as a maternal figure holding the infant body of her own deceased mother in her arms. In the dream, the infant mother's bare and icy feet represent the daughter-mother's inadequacy as a caregiver.[100]

Not only in this aspect of her biography but also in her own treatment of the maternal in poetry, Nelly Sachs revealed the arbitrary nature of the maternal signifier. The roles the poet and the poetic persona appropriate are not limited by labels and the expectations these evoke, but rather the daughter-poet assumes the role of mother, manipulating the labels themselves through acts of agency and creation in both life and art. The poet re-defines these terms for her own use through the medium of a poetic

---

[97] Patterson, 79.

[98] Cf. Nelly Sachs's own report on her mother's worsening condition already in 1946 in her letter to her close friend Gudrun Dähnert (*Briefe*, 58): "Die Lu kommt inzwischen zu Muttchen, aber sie muß ja vollkommen wie ein Kind gepflegt werden, es wird mir unendlich schwer, wenn auch nur für Tage sie zu verlassen."

[99] See Dinesen, *Nelly Sachs*, 190: "'Das Kind' in ihrer Beziehung ist jedoch die Mutter." Cf. also Fritsch-Vivié on this point, 94–95: ". . . die Mutter ist am Ende ihr Kind geworden. Sie haben die Rollen getauscht, das symbiotische Ineinander ist geblieben."

[100] Quoted in Dinesen, *Nelly Sachs*, 196: "ich habe die Strümpfe vergessen — ich halte den Tod."

language that strives for what Judith Butler referred to as "the recovery of
the maternal body within the terms of language, one that has the potential
to disrupt, subvert and displace the paternal law."[101] The paternal law
would dictate death as finality, the endpoint of a linear perception of existence, but the poetic persona resists this defined finitude and assumes
control of her sorrow by transforming her memories into text in an act
that is at once one of defiance and one of mourning.

This strategy is also practiced by Rose Ausländer in poems thema-
tizing the mother/daughter-poet relationship. In "Brennpunkt" (VI
227), the poetic persona fantasizes a reunion with the lost beloved
mother in a fusion that implies the re-birth of the mother as the
daughter's child conceived through the regenerative power of love:

> Wir treffen uns
> im Brennpunkt
>
> Er glüht im Kristall
> unsrer geretteten
> Liebe
>
> Du kennst die Entfernung
> zur nächsten Nähe
>
> Mutter mein Kind

The collective We of the first lines splits into a You and I at the very
moment where mother and daughter have allegedly been re-joined.
The heat of their affections, even in the imagination of the poetic persona, is not sufficient to melt away the division that still exists even in
the most intimate bond. Despite the persistent nature of this division,
however, the poetic persona constructs a vision of melding through
language in which the boundaries between the realms of mother and
child are both traversable and interchangeable. Poetic language becomes the last outpost of identification as well as the means to enact
subjectivity. The language the poetic persona appropriates represents
the (pro)creative legacy left her by the mother/muse and serves as the
medium in which she strives to control and fashion her own versions of
memory and future possibility.

---

[101] Butler, *Gender Trouble*, 80.

Procreation and Poetry

In a kind of infinite, mystical regress, a layering or palimpsest of concentric images, a woman writing creates/becomes a great mother who thrusts herself both around the story and into it: inside the mother is child/writer; within her is the unborn text and within that story, herself again, both mother and daughter, parthenogenic, birthing the word, born of the word. . . .

— Deborah Kloepfer[102]

In the beginning was the Word and the Word was with God and the Word was God.

— Gospel of John 1:1

"Die Sprache ist das einzige, was du jetzt besitzt, denke daran!"

— a friend to Nelly Sachs after her escape to Sweden[103]

Nelly Sachs and Rose Ausländer were both motivated by a search for means to express and engage their hopes, sufferings, memories, and desires. The poetic formulations they repeatedly returned to, experimenting with variations and transformations of language and imagery, were their attempts to give voice to the tensions and overlaps within the matrix of spirituality, history, and community they encountered. In this context, Sachs and Ausländer perceived their poetry as an outlet for remembrance and a vehicle for continuity. The past is mourned as a vanished state of security and innocence, but the lyrical voices that rise out of the ashes are nevertheless strong with a sense of mission. The mission to bear witness, to sustain and nurture memory as a maternalized act of creation in the transmogrified form of the poetic text, is characteristic of writers, regardless of gender, who sought to represent the experience of the Holocaust.[104] But for Rose Ausländer and to some extent for Nelly Sachs, the use of and belief in language develops from medium to message, in that language itself assumes a kind of maternal quality, serving as the locus of regenerative remembrance and an oth-

---

[102] Kloepfer, 92.

[103] Quoted in Lagercrantz, *Versuch über die Lyrik der Nelly Sachs*, 75.

[104] David Patterson in his study of the Holocaust novel, *The Shriek of Silence*, 79, asserts that the Holocaust writer is always already in some sense playing a maternal role in that any act of bearing witness is a symbolic rebirth of the experience of oppression and suffering.

erwise ungratified desire for home. Language, like the Cosmic Mother, embodies the dual capacity for good and evil and the simultaneity of creative and destructive forces in an unresolved opposition. Although both poets shared a belief in the creative capacity of the word, for Sachs writing and poetic language were manifestations of Divine presence, inspired by a cosmic Otherness that endowed the poet with almost visionary acuity of perception. While Sachs sought a path to transcendence through the poetic word,[105] Ausländer retreated into language as an encapsulation of all she expected from life and the world. For Ausländer, the poem served both as a surrogate home and as a place from which to launch her flights of imagination.

The use and abuse of language during the Nazi period and the continuity of language as a mode of aesthetic expression despite its deformations through history is the theme of Rose Ausländer's poem "Doppelspiel" (V 26). This poem demonstrates Ausländer's favored use of paradox as a technique to portray the coexistence and simultaneity of opposing forces that shape and guide human existence:

> Wir verwalten
> die Erde
>
> verwandeln sie
> in Gärten Worte Scheiterhaufen
>
> Dieses Doppelspiel
> Blumenworte
> Kriegsgestammel

The use of the pronoun We in the opening lines conflates the poetic speaker with the human agents of creation and destruction, the gardeners and the executioners. This simple and concise juxtaposition of actions in the first strophe is then abstracted to the level of language in the second, thereby connecting actions with words and emphasizing the contradictory powers inherent in human speech. The double game of life and death has no end and no resolution, but it does have a linguistic context that enables the poetic persona's access to it. Here the lyrical voice speaks in a factual, objective tone without moral judgment. From an enlightened perspective and without falsification, she recognizes the potential and real ambivalence of her medium.

The poetic persona in Ausländer's poems does not always maintain this attitude of objective yet informed detachment. In "Versöhnung" (IV 110), the poetic persona reflects on her position as both creature and creator. As a creature, she is aware of the forces at work upon her;

---

[105] Cf. Beil, esp. 412.

as a creator she feels her own power to transform and direct her future. She is both a subject determined by the world in which she exists and creator of her own realm of images and memory through language. The poem begins with a reference to the past. The ghosts of the dead have been increasingly absent from her waking hours and the poetic persona reads this as a signal of hope that she will be reconciled with the memories that had previously haunted her:

> Wieder ein Morgen
> ohne Gespenster
> im Tau funkelt der Regenbogen
> als Zeichen der Versöhnung
>
> Du darfst dich freuen
> über den vollkommenen Bau der Rose
> darfst dich im grünen Labyrinth
> verlieren und wiederfinden
> in klarerer Gestalt
>
> Du darfst ein Mensch sein
> arglos
>
> Der Morgentraum erzählt dir
> Märchen du darfst
> die Dinge neu ordnen
> Farben verteilen
> und wieder
> *schön* sagen
>
> an diesem Morgen
> du Schöpfer und Geschöpf

The absence of ghosts in the first strophe enables the lyrical voice to see the world in a new way, perhaps not really new but rather a return of a lost capacity for appreciation. The second strophe reinforces the theme of return and recovery, as if the poetic being had been reborn after an unspeakable experience, yet the return to a sense of humanity is both old and new. The poetic voice's self-address is one of encouragement and empowerment, granting permission to enjoy existence with a heightened consciousness that is generally taken for granted. The dawning of this reconciliation with the ghosts of the past simultaneously marks the moment in which the poetic persona has assumed control over her environment via the word, a kind of linguistic, poetic agency that gives her a sense of power: "du Schöpfer und Geschöpf."

This self-characterization as creator *and* creature reflects what Michaela Kessner described as Ausländer's belief in the creative power of language and the subsequent role of the poet as the creator of

words.[106] In Kessner's reading, Ausländer's faith in the power of the
poetic word was a substitution or transference of her earlier belief in the
creative power of the Divine Word.[107] The shift in belief from the Father's word to a self-perceived role as creator in and through the
mother tongue reinforces and illustrates the continued oscillation between paternal and maternal-centered models of representing and in-
teracting with the world that characterizes the breadth of both
Ausländer's and Sachs's œuvres.

In the poem "Mutter Sprache" (III 104), Ausländer presents the
mother tongue as the means and medium of the poetic persona's self-
identification and identity formation:

> MUTTER SPRACHE
> Ich habe mich
> in mich verwandelt
> von Augenblick zu Augenblick
>
> in Stücke zersplittert
> auf dem Wortweg
>
> Mutter Sprache
> setzt mich zusammen
>
> Menschmosaik

The poetic persona clearly acknowledges and celebrates the forma-
tive and transformative power of language, while simultaneously recognizing the transcience of the self-configurations she creates. Language
leads to both cohesion and fragmentation in a never-ending process
that divides and combines. The dual nature of language as the
"mother" of identity and the originator of a split either in perception
or the self is visually illustrated in the poem's title, where "Mutter" and
"Sprache" are presented as contiguous but nevertheless distinctly separate entities. The mother tongue presented in this juxtaposition of
words can be read as the literal "mother" as well as the native idiom the
poetic persona identifies with. The figuration of the mother tongue as
two separate words parallels the Yiddish rendering of this concept in
the term *mame loshn*. Yiddish as a mother tongue is a language of synthesis, one that continually modifies itself, adopting from and adapting
to the other languages with which it comes into contact. The blending
quality of the mother tongue itself is transmitted or translated into the

---

[106] Kessner, 97.

[107] Kessner, 100: "daß der Glaube an Gott durch den Glauben an die Sprache er-
setzt wird."

character of the speaker, such that the one mirrors the other.[108] In its manifestation as native idiom, the mother tongue in "Mutter Sprache" reflects the poetic persona's self-perceptions but simultaneously precedes and exceeds them. Despite her own powers of transformation, she is subordinate to the artistic limitations of the language she is imbedded in, where her contributions are just bits of color in a larger, infinitely expandable mosaic. This mosaic is constituted by language itself and the self-creating and shaping endeavors of its speakers.

The absoluteness of the speaker's involvement within language in this poem leaves out the immediate issues of history and temporality, implying instead that identity is purely discursive, but thereby also implicitly fragmentary and mutable. Language has in fact so thoroughly permeated human existence that humanity has become like a collage comprised of words. The division illustrated in the poem's title is healed in the final line, but only in so far as the space has been closed. The semantic sense of fragmentation artificially held in place by poetic language is evoked by the neologism "Menschmosaik." The human subject is rendered coherent and cohesive through the intervention of language, without which the poem implies the self would fall to pieces. But this is only an isolated facet of Ausländer's perspective on the matrix of language, self, nation, and the complex of social and psychological forces that position the social subject.

Language for Ausländer came to represent both a reminder and a remainder of her perpetual exile and her unstilled longing for the motherland. Ausländer's concept of the motherland and its affinity to the mother tongue closely parallels the figuration Dagmar Lorenz addresses in her study of German-Jewish women writers. In Lorenz's analysis, intellectual Jewish women in Germany confronted with their inferior status both within the Jewish community and in the society at large sought to carve out another dimension for themselves by laying claim to the German language which they regarded as distinct and culturally separate from the German "Vaterland."[109] For Ausländer following the war and the destruction of her homeland in the Bukovina, the mother tongue was the only home she could claim. In "Mutterland" (V 98), Ausländer portrays the shift in allegiance from paternal to

---

[108] Maeera Shreiber discusses this synthetic quality of Yiddish and the gender implications of the term *mame loshn* in her article "The End of Exile: Jewish Identity and Its Diasporic Poetics," *PMLA* 113.2 (1998): 278–79.

[109] See Dagmar Lorenz, *Keepers of the Motherland: German Texts by Jewish Women Writers* (Lincoln/London: U of Nebraska P, 1997), xix.

maternal processes and laws by playing with associative connections among fatherland, mother country, and mother tongue:

> Mein Vaterland ist tot
> sie haben es begraben
> im Feuer
>
> Ich lebe
> in meinem Mutterland
> Wort

Here the historical background underlying the poetic persona's retreat into the realm of language is spelled out. With the allusion to the fatherland as having been consumed by conflagration, the poetic persona makes an unveiled reference to the facticity of the Holocaust and the consequences of war. The juxtaposition of the terms fatherland and motherland dramatically emphasizes the conflicting loyalties at work upon the poetic persona. The proximity of the borders between the concretely geographical but never to be re-settled fatherland contrast with the abstract, linguistic realm of the motherland. The conflation of motherland and mother tongue illustrates the difficulty of trying to isolate factors of nationality, birth, and language as clearly demarcated and separate entities.[110]

The love of the (lost) homeland is closely related to the love of a (mother) language. In her comparative study of Rose Ausländer and Nelly Sachs, Claudia Beil argues rather pragmatically that for the poet in exile, the mother tongue assumes a compensatory function, substituting for the home the poet has lost: the love of country is displaced onto a love of the language associated with that country.[111] This substitution principle, however, is not as simple as Beil makes it appear and becomes especially blurred and confused in Rose Ausländer's peripatetic biography that culminates in her "return" to Germany. Ausländer's decision to settle in Germany in 1965 has been touted as a literal return to the German language.[112] It is important to distinguish, however, that language

---

[110] From Lorenz's discussion in *Keepers of the Motherland* of Ilse Aichinger's work contemporary with that of Ausländer's, it is apparent that the conceptualization of the motherland that Ausländer presents here and elsewhere enjoyed a wider currency among German-Jewish women writers. Aichinger's distinction positions the "motherland" as "the domain of her native language, regardless of political or ethnic boundaries" whereas the "fatherland" is implicitly tainted by its implication in "power structures" (156).

[111] Beil, 62.

[112] This is the view presented by Helmut Braun and is echoed in several secondary studies, cf. Kessner, Beil, and Helfrich. It should be noted that Ausländer first

in this instance is no longer an abstract, surrogate homeland, but has become conflated with a geographical place that in this case had never been Ausländer's home. Yet by this act of relocation understood as a return to a German language context, the poet hopes to overcome the disjunction of language and home. The displacement moves between the literary and the literal, where the physical context takes on a level of meaning for the poet that cannot be isolated into the realm of the referent (and the word). Therefore Ausländer's retreat into language, although apparent, cannot be viewed as absolute. The discursive space was not enough: she required a locus, a place of association that reinforced her artistic sense of being in the word.

The poetic gesture of merging maternal associations is one that Nelly Sachs also practiced, albeit without the direct emphasis on the mother tongue as a metaphorical place of refuge.[113] In "LINIE WIE" (*FS* 308), Sachs arrays a series of associative images that evoke alternatively the mother-child bond, the alienation of the poetic persona in exile, and the fantasized reunion with a motherland that is a composite of mother, mother country, and mother tongue:

> LINIE WIE
> lebendiges Haar
> gezogen
> todnachtgedunkelt
> von dir
> zu mir.
>
> Gegängelt
> außerhalb
> bin ich hinübergeneigt
> durstend
> das Ende der Fernen zu küssen.

---

planned on settling in Vienna, but when she arrived there in 1964, she did not find the literary environment that she had hoped for. After almost a year in Vienna trying to establish the necessary connections to proceed with her writerly ambitions, she decided to move to Düsseldorf where she had both friends and contacts. See Cilly Helfrich, *Rose Ausländer. Biographie*, 254–56.

[113] The figuration of the mother in poetic representations of nation and its significance for the poetic persona's sense of identity in Sach's and Ausländer's poems is discussed in detail in Chapter 4.

Der Abend
wirft das Sprungbrett
der Nacht über das Rot
verlängert deine Landzunge
und ich setze meinen Fuß zagend
auf die zitternde Saite
des schon begonnenen Todes.

Aber so ist die Liebe —

The mother-child bond alluded to in the first strophe, in which the two are connected by living hair that stretches between the You and the I like an umbilical cord, has already been severed in the second strophe. There the poetic persona is alone, bereft of both mother and other, yet this separation has not led to her emancipation: she appears neither autonomous nor free to act as an individual. Maternal absence has not granted her independence, but has instead bound her yet more tightly because of the intensity of her longing and her paralyzing sense of banishment. This longing escalates with the temporal progression of day into night, a gradual dissipation of light that serves as the bridge between the reality of her solitude and the wistful unity of her dreams. Evening, harbinger of dreams and unleasher of wishes, is here the springboard for the poetic persona's fantasy of reunion with the protean and shifting ground of the mother country, a tongue of land that metamorphoses into a quivering string vibrating with the imminence of death.[114] The calculated choice of the word "Landzunge" evokes associations to both country and speech while the poetic persona's appeal to an absent "Du" expands to include all her absent "mothers" in their various manifestations.

The poetic persona's mourning and desire are inspired by loss yet imbued with love, and she recognizes with a tone of resignation that the tenacity of her love is what has engendered both her longing and her pain. Viewed from another perspective, however, her love proves powerful enough to test or even transgress the temporal and physical boundaries of death. In breaking off the final line with a dash, Sachs again resorts to the tactic of representing what exceeds or eludes poetic expression through a visual break. The stark bluntness of this jutting dash is less an ending than a beginning and a symbol of defiance testifying to the endurance of the poetic persona's love that bursts through

---

[114] The connection of death with a resonant mode of communication beyond speech made here by Nelly Sachs anticipates the Jewish philosopher and writer Edmond Jabès's conception of death as the infinitude of the un-said. Cf. Edmond Jabès, *The Book of Margins*, 42: "Death has its heyday where everything remains to be said."

the limits of language. By apparently cutting off the speech or the thoughts of the poetic persona she has created, Sachs illustrates that there are emotions and desires that defy articulation. Still, this dash as a pregnant pause implies that these unspeakable sensations can nevertheless be felt, understood, and experienced in some realm of pre- or perhaps even post-linguistic identification.

For Rose Ausländer, as is characteristic for many authors who continue to practice their craft in exile, the language of her childhood, her mother tongue, retained its persuasive and aesthetic capacities despite the complications that surrounded and impeded its continued use. As a poet, Ausländer sought to create her own discursive realm as a kind of "new" or regenerated language within the "old" language, a daunting and never-ending self-assigned project that provided her with the incentive to continue writing. The difficulty of continuing within the medium of the "old" language was, unsurprisingly, especially powerful for those German-speaking Jewish writers during and after the Holocaust who continued to produce literature in German despite the associations that language held for them.

Nelly Sachs was only too aware of this dilemma and its potential effects on her own reception as a writer. In a letter to Kurt Pinthus in 1952, Sachs described the contradiction within herself as a division between country and language. She firmly rejected the idea of returning to Germany or of leaving her adopted homeland in Sweden for another substitute "Heimat" such as Israel.[115] At the same time, she pointed out the problematic, special situation of German Jews writing in their mother tongue in exile, where they were in effect writing for a void, for an audience notable by its absence: "Aber wohin mit allem. An die deutsche Sprache gebunden hat man als jüdischer Mensch nicht viel Aussicht. So muß alles warten, was in die Luft geatmet wurde."[116]

Nelly Sachs's belief in language was one repeatedly assailed by doubt and despair. As a result, she never invested the poetic word with the same enduring transformative and generative properties that Rose Ausländer associated with creative writing. In contrast to Ausländer's

---

[115] In a letter of November 1946, Sachs reports on the openness of the Swedish literary scene and remarks on how beautiful the country is. But she also notes how difficult it is to be bound to the German language in a foreign land that does not have a large community of exile writers. See *Briefe*, 71. Once she had finally been successful in her bid for Swedish citizenship in 1952, Sachs also dismissed the possibility of emigrating anywhere else. She had no desire to return to Germany and considered herself too old to start a new life in Israel. See *Briefe*, 143.

[116] *Briefe*, 144.

increasing retreat into language as the last refuge of hope and outlet for subjective if sublimated agency, Sachs's relationship to language was characterized by repeated ruptures, questions, and fundamental doubts about its expressive possibilities. This was especially true of her poetological self-understanding in the years immediately following the Nazi genocide and the traumatizing knowledge that accompanied it. She despaired that the language available, worn thin and meaningless with use, abuse, and time, could ever be adequate to the task of representing experience.

For Nelly Sachs, the trauma of the Holocaust was like a wound, whereby suffering became inseparable from its articulation, an intertwining of experience and representation that she expressed vividly in reference to the physicality of her own relationship to poetic language: "meine Metaphern sind meine Wunden."[117] Not only were representation and suffering indistinguishable for Sachs, but both were connected to the religious associations called forth by the Word. This mystical word, the Divine Word made flesh, as the articulation of the heterogeneous multiplicity of human experience and suffering could, however, only be approximated in the language available to the poet. Thus Sachs's lines often trail off into silence, echoing in the void beyond which lies the unrepresentable means of expression for what she both despaired of describing and strove to portray. Through language, she sought to probe and fathom that Other realm which she sensed beyond language, to communicate her deepest fears, desires, hopes, and beliefs.[118]

In pursuit of this purpose, Nelly Sachs used whatever representational means were available to approximate what she sought to express, mixing Christian iconography and Hasidic mysticism with Romanticist conceptions of transcendence. The elements of Jewish mysticism she adopted into her poetic vocabulary became central to her sense of spiritual survival. In her conception, mysticism was a form of spirituality bearing characteristically maternal aspects. The configuration of the originary maternal force as simultaneously the representation of the mystical is a conflation of attributes and aspects that goes back to early spiritual tradi-

---

[117] Quoted in Fritsch-Vivié, 99.

[118] In contrast to my reading of Nelly Sachs's relationship to language as equivocal, oscillating between belief and doubt, Claudia Beil argues solely from the perception of Sachs's mystical faith in the word and view of the world as semiotic in her study *Sprache als Heimat* (196): "Da die Welt wie das Dichter-Ich durch das 'Anfangswort' Gottes entstanden ist . . . kann alles Geschaffene ebenfalls als Zeichen, Schrift oder Wort angesehen, die Welt, ja der Kosmos schlechthin, als 'Buch' betrachtet werden . . . (. . .) Es gibt demnach eine Sprache, die allen Dingen und Wesen im Kosmos gemeinsam ist."

tions. In Sachs's particular combination, however, the maternal-mystical became transposed with Hasidic mysticism, which she relied on as a supportive crutch during times of severe crisis. In a letter to Margit Abenius in 1957, Sachs explains her connection to mysticism:

> Aus meinem eignen Volk kam mir die chassidische Mystik zu Hilfe, die eng im Zusammenhang mit aller Mystik die Quelle aller existentiellen Durchströmung des Alltagsaugenblickes ist und sich ihren Wohnort weit fort von allen Institutionen und Dogmen immer aufs neue in Geburtswehen schaffen muß.[119]

The regenerative and revolutionary quality she attributed to all forms of mysticism was the reason for its appeal and her affinity with its precepts. Sachs's efforts to give voice to the multiplicity and contradictions of experience in the anomie of the post-Holocaust world cannot be separated from her mystical self-understanding and her belief that the capacity to achieve such representation was somehow a demonstration of divine grace: "Wer leidet und wer liebt, muß sich überlassen können bis zum letzten Atemzug, den Staub zu durchseelen ist eine Mission — das Wort zu finden — Gnade."[120] This connection of suffering and grace, aspiration and language, is what Alvin Rosenfeld referred to as Sachs's unique yet ultimately poetic construct of language as a surrogate home in an atmosphere of absence. He described the metaphorical landscapes she conveyed in her lyric as abstract and transitory, yet nevertheless true to the existential condition she strove to express:

> Life in this landscape of abstract and fragile dimensions is itself highly abstract and fragile and is constituted principally of ephemeral and fading things. . . . There is not much permanence in such a world and certainly little comfort, yet it is an authentic world and honestly reflective of Nelly Sachs's experience. An exile herself, searching but never finding a true return to home, she finally lived a poet's existence in the sheer "language of breath."[121]

Yet the more general poetological tendency that Rosenfeld asserts here in relation to Nelly Sachs's retreat into language is not the purely literary, aesthetic gesture his observation would seem to imply. Language for Sachs was inextricable from suffering. At once pierced with pain, implicated in violence, and steeped in faith, it was never merely a medium of

---

[119] *Briefe*, 181.

[120] Letter of 30 October 1957 to Walter Berendsohn, *Briefe*, 173.

[121] Alvin Rosenfeld, "The Poetry of Nelly Sachs," *Judaism* 20.3 (1971): 364.

literary expression, but always and more importantly her spiritual connection both to lived existence and to a livable, survivable future.

In the poem "Einmal" (*SL* 88), Sachs portrays the sorrowful process
of regenerative yet future-oriented remembrance through the image of
a sunset that offers a temporal melding of present, past, and future
resonating with melodies of oceanic origin. The poetic persona in this
poem acknowledges her creative power as well as her ability to repossess the maternal in her own vision by reflecting and projecting herself back through language and memory to the prenatal condition of
unity and harmony that has since been irrevocably lost:

> Einmal
> als Abend im Rot den Tag vergaß
> gründete ich auf dem Stein der Schwermut
> die Zukunft
>
> Vorgeburtliches Wiedersehen —
> eine Melodie aus Meer gemacht
> lief ihre Bahn —

But the reunion with the oceanic maternal other is short-lived, slippery,
lost in and because of the inadequacy and insubstantiality of the poet's
linguistic nets. The language available to the poet, although permeated
with longing, melancholy, and sorrow, is nevertheless incapable of res-
cuing or resuscitating the "Du", and the poetic persona is portrayed as
experiencing an even greater sense of bereavement and finality in the
silence that follows:[122]

> Vielleicht ein Fisch am Äquator
> an der Angel eine Menschenschuld bezahlte
> und dann mein Du
> das man gefangen hielt
> und das zu retten ich erkoren war
> und das in Rätseln weiter ich verlor
> bis hartes Schweigen sich auf Schweigen senkte
> und eine Liebe ihren Sarg bekam —

The visual structure of these lines, staggered like steps that descend into
a nothingness that cannot be described, echo the poetic voice's gradual,
fading diminution into silence, a silence akin to the silence of death and
the finality of lost love.[123]

---

[122] Cf. Lawrence Langer's assertion that in Sachs's poetry the desire for rebirth is
destined to remain forever unfulfilled, and is sublimated instead into "a state of permanent yearning." *Versions of Survival*, 227.

[123] The visual descent evidenced in the structure of the strophe reinforces the at-

The pain of loss comes with its recognition, a recognition that comes to the sufferer both spiritually and discursively. The act of transmitting or attempting to represent experiences of terror and sorrow cannot be separated from the pain and sorrow associated with the experiences themselves, thus the act of writing becomes a re-enactment, a regenerating process of suffering which ensures that the wounds of memory will not heal. The brutal clarity with which Sachs described her relationship to remembering is therefore simultaneously a dismembering (*SL* 86): "Dies ist nur mit einem ausgerissenen Auge / aufs Papier zu bringen —." Here again, the differences between Nelly Sachs's relationship to language and that of Rose Ausländer become clear. While Sachs looked horror in the eye and then displayed the wounds it left upon her language, Ausländer, with the ever-increasing temporal distance to the Holocaust, demonstrated a growing tendency to retreat into a secular, fictional homeland of language with a seemingly naive belief in the still intact power of the word.[124]

Despite these differences, there is a discernible tendency in the works of both poets to nevertheless seek out in language the nurturing and sustaining properties they required in order to maintain their sense of being-in-the-world. Their writing not only served as a means of bearing witness to their personal experiences of history, it also provided them with a self-created support system of identification, empathy, and remembrance. In the realm of poetry, they were able to exercise an agency and generative control that was denied them in their isolation as displaced German-Jewish "others." In an environment that deprived them of their ability to choose, writing represented an act of choice.[125]

---

titude of despair and supports an observation made by Lawrence Langer regarding the direction of Sachs's work in general: "the dominant spatial impulse of Nelly Sachs's imagination is descent . . . as an acceptance of the reservoir of human anguish where all immersions of the modern spirit must begin — and often end. (. . .) there is no simple turning from despair to hope, but only another encounter with simultaneity: her version of survival requires the spirit to plunge *as* it mounts . . . ." (Langer, *Versions of Survival*, 243–44).

[124] Cf. esp. the third strophe of Ausländer's poem "Glauben" from her 1978 collection, *Mutterland*. In this strophe, Ausländer's poetic persona openly professes her belief in the generative and transformative power of the word: "Ich glaube an die Wunder / der Worte / die in der Welt wirken / und die Welten erschaffen" (V 93). See also Kessner (104) where she describes Ausländer's treatment of language as the last outlet for the articulation of her lyrical selves to such an extreme that the poet's own life became almost exclusively focussed in language.

[125] This turn to writing as a conscious choice in an atmosphere otherwise lacking in choices is also apparent in Anne Frank's and Etty Hillesum's diaries, as Rachel

Ultimately, Rose Ausländer, more so than Nelly Sachs, looked to language as the means of forming, transforming, naming, and refuting the constantly shifting identities that constitute the self, a self that is never static, but always "in-process."[126]

This plural self was, however, not to be isolated from an equally multidimensional environment, and both poets attempt to give shape and meaning to the chaotic diversity of experiences that resist fixity and elude representation.[127] The poetic selves they fashioned along an oscillating continuum between identification and extrapolation were expansions and inclusions of this multiplicity of historical and personal experience, as well as strategies for the poets themselves to come to terms with their individual feelings of isolation and alienation.[128] The desire for or fantasy of self-expansion to the point of all-inclusiveness goes back to the desire for a reunion with maternal infinitude, here evidenced as a desire to lay claim to maternal power. The daughter-as-poet appropriates the mother as tongue and body, absorbing the maternal qualities she both fears and admires with an embracing gesture, thereby collapsing the boundaries between subject and object, self and other, secular and spiritual. The worlds these poetic daughters aspired to create through language were lyrical spaces parallel to the hybrid mystical-earthly world in which they lived and suffered, with the differ-

---

Brenner points out in her study *Writing as Resistance: Four Women Confronting the Holocaust*, esp. 134–35.

[126] Cf. Julia Kristeva's discussion of the "subject-in-process" in *In the Beginning Was Love: Psychology and Faith*, trans. Arthur Goldhammer (New York: Columbia UP, 1987), 9: "We are no doubt permanent subjects of a language that holds us in its power. But we are subjects *in process*, ceaselessly losing our identity, destabilized by fluctuations in our relations to the other, to whom we nevertheless remain bound by a kind of homeostasis."

[127] Cf. Dinesen's discussion of Nelly Sachs's poetic project to give meaning to chaos in *Nelly Sachs*, 208: "Der Dichter, der die Worte zusammenstellt und sprachliche Strukturen bildet, der den Kosmos gleichzeitig heilt und neu erschafft, schafft Struktur im Chaos, einen Ort, eine sprachliche Begegnungsstätte, wo das Göttliche und die erschaffene Welt sich zu einer lebenden Ganzheit verbinden."

[128] Cf. Kessner's argument that for Ausländer this exercise of self-expansion was a means of compensating or even recompensing the loss of her homeland (68): "Erweitert das Ich seine Perspektive ins Unendliche, wird folgerichtig auch der Verlust der konkreten Heimat bedeutungslos." In Kessner's view the poetic persona in exile becomes the nexus of opposing forces and therefore is capable of mediating or negotiating the split within herself. The exile survivor is suspended between the cosmic and the concrete ("Stern und Stein") and between death and rebirth ("Grab und Grün"), a condition illustrated in Ausländer's "Ohne Hinterhalt" (IV 107).

ence, however, that their creations contained the potential and promise for mutual understanding, and unalienated self-expression.

By experimenting with identity transformations and by giving voice to multi-vocalic memory, Sachs and Ausländer created a community within language that allowed them a presence as powerful, active, and self-determining subjects. An analysis of the varying ways in which they transformed and nurtured memory in their pursuit of livable alternatives to the world-as-it-was and their differing efforts to provide a linguistic terrain conducive to tolerance, multiplicity, responsible coexistence, and "truth" is the subject of the next chapter.

3: Memory and Transformation

Memory is always problematic, usually deceptive, sometimes treacherous.

— Yosef Yerushalmi[1]

No matter what material or other public debts are paid, confessional memory is demanded as the only valid reparation. And as a claim upon official memory, the victim's anguish comes to be seen as a valuable possession. Other peoples also want the status of victimhood. (. . .) Can there be too much memory?

— Charles Maier[2]

. . . da habe ich mir die Formel ausgedacht, daß man für Amnestie und gegen Amnesie sein muß. (. . .) Anders kann man nicht leben. Man muß sich erinnern, aber man muß über den Horizont des eigenen Leids hinausgehen können, man darf nicht in der Welt des eigenen Leids verharren.

— Adam Michnik[3]

BOTH HISTORIOGRAPHY AND REMEMBRANCE are transformations of the traces left by the past into some form of discursive artifact. Historiography struggles to understand events on the basis of documented and verifiable evidence and thereby lend them a certain objective permanence. In contrast, remembrance dips into a past that exists as fragments of experiences that have been molded into a given form at the time of their storage, but these fragments of experience are simultaneously subject to the vicissitudes of the psychological environment that suspends and sustains them. As discursive phenomena, historiography and remembrance are both representational, insofar as discourse seeks to approximate an impression of "reality," even if the validity of any given "reality" can be called into question not only when it is transformed into remembrance but also in the moment of its percep-

---

[1] Yerushalmi, *Zakhor*, 5.

[2] Charles Maier, *The Unmasterable Past: History, Holocaust, and German National Identity* (Cambridge: Harvard UP, 1988), 161.

[3] In an interview with Jürgen Habermas, *Die Zeit*, Overseas Ed. 24 December 1993, 8.

tion.[4] As representational processes historiography and remembrance are limiting and selective: the choices between which aspects of the past to preserve and which to repress, consciously or unconsciously, influence and alter the record and recording of the past over time.

My purpose in contrasting the representational processes at work in historiography and remembrance is to underscore the necessity of addressing the question of how history and memory, historiography and remembrance, interrelate and influence each other in any analysis of texts within the context of their historical situatedness. The refusal to participate in a rigid dichotomization of history and memory does not exempt us from questioning and analyzing how remembrance is to be defined and understood vis-à-vis historiography, and to the extent that both are discursive or, more particularly, textual, how they should be read and interpreted.

What I am interested in here has to do with the representational, textual quality of memory as remembrance evidenced in traces and inscriptions of remembered and imagined trauma in poetry after the Holocaust. Lyric poetry as a genre is not the form one would immediately associate with the representation or preservation of memory if one considers memory in epic or narrative terms.[5] The compression and layering of multiple meanings that the lyric poem allows, however, enables a representation of the emotional and traumatic aspects of memory where the blurred boundaries between the conscious and unconscious are translated into images and where the elusiveness of language allows the poet to negotiate the space between repression and recovery. But just as lyric poetry can be read as inscribed with and responding to traumatic memory in a faltering complex of confrontation and denial, it can and has been used in the service of ideologically prescribed remembrance, most blatantly in the poetics of propaganda fostered by the Nazis.[6] It is therefore necessary to keep in mind not only the question "remembrance of what" but also "remembrance of and for whom."

---

[4] Primo Levi, in his self-reflective study of Holocaust remembrance, *The Drowned and the Saved*, notes a phenomenon among victims whereby the condition of experience is denied or altered even as it is occurring, i.e. the distortion does not first occur in the transformation of experience into memory, but already at the level of immediate perception of the experience. Cf. Levi, *The Drowned and the Saved*, trans. Raymond Rosenthal (London: Abacus, 1989), 19.

[5] Cf. Charles S. Maier, "A Surfeit of Memory? Reflections on History, Melancholy and Denial," *History and Memory* 5.2 (1993): 149; and Richard Terdiman, *Present Past: Modernity and the Memory Crisis* (Ithaca/London: Cornell UP, 1993), 25.

[6] Cf. Sander Gilman, *Inscribing the Other* (Lincoln/London: U of Nebraska P, 1991), 225.

One must distinguish the remembrance of the victims from that of the perpetrators while remaining aware that even as these differ in quality they share a heterogeneity that is erased when one voice claims to speak for all.

The inscription of memory traces into poetry runs yet another risk. As symbolic representations of that which cannot be recovered, poetic articulations of remembrance oscillate between the desire to sublimate the trace into art and the wish to repossess it by naming and confronting it. The tension between the moral imperative to bear witness and the artistic impulse toward symbolic representation remains unresolved, although the former exerts a limitation on the latter.[7] I see Nelly Sachs's and Rose Ausländer's poetry as situated in that intermediate region between confrontation and transmutation. Their post-Holocaust poetic texts can in part be read as acts of transference in which traumatic memories that threaten to overwhelm the subject are mediated by their transformation into images that remain suspended between projection and reflection.[8]

Nelly Sachs and Rose Ausländer experimented with multiple traditions in their poetry, becoming like poetic alchemists in their efforts to transform and renew the tarnished past by melding elements appropriated from mysticism, literary romanticism and modernism, religion and philosophy. For Ausländer this meant a conception of writing as a direct process of linguistic transformation, within which morphological and elemental components combined in a kind of metaphorical or-

---

[7] Saul Friedländer, in an extension of Adorno's now well-worn caveat against writing poetry after the Holocaust ["Kulturkritik und Gesellschaft," *Prismen* (Frankfurt am Main: Suhrkamp, 1955), 31] maintained that the "moral imperative" to remember the Holocaust in and of itself imposed limits on aestheticization, with the underlying implication that it is in the transformation of memory into poetry that ethics and aesthetics meet. Cf. Friedländer, *Memory, History, and the Extermination of the Jews of Europe* (Bloomington: Indiana UP, 1993), 55.

[8] In his essay "Remembering, Repeating and Working-Through (Further Recommendations on the Technique of Psycho-Analysis II)" Sigmund Freud remarks that transference can be harnessed in the service of treatment of repetition compulsions associated with traumatic memory. The constructed "transference neurosis" would create "an intermediate region between illness and real life through which the transition from one to the other is made." Cf. *The Standard Edition of the Complete Psychological Works of Sigmund Freud*, Vol. XII, trans. and ed. by James Strachey (1958; London: The Hogarth Press, 1971), 154. In my use of the term transference here I am arguing that the poetry of Nelly Sachs and Rose Ausländer demonstrates this intermediate nature of transference and serves as a means of negotiating the rift between the traumatic wounds of the past and the desire to transcend these in order to survive in the present.

ganicity. Sachs, in contrast, characterized the relationship between language and representation as necessarily mediated by perception. In Sachs's conception of writing as representation, the visual or envisioned is both informed by and prior to its linguistic articulation, i.e. the transformation of image into language is an interactive process continually negotiating the gaps between and among perception, reception, and articulation. Through a mutual faith in the creative and transformative power of language conjoined with a conception of the word as a synthesis of Biblical, mystical, and matriarchal originary myths, both poets gave expression to their convictions and their perceived moral responsibility as bearers of witness and guardians of memory.[9] The crises of faith they experienced in response to the Holocaust, toward God as well as toward humanity, and the resulting destabilization of their sense of identity catalyzed a search for a means to a new beginning via a rejuvenation of language. The progression of their respective poetic projects is marked by reflections on the explanatory models that had shaped past attitudes toward history and religion and which continued to influence and inform subsequent experimentations with alternatives.

The experiences of loss and trauma generated by living through and surviving the Holocaust destabilized Sachs's and Ausländer's senses of identity in relation to their destroyed pasts and in relation to their troubled futures as necessary exiles, necessary because the places they had respectively called home had been forever changed or erased by the impact of the Third Reich. The condition of destabilization was marked not only by mourning but also by the desire to reconstruct an identity out of the ashes, to search for a means of renewal or restoration, a kind of secular, personal *tikkun*[10] via the word in a conscious emulation of the regenerative capacity of the Divine Word. One of the motivations behind their projects of revitalization and renewal was a concern with the diversity of memories of the catastrophe and a dedication to their preservation, both out of respect for the dead and out of a sense of moral obligation to provide a commemorative legacy for the future.

The transformation of memory — as an amorphous colloid of remembered events — into poetry is bounded by the expressive limits of

---

[9] For a discussion of the mystical conception of alchemy in the Jewish tradition, see Gershom Scholem, "Alchemie und Kabbala," *Judaica IV*, ed. Rolf Tiedemann (Frankfurt am Main: Suhrkamp, 1984), 19–128.

[10] The Hebrew term *tikkun* means restoration or reintegration and represents one of the three central doctrines describing the origins of the world in Lurianic Kabbalah. See Gershom Scholem, *Kabbalah* (Jerusalem: Keter Publishing, 1974), esp. 129, 140.

language as well as by the extent of the poet's understanding, experiences, and resistances. Remembrances that are translated or transformed into language with its capacity to absorb and appropriate the "once-new" are inevitably diminished or relativized in some way. In the case of mourning, the absorption of the particularity of experience into the totality of language divests the painful experience of its impact but also of the opportunity to work through it.[11] Any act of representation is always already a reduction which is then further reduced by the blunting effects that follow the "putting-into-language" of experience. Here Primo Levi's observations are relevant to the task of evaluating and reading not only narrative but also poetic testimony, where testimony is understood as the discursive process of approximating or recollecting past experience. Levi notes that repeated recall can have a strengthening effect akin to the exercise of a muscle. Too much repetition, however, can result in the ossification of the remembrance as a fixed narrative, leading to stereotyped memory and to the atrophy of what Levi terms "raw memory."[12] This danger is compounded by language's susceptibility to both functionalization and ambiguity. The special circumstances of the poem as the medium for transformed memories must be addressed, although first it should be noted that what is being transformed or represented in the poem is not the memory itself, but rather a scripting of an affective response to a traumatic situation or condition.

The translation of this kind of "memory" into poetry is therefore not to be confused with testimony to specific events. And even if understood as a transformation of a psychological response to these events, the poem is always already abstracted from the emotional and psychological response, necessarily transformed by the language of representation. The poet's mission to give voice to memory becomes an unresolvable communicative task because of the nature of language as a medium that continually accumulates new layers of meaning and simultaneously reifies linguistic innovations. The aspiration to truthful

---

[11] Ewa Ziarek offers a view on the totalizing nature of language specifically in relation to mourning and by extension to memory in her essay "Kristeva and Levinas: Mourning, Ethics, and the Feminine" in *Ethics, Politics, and Difference in Julia Kristeva's Writing*, ed. Kelly Oliver (New York/London: Routledge, 1993), 72: "Mourning posits language as a process of distancing from the other and opens a way of neutralizing this alterity through translation. As a result of such symbolic mediation, alterity becomes absorbed in the immanence of linguistic totality." The absorption of experience as immediacy is also implicated in this totalizing tendency of language with its double capacity for appropriation and estrangement.

[12] Primo Levi, *The Drowned and the Saved*, 11–12.

representation is further complicated by the elusive fluctuation that characterizes memory itself. In using the poem as a medium for "working through" memories of trauma,[13] the poet is also attempting to reconstruct an identity for herself out of the fragments that are left to her from the past. These fragments may come from her own experience or stem from events that she did not witness first-hand, but yet has appropriated *as if* they were a part of her own past.[14] In identifying and identifying with the scripting of emotionally charged phenomena as a simultaneously subjective and collective act, the poet seeks to both represent the Other and regain or sustain a certain cohesion of self.

The nurturing of memory is a nurturing of the multiply lost: childhood, homeland, maternal presence, beloved. The textualization of memory, with its tacit bid for permanence, is a strategy of retaliation and an attempt to subvert the forces of relativization and erasure that follow in the wake of time. The diversity of these memories is a central concern in the consideration of the representability of the catastrophe within the constraints of existing language. The tensions inherent in the mother/daughter relationship outlined in the preceding chapter also inform the poetic struggle to come to terms with memory as a complex of shifting voices, alliances, and emphases. The dialectic between identification and alienation that characterized the daughter's quest for identity vis-à-vis the mother is paradigmatic for the interactive communication between the poetic persona and the We of the collective as the mass of the victims and the insignia of the tribe of Israel. The oscillation between identification and alienation characterizing the mother/daughter bond comes then to mark also the poet-survivor's position in relation to individual and collective memories, to her Jewish heritage, and to the complex of German-Jewish identity. Caught in the web of these conflicting directives and desires, Sachs and Ausländer responded in different ways to the call for a mode of expression adequate to these memories that would not obscure the particularities of historical experience behind the mask of comfortable coherence or redemptive closure.

---

[13] In my use of the Freudian concept of "working through" here, I am following Dominick LaCapra's lead in employing it in a more socially applied sense, i.e. as an act with both personal and collective implications. See LaCapra, *Representing the Holocaust: History, Theory, Trauma* (Ithaca/London: Cornell UP, 1994), esp. 173–74.

[14] This kind of vicarious or appropriative memory is particularly evident in Nelly Sachs's poetry of witness in which the events she testifies to are not part of her direct experience, but which nevertheless have undeniably affected her personally.

In this chapter I first examine how the poetic persona is constructed and situated in relation to itself as a real or implied I and to the collective We of a group whose configuration is continually shifting, but which implicitly signifies *the* Jewish community. The appeal to the pronoun We can be viewed as a kind of relativization through collectivization, a linguistic move that obscures individuality and difference by blending the distinctive voices of the many into the united cry of the group. The negativity of such an absorption of difference through collectivization can be countered by a different reading of the We as an acknowledgment of and identification with a group solidarity that is especially empowering and therapeutic for a people whose existence on earth had been "willed to extinction" in the racial ideology instrumentalized by the Nazis.[15] Nevertheless, the tension between these negative and positive conceptions of the I/We relation remains unresolved, both in the poems addressed here and in the social reality that they confront.

Part of the difficulty involved in representing the memory of an historical catastrophe with collective and individual aspects and implications lies in the limits of representation and ultimately in the constraints of language. Sachs's and Ausländer's poetic treatments of these linguistic constraints and their confrontations with the limits of representation are the focus of the final two sections of this chapter. In an extension of the I/We interaction and identification discussed above, the lyrical selves in the poems addressed in the first of these sections assume positions as mouthpiece and messenger for a force or phenomenon greater than themselves. Through the appropriation of a privileged and powerful voice, they demonstrate their acceptance of the moral imperative to speak, albeit one complicated by doubts that further destabilize their already shaken conviction in the adequacy of the linguistic medium available to them. These doubts culminate in a void of silence that both attracts and repels them even as it comes to signify the locus of their faith. The echoes of their words in this void replete with paradoxes (silence as both absence and infinitude of meaning; Nothingness as simultaneously absolute emptiness and Divine presence; lack as both negation and undetermined potential) reflect the multiplicity of reactions to the disaster and the questions it raised.

The act of poetic transformation of memory, defined here by the traces it both leaves and suggests of trauma, empathy, and longing, rep-

---

[15] Cf. Berel Lang's discussion of the situation of the survivors of the Nazi genocide and the arbitrariness of their survival of a systematic extermination aimed at the extinction of the Jewish people, *Act and Idea in the Nazi Genocide* (Chicago: U of Chicago P, 1990), xiv.

resents a negotiation of what Saul Friedländer describes as the difference between "deep memory" and "common memory." Deep memory is that which is repressed yet recurs and resurfaces at the individual level, while common memory attempts to establish coherence and closure as well as justification for the events remembered.[16] The transformation of remembrances, especially of traumatic experiences, into poetry takes place in an atmosphere of tension between conflicting forces: on the one hand, the fear of recalling extreme and painful experience, and on the other the desire to confront it. One means of coming to terms with this conflict is by transforming the negativity of the remembrance into a positive projection for the future. This redemptive metamorphosis of pain and trauma is evident in Rose Ausländer's poem "Versöhnlich" (III 14) written around 1966, the year in which the German Federal Republic awarded her reparations payment and a pension as victim of Nazi persecution:[17]

> Versöhnlich
> mein Gettoherz
> will sich verwandeln
> in eine hellere Kraft

The poem, in fact a single sentence interrupting itself by line breaks, portrays through these breaks the hesitancy of the poetic persona, the difficulty of expressing this wish for reconciliation that cannot be expressed directly as a continuous line. Yet this doubt and hesitancy is offset by the decreasing parsimony of each successive line — the number of words the poetic I speaks in succession increases from one to four, as if the desire for reconciliation that inspires her words contributes to an increase in fluency and a less fragmented relation to language. But the poetic persona expresses this wish for reconciliation while simultaneously hinting at the impossibility of its fulfillment. The "Gettoherz" as the affective center has become identified with the experience of persecution and suffering. Inscribed with that extreme experience, it can only long for a transformation or a return to a condition of lightheartedness. The brighter, lighter power of the final line offers a foil to the implicit darkness of the ghetto heart, a disparity suspended and sustained by a single line that wills but does not achieve the reconciliation the poetic persona desires.

---

[16] Saul Friedländer, *Memory, History, and the Extermination of the Jews of Europe*, 119.

[17] See Helfrich, 247.

The degree to which the poetic persona has been affected and transformed by the multiple levels of suffering is revealed in the synecdoche "Gettoherz" that signifies both the poetic persona and the experience that has internally marked her. This internal marking in "Versöhnlich" becomes an external one in Nelly Sachs's claim: "Meine Metaphern sind meine Wunden."[18] Sachs's assertion speaks to the complex of remembered suffering and its transformation into language. Yet her metaphors were also her bandages, covering wounds that refused to heal, the wounds of otherwise unbearable memories of trauma and loss, with a thin veneer of abstraction that both enabled and constituted her art and her strategy for survival.

The translation of memory traces into poetry thus offers not only a means of responding to a call to witness, but also serves as a coping strategy, a means by which the poets could both reveal and conceal their wounds behind a shield of metaphor often simultaneously translucent and opaque. Without this mediation (as a kind of poetics of transference[19]) through a textualization that constructs or enables a temporal simultaneity of past, present, and future, the compulsion to remember and confront the suffering of the past threatens to overwhelm the present and transform, in Walter Benjamin's words, "existence into a preserve of memory."[20] As a genre, lyric poetry provides the medium in which a simultaneity or superimposition of temporal levels can take place. Emil Staiger, in his classic study on poetics, posited the concept of "interiorization" which he defined as an interpenetration both of subject and object and of temporal levels within the context of the lyric poem.[21] This braiding of strands of time knotted together in the moment of poetic figuration subverts progressive, linear conceptions of temporality and history.[22]

---

[18] Referred to above and quoted in Fritsch-Vivié, 99, and in Bengt Holmqvist, "Die Sprache der Sehnsucht," *Das Buch der Nelly Sachs*, 29.

[19] See reference to Freud's essay "Remembering, Repeating and Working-Through" in note 8 above.

[20] Walter Benjamin, *Illuminations*, ed. Hannah Arendt, (1955; New York: Schocken, 1969), 203.

[21] Emil Staiger, *Basic Concepts of Poetics*, trans. Janette C. Hudson and Luanne T. Frank, intro. by Luanne T. Frank (1946; University Park: The Pennsylvania State UP, 1991), 82: "We shall use the word 'interiorization' [*Erinnerung*] for the absence of distance between subject and object, for the lyric interpenetration (*Ineinander*). The present, the past, even the future can be interiorized and remembered in lyric poetry."

[22] This conflation of temporal levels in a single point as a concentration of mem-

Nelly Sachs's poem "WENN DIE PROPHETEN einbrächen" (*FS* 92–93) from the collection *Sternverdunkelung* demonstrates in its three central strophes a diffusion and inversion of temporality that is represented both figuratively and grammatically (*FS* 93):

Wenn die Propheten einbrächen
durch Türen der Nacht
und ein Ohr wie eine Heimat suchten —

Ohr der Menschheit
du nesselverwachsenes,
würdest du hören?
Wenn die Stimme der Propheten
auf dem Flötengebein der ermordeten Kinder
blasen würde,
die vom Märtyrerschrei verbrannten Lüfte
ausatmete —
wenn sie eine Brücke aus verendeten Greisenseufzern
baute —

Ohr der Menschheit
du mit dem kleinen Lauschen beschäftigtes,
würdest du hören?[23]

By using the conditional subjunctive in this litany of images of suffering, death, and indifference, the poetic voice is able to speak for the prophets in an anticipation of a prophecy that is already past. The as-if of the prophetic becomes then not prophecy but remembrance and an exhortation against deafness and indifference to the pain and suffering of the victims of past persecution. The truth-value of the result is, however, constantly destabilized by the dynamic and mutable nature of memory as a process that shifts its allegiances and emphases with the passage of time as well as in response to ever-changing situational factors. The tensions that bind and separate history, memory, and poetry are ever present and unresolvable. The poet's refusal of healable suffer-

---

ory is termed "kairós" in Gisela Dischner's study of Nelly Sachs's poetry in the context of modernism, *Poetik des modernen Gedichts. Zur Lyrik von Nelly Sachs.* Her reading of "kairós," however, emphasizes the nature of a spontaneous moment of remembrance that involuntarily expands into a paradigm (7): "Ein scheinbar beliebiger Moment des Lebens wird in der Erinnerung plötzlich zum Kairós, in dem alles Vergangene und Gegenwärtige zu einem Punkt gerinnt, um den sich Assoziationen lagern, bis dieser Moment . . . zu einer Modellsituation wird."

[23] In its pointed allusions to humanity's deaf ear, this poem recalls Rose Ausländer's indictment of the bystander's silence in "Wo waren" (IV 92): "Wo waren / die laut schweigenden / Menschen." Taken in combination, these two poems reflect on the inaction of those who stood by, deaf and dumb in the face of victimization.

ing becomes a means of mediating these tensions while keeping them in suspension despite the recognition that the linguistic means available are ultimately incapable of doing justice to experience. Sachs's repeated associations between poetic language, the suffering of memory, and wounds can be further extended by the symbolic associations of the wound in Christian iconography, where it serves as a metaphor for transcendence and resurrection as well as a representation of that which cannot be erased or denied.[24]

Elective or Collective Affinities

It is necessary not to be "myself," still less to be "ourselves." The city gives one the feeling of being at home. We must take the feeling of being at home into exile. We must be rooted in the absence of place.

— Simone Weil[25]

The I can be wholly I, can descend wholly into the depth of its solitary one — as the Psalmist calls his soul — only because, as the I that it is, it dares to speak with the mouth of the congregation. (. . .) This intensification of the individual soul into the soul of all is what first gives the individual soul the audacity to express its own distress — because it is, precisely, more than just its own individual distress. In revelation, the soul acquiesces; it surrenders its individuality so that it might be forgiven its individuality.

— Franz Rosenzweig[26]

The traditional Jewish relationship to history and memory is one that is intimately bound up with notions of identity. The injunction to remember is central to a sense of belonging to the community of Judaism and forges a connection to the past in which an eschatological view of history prevails over a secular one. The recurrence of catastrophe is perceived as part of a cyclical, biblically validated alternation of disaster and redemption, with the result that temporal distinctions in terms of secular time are significant only insofar as they represent events in the recognized chronology of religious history. The remembrance enjoined in

[24] Shoshana Felman's discussion of the associative nature of the wound in Christian symbolism as it relates to Paul Celan's metaphorics of witness in "Todesfuge" parallels Sachs's conception and representation of the wound as a metaphor for memory in the poems addressed in this chapter. Cf. Felman and Laub, *Testimony*, 30.

[25] Weil, 86.

[26] Franz Rosenzweig, *The Star of Redemption*, trans. William Hallo (Boston: Beacon Press, 1972), 250–51.

Deuteronomy[27] is thus an injunction to remain aware of the biblical past which the historical past merely replicates. The preservation of this past is not only vital to a sense of group identity, it is also presented as the prerequisite for achieving a redemptive future.[28]

The stigmatization of Jewish identity under the racist ideology of the Third Reich forced many assimilated Jews to confront a heritage they had repressed, denied, or forgotten. For some Jews, this obligatory assumption of an ethnic identity inspired an awakening to Judaism. For others, it led to an even more pronounced antipathy and renunciation of a collective association that had only brought suffering and death to the Chosen People.[29] The plight of the Jews under National Socialism did not only stem from the external threat to their existence, but was also compounded and complicated by internal conflicts, both individual and collective, as to the nature and constitution of Jewish identity. The I assumed through the process of assimilation had in many ways been an appropriation of characteristics privileged by the dominant, socially powerful They with a concomitant rejection of those characteristics of a We labelled and perceived as inferior or negative in that social context. The so-called emancipation of the Jews in Western Europe therefore did not lead to an increased tolerance for pluralism and difference, but rather to an eradication or denial of those qualities that disrupted the ideal of homogeneity necessary to the construction of national identity.[30]

The I of assimilation achieved a position of perceived privilege through participation and complicity in the stigmatization of the We — a phenomenon that became disturbingly evident in the perpetuation of prejudices and lack of solidarity many Jews in Western Europe showed toward the Jewish refugees and immigrants from Eastern Europe even

[27] Cf. esp. Deut. 6:12: "Then beware lest thou forget the LORD, which brought thee forth out of the Land of Egypt. . . ."

[28] Cf. Aleida Assmann, "Zur Metaphorik der Erinnerung," where she discusses Jewish memory as a connection to the past that simultaneously anticipates a redemptive future (23): "Das Geschehen am Sinai liegt lange zurück, es gehört einer fernen Vergangenheit an; durch die Erinnerung allein wird es zur verpflichtenden Gegenwart und zur hoffnungsträchtigen Zukunft. (. . .) Im Exil wurde die Erinnerung zum einzigen Band mit der anderen, der wahren Zeit."

[29] Cf. Aharon Appelfeld, "After the Holocaust," trans. Jeffrey Green, *Writing and the Holocaust*, ed. Berel Lang, 91.

[30] Cf. Zygmunt Bauman, *Modernity and the Holocaust* (Cambridge: Polity Press, 1989), 128; and Bauman, *Modernity and Ambivalence* (Ithaca, NY: Cornell UP, 1991), 141–42.

before Hitler came to power.[31] The privileging of certain identities over others in the modern multicultural nation-state resulted in factionaliza- tion and internal conflict within groups that were by narrow definition regarded as collectives. Jealous of their acquired privilege as assimilated Jews and citizens of their respective countries, Western European Jews allied themselves with nationality and not with religious heritage. They thereby further intensified and deepened the "Us versus Them" polar- ity that underlay the ethnocentric and nationalistic policies of European nation states, most prominently Germany, by allying themselves with the artificial image of national homogeneity over against what they per- ceived to be an inchoate mass of backwards, uncultivated, and unas- similated Eastern Jewry.[32]

In Germany, the Nazi propaganda and the development of repres- sive, discriminatory policies against the Jews did not lead to an atti- tude of common suffering and solidarity among Jews, but rather further reinforced the internal prejudices and dichotomies that already pitted "the Jews" against each other: West vs. East; assimilated vs. un- assimilated; reformed vs. orthodox. Nazi policies clearly established the Jews as Other to the Aryan ideal. By using "Jew" as a collective term for the absolute Other vis-à-vis "German" or "Aryan," these dis- criminatory policies and practices produced a hierarchy of otherness not only between Jew and German but also subsumed within the category of "Jew" itself as "Other." The assimilated (Western) Jews saw themselves as closer to the ideal privileged as German and strove to distance themselves from the Other, i.e. the Jew portrayed by Nazi propaganda, a figuration they associated with unconforming and unas- similated Eastern Jewry. Here the irony of the collective label used to

---

[31] Cf. Steven Aschheim, *Brothers and Strangers: The Eastern European Jew in German and German Jewish Consciousness, 1800–1923* (Madison: U of Wisconsin P, 1982); and Juliane Wetzel, "Auswanderung aus Deutschland," in *Die Juden in Deutschland: 1933–1945*, ed. Wolfgang Benz (Munich: C.H. Beck, 1989), 436–37.

[32] Cf. Zygmunt Bauman, *Modernity and the Holocaust*, 132. Earlier in this study, Bauman argues for the unique non-nationality of the Jews, who by their very exis- tence were a provocation to the construct of a homogeneous national identity (52): "*The Jews were not just unlike any other nation; they were also unlike any other foreign- ers.*" In short, they undermined the very difference between hosts and guests, the na- tive and the foreign. And as nationhood became the paramount basis of group self- constitution, they came to undermine the most basic of differences: the difference between 'Us' and 'Them'." This disruption of the Us/Them polarity does not con- tradict its intensification as discussed above, rather it complicates the distinction by introducing new fields of difference. The process of assimilation is akin to perform- ance where an "other" identity is studied, learned, and practiced until it becomes difficult to distinguish the boundary between the performed and the performance.

homogenize the victims in the name of genocide is revealed — the collective label foisted upon the Jews in order to segregate them and set them apart obstructed rather than promoted the development of an internal group solidarity.

In light of the conflicts and tensions that divided European Jewry, it would be fallacious and precipitate to disregard the internal prejudices that marked the diverse European Jewish population in favor of an idealized construct of group solidarity united against a common enemy. The We of a collective Jewry is thus a patchy fabrication of totality, useful and necessary for a coherent discussion of a heterogeneous people, but nevertheless constantly called into question by the particularities and peculiarities of the individuals it claims to conjoin and define.[33] The coerced nature of this grouping as a kind of We by default resulted in an attitude of ambivalence towards an artificially collectivized identity, one which obscured an underlying resistance to categorization and fixity. The internal divisiveness of the We highlights the constructed nature of the collective and serves to disrupt the alleged clear demarcations separating the We and the They. The acquisition of an identity through assimilation contributed to a kind of group ambivalence toward the Jew as Other, an Other that came to be identified with the unassimilated, orthodox Jew. This attitude of ambivalence is evidenced in the oscillation between solidarity and alienation, in vocalic confrontations between I and We, I and You, and We and They in the poems addressed in the following analysis.

The figuration of the Jewish people as a people of memory and their accompanying identification with the injunction to remember are central themes in Nelly Sachs's 1946 poem cycle *Chöre der Mitternacht*. The first two strophes of the poem at the midpoint in the cycle, "Chor der Steine" (*FS* 58–59), exemplify the poetic identification with and representation of the Chosen People as the people of memory.

[33] Cf. Hannah Arendt's incisive discussion of Jewish identity and the divisiveness characteristic of the European Jewish population around the time of World War II in her essay "We Refugees" of January 1943, reprinted in *The Jew as Pariah: Jewish Identity and Politics in the Modern Age*, ed. Ron Feldman (New York: Grove Press, 1978), 55–66. Arendt argues here that because of their rootlessness and permanent exile status, the Jews are the representatives of the purely human in a world in which purely human beings have ceased to exist (65).

WIR STEINE
Wenn einer uns hebt
Hebt er Urzeiten empor —
Wenn einer uns hebt
Hebt er den Garten Eden empor —
Wenn einer uns hebt
Hebt er Adam und Evas Erkenntnis empor
Und der Schlange staubessende Verführung.

Wenn einer uns hebt
Hebt er Billionen Erinnerungen in seiner Hand
Die sich nicht auflösen im Blute
Wie der Abend.
Denn Gedenksteine sind wir
Alles Sterben umfassend.

The use of We in the very first line immediately establishes a sense of belonging — the poetic voice speaks not as an individual but for a group, allying itself with a legacy rooted in biblical history. The We in its likeness to memorial stones embodies and implies an agelessness that is the privilege of a people whose claim to origin dates back to the specifically biblical genesis of humankind. The We of stones is both part of and party to this past, cognizant in retrospect of the Fall and the consequences of this primordial banishment and the loss of "innocence" that incited it. In the second strophe the parallels between the stones and the Chosen People as a people of memory are expanded in an associative chain such that the collective We refers not just to the Jewish past but to the legacy of mortality that is common to all humanity. The stones as monuments to a lost yet preserved past are at once the receptacles of memory and self-conscious of their function as such.

Although the poetic voice in Sachs's "Chor der Steine" speaks through a We to indicate an identification with a collective, here signifying both a collective past and people, this relationship of affiliation is not consistent, but is instead complicated by questions of belonging, crises of identity, and desires for emancipation from the heavy burden of the past that is both the heritage and essence of the We. Vibrating along a continuum stretching from identification to alienation the voiced or implied I alternately appeals to and denies a relationship to a We. Despite the ambivalence inherent in this relation, it can be read as the attempt on the part of the I to reconstruct or define a self in relation to a group, regardless of whether this relation is perceived as positive or negative.

As the convenience of the We by default is revealed to be an oversimplification, so too is the claim to an identity as an I problematic. The implied totality of these labels must be questioned if the ambivalent relationship of the individual, as a subject (albeit one subject to conflicting forces and positions, to the group, as a variegated and necessarily obstreperous collective), is to be understood in the poetic representation of traumatic memory as inextricably connected and identified with the oppressed group. Many of the poems that address the I/We relationship figure the poetic persona's identification with her people as one of solidarity with the oppressed, implying a call for survival in defiance of the oppressors.

Rose Ausländer's "Lassen uns nicht" (VIII 226) offers an illustration of this move toward solidarity and resistance:

> Mein Volk
>
> Mein Sandvolk
> mein Grasvolk
>
> wir lassen uns nicht
> vernichten

The presence of the I is apparent in an assertion of possession over the collective term "Volk." The choice of the phrase "mein Volk" evokes associations to Else Lasker-Schüler's poem "Mein Volk" in which Lasker-Schüler likens the Jewish people to a crumbling cliff on the edge of the sea. The poetic I in Lasker-Schüler's poem avows her connection to this disintegrating yet spiritually extant heritage, a connection that she has internalized to the extent that she experiences its decay as an inner decomposition:

> Der Fels wird morsch,
> Dem ich entspringe
> Und meine Gotteslieder singe . . .
> Jäh stürz ich vom Weg
> Und riesele ganz in mir
> Fernab, allein über Klagegestein
> Dem Meer zu.
>
> Hab mich so abgeströmt
> Von meines Blutes
> Mostvergorenheit.
> Und immer, immer noch der Widerhall
> In mir,
> Wenn schauerlich gen Ost
> Das morsche Felsgebein,
> Mein Volk,
> Zu Gott schreit.[34]

---

[34] Else Lasker-Schüler, *Sämtliche Gedichte* (Munich: Kösel Verlag, 1984), 135.

The association between an I and a collective here is suspended in the tension between internalization and alienation — there is no explicit We but rather an I which is unwillingly affected by and imbued with the collective people. The "Volk" has lost its stability and strength, and while the parallel to the sand image in Ausländer's poem is evoked by the verb "riesele" in the fifth line, Lasker-Schüler's trickling sand is unequivocal in its figuration of decay and the dissolution or erosion that comes with the passage of time. The image of dissolution in the first strophe is a flowing away from the source of origin in the second: "Hab mich so abgeströmt / Von meines Blutes / Mostvergorenheit." Here Lasker-Schüler shifts elemental relations from earth (stone cliff) to water (ocean), to illustrate the transition from static stability to fluid motion, a fluidity not only evoked by the choice of verb "abgeströmt" but also in the noun neologism "Mostvergorenheit" which signals an effervescence within the fluid state itself. Unlike the voluntary and even defiant claim to association with the "Volk" in Ausländer's "Lassen uns nicht," the poetic I in Lasker-Schüler's poem is not the agent of this relationship, but must rather suffer through it as the poem's closing lines imply. In her reading of this poem, Dagmar Lorenz offers it as a demonstration of Lasker-Schüler's unique understanding of her Jewishness, not as a religious affiliation, but rather as "an ethnic, historical, and mythical perspective."[35] This fusion of strands into an almost elemental conception of Judaism both supports Lasker-Schüler's affiliation with her people and allows for a wide embrace of other religious traditions (and here too there are parallels to both Ausländer and Sachs), particularly Christianity.

In Rose Ausländer's "Lassen uns nicht" the use of "mein" demonstrates the association of the poetic voice with the people, while the pairings of "Sand" and "Gras" in the formation of compounds with "Volk" distinguish Ausländer's re-appropriation of the word from its ideologically infused usage under Nazism. These compounds not only represent an assertion of Jewish rights to the term "Volk," a claim to recognition of their status as a people — but also, in defiance of the Nazis' genocidal project, attest to the continuity and resilience of the Jewish people. But there is also an ambivalence inherent in the images of sand and grass as metaphors for both insignificance and numberlessness. This ambivalence can be traced back to the biblical symbolism in Isaiah where sand and grass are used interchangeably as reminders to the people of their smallness and worthlessness in relation to God and

---

All rights held by Suhrkamp Verlag, Frankfurt am Main.

[35] Lorenz, *Keepers of the Motherland*, 74.

as encouragements to their obedience and the manner in which it
would be rewarded — by great prosperity and fecundity.[36] In
Ausländer's poem, however, there is a tone of resistance that is absent
from the biblical passages and that is unmistakably a response to the attempt to eradicate the Jews not by God's hand but by man's. The near
infinitude of sand and grass implies not only the ineradicable nature of
the Chosen People, but in its association to multiplicity also offers a
metaphorical means of getting beyond the totalizing and collectivizing
implications of the words "people" and We.

The use of the I as voice and medium for the textualization of collective memory, with the tacit understanding that this memory must be
passed on as a legacy to future generations, is, however, problematic.
Although it could be argued that the first-person singular offers a better
identificatory model for the reader and encourages greater empathy than
an amorphous, impersonal or choral voice might,[37] the I itself must be
regarded as in flux, unstable, and an abstraction constructed by the poet
in what is sometimes an attempt to lend greater authority to the poetic
voice by implying that it is the voice of (personal) experience. Further,
the privileging of the first person can also serve to obscure the cacophony of voices that make up the text and texture of memory.

This potential erasure of the plurality of the multitude in the moment where the I speaks for the We is refuted, even reversed, in
Ausländer's posthumously published poem "Drei" (VIII 111). This
poem explicitly identifies and allies I and We, but simultaneously indicates that the conjoining of the I with the We is accompanied by the
disappearance of the "self":

> Die Tafel mit dem Griffel verwundbar
> drei Worte
> ich
> bin
> wir
> Weggewischt
>
> zähl ich nicht mehr

---

[36] See Isaiah 40:7 "surely the people is grass"; 44:4 "They shall spring up like grass
amid waters"; 48:19 "Your offspring would have been like the sand"; as well as 1. Moses
13:16 "if a man can number the dust of the earth, so shall thy seed be numbered."

[37] Cf. Yosef Yerushalmi, *Zakhor*, 44; and Hayden White, "Historical Emplotment
and the Problem of Truth," in *Probing the Limits of Representation*, ed. Saul
Friedländer (Cambridge: Harvard UP, 1992), 45.

Ich zähle bis drei und mehr
auf der Tafel
schreiben
drei Finger
weiß auf schwarz

The identification of the self with the collective here obscures the particularity of the I, dissolving individuality into anonymity. This dissolution of independent existence can be read both negatively and positively. The disappearance of the I behind or into a collective We can be read as an evasion of individual responsibility; or as a recognition of the minimal significance of the one versus the many and the subsequent denial of the self in favor of the collective. These negative associations with the disappearance of the I as singularity can, however, also be viewed as an expression of solidarity with a group acknowledged as having greater relevance and worth than the individual ego and which therefore deserves and inspires the individual's self-subordination and allegiance. In addition to these, I would propose yet another reading, that the erasure of the I is made possible by its identification, whether voluntary or coerced, with the collective identity of the group, much the same way that the Nazis set about achieving their genocidal purposes by forcing all of Jewish lineage to assume a Jewish "identity." By collectivizing the Jews and marking them with clearly visible signifiers, the Nazis succeeded in obscuring the particularity and singularity of the individual which then allowed them to proceed to eradicate a categorized, depersonalized group of their own construction. Ironically, the Nazis here were at least ideologically able to homogenize a group that they perceived as a threat to the realization of the homogeneous ideal of Aryan "German" identity that they were striving for.[38] In the case of the Jews, the (forced) assumption of a designated group identity thus became the prerequisite for the erasure of the individual.

But these are just several of many possible readings of voice in a poem where the continually shifting alliances and emphases resist fixity. The I disappears and reappears, serving as the writer, the written, and the erased, yet paradoxically appears as a tangible, corporeal presence in the closing strophe. The diminished significance or even disappearance

---

[38] Steven Katz, in his essay "The 'Unique' Intentionality of the Holocaust," discusses the underlying assumption regarding Hitler's stigmatization of the Jews, namely, by categorizing them as a group and then insisting on the unalterable character of its members in regard to assimilation, Hitler denied the Jews any possibility of integration even at the price of their Jewish identity. The definition of ethnic identity as inherited and not learned was therefore central to the Nazi genocidal agenda. Cf. Katz, *Post-Holocaust Dialogues* (New York: New York UP, 1985), 300.

of the self implied in the opening lines of the poem is belied by the intervening material presence of the I, represented pars pro toto by the poetic persona's three pale fingers writing. This poem in its brevity distills a complex of images inspiring multiple associations and readings that both complement and contradict each other. The choice of "Drei" as a title evokes associations to the Holy Trinity, unity in plurality, communicative triangles, and the mystical power attributed to numbers. In a conscious play with the evocative aura surrounding the number three, the poet both anticipates these associations and calls them into question. Three is mentioned all of three times, a repetition that adds yet another dimension to the numbers game, but the apparent power of this cipher is undermined in the third strophe by the return or resurrection of the erased I who counts (yet paradoxically does not "count," in the sense of being counted among the existing, as the wordplay in the second strophe intimates) to three and beyond, thereby exceeding the limits and disrupting the hegemony of the triad. This gesture into the beyond is momentary, however, and is immediately displaced and superseded by the starkly visual image of the three white fingers which inscribe the poetic testimonial. In the end, the boundaries between the writer and the text are dissolved and the poem appears to write itself.

The ambivalent desire of the I to merge with the anonymous mass of the collective We recalls the wish for union with an archetypal maternal force discussed in the preceding chapter. The oscillation between attraction and repulsion evident in the maternal poems is also characteristic of those that portray the I/We relationship as a connection between the poetic persona and her people. The ambivalence evident in the I/We interaction characterizes many of Nelly Sachs's lyrical representations of the I/We encounter and her poetic self-understanding as a representative voice for her people. In her letters Sachs repeatedly insisted on the insignificance of her person in relation to the message she was trying to convey through her lyric,[39] a biographical parallel to the process at work in Ausländer's "Drei." Sachs's poems bear witness both to the suffering of the victims and to the unresolved tensions that connect and divide the

---

[39] Cf. *Briefe,* 177: "Auf meine Art kämpfe ich für mein Volk. Am liebsten hätte ich das ohne meinen Namen getan. (. . .) Meine Person ist ganz unwichtig dabei, und ich lehne ja auch immer ab, wenn ich persönlich herangezogen werden soll." See also (*Briefe,* 217–18): ". . . daß ich hinter meinem Werk verschwinden will, daß ich anonym bleiben will. (. . .) ich . . . will, daß man mich gänzlich ausschaltet — nur eine Stimme, ein Seufzer für die, die lauschen wollen. Eine Tragödie soll man so leise wie möglich behandeln — niemals darf sie mit Unwesentlichkeiten umkränzt werden."

poet as individual and exile-survivor and the collective in its manifestation as an uneasy, conglomerate identity.

One of Sachs's strategies for articulating a kind of unity in diversity
is through the appeal to a choral voice, a tactic most evident in the cycle of poems *Chöre der Mitternacht* (*FS* 47–68). In this group of four-
teen poems, beginning with an image of abandoned objects and closing
with the call of the Promised Land, Sachs offers a composition of in-
termixed voices marked by moments of solo, unison, and polyphony.
The first poem of the cycle, "CHOR DER VERLASSENEN DINGE"
(*FS* 48–49), opens with the poetic persona's speculations about the stories behind the abandoned objects she sees, and while considering her
own sense of loss, she identifies with their abandonment and loneliness:

> *Krug im Schutt*
> WAR ICH DER KRUG, daraus der Abend floß wie Wein
> Und manchmal ein gefangner Mond zum Rosenstock?
> Die Sterbenacht der Greisin fing ich ein
> Al schon ihr Atem keuchte wie die Geiß am Pflock.
> O Krüge, Krüge! in ein Abschiedsmaß gezwängt
> Ist was wir halten; rinnende Natur.
> Wir sind wie Herzen, draus es weiter drängt
> Und stille steht wie Zeit in einer Uhr.

The singularity of the I empathizing with the single jug in the opening
lines is quickly displaced by a plurality of jugs that are both objects and
signifiers for the lives and hearts of a We: "Wir sind wie Herzen, draus es
weiter drängt / Und stille steht wie Zeit in einer Uhr." The plurality
that marks the We cannot only be equated with a logic of numbers;
rather the I herself is characterized by an internal division or multiplicity
that calls the presumed homogeneity of individual identity into question.

This fragmentation of the self is represented in the next strophe
through the dialogue between the voice of the I and the You of her
shadow (*FS* 48):

> *Ein halbverbranntes Licht*
> O Schattenspiegel mein! ich sah in dir, ich sah —
> Die Hand aus Grabesstaub, die sich an einem Stern verging.
> Die Zeit in ihrer Sterbewiege schrie — ich sah
> Israels Mund in Qual, gebogen wie ein Ring.

The chain of associations sparked by the recognition of the otherness of
and within the self as seen in the shadow reflected by the dim light of a
candle stump moves from an identification as an individual to one as a
victim to finally that of an archetypal entity, Israel. The I is not only self
and other to itself, but is also, more expansively, the personification of

Israel with all its accompanying associations: biblical, historical, geographical, and messianic.

In regarding a single, empty shoe in the third strophe, the poetic voice identifies with the solitariness of the object, but also conflates its isolation with her own. The shoe in post-Holocaust iconography echoes with the extinguished steps of wandering peoples and represents associatively the piles of shoes in museums and memorials that testify to the persecution, flight, and extermination of victims whose mute stories are poignantly encapsulated in the apparent banality of abandoned everyday objects:

> *Ein Schuh*
> Verlornes Menschenmaß; ich bin die Einsamkeit
> Die ihr Geschwister sucht auf dieser Welt —[40]
> O Israel, von deiner Füße Leid
> Bin ich ein Echo, das zum Himmel gellt.

These forlorn and isolated things, like the poetic persona, have escaped destruction. As remnants of a lost past they stand as reminders of what once was and as testimonials to the suffering and deaths of the victims. The alternating rhyme scheme further reinforces the parallels between the past and the present and the searching longing of the poetic I that is obstructed by the intervention of catastrophe, visually indicated by the dash in the second line. This dash further indicates a break, temporal and existential, which, in combination with the poet's use of rhyme, renders the plaintive echo expressed by the poetic persona both figuratively and literally audible.

The complex of identifications developed in the first three strophes of this poem shifts between and among objects, interior and exterior otherness, the collective multiplicity of the victims, and an archetypal Israel that is figured as at once singular and plural. In her reading of this poem, Birgit Lermen places it in the context of the Hasidic narrative of creation which came about through the transition from Divine wholeness to Divine fragmentation. In Hasidic mysticism, God's contraction or *zimzum* results in a compression of Divine power that is too great to be contained. What follows is the breaking of the vessels or *shevirah* which causes the holy sparks to be dissipated into the atmosphere, imbuing all

---

[40] The concept of loneliness as the collective fate of the Jewish people was one that preoccupied Nelly Sachs also in her letters. In a letter to her close friend Gudrun Dähnert in 1948 she wrote of her own identification with this fate of solitariness that is both personal and universal (*Briefe*, 95): "Aber mein Schicksal ist Einsamsein, so wie es das Schicksal meines Volkes ist."

things with particles of spiritual energy.[41] Lermen extrapolates from this
premise of the Divinely invested nature of all things to an interpretation
of the objects in Sachs's poem as silent witnesses to extreme events, but
people have forgotten how to hear their testimony. [42] This convergence
of voices and identities culminates in the unison of a choral We spoken
by the dead in the poem's closing strophe (FS 49):

> Chor
> Wir aber sind, seitdem wir Erde waren
> Getrieben schon von euch durch soviel Tod —
> Bist du ein Band, gepflückt aus Totenhaaren
> Geh ein zum Wunder, werde Brot.
> Hier ist ein Buch, darin die Welten kreisen
> Und das Geheimnis flüstert hinter einem Spalt —
> Wirf es ins Feuer, Licht wird nicht verwaisen
> Und Asche schläft sich neu zur Sterngestalt.
> Und tragen wir der Menschenhände Siegel
> Und ihre Augen-Blicke eingesenkt wie Raub —
> so lest uns wie verkehrte Schrift im Spiegel
> Erst totes Ding und dann den Menschenstaub.

The We of dead voices issues instructions to the living as to how to
read the traces of their lives in the residue of objects and ashes they
have left behind. Their words have the phoenix-like quality of the mystical alphabet[43] in that they cannot be consumed by fire, but rather retain the substance of their cosmic secrets in transmogrified form. The
book that is their legacy represents the point of intersection between
the mystical and the mortal. The text inherent in these lifeless things is
likened to a backwards script that can only be deciphered in a mirror
("So lest uns wie verkehrte Schrift im Spiegel"). This image of a backward script is yet another representation of the dialectical relations between presence and absence, memory and existence, repression and
recovery impelling the poem. The reading of the backwards script in
the mirror is thus also an act of reversal, controverting the erasure of
the victims so that their existence as remembrance is recuperated
through the deciphered word. The reversed writing evoked in the

---

[41] For a detailed discussion of these concepts, see Gershom Scholem, *The Origins
of the Kabbalah*, 129, and *On the Kabbalah*, 137.

[42] See Lermen and Braun, *Nelly Sachs "an letzter Atemspitze des Lebens"*, 74–76.

[43] Cf. David Roskies' discussion of the indestructible nature attributed to the letters
of the Torah in Jewish belief in *Against the Apocalypse*, 32: "The letters of the Torah have
a life of their own and take leave of the burning scroll in the same way as the soul departs
from the human body. The scroll is mere flesh, but its spirit is indestructible."

poem is also a mirroring of the poem itself which through its various configurations has the capacity to simultaneously reflect backward, forward, and inward: as a testimonial to the past, an exhortation to the present, and as a warning to the future.

Ultimately, however, the poem questions its own presence and its limitations as an adequate medium for the messages and memories it seeks to convey. Despite the apparent indestructibility of the book, which is associatively also the Book, thrown into the flames, the We recognizes that their words are not imbued with a similar immortality, but are instead destined to disintegrate into lifeless dust. With this question of the viability of the poem as representation, the voices of the We speak to the difficulty of negotiating the inexpressibility of an incomprehensible past and the moral obligation to remember.

In "DIE AUGEN ZU," a later poem from the 1961 cycle *Noch feiert der Tod das Leben*, Sachs re-visioned the images illustrating the themes of memory, loss, and witness-bearing from "CHOR DER VERLASSENEN DINGE" and eliminated the alternation between the I and the We of the earlier text. The voice speaking in "DIE AUGEN ZU" is anonymous yet inscribed with suffering and the message is one of remembered pain and current despair as to the possibility of ever vanquishing the hegemony of the oppressors (*FS* 375):

DIE AUGEN ZU
und dann —
Die Wunde geht auf
und dann —

Man angelt mit Blitzen
O
die Geheimnisse des Blutes
O
für Fische[44]
Alles im Grab der Luft
Opfer
Henker
Finger
Finger

[44] For a discussion of "fish" as a trope for martyrdom and suffering in Nelly Sachs's poetry see Olof Lagercrantz, *Versuch über die Lyrik der Nelly Sachs*, esp. 26; and Ruth Dinesen, "Das Ziel des Kosmos. Zum Element 'Fisch' in der Lyrik von Nelly Sachs," *Jahrbuch der Deutschen Schiller-Gesellschaft* 26 (1982): 445–66.

Das Kind malt im Sarg mit Staub
den Nabel der Welt —
und im Geheg der Zähne hält
der Henker den letzten Fluch —

Was nun?

Night is the harbinger of dreams and memories that torment the unnamed poetic persona. The very lack of specific traits characterizing this poetic persona creates an impression of anonymity, which ironically, because of its very featurelessness, enables a wider identification with differentiated experiences of suffering both past and present. The one-for-all image of Israel from "CHOR DER VERLASSENEN DINGE" has been condensed but not erased and is here represented in the single letter "O" in the second strophe, recalling the lines "Israels Mund in Qual, gebogen wie ein Ring" of the earlier poem. In the later work, the poet no longer relies on metaphorical representation, but instead appeals to the latent polyvalence of the letter itself with all its aural and visual associations. This resonant "O" that recurs twice in the second strophe is the circle that rounds up the victims, the facial appearance of their outcries of sorrow and despair, and the shape of the mouths forming these sounds.

The repetition of the word "Finger" in the second strophe is also a tactic of evoking multiple meanings and in its contiguity with the words that precede it ("Opfer / Henker") both confuses and disrupts the implied polarity between persecuted and persecutor. The victims and the perpetrators are all destined for a common mortal fate ("Alles im Grab der Luft"), a mortality dictated by their shared humanness, here represented through the synecdochical finger. But these human and mortal similarities are set in sharp opposition to their implied differences, especially the manner of their respective deaths. The gestures made by the executioner's fingers are not equivalent to those made by the executed. The fingers that select those designated for death are fingers similar to those of the victims, but their power and significance are fundamentally different.[45] An appeal to the common humanity implied by the similarity of the "finger" image is here put into question: the paralleling of the fingers does not imply an equivalence, but instead undermines any presumed singularity of meaning in the signifier.

---

[45] The synecdochical representation of the executioner through the crooked gesturing finger appears also in Sachs's only narrative description of the conditions of persecution under Nazism. In "Leben unter Bedrohung," Sachs refers to that time of danger as "die Zeit der gekrümmten Finger und der starken Schritte." Cf. Walter Berendsohn, *Nelly Sachs* (Darmstadt: Agora Verlag, 1974), 10.

The last strophe of the poem plays with paradoxical images of human mortality and concludes with a question seemingly echoing with despair: "Was nun?" The voice of the poet, present yet disembodied and depersonalized, attempts to speak the memories of the past in the present, all the while overwhelmed with the recognition that these are not just memories but realities. The past is not past, the wounds have not healed, and all is not right with the world. Yet the final line of the poem, although evocative of despair, is still an open question that can be read either with a tone of resignation or one of defiance. The open-endedness of this "Was nun?" allows for a variety of responses, and, like Hölderlin's "Wozu Dichter in dürftiger Zeit?,"[46] is a provocation to the poet as well as an appeal to her readers to continue striving for transformation, within and against a language that has been abused and instrumentalized in the construction and perpetuation of a hegemonic system of exclusion, oppression, and eradication.

The theme of persistence in spite of the forces of eradication is expressed as the persistence of memory traces in the poetic persona's consciousness in Rose Ausländer's "Schatten im Spiegel" (III 42). The encounter between the present and past takes place in the act of self-reflection where the shadowy images of the past superimpose themselves on the reflections of the poetic I, mirroring her confrontation with a fragmented identity.

> Schaut mich an
> mit vielen Augen
> der Spiegel
>
> Ich geh von
> Gesicht zu Gesicht
> sie kennen mich nicht
>
> Ich frage jedes
> wer du bist
>
> Sie sagen
> lösch unsern Schatten
>
> Ich schöpfe den Spiegel leer
> bis kein Bild bleibt
> aber die Schatten sind da
>
> schaun mich an
> mit vielen Augen

---

[46] Friedrich Hölderlin, *Sämtliche Werke.* Vol. 2.1 (Stuttgart: Cotta, 1951), 94.

This poem conjoins several representational strategies for figuring the inscriptions of the past and the lost: the address to a You as a means of transcending temporal boundaries and the metaphorical imaging of the trace as the shadow of undecidability between presence and absence, as the external, invisible yet influential power of a force associated with collective fate and belief. The mirror here is both an entity in itself and the locus for a conglomeration of entities who have left their images on its surface. The poetic persona, in regarding the mirror, sees therefore not only the mirror and her self-reflection but also the faces of those before her whose ineradicable shadows have become unwilling yet persistent accomplices to memory. In the self-searching implied by the poetic persona's interaction with the mirror, the I splits revealing the multiplicity of her identity as it is effected and affected by the past.

In "Schatten im Spiegel" the distinctiveness of the I and the unity of the self are called into question — the voice that speaks as I does not do so from a position of sovereignty or stability. Any apparent distinctiveness is revealed to be merely a brief moment in a process where the self in relation to itself and to the collective is constantly being shifted, altered, and displaced.[47] This becomes most apparent in the third strophe, where the voice of the poetic I inquires after the identity of the You who is at once the I and an Other. The encounter with the mirror as vessel for re-membered visages from the past reflects the estrangement of the I from herself, a splitting of the I into a mixed recognition of multiple, multiplying identities. In order to determine the identity of the You, the shadowy denizens of the mirror enjoin the I to erase them — paradoxically stated in the fourth strophe through the juxtaposition of They and We: "Sie sagen / lösch unsern Schatten." The division of They and We is to be extinguished with the collective shadow left by the faces of the past — strangely, the shadow is singular, while the voice implies plurality. The mirror gives back the image of the self as a collectivized construct of others thereby thwarting any desire for self-affirmation or self-idealization the I might have had in approaching the mirror in the first place.[48] The distinction between singularity and plu-

---

[47] In this I would argue with Berel Lang's conception of the identification with "another" as a process that at once preserves and reflects difference (cf. Lang, *Act and Idea in the Nazi Genocide*, esp. xv). His reading of identity as mutable *and* dependent on the existence of the Other is, however, central to recognizing how these complexities and dynamics of self-understanding influence the articulation and transmission of memory.

[48] Contrast this use of a single mirror to reveal the plurality of the "I" and the use of multiple mirrors to depict an ideal, powerful self in Ausländer's poem "Treue I" (VIII 139) discussed in the preceding chapter.

rality is thus further undermined by the internal multiplicity of the I, an I that is also a You even if that You is invisible or obscured. Thus the difficulty of the poetic task, namely the ambition to give voice to silent or silenced meaning using a linguistic medium ultimately incapable of fulfilling the moral and representational demands of remembrance, is further complicated by the self's internal multiplicity.

The totality and singularity of the I are thus put into question both by the existence of the collective and by the internal divisiveness of the self. In a prose text entitled "Hier und Dort" (III 185), Rose Ausländer compares the dislocation of a stable self-conception characterizing the fragmented self with the arbitrariness of place as an anchoring locus of identification. Just as it is unjustifiable to insist upon the autonomous singularity of the I recognizing that the self is constituted by an accumulation of relationships with others, so too is it untenable to maintain the alleged stability of an identity grounded in a fixed spatial location:

> Wäre ich nur ich, wie einfach wäre alles. Aber ich bin auch jedes mögliche Du und Er und Sie. Ich habe mich nicht in der Hand. (. . .) Das Wo ist ebenso ungewiß. Es sagt zwar: hier bin ich, aber wer weiß, was *hier* ist. Auch das Dort kann hier sein.[49]

The lack of control and self-determination and the arbitrariness of fate implied in this passage anticipate another aspect of the treatment of memory in Sachs's and Ausländer's works. The overwhelming power of the forces of destruction against which individual efforts at resistance were futile continues to threaten the poet's testimony with obliteration, even as the event and its consequences are re-enacted through remembrance. This situation is further complicated by the burden of responsibility to account for the past that has itself become an obstacle to representation and expression. The moral obligation the poet feels toward the dead, together with the expectations the dead are perceived to have toward the preservation of their own memory contribute to the silencing of the poetic persona in Rose Ausländer's poem "Graues Haar" (III 28). Here the alternation of voices is no longer between I and We, with the concomitant implied identification via the first person, but rather one between I and They. The ancestors, here specifi-

---

[49] Contrast Ausländer's open, almost playful treatment of dislocation with Sachs's more disturbed, if cosmic one in the poem "Nicht HIER noch DORT" (*SL* 72): "Nicht HIER noch DORT / aber im Schlaf doppelzüngig / die Natur stottert in ihren Untergang / der Schatten geht nach Haus / Auf den Lebenslinien wandert der Planet / saugt königliche Botschaften ein / wird reicher —"

cally identified as father and mother, call upon the poetic persona to join in the mourning ritual for the victims of the Holocaust.

> Auf der Flucht
> aus dem Feuerland
> in den Himmel verirrt
>
> Sitzen Vater und Mutter
> SCHIWE
> Asche im Haar
>
> Ich frage sie nicht —
> sie antworten:
> Wer hat sie begraben
> wer sagt den KADDISCH[50]
> wo steht der Stein mit der Inschrift
> HIER LIEGEN DIE NAMENLOSEN
>
> Ich antworte nicht
> Sie fragen
> sie streuen mir
> Asche ins Haar

The insertion of the Other, or more specifically, the "Jew" as Other, is made visibly and linguistically manifest by the use of two Hebrew words, "SCHIWE" and "KADDISCH," both of which have to do with mourning. The transliterated Hebrew term "Schiwe" comes from the number seven and refers to the practice of mourning the dead for seven days after the funeral, a ritual referred to as "sitting *schiwe*" during which the *kaddisch* is recited. The dissonance between the poem's title and the transliterated Hebrew term in the body of the text arises out of the ambiguity in the spelling of the Hebrew words for "seven" and "gray hair, old age," the first of which is written with the letter "shin" and the second with the letter "sin," so that the Hebrew pronunciation of the latter would be "seva." In Yiddish, however, the pronunciation of this letter combination preserved the ambiguity of the written form: both meanings were embodied by the spoken form "schiwe." This apparent contradiction between title and text not only points to Ausländer's familiarity with both Hebrew and Yiddish, but also high-

---

[50] Jewish prayer recited for the dead, although in content it makes no reference to death but is rather a reaffirmation of faith in God. Contrary to popular understanding, the Kaddisch is not only recited in connection with mourning, but also occurs in the context of common prayer as the sanctification of God's name.

lights her exploration of simultaneity and ambiguity as othering processes within and between languages. [51]

In "Graues Haar," the aging parents carry out the ritual of mourning and their sorrow is represented by the ashes in their hair, while their
gray, ashen hair becomes a signal of their identification with the ashes
and associatively also with the suffering of the victims. But these parents, also representing the elders, not only mourn the deaths of the
victims, but also the death of tradition, the absence of those who would
carry on the Jewish cultural legacy. This disappearance of collective
identity in adherence to tradition is reinforced in the absence of a We in
the second strophe. The poetic I is mute in response to the questions
about the future of the Jewish tradition: the fate of the They does not
encompass the I — the sense of a collective identity has been severed.
The loss of identity is then further exposed in the reference to the dead
as the "NAMENLOSEN." The mixture of moral consciousness and a
sense of guilt at having survived that characterize the poet-as-witness
inform the poetic persona's relationship and attitude toward the victims
as "other." The use of the They is thus a defense mechanism against
this sense of guilt as well as a means of speaking for a collective without
explicitly joining it.

In the poem's final strophe the parents draw the poetic persona into
their ritual of mourning, forcing her to identify with the tradition, to
share in the legacy of ashes. Figuratively these ashes are multivalent as
symbols of mortality, residue of catastrophe, penance and atonement,
while also serving literally as ashes in her hair which invoke the graying of
age as well as an association with the ashen hair of the Holocaust victims.
The appeal to tradition is not just a ritual one. The allusion to ashen hair
is an allusion to another legacy, the poetic legacy of writing and representing the Holocaust with a reference to one of its most celebrated examples: Paul Celan's "Todesfuge" and the figuring the fate of the Jews
synecdochically in contrast to that of the Aryan/Germans: "dein golde-
nes Haar Margarete / dein aschenes Haar Sulamith."[52] In Ausländer's
poem, the semantic plurality of the ashes mediates the poetic persona's
ambivalent relationship to the past and to her heritage. The remembrance of her ashen-haired parents, themselves turned to ash, associatively ages, implicates, and marks her as well. Yet the lyrical I both
recognizes and denies the legacy of her people represented by her par-

---

[51] I am indebted to Rabbi Lederman of Jerusalem for the linguistic explication of
these semantic differences.

[52] Celan, *Gedichte*, Vol. 1 (1975; Frankfurt am Main: Suhrkamp, 1991) 42.

ents, and her silence in response to their questions can be read as a resistance to as well as an acknowledgment of their bitterness.[53]

The use of the term "NAMENLOSEN" for the victims of the Holocaust in the poem "Graues Haar" recurs throughout Rose Ausländer's poetry, and is one with which the poetic persona explicitly identifies in the poem "Auch ich" (III 135).

> Auch ich bin
> in Arkadien geboren
> bei Sonnenaufgang
> friedlich im Fruchtwasser
> die Luft eine Herausforderung
> an den Atem
>
> Auch mir
> blühten duftige Mutterworte
> Auch ich wuchs auf
> unter phantastischen Legenden
>
> Das Gruseln erlernte
> auch ich
> als Menschen
> Gesicht und Gewicht
> verloren
>
> Auch ich verlor
> meinen Namen
> unter Namenlosen
>
> Auch ich
> fragte das Nichts
> nach dem Sein
>
> frage und
> höre
> höre
> höre
> die Antwort
> des Echos

---

[53] The figuration of the poetic persona and her forebears in this poem anticipates the complexity of the relation between self and parents as others and ancestors in Julia Kristeva's theorization of foreignness and identity in *Strangers to Ourselves*, trans. Leon Roudiez (New York: Columbia UP, 1991), 22: ". . . there is a fondness that binds to the grave what is beyond the grave, the survivor that I am to my forebears. (. . .) And nevertheless, no, I have nothing to say to them, to my parents. Nothing. Nothing and everything, as always."

In "Auch ich" the poetic persona lays claim to a paradisiacal past that she shares with the implied other she is addressing. By stating her position as "auch ich" she implies an Other whose experience of coming into being was similar to hers. This appeal to a shared, idyllic past is, however, progressively deconstructed by linking the anaphoral "auch ich" with ever bleaker associations and images. In the second strophe the mythical idyll of Arcadia is displaced by the innocence and security of childhood represented as "duftige Mutterworte." What at first appears as a nostalgic reflection on a childhood idyll embraced within the mother tongue is quickly dispatched by the twisted transformation of that remembered idiom into a language of horror and death in the third strophe. Here the environment is no longer warm and nurturing but rather characterized by dehumanization and erasure, referred to as a temporal space where "Menschen / Gesicht und Gewicht / verloren."

The alliance of the I with the implied Other outside of the poem is a gesture that is at once self-reflectively other-directed (in reference to the author's own cultivation of a foreigner's mystique and the pose of the "outsider" in her retention of her married name, Ausländer) and literally other-directed (in the appeal to the reader). This kinship with the "outsider" is then turned into an alliance with all those lost selves who were "othered" and deprived of their individuality in the Holocaust. The lyrical I, although speaking in the present as a distinctive self, as an I, was at one time also a part of that historical experience of collective categorization and the subsequent loss of independent identity: "Auch ich verlor / meinen Namen / unter Namenlosen." The result of this experience of erasure is a confrontation with nihilism, with the nothingness and meaninglessness of an existence that is without justice or "moral" righteousness. The existential question on the nature of being and existence is left an unresolved and unresolvable existential dilemma resonating in the void. The echo that is that question's legacy can be read as both the inspiration for and manifestation of a series of unanswered and perhaps unanswerable questions about meaning, belief, and the existence of an Other outside of the poem to whom the poetic persona implicitly refers in her assertion of her status as I. The validity of her claim to this I is dependent upon the relation to the implied Other who in this poem does not or cannot speak. The complexity of the poetic persona's attitudes towards her memories of the past combine with the tension between speech and silence to culminate in an echo that is both a simulation and a parody of the dialogue she seeks. Her articulations are confrontations with potential erasure; her words emerge as questions echoing in the mocking or sublime silence of the void.

Confronting the Void

All plenitude turns out to be inscribed upon a "void" which is simply what remains when the overabundance of meaning, desire, violence, and anguish is drained by means of language.

— Julia Kristeva[54]

But the urn of language is so fragile. It crumbles and immediately you blow into the dust of words which are the cinder itself. And if you entrust it to paper, it is all the better to inflame you with. . . . No this is not the tomb he would have dreamed of in order that there may be a place . . . for the work of mourning to take its time. In this sentence I see the tomb of a tomb, the monument of an impossible tomb —

— Jacques Derrida[55]

He stretcheth out the north over the empty place, and hangeth the earth upon nothing.

— Job 26:7[56]

The identification of the poetic persona with a collective is one strategy of articulating and questioning representations of memory and could be read as an attempt to lend the poetic message greater significance by referring beyond the individual ultimately to humanity as a whole. The appeal to a superior external force that speaks through the poetic persona represents another approach to enhancing the power and credibility of the poetic word. The poetic persona's speech act is, by virtue of its exterior inspiration, implicitly greater than the words that constitute it, and the poem as lyrical text is transformed into a vessel for the Word from beyond that brought it into being.[57] The poem as a figurative and literary vessel also serves to contain the victims' suffering vicariously experienced and concentrated in the body of the poetic persona. In this

---

[54] Kristeva, *In the Beginning Was Love*, 34.

[55] Derrida, *Cinders*, trans. Ned Lukacher (Lincoln: U of Nebraska P, 1991), 53.

[56] Deborah Lipstadt in "Facing the Void," in *Different Voices: Women and the Holocaust*, eds. Carol Rittner and John K. Roth (New York: Paragon House, 1993), offers a slightly different translation of this passage from the Book of Job (351): "God suspends the earth over a void."

[57] This is a conception of the task of the poet that has its roots in Hasidic belief. Cf. Martin Buber, ed. *Ten Rungs: Hasidic Sayings* (New York: Schocken Books, 1947), 32: "Remember that you are only a vessel, and that your thought and your word are worlds that spread out: the world of the word — that is the Divine Presence which, when it is uttered, desires something from the world of thought."

play of constellations, the poetic persona is at once scribe and inscription, body and text, while the poem as figure and ground is fashioned into an urn of memory.[58]

Sachs and Ausländer both claimed that they often felt their writings were dictated to them by some exterior force and came to them as nocturnal inspirations for which they served as transmitters rather than inventors. In a letter to Gudrun Dähnert of May 1946, Nelly Sachs described her work as dictated by the voice of the Jewish people and given to her by God:

> Daß ich dies alles schrieb, ist vollkommen nebensächlich, die Stimme des jüdischen Volkes spricht und weiter nichts. (. . .) Ich habe wirklich fast alle meine eigenen Dinge in der Nacht geschrieben und . . . in der Dunkelheit. Aber Er war bei mir und gab mir die Worte.[59]

Although Rose Ausländer shared Sachs's propensity for nocturnal productivity, in her case these writings in the night were also catalyzed by chronic insomnia.[60] In an interview with Raimund Hoghe in 1983 she maintained: "Ich arbeite immer in der Nacht — ich kann tagsüber nicht schreiben. (. . .) Ich komme nicht zu den Gedichten, die Gedichte kommen zu mir."[61] This portrayal of poetic creation as reception rather than conception is repeatedly addressed in Ausländer's poetological contemplations. In one of her best known prose texts entitled "Alles kann Motiv sein" (III 284), she experimented with answers to the hypothetical question "Warum ich schreibe?" and offered a number of reasons, ultimately refusing, however, to privilege any one response over others. In contrast to Sachs's portrayal of divinely inspired words, Ausländer in this text both secularized and anthropomorphized the Word in favor of an autonomous poetic language: "Warum ich schreibe? Weil Wörter mir diktieren: schreib uns. Sie wollen verbunden sein, Verbündete. Wort mit Wort mit Wort."

This belief in language as a living, autonomous, and exterior power informs the entire breadth of Ausländer's œuvre and becomes more pronounced in her late works. Toward the end of her literary life, poetry became a last refuge, a realm that Ausländer perceived from her subjective position as a perpetual exile to be the only remaining alter-

---

[58] This phrase is borrowed from Rose Ausländer's poem "Urne Erinnerung" (III 54) discussed later in this chapter.

[59] *Briefe*, 54–55.

[60] Conversation with Helmut Braun, August 1993.

[61] Raimund Hoghe, "Nachwort," *Ich zähl die Sterne meiner Worte,* by Rose Ausländer (Frankfurt am Main: Fischer, 1987), 85.

native to an external reality whose rhythm and routine she no longer shared. Still, like Sachs, she experienced and questioned the tensions inherent in language with its dual capacity for creation and destruction, hope and despair. And like Sachs, she celebrated and pursued existing language as the shadowy approximation of the Word, tending toward a silence resonant with the potential for infinite meaning and interpretative possibilities. The polysemous nature of language in conjunction with its quality as a kind of speaking silence caused her to question her ability to receive, interpret, and transmit the "word."

In the poem "Verbunden" (VIII 112) Rose Ausländer portrays the poetic persona as full of doubt as to whether she is capable and worthy of serving as the mouthpiece or transmitter for a message that exceeds her powers of expression:

> Immer verbunden
> mit dem Nichts
> aus dem du heraufblühst
> und sieh es ist schön
> und sieh die Angst
> hinter der heiteren Maske
> das geliebte Gesicht
> das stets lebendig
> verbunden mit dem Nichts
> diesseits und jenseits
>
> Mein Gott sagst du
> als wüßtest du seinen Namen
> der zu dir spricht und
> schweigt

The lyrical Thou acknowledges her affinity with the originary void of creation, but sees this affinity as neither comforting nor secure. Confronted with the face of the other, a double doubly figured by representation and self-representation in which the voice of the poem as an absent I addresses herself as You, the lyrical voice encounters the otherness in herself. This otherness becomes manifest in the doubt that destabilizes her sense of identity and her belief. The uncertainty of the poetic persona's own internal communication and self-understanding is further intensified by the realization that the Voice for which she serves as a mouthpiece is neither unequivocal in its utterances, nor is the Word that it gives voice to clearly recognizable as speech. The dialectic of speech and silence that characterizes the poet's individual efforts at representing memory and suffering is here portrayed as the legacy of her relationship to the Divine Word and Voice. Both the poetic persona's words and her silences are evidence of this inheritance, bequeathed by a power exterior to herself that simultaneously inspires and eludes poetic representation. Although this external Voice cannot be coerced or commanded, the poetic persona longs for the regenerative strength inherent in the Divine Word.

The poet's desire for divine inspiration in her pursuit of divine emulation is portrayed with unabashed directness in Rose Ausländer's "Gib mir" (V 45):

> Gib mir
> den Blick
> auf das Bild
> unsrer Zeit
>
> Gib mir
> Worte
> es nachzubilden
>
> Worte
> stark
> wie der Atem
> der Erde

Here the poetic persona asks not only for the Word, but also for insight, for a visionary power to grasp the panorama of experience in a finite world bounded by time. The words she seeks in order to give life to this vision are dynamic and mutable. The kind of representation she aspires to is one of living mimesis: organic and elusive yet imbued with the same permanence as the subject it is to represent. The connection between Divine inspiration, poetic language, and representational memory is neither static nor uni-directional. The memory invested in the poetic persona mediates both a primal and an historical past and an anticipatory future and serves as a tool with which to locate Divine presence or godliness in the world of the here-and-now. Memory in this sense transcends temporal boundaries and purports to reverse or recuperate the losses of the past by locating the past in the present.

The drive to recuperate the past through remembrance cannot be viewed separately from an equally powerful drive to forget. This is especially true of traumatic extremes that are smoothed over in appeals to a past that is somehow outside of history, such as the idyll of a lost childhood and the unlived mystique of a primordial homeland. In order for the work of mourning to take place, however, the seductive pull of amnesia must be resisted, not only out of a sense of duty to the dead but out of an awareness of the significance the past carries for the present and the future. A refusal to succumb to the conciliatory tendency that accompanies forgetting and the levelling effects of time is the central theme in Nelly Sachs's "CHOR DER TRÖSTER" (*FS* 65), discussed in Chapter One, and is most clearly expressed in the warning near the end of the poem:

> Nicht einschlafen lassen die Blitze der Trauer
> Das Feld des Vergessens.
>
> Wer von uns darf trösten?

The question "Wer von uns darf trösten?" following the caveat against forgetting points to the impossibility of consolation while implicitly questioning a "forgive-and-forget" attitude toward the past. The suffering was too powerful to be relegated to the dark recesses of memory, and the crime exceeded any possibility of recompense or reconciliation. Not to be forgotten, not to be forgiven, but to be mourned — this is the situation we are left with in the poem's closing lines (*FS* 66):

> Gärtner sind wir, blumenlos gewordene
> Und stehn auf einem Stern, der strahlt
> Und weinen.

The conscious resistance against forgetting in Sachs's "CHOR DER TRÖSTER" is one strategy of confronting a past so recently and deeply marked by dehumanization and genocide. The refusal to let this fact disappear from public consciousness is an attempt to wrest some retroactive control away from the executioners who sought not only racial supremacy but also hegemony over historiography and remembrance.[62] Yet the process of remembrance is inseparable from that of forgetting. Forgetting itself is a complex layering of conscious and unconscious forces acting to erase memory traces that generate conflict or tension within the self. The desire to avoid the conflict triggered by the memory of trauma can lead to its denial or repression. In a poem entitled "Das Fest" (III 32) Rose Ausländer portrays the interaction of denial and forgetting and implicitly addresses the phenomenon of repression.

DAS FEST

Wir feiern das Fest der Abwesenden
mit verschollenen Freunden

Vergessen die Uhren aufzuziehn
die Zeit wird auch ohne Zeiger uns finden
zur Unzeit entführen wird uns der Tod

---

[62] Cf. Elisabeth Domansky's discussion of the Nazis plans to erect a museum of Jewish culture after they had implemented the 'Final Solution'. Domansky, "Die gespaltene Erinnerung," in *Kunst und Literatur nach Auschwitz*, ed. Manuel Köppen (Berlin: Erich Schmidt, 1993), 194–95.

Vergessen daß wir gestern die Rose rühmten
morgen den Mond besuchen wollten
was wollten wir übermorgen

Erhoffte Botschaften
die uns nicht erreichten
gefürchtete
die uns erreichten
vergessen

Wir erkennen uns nicht mehr im Spiegel
erkennen den Spiegel nicht an
die vorgespiegelten Länder
vergessen

Hinter dem Himmel
wir feiern wir zechen
mit den Schemen
verschollener Freunde

The dialectic of remembrance and forgetting is revealed here in the juxtaposition of recollection and denial of recollection. The memory process the poet reveals is one conscious of its own desire to forget, one that reflects on itself as subject to psychological forces that seek to obscure the incommensurability of good and evil behind a tenuous screen of denial. The claim to have forgotten is a bid for exculpation from a past that the We here wishes could be erased, yet the borders between "forgetting" and denial are made visible by the interweaving of articulation and protestation. This process of repression as an alienation from memory leads to an identity crisis expressed as a loss of a coherent sense of self and a grounded sense of connection to the reality of the "here-and-now" in the fifth strophe ("Wir erkennen uns nicht mehr im Spiegel / erkennen den Spiegel nicht an"). Because of the extent of the denial illustrated by the We, the realm of the present becomes implicated in the displacement of the past. The lyrical We can only locate itself in a despatialized, detemporalized "Jenseits" that is almost cynically portrayed in the closing strophe as a beyond in which lost selves and lost souls revel with abandon. The reiteration of claims to forgetting stand in uneasy opposition to the revelatory statements that precede them, revealing the repression of the past to be unsuccessful: the denial is a thin veneer on the surface of despair. Thus the implication at the end of the poem is that there is no abandon, but rather a sad shadow of celebration, just as the lost souls, the lost friends are reduced to mere silhouettes. In its portrayal of a relationship to the past as one of denial and repression culminating in a fantastical party beyond the limits of

time and space ("Hinter dem Himmel"), the poem questions and reveals the persistence of the past in the present and the transformation of
remembrance as the return of the repressed.

The refusal to become a part of the forgetting and the forgotten represents an aspect of the poetic persona's perceived role as a vessel for the
sufferings of her people. In poems that address this aspect of memory,
the poetic persona is both the embodiment of and the vehicle for the
voice of sorrow. Speaking through metaphors, the poetic persona becomes both the scribe and the inscripted, the artisan and the urn. The
sorrows she speaks for are as mutable and heterogeneous as her own
multiple poetic representations, and are constituted by a complex of images that evoke and question the depth and extent of her loss: people,
homeland, identity, and belief. The protean character of the poetic persona as simultaneously messenger and message, voice and mouthpiece,
echoes the plurality of suffering which these poems express.

In "Der hervorstürzende" (SL 95), already discussed briefly in
chapter one, Sachs lends the poetic persona a body which is then
transformatively portrayed as the receptacle for a collective experience
of suffering.

> Der hervorstürzende
> Fackelzug der Ahnen
> in den Ysopgärten schimmerten ihre Köpfe
> in den Verstecken des Blutes landsflüchtig den Gott
> Auf den Küsten der Mitternacht
> auf den verbannten Inseln
> getauft mit den Wetterfahnen des Blitzes
> Agonie in brennenden Tempeln
> eure Heimat in meine Adern verlegt —
>
> Reich bin ich wie das Meer
> aus Vergangenheit und Zukunft
> und ganz aus Sterbestoff
> singe ich euer Lied —

The poem begins with an image of a torchlight parade of ancestors
whose pain and persecution are the poetic self's legacy. The agonies of
past torture and annihilation are in her blood, intimating that memory is
not learned, but rather inherited. The memories of victimization have an
archetypal quality: the images of burning temples and a lost primordial
homeland are not given any historical specificity, but rather evoke a kind
of cosmic time outside of history. The mythologized space of the
"Ysopsgärten" in which the ancestors resided is gradually transformed
into more and more concrete spatial figurations, culminating in the architectonic image of the burning temples in the last lines of the first

strophe. The transition from a mythological space to the body of the poetic persona is achieved by passing through a spatialized temporality: the
"Küsten der Mitternacht" as the point of crossing between dimensions
of time and space. The fire of the ancestral torches merges with the
flames consuming the burning temples, the boundaries of time and space
become blurred, even merge, in the body of the poetic persona in whose
veins flow memories beyond her experience. The reference to the ancestors as a plural You establishes an Other to the lyrical I, a You of the
timeless past which supports the identity of the I in the present and
whose legacy is so powerful that it permeates the lifeblood of the self.

But this figuration of the poetic persona as a receptacle for suffering
and memory is complicated and expanded in the second strophe, where
the poetic persona is no longer defined by the finite bounds of a human
body, but instead assumes a metaphorical vastness akin to that of the
ocean: "Reich bin ich wie das Meer / aus Vergangenheit und Zukunft." The veins referred to in the first strophe have swollen into a sea
that suspends and dissolves temporal distinctions. The timeless quality
of the ancestral pageant in the opening strophe is displaced and sup-
planted through the self-representation the poetic I constructs as both
mediator and nexus of past and future in the poem's closing lines. The
condition of suspended temporality and the inextricable linking of
temporal and spatial aspects of memory embodied in the poetic persona, however, are paradoxically limited by the finitude of mortal existence. Her undeniable mortality ("und ganz aus Sterbestoff / singe ich
euer Lied —") calls into question the poet's pretension of generating a
text that will endure.

In the conflation of mortal and transtemporal aspects within the poetic persona she creates, the poet as the voice speaking the poetic text
implicitly aspires to transcend her own mortal finitude. Through the act
of poetic creation, however engendered, the poet obtains a means and a
medium of bearing a message that has at least a potential for continuity
beyond her bounded physical existence. The blood of suffering she in-
herits from her ancestors is passed on as a poetic legacy attesting not
only to their experiences and her own, but also as one which serves as
an admonition and a testimonial to those who come after her.

The figuration of the poetic persona as a body imbued with the
memories of the victims oscillates and alternates with the figuration of
the poetic text as an urn for the metaphorical ashes of the dead,
whereby the poem itself as textual materiality becomes the reliquary for
sorrow and remembered pain. The boundaries between the poetic persona and the poetic text are permeable, often merging in complex constellations of image and imaged where divisions are blurred or

obscured. Rose Ausländer's poem "Bis an den Nagelmond" (III 36) illustrates this tactic of melding body and text and merging these with images of death, suffering, and the preservation of memory. The poetic persona here remembers a lost loved one, who is addressed in the second person but whose namelessness in the poem allows for a collective identification with the victims of the Holocaust:

Bis an den Nagelmond
denk ich an dich
wenn die Nacht mich nimmt

Sie haben dich begraben
im Feuer

Ich halte den Gedanken
deiner Asche
im Blutgefäß
das rastlos zum Herzen führt
deinen Namen

Wie schön
Asche blühn kann
im Blut

The image of the "Nagelmond" in conjunction with the night indicates that the darkness that encourages dreams also allows for recollections of the lost that are potentially painful and anxious: the poetic persona's thoughts on the absent You are accompanied by a metaphorical nail-biting. Night, already alluded to above as a time of poetic inspiration and productivity, is here presented with ambivalence, in that it offers the potential for a momentary reunion with the past while simultaneously allowing for a return of repressed memories and fears. In the poem's third strophe, a reunion with the lost is represented in the image of the poetic persona figuratively invested with the ashes of the dead which she imagines mingled with her blood: "Ich halte den Gedanken / deiner Asche / im Blutgefäß."

The ashes of memory are imaged as an inversion of their conventional association with lifeless residue and evidence of absence, and instead signify both loss and an inextinguishable life force propelling memory that flourishes in the blood of the poetic persona: "Wie schön / Asche blühn kann / im Blut." This paradoxical image of ashes as living memory appears frequently in Ausländer's poetry. In the concluding strophe of a poem from the same period entitled "Urne Erinnerung" (III 54), ashes are figured as the very stuff of memory, collected and preserved in an urn that breathes with the remembrance of the consumed:

> Nichts verloren
> in der Urne
> die Asche atmet

This image of the urn conflates present, past, and future in a convergence of signifier and signified, body and text, memory and articulation.

The inversion of the ash image and the figuration of the urn as a positively valued receptacle containing living and even expressible memory in Ausländer's poetry appear but are rendered with much greater equivocation in Sachs's lyric. In "Hinter den Lippen" (*FS* 319), the merging of the poetic persona with the poem's central metaphors occurs in the context of the imaged urn, an urn, however, which is at once an urn and the poetic persona's mouth. The mouth as the origin of speech has become the reliquary of spent language. In contrast to the representational optimism of Ausländer's poetic persona, Sachs's despairs of her capacity to give expression to her sorrow and sense of loss:

> HINTER DEN LIPPEN
> Unsagbares wartet
> reißt an den Nabelsträngen
> der Worte
>
> Märtyrersterben der Buchstaben
> in der Urne des Mundes
> geistige Himmelfahrt
> aus schneidendem Schmerz —
>
> Aber der Atem der inneren Rede
> durch die Klagemauer der Luft
> haucht geheimnisentbundene Beichte
> sinkt ins Asyl
> der Weltwunde
> noch im Untergang
> Gott abgelauscht —

The poetic persona's struggle to give voice to the inexpressible is likened to a martyrdom of letters, an image that recalls Kabbalistic linguistic mysticism with its teaching that the "true" and Holy letter is both indestructible and possessed of self-regenerating, reconstructive power.[63] The second strophe depicts the aftermath of the sacrifice of existing language, where only a speechless residue remains as a spiritual trace of the suffering and pain it cannot or can no longer express. The complete absence of verbs in this strophe is striking — the martyrdom of the letter is simultaneous with a reduction to nominalism: the tri-

---

[63] Cf. Roskies, 32.

umph of the name over the agency granted by the verb. The inability to
speak in this dead, inactive idiom causes the poetic persona to turn inward in the third strophe, retreating from the alienating encounter with
the external, unrepresentable world to an internalized state of silent
communion with a remembered past and an absent God. The nature of
the poetic persona's retreat is both resigned and transcendent. The absence of a spoken idiom in which to voice her sorrow in the existing
world is transformed into a demystified confession and an unmediated
connection with suffering that enables her to finally discern the presence of God.

In "HINTER DEN LIPPEN" Nelly Sachs offers a poetic figuration
of her own religious view that the believer's relationship to God is
characterized by suffering, and that it is through suffering that one
achieves revelation and a state of grace.[64] This relationship of divine
grace and human pain is one often characterized in Jewish theological
writings as specific to the Chosenness of the Jews, but Sachs extrapolates it to the condition shared by all who believe in a theology of love
and suffering. In a letter to Manfred George of October 1947, she described the interaction of suffering and expression in the context of her
own efforts at representation:

> Wir nach dem Martyrium unseres Volkes sind geschieden von allen
> früheren Aussagen durch eine tiefe Schlucht, nichts reicht mehr zu,
> kein Wort, kein Stab, kein Ton . . . schrecklich arm wie wir sind, wir
> müssen es herausbringen . . . . denn der Äon der Schmerzen darf nicht
> mehr gesagt, gedacht, er muß durchlitten werden.[65]

The figuration of suffering and memory as vessels occurs repeatedly
in both Sachs's and Ausländer's œuvres. The tactic of merging the figure of the poetic persona with that of her creation is one that instru-
mentalizes each as a vehicle for a message external to both of them.
This strategy of instrumentalization becomes a literal *instrument*alization of the re-membered dead in Sachs's poems "DAS FLÖTEN-
GERIPPE DER TOTEN" (*SL* 123) and "WIEDER MITTE" (*SL*
131). Already in the first line of "DAS FLÖTENGERIPPE" the image
of the dead as instruments (significantly figured as flutes and invoking

---

[64] In this, Sachs echoes Simone Weil's conception of the relationship between
humanity and the true God as one of suffering (cf. Simone Weil, *Gravity and Grace*,
esp. 122, 141, 164–5). The connection between faith and suffering appears again
and again in Sachs's poetry, e.g. "Zwischen" (*FS* 267) which ends with the lines:
"Der Himmel übt an dir / Zerbrechen. // Du bist in der Gnade."

[65] *Briefe*, 83–84

the symbolic tradition in which flutes are associated with the cries of lost souls seeking heaven[66]) is evoked.

> DAS FLÖTENGERIPPE DER TOTEN
> plötzlich über die Grenze gezogen
> das geistige Alphabet am Gehör des Schweigens leuchtet
> Hier vorne Asche des Grauens die Hinterlassenschaft —

The dead, whose musical skeletons are somehow audible to the silence-sensitive ear of the poetic persona, are both beyond and evanescently present in the polysemous, spiritual silence that surrounds the poetic space. The presence of these dead souls in the here-and-now realm spatially imaged as "Hier vorne" is one of residual existence: they are disembodied fragments. Like the contents of the urns of memory discussed above, there are only ashes left. The residue of ashes represents the traces of horror and with a dash into the void that could mean extinction or infinitude, the poem ends without conclusion. Ashes as a favored image for memories in the works discussed here serve as both remainder and reminder of the lost, as the tenuous and fragile legacy of the past that must be preserved and passed on to the reader in the urn of the poem and via the figurative body of the poet. Through the transmission of the ashes as memory and body, the poet reenacts a communion, both with the past and with the reader.

In contrast to the figuration of ashes as a trope for paradoxically tangible absence in "DAS FLÖTENGERIPPE," the remains of the dead leave only musical traces of their presence and passing in "WIEDER MITTE" (SL 131). The musical message from the dead is received and comprehended by the lyrical observer who recognizes in her own poetic space the collecting point for the tormenting resonances of the past:

> WIEDER MITTE geworden
> für abgezogene Musikskelette
> im Gehörraum
> die Hölle gegründet
> mit Bienensang
> verirrt im Ohr —
> Oasen wo Tod die Raumräuber
> Schweigen lehrt
> Ihr göttlichen Verstecke
> schlagt die Augenlider auf —

---

[66] *Herder-Lexikon Symbole* (Freiburg: Verlag Herder, 1978), 54.

The insistent reminders of the past are hardly music to the poetic persona's tortured ear, but are instead associated with the insistent and aggravating buzzing of trapped bees. The poetic persona is haunted and tormented by these voices that are apparently independent of her and beyond her control, yet through her suffering, she is made to acknowledge her affinity with them. The pathology implied in this condition of hearing internal voices that cannot be dispelled has a basis in Nelly Sachs's own experience. She suffered from periodic delusions of persecution and deep depression, the result of her identification with the horrors of the past and her fear that she as a survivor had been singled out for particular abuse as the object of the persecutors' revenge. This poem and the one discussed above were written during one of these periods in Sachs's life where she was suffering from such extreme psychological torment that she sought psychiatric treatment. Many of her poems published in the 1960s were written either during or after these bouts of nervous collapse followed by institutional convalescence. The confluence of identification with the past and present suffering voiced in "WIEDER MITTE" is thus a reflection of the interpenetration of representation and reality and the parallels between the poet and the poem and underscores yet again the function of writing as a coping strategy.

The interconnection of poet and poem is effected by suffering, empathy, and memory which combine in the construct of the poetic persona as well as in the articulation of the poem. In "Verzeiht ihr meine Schwestern" (*SL* 27), a poem mentioned in contrast to Rose Ausländer's "Meer II" in the previous chapter, Nelly Sachs once again addresses the interrelationship of testimonial responsibility, suffering, and silence that informs her poetic project to its end. The poetic persona assumes the role of representative or speaker for a mute or absent collective likened to a sisterhood. The persecution of the victims of the past and their concomitant silencing is both feminized and oceanized in the appeal to the "Schwestern," a poetic move that recalls the daughter-poet's desire for and identification with the oceanic mother.

> Verzeiht ihr meine Schwestern
> ich habe euer Schweigen in mein Herz genommen
> Dort wohnt es und leidet die Perlen eures Leides
> klopft Herzweh
> so laut so zerreißend schrill
> Es reitet eine Löwin auf den Wogen Oceanas
> eine Löwin der Schmerzen
> die ihre Tränen längst dem Meer gab —

The opening lines of "Verzeiht ihr meine Schwestern" imply some wrongdoing or failure on the part of the poetic persona, a foreseeable flaw latent in the poet's situation of emotional restraint and linguistic limitation that obstructs her efforts at representing the suffering of her people, her "sisters." Again the poetic persona is presented as the vessel for the suffering of a collective, a collective which cannot speak because it has been silenced by oppression and death. Yet the invisible, inaudible presence of these victims speaks to and through the poetic voice with the piercing insistence of a moral imperative to remember. The cacophony of remembered pain threatens to engulf and overwhelm the poetic persona, recalling the situation of the daughter-poet in the preceding chapter, where the longing for reunion with her oceanic origins carried with it also the potential danger of self-dissolution.

Sachs employs strikingly similar imagery to convey different impressions, but still the figuration of the ocean remains a point of connection as well as convergence. The ocean in Sachs's poetry is a multivalent trope evoking positive and negative associations. In this particular poem it signifies a vessel for an immeasurable sorrow. In its vastness, this vessel represents in macro-scale the container for suffering that the poetic persona and the poem had embodied on a smaller scale in the analyses above. The image of the sea as a receptacle for tears, however, also connotes a certain reassurance and consolation. Its apparently immeasurable vastness and volume imply that there is a place and a space in the world large enough for the venting of such enormous suffering. This image by virtue of its very earthliness also insists on the permanence of these memories in the world and thereby refuses, at least in this poem, the seductive gesture in the direction of transcendence.

The transformation of overwhelming remembrances into poetic language is a complex and variegated process compelled by conflicting desires. The resulting lyrical figurations differ in their emphases and offer a diverse array of gestures that indicate direction but not resolution: towards transcendence, reconciliation, despair, and redemption. The Voices that speak to and through the poetic persona are at once cosmic and terrestrial, pantheistic and human, insistent and absent. They are the differentiated manifestations of the Other as both exterior and intrinsic to the Self, an other whom the poetic persona encounters with an ambivalence fluctuating between identification and alienation.

In Rose Ausländer's "Du bist die Stimme" (V 149), the poetic persona identifies with the other as the stranger whose ubiquitous presence is signalled by the disembodied voice that speaks to her:

Sei mir gewogen
Fremdling
ich liebe dich
den ich nicht kenne

Du bist die Stimme
die mich betört
Ich hab dich gehört
ruhend auf grünem Samt
du Moosatem
du Glocke des Glücks
und der unsterblichen Trauer

The pantheistic nature of this "stranger" implied by the association to "Moosatem" adds another dimension to the conception of a monolithic deity evoked in appeals to an external Voice in other poems. The stranger here as exterior force embraces the plurality of affect characterizing both human memory and experience, one ranging from extreme happiness to inextinguishable sorrow. It is within this dynamic spectrum of emotions that the poet seeks to mediate the tensions inherent in the mixture of desires for peace, redemption, transcendence, and the transformation of the world.[67] The articulation and textualization of these conflicting desires and the poetological attitudes towards the possibility and viability of such representations that accompany these shifting experimentations with words, images, and temporality are the subject of the following section.

---

[67] Lawrence Langer's assessment of this complex of emotions and desires in Nelly Sachs's poetry in his *Versions of Survival* (239) could apply equally well to the processes at work in Ausländer's writings: "Nelly Sachs's survivors inherit a legacy of annihilation, a sharing of the feeling of already-having-died: they are vessels of memory and longing who seek an equilibrium between an unaccountable past and an indefinable future."

Transformation, Transcendence, Redemption?

There is hurt within the word.
Word that hurts and, strangely, comforts.
Mystery of its strangeness.

— Edmond Jabès[68]

Transforming events into a fictional mode was a means of detaching
oneself from the pain, a way of becoming an "other." For the generation
of Auschwitz, the act of writing . . . seemed to bestow an order on a real-
ity that had none.

— Ellen S. Fine[69]

Memory itself is a representational process and hence limiting and selective, i.e. the choices made as to which aspects of the past are preserved versus those that are consciously or unconsciously repressed
influence and alter the transmission of memory over time. Because of
the representational nature of memory, it continually slips between the
veneer of aestheticization and the surface of "truth." The bulk of collective memory cannot and does not equal the sum of individual
memories. While the recollections of individuals are necessarily selective
and incommensurate with the multifaceted reality of the event itself,
the effort to give expression to the heterogeneity of voices and experiences via poetic language demonstrates an attempt at representing the
complexities of the past. The poets' remembrances of the past are not
only remembrances of horror and catastrophe, but also nostalgic recollections of the lost: childhood, family, beloved, and "home." Horror
and nostalgia are not only juxtaposed, but are also intertwined in the
reproduction of memory, adding another twist to the convoluted process of representation.

   In the poems discussed in this section, the conceptualization of remembrance as a process that looks to the past in order to preserve hope
for the future is explored in its various manifestations. Remembrance as
a bid for recuperation and justification is here affiliated with the poetic
depictions of childhood, home, and death. The nostalgia that transfigures re-collections of childhood and "home" into idealized visions of a
lost harmony simultaneously disfigures and is disfigured by the memo-

---

[68] Edmond Jabès, *A Foreigner Carrying in the Crook of His Arm a Tiny Book*,
trans. Rosmarie Waldrop (Hanover, NH: Wesleyan UP, 1993), 27.

[69] Ellen S. Fine, "The Absent Memory," in *Writing and the Holocaust*, ed. Berel
Lang, 43.

ries of suffering that the poet seeks to both represent and transcend.
This interplay and interaction between different levels of remembrance
is the distinguishing feature of Ausländer's poem "Biographische No-
tiz" (IV 212) which writes and reads the text of the poet's life through
the harsh lens of the Holocaust:

> Ich rede
> von der brennenden Nacht
> die gelöscht hat
> der Pruth
>
> von Trauerweiden
> Blutbuchen
> verstummten Nachtigallsang
>
> vom gelben Stern
> auf dem wir
> stündlich starben
> in der Galgenzeit
>
> nicht über Rosen
> red ich
>
> Fliegend
> auf einer Luftschaukel
> Europa Amerika Europa
>
> ich wohne nicht
> ich lebe

For the poetic persona in the lyrical present of the text, there is no
space for aestheticization in her articulation of the past. She does not
write of roses, although she is indeed associatively speaking of a "rose,"
namely Rose the author whose abbreviated and poeticized biography
we are being presented with here. The past informs the present in that
the poetic voice is unable to speak of anything without memories per-
meating her perceptions, but the closing strophes indicate a life-energy
that goes beyond a mere will to survival. The oscillation between Europe
and America reflects the migration and flight pattern of the poet herself, while the poetic persona she creates as her representative is paradigmatic of the rootless wanderer. The closing lines of the poem can be
read in several ways, depending on the meanings and emphases one attributes to the verbs "wohnen" and "leben." In a reading emphasizing
the connotation of "wohnen" as to dwell in a place one can call home,
the poem's finale is the culmination of a bitter life of persecution. Not
only is she chronically confronted with the dark memories of death and
violence stemming from the Holocaust, but even in the present there is
no final resting place, no realm in which she can experience a sense of

belonging. Another interpretation, one focussing on the life-affirming connotations of "leben," offers a different reading of the ending. The poetic persona's vitality despite the extremity of her experience enables her to continue to embrace life, and the voyages she has both behind and before her represent not escape but the mobility of freedom. In a more concretely biographical reading of these closing lines, Cilly Helfrich argues that the opposition between the verbs reflects Ausländer's restless habit of living out of suitcases and never establishing a residence of her own after "settling" in Germany.[70]

Rose Ausländer alternated between moments of negativity and optimism across the span of her work, but she never approached the degree of despair evident in Sachs's œuvre. Sachs and Ausländer responded differently to the challenge of poetic re-creation within the languages that both inspired and discouraged their efforts at representation. While Ausländer projected her longing for an environment of freedom, security, and happiness back to an idyllic vision of childhood in the Bukovina, Sachs's portrayals of childhood are more archetypal, projecting ultimately toward a realm or condition that transcends the profane images she conveys. This difference in their treatment of childhood as a "time before" or a temporal space somehow outside of history parallels a fundamental difference in their poetological views on language and representation.

As time progressed, Sachs's writings tended more and more toward the willful incoherence and silence of the unrepresentable, evidence of her deep-seated doubt as to the expressive capacity of existing language. In this tendency toward growing inscrutability, her work demonstrates a similarity to that of Paul Celan, whose increasing hermeticism over time can be read as a resistance to the absorption or adulteration of his poetic articulations by conventional discourse.[71] In contrast to this quality of the later works of Sachs and Celan, Ausländer persisted in her apparently unshakeable faith in the representational power of poetic language, although one not untroubled by moments of despair and

---

[70] Cilly Helfrich further traces this restlessness and resistance to belonging back to Ausländer's childhood and her parents' insistence that she keep her distance from the neighborhood children. See Helfrich, 57–58, 274–75.

[71] Cf. Sidra DeKoven Ezrahi's discussion of Celan in her essay "'The Grave in the Air': Unbound Metaphors in Post-Holocaust Poetry," in *Probing the Limits of Representation*, ed. Saul Friedländer. Ezrahi's concluding comments on the implications of Celan's apparent hermeticism could equally well apply to the poetic tendency towards privatized allegory observable in Nelly Sachs's work (276): "The more personal or idiosyncratic the inscription, then, the more immune it is meant to be to both the debasement of metaphor and its reification in history."

questioning as to the adequacy of both her medium and her own expressive powers. This difference in attitudes toward language reflects
and parallels a difference in direction that strongly distinguishes their
poetic projects. Despite Sachs's concern for the future of the world and
her empathy with human sufferers both past and present, her poetry
looks more toward a beyond, a cosmic realm where silence speaks and
the conflicts of earthly existence are rendered irrelevant in a demateri-
alized space free of the tensions caused by human peculiarities, prejudices, aspirations, and crises.[72]

It is this gesture toward transcendence that has been conflated with
what several scholars interpret as evidence of Sachs's longing for
death.[73] Claudia Beil, in her comparative study of the two poets, distinguishes Sachs from Ausländer on this very point, attributing to the
former a strong tendency toward "Todessehnsucht" while placing the
latter at the opposite extreme in the category of "Lebensbejahung."[74]
While the longing for death is a central theme in many of Sachs's late
poems, particularly foregrounded in "TOD — ich sehne mich weiß
nach dir" (SL 128), Beil's polarization overlooks Ausländer's own
withdrawal from life in her later years, a willed retreat into the past and
the self-created space of her writing. In Sachs's "TOD — ich sehne
mich weiß nach dir" the poetic persona looks to death as a release into
a transcendent beyond, as a reincarnation into a different plane of existence that cannot be figured in physical terms.

> TOD — ich sehne mich weiß nach dir
> bis über dein letztes sterbendes Licht
> alle Blutstropfen in den Augenblick deines Nichts vergießen
> Leblose Jenseitsentdeckung —
> Auferstehung —

[72] Christa Vaerst offers the interpretation that Nelly Sachs constructs an alternative
reality in and through her poetry as a reaction against the reality that denies self-
actualization and spiritual fulfillment. The autonomous linguistic realm that results is a
response to a historical reality "die das vereinsamte dichterische Subjekt zwingt, in der
Dichtung das zu suchen, was in Wirklichkeit zerstört ist." Cf. *Dichtungs- und Spra-*
chreflexion im Werk von Nelly Sachs (Frankfurt am Main: Peter Lang, 1977), 166.

[73] Cf. esp. Gisela Dischner, *Poetik des modernen Gedichts: Zur Lyrik von Nelly Sachs;*
Ehrhard Bahr, Nelly Sachs (Munich: C. H. Beck, 1980); Claudia Beil, *Sprache als Heimat:*
Jüdische Tradition und Exilerfahrung in der Lyrik von Nelly Sachs und Rose Ausländer.

[74] Beil, 259–60, 280, 299, 325. Beil's study focusses on the German-Jewish
identity of the two poets and the complexity of this identity in the context of German cultural history. She argues that the works of both poets demonstrate successful
syntheses of intercultural influences, emphasizing German Romanticism, Christian
mysticism, and the Kabbalah.

The whiteness of the poetic persona's longing is not only the result of the outpouring of blood referred to in the third line, but is on another level a merging of the body of the poetic persona with the materiality of the text. The whiteness of her longing is akin to the white blankness of the page surrounding the written. The allusion to whiteness thus inspires images of both bloodlessness and wordlessness, establishing a parallel between blood and language that recalls the correlation of blood and poetry made in the sixth strophe of "WAS STIEG aus deines Leibes weißen Blättern" (*FS* 227): "Auf welchen Spuren / soll ich deines Blutes Dichtung suchen?"[75] Death and life are inextricably linked within the body of the poetic persona and the text, so that the longing for death in this life comes to signal a longing for a new life after death in Sachs's works. This view is echoed in Johannes Anderegg's reading of longing ("Sehnsucht") in Sachs's œuvre. Anderegg argues that for Sachs "Sehnsucht" is a multifaceted construct that combines a longing for death with a longing for "being-under-way" in a distinctly spiritual sense, i.e. as a journey toward God.[76]

Whereas Sachs's longing for death can be seen as a spiritual desire to join in a mystical union with God, Ausländer's withdrawal from life was not a deferral of fulfillment until death, but rather an act of will that she carried out in her declining years. After a fall in 1972 in which she suffered a serious bone fracture, Ausländer's mobility was greatly impaired. She moved into the Nelly-Sachs-Haus, a Jewish convalescent home in Düsseldorf, and by degrees retracted herself from public life. In May 1977 she left her room for the last time in order to attend the opening of an exhibition in her honor at the Heinrich-Heine-Institut in Düsseldorf. After this appearance, she confined herself to bed, where she remained until her death in 1988.[77]

That the two poets ultimately resist categorization according to such dichotomous criteria as longing for death or affirmation of life is made clear in "Stark" (VI 209), a late work by Rose Ausländer in which she juxtaposes sorrow and joy through a paradoxical equation of life and death, thereby revealing not only the proximity of these emotional states to each other but also their equivalence in terms of the power that compels them.

---

[75] For a detailed discussion of this poem, see Chapter 2.

[76] See Johannes Anderegg, "Nelly Sachs: The Poem and Transformation," *Jewish Writers, German Literature*, ed. Timothy Bahti and Marilyn Sibley Fries, 67.

[77] See Helfrich, 287–98. This was also confirmed in a personal conversation with Helmut Braun, one of the few people Ausländer permitted to visit her during her last years.

> Trauer
> stark wie der Tod
>
> Freude
> stark wie das Leben

In "Stark" Ausländer condenses the complexity and conflicts that characterize the intertwined processes of memory, mourning, and survival into two compact strophes incisive in their simplicity. The strategy of using a parallel structure in these two strophes is intensified by the repetition of the word "stark" which allots the opposing forces of death and life equal strength both literally and figuratively. Hamida Bosmajian has argued that the yearning for transcendence evident in much Holocaust poetry ultimately signals a search for an escape from memory, while a strong commitment to remembering the catastrophe by necessity "denies the possibility of transcendence."[78] This portrayal of the relationship between transcendence and memory illustrates a tendency toward dichotomization in many critical studies of Holocaust literature and the subsequent establishment of clear-cut and fixed categories that often give rise to oversimplified analyses.[79] I would argue that the desire for transcendence can and does coexist with a powerful moral obligation to remember, and that the one does not necessarily preclude the other.[80] It is effectively through the oscillation between these impulses that the complexity of the poet's endeavor and the reflective nature of her efforts at representation are revealed.

---

[78] Bosmajian, *Metaphors of Evil*, 22.

[79] Christa Vaerst, however, is to be credited for her investigation of the dualistic language in Nelly Sachs's poetry. In her study, she sets out to address the simultaneity of the spiritual and historical aspects in Sachs's work. Vaerst questions the contentions of earlier studies that Sachs's writing evidences an estrangement from reality culminating in an "absolutization" of language (14).

[80] Here I would also question the dichotomy that Emmanuel Levinas established in his 1950 essay "Place and Utopia" where he disallows an ethical active principle in utopian thinking: "One can choose utopia. On the other hand, in the name of spirit, one can choose not to flee the conditions from which one's work draws its meaning, and remain here below. And that means choosing ethical action." Cf. Levinas, *Difficult Freedom*, 100. Cf. also Seymour Cain's discussion of the command for hope in post-Holocaust anticipations of the future in "The Question and the Answers After Auschwitz," 278: "hope, of course, being understood not as a self-deceptive, sentimental optimism, but as an ontological virtue and function, rooted in personal, human, and universal being, and ultimately in the bond with, or aspiration toward, the transcendent that may become present. This means to say 'Yes' to reality, no matter what."

The transformative idiom Nelly Sachs aspired to is one intimately connected to the metaphysical Voice of divinity that speaks through the poetic personas she constructed. By virtue of its inspirational relationship to this exterior and implicitly superior force, the poetic text becomes something greater than itself: imbued with the spiritual significance of that otherworldly power, it acquires the capacity to transcend its own potential destruction. In "VERGEBENS" (*FS* 335–36), Nelly Sachs conjoins divine grace and love within an idealized linguistic realm where the word is portrayed as resistant to annihilation. Like the indestructible book whose cosmic meaning rises from the flames in the poem "CHOR DER VERLASSENEN DINGE" (*FS* 49) discussed above, words as figures in this poem are transformed rather than consumed by fire. Sachs's depiction of the regenerative capacity of the letter here is informed by Kabbalistic belief in the magical power and resilience of script.[81]

> VERGEBENS
> verbrennen die Briefe
> in der Nacht der Nächte
> auf dem Scheiterhaufen der Flucht
> denn die Liebe windet sich aus ihrem Dornenstrauch
> gestäupt im Martyrium
> und beginnt schon mit Flammenzungen
> ihren unsichtbaren Himmel zu küssen
> wenn nachtwache Finsternisse an die Wand wirft
> und die Luft
> zitternd vor Ahnungen
> mit der Schlinge des anwehenden Verfolgers
> betet:
>
> Warte
> bis die Buchstaben heimgekehrt sind
> aus der lodernden Wüste
> und gegessen von heiligen Mündern
> Warte
> bis die Geistergeologie der Liebe
> aufgerissen
> und ihre Zeitalter durchglüht
> und leuchtend von seligen Fingerzeigen
> wieder ihr Schöpfungswort fand:
>
> da auf dem Papier
> das sterben singt:

---

[81] Cf. Roskies, 32.

> Es war
> am Anfang
>   Es war
>   Geliebter
>   Es war —

The opening line already establishes the tone of ambiguity and undecidability that permeates the entire poem. The futility of the burning epistles could be understood as the futility of their having been written, since the medium for the message they contain is so ephemeral. Or it could be read as the futility of any attempts to destroy them, as a defiant tribute to their immortality, in that the letters separate from the paper in the moment of combustion. The portrayal of loss and resurrection as simultaneous and coterminous phenomena recurs frequently in Sachs's poetry and here serves as both a lament and a tribute to the transcendence of the soul. This depiction is reminiscent of an earlier poem, "CHOR DER TOTEN" (*FS* 56), commemorating the deaths of Holocaust victims, where the dead victims are portrayed as having triumphed in the end, because through their suffering and death they have come closer to their God.[82]

The connection between suffering and revelation made in other poems is portrayed in "VERGEBENS" as a conglomeration of disparate images where sacrifice by fire and the martyrdom of Christ are bound up with allusions to resurrection, cosmic mysteries, and the omnipresent threat of persecution. This complex string of associations is then further complicated and estranged by the anthropomorphization of the air, as the element that surrounds and gives life to the forces of both love and destruction. The air is witness and accomplice to the scene the poetic persona spreads before us, it gives breath to the living even as it enables the flames to burn and consume. Because of this duplicity, the personified air is confronted with the moral dilemma inherent in its very nature. It is perhaps for this reason that air is portrayed in the poem as a kind of prescient consciousness praying for the return to the originary moment where all being was suspended in an undetermined and still uncorrupted condition of becoming.

Love, like the Divine Word, proves stronger than Death even after its beloved materiality has passed into the preterite of the poem's final

---

[82] "Wir Toten Israels sagen euch: / Wir reichen schon einen Stern weiter / In unseren verborgenen Gott hinein" (*FS* 56). For a more detailed treatment of this poem, refer to the discussion in Chapter 1.

lines.[83] The injunction to the implied listener, other or reader to wait until the time when the lost alphabet has returned implies that the return of the letters will enable a different, if not more immediate, relationship to the world through the reconstituted word. Lawrence Langer attributes this concern with the individual letters of the alphabet in Sachs's poetry to the belief that "we must return to the separate letters of the alphabet if we are to reestablish a link between words and spiritual reality."[84] This sought-for reunion between word and reality represents a desire for a relationship of phenomenological immediacy in which language becomes a window rather than an obstacle to the perception of the world.

The desire for a language with which to meet the world is simultaneously one longing for the revival of the spiritual power of the word as a manifestation of the divine in human speech.[85] The poetic representation of the word, however, is limited by the confines of the medium and its manufacture as textual product. The resulting image on paper is the only approximation available to the poetic persona, who, despite the recognition of the fragility of her creation, nevertheless perceives its kinship to the infinity of the Word. This connection between the poetic and the divine emerges in the poem's closing lines, where a remembrance of an unspoken if not unsung time past is offered in terms invoking biblical associations to the creation myth: "Es war / am Anfang / Es war/ Geliebter / Es war —."

In the beginning was the word, but the paradoxically prophetic quality of the past tense in the biblical passage, one indicating a generative moment before time began and after which the world came into being is absent here and only the reminiscence of that pretemporal time remains. Syntactically the beginning here is past, it "was," but semantically it still "is," in that it still has the power to evoke genesis, plenitude, and primordial harmony. With the address to the absent beloved

---

[83] As Gisela Dischner points out in her insightful reading of this poem, this is not the first instance of a shift in tense. Dischner argues that the choice of the preterite in the word "fand" at the end of the second strophe where one might expect to find the future tense is evidence of Sachs's mystical conception of time in which the progression of past, present, and future no longer holds. See *apropos Nelly Sachs*, 45.

[84] Langer, *Versions of Survival*, 224.

[85] The conception of the alphabet as the dwelling place of the divine as a latent presence in language is one Nelly Sachs took up in her lyrical drama, *Beryll sieht in der Nacht*, as evidenced in her explanatory notes on the play. Cf. Nelly Sachs, *Zeichen im Sand: Die szenischen Dichtungen der Nelly Sachs* (Frankfurt am Main: Suhrkamp, 1962), 354: "Das Alphabet ist das Land, wo der Geist siedelt und der heilige Name blüht. Es ist die verlorene Welt nach jeder Sintflut."

as a substitute for or displacement of the absent but implied word, the expectations of the reader are deflected away from the Word to the poet's word. By inserting the beloved in a line that recalls the Scripture, the poet is both appropriating and transforming the written as tradition and medium. Her word comes to replace the Word in an act of poetic agency that seeks a message appropriate to the complex of suffering, loss, desire, and intense longing that characterizes the poem as a whole. Genesis past is brought into the present by the act of address, yet the poetic persona speaks to a beloved whose material presence in the poem can only be manifested in the word.

Through this substitution of signifiers and signification, the poet both transfigures and reinstates the word, making the slippage between and among her choices of signifiers visibly obvious by staggering the lines. The staggering descent of the closing lines abruptly breaks with a visual and punctual signal, the dash, which Sachs often used to indicate the boundary between speech and silence, finitude and infinitude, being and nothingness. In this last suspended "Es war —" we are left with the uncertainty of re-collection: the word as representation and regenerative power is there and not there, immortal and mortal, and the tension between these opposites remains intentionally unresolved. Through its very undecidability, the word, both divine and poetic, retains its multiplicity and thereby its potential to effect change.

The materiality of the poem as product and the divine power of the Word are themes that recur in Sachs's and Ausländer's poetological works albeit in markedly different manifestations. The oscillation between hope and despair informing Sachs's poetological contemplations is absent in Ausländer's vision of a realizable and more immediate language. Claudia Beil distinguishes Sachs's and Ausländer's relationship to language based on religio-temporal criteria, whereby she maintains that Sachs acknowledges the ephemeral nature of linguistic power and its capacity as a medium of transcendence, while for Ausländer human language is already a divine manifestation and offers an immediate connection to the world or, more specifically, a path to home.[86] Although Ausländer too questions the expressive capacity of words, her pronouncements are direct, straightforward, often even playful, regardless of whether they are statements on poetic powers of perception or the ultimate unrepresentability of the world. The poetic persona she assumes in these poems is unselfconscious in her aspirations to represent the world, as in "Das Netz" (IV 154):

[86] Beil, 412.

Ich möchte etwas sagen
ein Wort
das alles sagt

Nicht
ich bin ich
nicht gebet mir
Funkeldinge Länder Geld

Das Wort fällt mir nicht ein
ich falle mir selber ins Wort

falle in ein Netz
aus zeitgeknüpften
Silbenmaschen

This directness, however, is not one stemming from an unwavering, unreflected belief in the feasibility of such a feat, but rather a frankly stated wish that is undermined by the cumbersome process of imagination and articulation in which the limitations of both cancel the capacity for expression in the third strophe.

The following two poems by Rose Ausländer are concerned with the materiality and regenerative capacity of language similar to Nelly Sachs's "VERGEBENS" discussed above, yet in their manner of articulation they also serve to illustrate some of the fundamental differences in poetological self-understanding that distinguish the two poets. In the posthumously published "Verfolgt" (VIII 196), Ausländer reflects on the contrast between the finitude of her work as material substance and the artistic conceit that aspires to eternal presence:

Mein Handwerk hat
einen papiernen Boden

Er bricht
nicht

Unverwüstliches Wort
immer auf der Flucht

verfolgt
vom Wahn der Ewigkeit

The imagery demonstrates certain parallels to Sachs's poem "VERGEBENS," most notably in the allusions to the indestructibility of the paper as the materialization of the Word and the characterization of the Word as in perpetual exile. Yet unlike the paper singing in the flames in "VERGEBENS," Ausländer's word is not put to the test of fire. The forces of destruction that pursue the word in her rendering are not external, but rather contained within the word itself in its inherent ambition to be immortalized. The word in "Verfolgt" is thus, paradoxically, in flight from itself. In these few deceptively simple lines, Ausländer implicitly questions the character of language as a medium that eludes not only the speaker but also itself. In contrast to the paper singing out its swan song of last words at the end of Sachs's "VERGEBENS," the poet's handiwork in "Verfolgt" asserts its durability ("Er / bricht nicht") albeit one simultaneously destabilized by its constantly fluctuating position or localization ("immer auf der Flucht"). The wandering letters whose return is awaited with expectancy in Sachs's poem are here joined together and embodied in the word figured as a perpetual fugitive from its own pretensions to eternity.

The veiled reference to the opening passage of the Gospel of John (1:1; "In the beginning was the Word") in the closing strophe of "VERGEBENS" is not only a temporal inversion of the sequence of beginnings and endings but also a gesture of destabilization. By literally and visually trailing off into silence with this allusion to a past generative power of the Word, Sachs expresses an uncertainty as to whether her own words can carry the message she longs to convey. Ausländer, in contrast, openly allies herself with the Word in a poem appropriately entitled "Das Wort" (VI 140), first by directly quoting the passage from the Gospel of John in the beginning strophe and then by pronouncing the existence of a God-given idiom implying a comparable creative power in human language:

> "Am Anfang
> war das Wort
> und das Wort
> war bei Gott"
>
> Und Gott gab uns
> das Wort
> und wir wohnen
> im Wort
>
> Und das Wort ist
> unser Traum
> und der Traum ist
> unser Leben

The gift of language is passed on by Divine will to humankind not only as a communicative medium but also as a dwelling place. This concept of language as a kind of surrogate home recurs frequently in Ausländer's work.[87] The fugitive quality of the word in "Verfolgt" anticipates or re-

---

[87] Cf. Beil, 410: "Sprachkraft fällt mit Lebenskraft zusammen und bildet so den

calls the image of the word as a kind of nomadic home, as the conflation of mobility and flight that became a way of life for the Chosen
People in the Diaspora. Just as the Torah became the substitute house
of God after the destruction of the second Temple in Jewish history,[88]
so too does the word become the portable home for the nomadic poetic persona, who represents not only the exiled poet but also the
broader mass of Jewry as a displaced people. The poetic voice undermines the conciliatory quality of this one-for-the-other substitution,
however, in the final lines of "Das Wort." The word as home is simultaneously a dream of security, or the linguistic home itself is always already a dream because of the ultimate intangibility and mutability of
language. By juxtaposing dream and lived existence in an unresolved
constellation, the poetic voice presents the undecidability of the human
condition both expressed and confined by the realm of the word.

This imbeddedness in language becomes the major poetological focus in Ausländer's late work where she no longer questions the nature
of language as surrogate home, but rather embraces it as her locus of
preference. The following untitled poem from the 1985 collection *Ich
zähl die Sterne meiner Worte* (VII 117) serves to illustrate this:

> Ich hab
> ein Wort gefunden
> das nicht weint
>
> Die andern trauern
> um den Verlust
> der Heimat

The poetic persona in this late poem is confident in her belief that she
possesses a privileged knowledge that recognizes the superiority of language as a realm of existence. Language here is no longer only the means
and medium of poetic representation but has become an end in itself.
The security of this conviction contrasts with the ambiguity of affect re-

---

Raum, in dem Gott und Mensch sich treffen — in dem sie, beide exiliert, ihre fragile
Heimat finden. Im Leben, dem Atem der Sprache verbirgt sich jene eigentliche, von
aller Geographie unabhängige Heimat, die nicht geraubt werden kann, solange man
existiert."

[88] Sidra DeKoven Ezrahi describes this displacement of home onto the Word as
Scripture in her essay "Considering the Apocalypse: Is the Writing on the Wall Only
Graffiti?" in *Writing and the Holocaust*, 138. After the destruction of the Temple
there was a reorientation away from the sacrificial altar and "onto the written word.
The Temple, which had been reconstructed once before from the ground up, could
not be rebuilt again and acquired the status of a governing myth: an edifice of words
was erected as a defense against the reality of ruin and desolation and as a movable
property that made the Diaspora possible as a shifting Jewish province."

garding the linguistic situatedness of the poetic persona in "Das Wort" where dream and reality are indistinguishable and the subject is suspended in a state of permanent undecidability. The tone of acceptance that echoes from these last lines holds much greater optimism and enjoyment for this fluctuating condition of uncertainty than does Sachs's poem "VERGEBENS" which heralds its tone of despair already in the title. But Sachs's poem also introduces a factor of hope absent in the Ausländer poems discussed above. This hopeful moment appears as if from nowhere in the second strophe and then again, unexpectedly, in the closing lines, and stems from a resilient belief in the power of love to triumph over the forces of destruction and death. In the end, love even seems to displace language as the privileged mode of transcendence.

The introduction of the beloved as a substitute or displacement of the Divine Word in "VERGEBENS" is expanded into a privileging of both the beloved and the poet in their access to the creative power of language and their comprehension of hidden meanings in Sachs's "SCHLAF WEBT das Atemnetz" (*FS* 296).

> SCHLAF WEBT das Atemnetz
> heilige Schrift
> aber niemand ist hier lesekundig
> außer den Liebenden
> die flüchten hinaus
> durch die singend kreisenden
> Kerker der Nächte
> traumgebunden die Gebirge
> der Toten
> übersteigend
>
> um dann nur noch
> in Geburt zu baden
> ihrer eigenen
> hervorgetöpferten Sonn —

Night, discussed above as the bearer of dreams and the temporal locus of inspiration for the poet, is here given an additional dimension as a realm in which a figurative reunion takes place. The sleep that engenders dreams is inscribed with a cryptic script that only expired lovers can decipher. The imagery Sachs uses to portray the escape of the lovers from the chains of the singing cells of darkness recalls the singing of the singed paper in "VERGEBENS." In both poems, singing serves as the prelude to transcendence. The night-singing in "SCHLAF WEBT" anticipates a moment of freedom where the lovers move to a new level of existence beyond the realm of the dead ("der Toten / übersteigend") but still within the realm of dream ("traumgebunden"). The move into another realm, whether understood as transcendence or resurrection, culminates in regeneration or rebirth into a space that is the product of the lovers' own creation and by association also of the poetic imagination. The light that redeems the lovers is not of this world or the next, but of an Other world that exists solely in and as poetic text. The representation of love here as a transgressive and regenerative force illustrates a recurrent theme in Sachs's poetry, namely a conception of love as a transcendent power akin to the divine power of the Word in its capacity to rejuvenate or transform the world.

The transcendent, expansive quality of love as it appears in Sachs's work is one aspect of a complex process in which love, longing, and language combine in a poetic gesture toward acceptance and tolerance of others in an idealized vision of an other social reality, an alternative homeland. Although the desire or longing for home is a strong element in Sachs's poetry, it would be a denial of the thematic variety inherent in her work to argue that this quest for home is the overarching impulse compelling her writing.[89] The creation of a surrogate homeland within the realm of language is just one of several strategies for coming to terms with loss and mourning and one which does not function in isolation. The thematization of love in Sachs's poetry is another tactic used to enact or transform memory into a positive force that affirms both the intensity of past experience and the lasting, determinative power of emotion in the present. Love serves as the medium with which to bridge the gaps between past, present, and future, individual and community, survivor and victim, persecuted and persecutor. In a letter to Hilde Domin in 1960, Nelly Sachs explicitly argued for an end to the destructive dichotimization of victim and oppressor: "Es muß der Schritt gewagt werden, wo Henker und Opfer ausgewischt werden als Begriffe. Dort kann und darf die Menschheit nicht stehen bleiben, wenn nicht dieser Stern seelisch zu Grunde gehen soll."[90] That this impulse was central to her thinking even in the immediate aftermath of the catastrophe is apparent in a passage from a much earlier letter of 1947 to Hugo Bergmann where she criticizes the categorical tendencies that isolate and alienate human beings from each other:

Diese von Menschen ausgedachten Einschränkungen mögen nur einmal fortfallen. Das historische und dogmatische Moment möge doch

---

[89] This is the emphasis of Claudia Beil's reading of Sachs in *Sprache als Heimat*, 186–87: "Denn alle 'Sehnsucht', alles 'Heimweh' in den Texten der Nelly Sachs gilt dieser transzendenten Vision, in sie mündet letztlich ihre Suche nach Heimat."

[90] *Briefe*, 260.

nicht mehr die Menschen trennen, die in ihrer seelenhaften Liebe ei-
nig sind.[91]

Sachs's situation as an exile-refugee in a land she could never truly call
home and where she was continually confronted with memories of the
past and a home that had ceased to exist catalyzed a conceptual turn away
from a concern with country as home to a focus on community as "Heimat." This shift from geography to intersubjectivity comes across clearly
in two letters that demonstrate the development of Sachs's thinking on
the connection between love and community. In a 1946 letter to Gudrun Dähnert written during the time when her sense of exile and loss
were most immediate, Sachs proclaimed: "Ich habe kein Land und im
Grunde auch keine Sprache. Nur die Inbrunst des Herzens, die über alle
Grenzen hinwegeilen will."[92] In the absence of a land and a language she
could unselfconsciously identify as her own, Sachs turned inward to the
realm of feelings which in their unlocalizable inexpressiblity possessed an
authenticity uncorrupted and undetermined by either spatial or linguistic
constraints. In the second letter, written over twenty years later to a
friend in New York, the connection between love and homeland, or
more accurately, the anticipation of love as a kind of surrogate homeland
implied in the earlier letter, is made explicit: "Denn ein Land kann uns
niemals mehr Heimat sein, das werden Sie sicher genau wie ich empfin-
den. Nur wo wir Liebe finden, sind wir zu Hause."[93] Ultimately, however, the articulation of love as community is one moment in a poetic
process of representation continually moving between desires for understanding, refuge, transformation, and redemption.

Through the textualization of memory, Sachs and Ausländer sought
in different ways to lay claims to a violently severed past as well as to a
future of still-to-be-realized possibilities. In the representation of a past
that informs and anticipates the future, the lyrical voice becomes a dialogical crossroads where the Self and the Other, the I and the Thou,
meet, converse, and converge. What emerges in the textualization of
memory then is a dialogue of remembrance (with the witness as vehicle
for memory) conveyed between the poet/poem and the reader/reading
as a variation of the Self/Other exchange transmitted via the lyrical text.
Lyric poetry, by virtue of its form and formulation, demands the active
involvement and commitment of the reader if there is to be a production
of meaning or an achievement of understanding. In the poems discussed

---

[91] Ibid., 86.

[92] Ibid., 65.

[93] Ibid., 308.

in this chapter, the dialogic connection between the Self and the Other serves as a poetic means for articulating a vision of a social reality that supports both communication and coexistence.

The extrapolation of the experience of victimization and ostracism from the Jews to humankind as a whole is achieved through the appeal to a universalized Self/Other relation and represents an attempt to overcome the "Us versus Them" dichotomy that foments intolerance and violence. The resulting figuration of interactive community grounded in a concept of love as ethical responsibility for the Other is the culmination of poetic and humane desires for an alternative to the destabilized society of the here-and-now. This alternative vision of responsible community would bring an end to the cruelty and suffering that grows out of the hegemonic pretensions of a totalizing concept of identity, both in regard to the individual and the group.

The diversity of positions that Sachs and Ausländer occupied as women, German-speakers, Jews, survivors, poets, selves, and others leave resonances and traces in the multiplicity of poetic representations they generated to give voice to their experiences and hopes. The results of their efforts reflect their aspirations to represent the complexity and heterogeneity of lived historical experience imbued with a consciously future-oriented impulse toward the establishment of a world community capable of both recognizing and supporting the unresolvable yet not unreconcilable differences that distinguish nations, languages, cultures, and individuals. The articulation of difference through varied representations of the I/Thou relationship and the implications of these for the formation of a community grounded in interactive responsibility, recognition, and remembrance are explored in the concluding chapter.

4: Tracks and Traces

*A trace is the insertion of space in time, the point at which the world in-
clines toward a past and a time. (. . .) Only a being that transcends the
world can leave a trace. A trace is a presence of that which properly
speaking has never been there, of what is always past.*

— Emmanuel Levinas[1]

*I will put my law in their inward parts, and write it in their hearts; and
will be their God, and they shall be my people.*

— Jeremiah 31:33

Das Gedächtnis hält die Erinnerung nicht aus.

— Elazar Benyoëtz[2]

IN A DISCUSSION OF MEMORY AND EXPERIENCE, the traces of the past
leave imprints on the present and fade into the future, fragile yet tenacious reminders of what has come before and admonishments against
what could occur again. The words of Emmanuel Levinas quoted
above demonstrate a complex understanding of what constitutes a
trace, ultimately undefinable and elusive, something both inside and
beyond time, a legacy without a verifiable origin. The articulation of
the trace in the poetry of Nelly Sachs and Rose Ausländer, while less
abstract and elusive than in Levinas's conception, shares in its transtemporal aspect, resisting fixity in time but still speaking to history. In
the dialogue of remembrance, the *poem* serves as a constructed Other or
witness with whom the poet shares her experiences, albeit as transliterated
emotional traces.

Language as the poet's artistic medium provides an arena in which
she can exercise a certain degree of control or agency in shaping and
preserving her memory traces. This agency of the poet and the interaction between the poet and the poem as witness to her testimony add
another dimension to the understanding of the Self/Other dialogue
alluded to in the preceding chapter. The trace in Sachs's and
Ausländer's poems discussed in this chapter alternates in its emphasis

---

[1] Emmanuel Levinas, "The Trace of the Other," in *Deconstruction in Context*,
ed. Mark C. Taylor (Chicago: U of Chicago P, 1986), 358.

[2] Elazar Benyoëtz, *Treffpunkt Scheideweg* (Munich/Vienna: Carl Hanser, 1990), 16.

on loss, destruction, indestructibility, transcendence, and continuity. The figurations of the trace as breath, ashes, footsteps in the sand, abandoned objects, fleeting images, numbers burned into the arms of prisoners, and words spoken into the wind create an associative chain of images whereby the poem as a text, as the residue of the act of writing, itself becomes a part of the legacy of traces it describes.

In this sense, Nelly Sachs's poem "DIES IST" (*FS* 254–55) is at once a trace and a tracing, marked by the destruction and wrongdoing it describes in the present but which can be traced back to the Biblical sins of Sodom. In the first two strophes of the poem, the poetic voice establishes a line of continuity from the sins and wrongdoings of Biblical ancestors to the present time using a technique of repetition. By beginning each strophe with the declaration "Dies ist" the speaker achieves a temporal presentness as a witness to events that can only be synchronous in a mystical conception of time.

> DIES IST der dunkle Atem
> von Sodom
> und die Last
> von Ninive
> abgelegt
> an der offenen Wunde
> unserer Tür.
>
> Dies ist die heilige Schrift
> in Landsflucht
> in den Himmel kletternd
> mit allen Buchstaben,
> die befiederte Seligkeit
> in einer Honigwabe bergend.

The loss of faith or its rejection implied in the reference to Sodom in the opening strophe is a legacy that still marks the people's relationship to God and is implicitly connected with the presence of evil in the world. The next strophe portrays the retraction of divine grace as a loss of pure language, the language of the Holy Scripture which at once represents the expressive power of divine language and the Law that identifies the Jews as the Chosen People. The betrayal of the Covenant implied by the allusion to Sodom and Ninive instigates God's withdrawal into a realm of mystery where the believer cannot follow. The poem ends with an image of desolation and dissipation where the poetic persona confronts the mortality and suffering that characterize human existence.

> Dies ist Seine Meeresschleppe
> zurückgezogen
> in die rauschende Kapsel der Geheimnisse.
>
> Dies ist unsere Ebbe
> Wehegestirn
> aus unserem zerfallenden Sand —

The withdrawal of God, here figured as a cosmic entity whose robes trail into the sea, leaves tracks in the sand, traces of the elusive mystery that exceeds mortal understanding and that is experienced as suffering. The trace of God's presence testifies both to Divine Being and Divine Absence and it is this unresolved tension between presence and absence that constitutes the poetic persona's faith. It is significant that the poetic voice first speaks of the loss of the Holy Script before mentioning God's retreat. The violation of sanctified language is at once the catalyst for and the culmination of a process of spiritual estrangement.

The connection between faith and language is a theme that pervades Sachs's poetry and the echoes of the Word the poetic voice continuously strives to approximate represent another revelation of the trace: the poet's words as shadows, echoes, distortions, and ashes of a lost generative power. This aspect of the trace is also evoked in Rose Ausländer's "Asche" (IV 97) in which the perfected, sublime, and Holy Name has been reduced to ashes by fire. The ashes left behind are the record and the residue of the Name that persists and continues to exercise its power through the poetic persona's representations.

> Im Aschenregen
> die Spur deines Namens
>
> Es war
> ein vollkommenes Wort
>
> Feuer
> hat es gefressen
>
> Ich warf mein Staubgewand
> in die Flamme
>
> Hinter blindem Blick
> deine Augen
> ziehen mich an

The images of fire and ashes here inspire associations to the many pseudo-sacrificial pyres that marked the Third Reich's history of burning books, buildings, reliquaries, and bodies, and the poetic persona symbolically joins in this tradition by making a ceremonial offering of her own mortality, her "Staubgewand." This act should not be read as a sacrifice of belief, but rather as an affirmation of the Name. Despite the devastation that has occurred and continues to occur, the You she addresses in the final strophe is the Divine Being who remains the object of her blind faith.

The image of ashes serves as the representation of a different kind of trace in Nelly Sachs's poem "Zahlen" (*FS* 110). Here the ashes of the victims as traces of their material existence are displaced by the numbers that had been burned into the victims' arms to identify them as prisoners. These numbers remain burned into the poetic persona's memory long after the bodies she associated with them have ceased to exist, an ironic triumph of a program of depersonalization which had succeeded in systematically effacing individual identities.

> ALS EURE FORMEN zu Asche versanken
> in die Nachtmeere,
> wo Ewigkeit in die Gezeiten
> Leben und Tod spült —
>
> erhoben sich Zahlen —
> (gebrannt einmal in eure Arme
> damit niemand der Qual entginge)
>
> erhoben sich Meteore aus Zahlen,
> gerufen in die Räume
> darin Lichterjahre wie Pfeile sich strecken
> und die Planeten
> aus den magischen Stoffen
> des Schmerzes geboren werden —
>
> Zahlen — mit ihren Wurzeln
> aus Mördergehirnen gezogen
> und schon eingerechnet
> in des himmlischen Kreislaufs
> blaugeäderter Bahn.

The numbers here have multiple meanings. They are ciphers of evil marking the fate of the prisoners of the death camps, but also serve as the symbolic representatives of a mystical order incomprehensible to human consciousness. Numbers in the tradition of Hasidic mysticism had a sacred meaning and it was believed that there was an intrinsic correspondence between the number of commandments in the Jewish law and the structure of the human body.[3] Nelly Sachs makes a direct reference to this belief in the epigraph to the poem cycle "CHASSIDISCHE SCHRIFTEN" (*FS* 141): "*Es heißt: die Gebote der Thora entsprechen der*

---

[3] Scholem, *On the Kabbalah*, 128.

Zahl der Knochen des Menschen, ihre Verbote der Zahl der Adern. So deckt das ganze Gesetz den ganzen Menschenleib." In a chilling perversion of this mystical belief in the sacred physicality of numbers, the Nazis devised a system of ordered and organized execution that made horribly real what was religious allegory for the Hasidim.

In Nelly Sachs's poem "DU GEDENKST" (*FS* 27) from the cycle *Gebete für den toten Bräutigam* written immediately after she learned that the man she loved and revered had been murdered in the death camps,[4] the poetic persona intones a series of images representing scattered traces of the past. In their disparateness and diversity, these traces testify to the extent of the losses suffered. The traces in this poem are synecdochical and mnemonic representations that retain their plasticity and power despite the absence of a concrete referent. They are imprints of what had been real, preserved by remembrance as both consolation and admonition.

> DU GEDENKST der Fußspur, die sich mit Tod füllte
> Bei dem Annahen des Häschers.
> Du gedenkst der bebenden Lippen des Kindes
> Als sie den Abschied von seiner Mutter erlernen mußten.
> Du gedenkst der Mutterhände, die ein Grab aushöhlten
> Für das an ihrer Brust Verhungerte.
> Du gedenkst der geistesverlorenen Worte,
> Die eine Braut in die Luft hineinredete zu ihrem toten Bräutigam.

In linking this series of images together in a litany of mourning, Sachs conveys the relationship between death and life in which the poem becomes an act of resistance against the facticity of death. The poetic persona's testimony to the ruptures and separations brought about through death bears witness to an unconsummated longing for an existence free of alienation and persecution. Like the orphaned child, the bereaved mother, and the widowed bride, the poetic persona feels denied the re-

---

[4] In 1908 Nelly Sachs met a man who has never been identified, but who was to remain the object of her love and admiration for the rest of her life. In her monograph on Nelly Sachs, Gabriele Fritsch-Vivié provides excerpts from remarks by Sachs's friends and acquaintances that shed some light on the mystery man and Sachs's relationship with him. It appears that this man was considerably older than Nelly, was a divorced non-Jew (42) and was later active in the resistance against Hitler (40). It is not clear what prevented Sachs from having an officially sanctioned relationship with this man, but she nevertheless continued to see him until she fled Germany in 1940. It was no doubt his involvement in the resistance that led to the arrest and interrogation by the Gestapo that Sachs speaks of in "Leben unter Bedrohung" (see here also Fritsch-Vivié, 73). When she learned of his death in the camps in 1943, this news served as the catalyst both for the collection *In den Wohnungen des Todes* and her lyrical drama *Eli*. (cf. *Briefe*, 157)

alization of companionship with those whom she loves. At the same time, by constructing the poem as an address to a You ("Du"), the implied poetic persona recuperates these relationships indirectly. The You of her imagination becomes the substitute for the beloved she has lost as well as the Other whom she has not relinquished hope of reaching through her words. This aspect of Sachs's poetry as dialogue with an absent Other serves as a strategy for representing memory while transcending temporality. The address to the You brings the past into the present, while the lack of either physical or temporal specificity of this Other allows for an extension of the present into a textual present that is at once here-and-now and an unspecified future.

Rose Ausländer also employs this communicative strategy in her search for an idiom that will transcend or transfix time. In the poem "Nicht Oktober nicht November" (II 298) Ausländer presents a dialogue between an I and a You, in which the I has privileged access to some knowledge that the You does not possess. The I assumes the role of a tutor or translator, revealing the complex reality hidden behind the deceptively simple observations made by the You:

> Herbst sagst du
> und meinst den Wind er schärft
> sein Messer an deiner Stirn
> meinst rostige Blätter sie rollen
> deinem Schritt voran
> meinst Frostnadeln sie stechen
> die Luft den Baum die Haut
>
> Herbst herber Laut
> brauner Geschmack
> Die Freunde an der Front
> werden bitter und braun
> nicht von Sonne gebräunt
>
> Die Erde rostet und rollt
> mondab
> in die Schlucht wo die
> Geschichte Burgen baut
> Schuldtürme Falltüren

The first strophe addresses the relationship between language and "reality." The multivalence of the word is revealed through the chain of associations evoked by the word "Herbst" where the utterance is a surface phenomenon for a process of meaning that the poetic persona discerns beneath its usage by the You. The voice of the lyrical I shifts in the second strophe to its own perceptions and associations between the visible and the historical. The images progress from the brownness of autumn to soldiers in the battle-darkened atmosphere of the front, whereby the color brown evokes associations with the Nazi brownshirts as well as the discoloration of death. Here the poetic persona reads the broader text of nature for messages from the past: nature itself becomes the locus of resonant metaphors in which every perceived object is a signifier for something else and serves as a catalyst for chains of associations. The poem makes use of this associative process in order to explore the implications of a single word, "Herbst," revealing the resistance to temporal specificity it conceals. Like the reification of history presented as constructing its own fortresses, towers of guilt, and trapdoors in the third strophe, "Herbst" hides its complexities behind approximations. Meanwhile the search continues for a language capable of addressing the disparity between perception and experience, history and time:

> Herbst sagst du
> aber ich sage dir
> nicht Oktober nicht November
> du mußt einen neuen Kalender erfinden
> ein andres Alphabet
> eine Sprache die Einhalt gebietet
> denn die Zeit fällt
> fällt ins Unabsehbare
> und wir fallen mit ihr

In their respective quests for poetic figurations of the past that would not only do justice to the memories of the victims but also transmit hope for engendering a better future, Nelly Sachs and Rose Ausländer experimented with voice, metaphor, and form. The oscillation of voice as a strategy of representing multi-vocalic memory discussed in the preceding chapter is one aspect of a central, underlying theme that compels the works of both poets: the dialogic potential of the Self/Other relationship. The interplay of voices and the exchanges between I and Thou in these poems reflect an attempt to simulate or constitute an ideal of relation within the realm of the poetic text.

The I/Thou relation that Sachs and Ausländer evoke in their writings has its roots in the theological philosophy of Martin Buber, whose pioneering work *Ich und Du*, published in 1923, exerted a powerful and lasting influence on philosophical and theological conceptions of the Self's encounter with the Other. In Buber's work, the relationship between the I and the Thou is both primary and constitutive for the self: the I realizes a genuine state of personhood only through its encounter with the Other as a "Thou." The interaction with the Thou is characterized by a mutual recognition of the Other as a subject and is founded upon acceptance and responsibility rather than appropriation or manipulation. The relation with the Thou as Other on an interpersonal level was, in Buber's view, simultaneously an entering into relation with God as the absolute Other. Through the medium of interaction with the human Thou[5] one approaches God. Buber's conception of the I-Thou relation as simultaneously representative of the connection between the Self and the human other as well as the Divine Other not only emphasizes the interconnectedness of human experience but also its religious resonance.[6]

The combination of experiential, existential, and mystical aspects inherent in Buber's I/Thou dyad offers a philosophical foundation for a poetics of dialogue and responsibility that is grounded in intersubjectivity and acceptance. The Self engages in a conversation with the Other that both reveals and transcends the connection between them: the act of entering into dialogue acknowledges the personhood of the other both independent of and in relation to the self. The recognition of the humanity of the Other both in response to and in spite of her/his similarity and difference is the prerequisite for non-violent coexistence in a pluralistic community. The ethics implied in the interaction between I and the Thou involves communication and exchange and is directed at the good of the social context in which these two find themselves. The "good" here is not to be understood as the cohesion of harmonious community, but rather as a recognition of the being of the Other that enables independent existence and autonomy.[7] I am using the term "community" here to designate a group of persons bound together by their mutual recognition of responsibility for each other as human beings. Community in this sense is not defined by geographic or demographic criteria, but refers rather to a kind of social relation based on

[5] Buber, *Werke I*, 170.

[6] The proximity and interrelationship of the human and the divine pervades Jewish mysticism, and perhaps most striking in the Kabbalistic injunction to married Jews to engage in sexual intercourse on the Sabbath eve. In this imitation of the *hieros gamos*, the man symbolically becomes God and his wife the Shekhinah, conjoined in a holy union. See Philip Beitchman, *Alchemy of the Word: Cabala of the Renaissance* (Albany: State U of New York P, 1998) 33.

[7] This critical concern about the nature of community and the implications of a concept of community based on mutual understanding is cogently addressed in Iris Young's "The Ideal of Community and the Politics of Difference," in *Feminism/Postmodernism*, ed. Linda Nicholson (New York/London: Routledge, 1990), 300–323, here esp. 311: "Racism, ethnic chauvinism, and class devaluation, I suggest, grow partly from a desire for community, that is, from the desire to understand others as they understand themselves and from the desire to be understood as I understand myself. Practically speaking, such mutual understanding can be approximated only within a homogeneous group that defines itself by common attributes."

respect for the shared humanity of the Other, or, in Buber's terms, the recognition of the other as a "Thou." The relationship with the Other is thus not based on sympathetic identification, but on difference.[8]

The encounter of the I with the Thou as the other exterior to itself is accompanied by the realization of "otherness" interior to the self as well. This aspect of the I/Thou encounter is already present in Buber's conception of the relation in which the I is characterized as always already split, divided, or what he terms "zwiefältig."[9] That the recognition of the other within is a prerequisite for establishing a community both accepting and respectful of difference is an insight that has grown out of this fundamental ontological relation and one that has been appropriated and adapted in the many analyses and theories of gender, ethnicity, and morality that seek to reconcile identity and difference, singularity and plurality, community and heterogeneity, politics and ethics.[10]

A key philosopher after Buber who conjoins Jewish faith with an ethical ontology expressed as "being for the other" is Emmanuel Levinas. Writing after the Holocaust, Levinas found himself confronted with the dilemma of how to reconcile faith, community, and belief in God with an ethics of human responsibility. In his essays on Judaism, Levinas addresses the question of evil and human sovereignty, arguing that no ritual can efface the horrors perpetrated by man and against man.[11] God cannot be instrumentalized as a substitute for the victims or as a deflection of individual responsibility and obligation toward the "other." Levinas warns against the flight from this responsibility in reaction to catastrophe. In the aftermath of destruction, to flee from the hard claims of reality into an illusory utopia is to choose the path of selfishness. Regardless of whether the time is one of peace or conflict,

---

[8] This is an essential aspect of the Self/Other relationship in Levinas's thought. See *Time and the Other*, esp. 75–76: "The relationship with the other is not an idyllic and harmonious relationship of communion, or a sympathy through which we put ourselves in the other's place; we recognize the other as resembling us, but exterior to us; the relationship with the other is a relationship with a Mystery. The other's entire being is constituted by its exteriority, or rather its alterity. . . ."

[9] Buber, *Werke I*, 122: "Kein Mensch ist reine Person, keiner reines Eigenwesen, keiner ganz wirklich, keiner ganz unwirklich. Jeder lebt im zwiefältigen Ich."

[10] Cf. esp. Julia Kristeva, *Strangers to Ourselves* and *Nations without Nationalism*, trans. Leon Roudiez (New York: Columbia UP, 1993); Iris Marion Young, *Justice and the Politics of Difference* (Princeton: Princeton UP, 1990); Anthony Cortese, *Ethnic Ethics: The Restructuring of Moral Theory* (Albany: State U of New York P, 1990); Joan Tronto, *Moral Boundaries: A Political Argument for an Ethic of Care* (New York/London: Routledge, 1993).

[11] Cf. Levinas, *Difficult Freedom*, 20.

the spiritual meaning of being is always drawn from the encounter with and responsibility for the "other." Therefore one must choose what Levinas terms "ethical action," which for him is part of the legacy of Jewish tradition.[12]

The conjoining of traditions, be they religious or philosophical, into a kind of synthetic spirituality, is as has been shown characteristic of both Nelly Sachs's and Rose Ausländer's faith which manifests itself as at once mutable and monotheistic. In her critical study of monotheism, Regina Schwartz argues that its tenets effectively demonize pluralism and form a bulwark against heterogeneity, phenomena that are perceived as threats to coherent identity and stable community.[13] The result is a theological creed grounded in exclusivity designed to ensure clear-cut boundaries of belief and belonging. By virtue of its demand for absolute allegiance and the agonistic construction of identity this gives rise to, monotheism functions according to a kind of "ethics of limitation." In contrast to this "ethics of limitation" the openness to a variety of spiritual traditions Sachs and Ausländer exhibit in combination with their critical attitudes toward orthodoxy can be read as an embrace of pluralism.

In the present discussion, the I/Thou or Self/Other[14] relationship also serves to support of plurality, and I argue that the figuration and recognition of the primacy of this relation in both Sachs's and Ausländer's poetry is evidence of their concerns not only with faith in a divine power but also with the future of a viable human society. Through the identification with the other within the self, the individual becomes more receptive to the other exterior to the self, which in turn enables a shift from appropriation and erasure of the Other to acknowledgment. According to Levinas, the other remains distinct and must remain distinct in her/his very alterity, for if "one could possess, grasp, and know the other, it would not be other."[15] Yet the responsibility to

---

[12] Ibid., 100, 109.

[13] See Regina Schwartz, *The Curse of Cain*, 46–47: "In the myth of monotheism, pluralism is betrayal, punishable with every kind of exile: loss of home, loss of land, even alienation from the earth itself."

[14] In contrast to Paul Ricoeur who defines the "self" as a reflexive condition, whereas the "I" is a construct that can be defended or denigrated, but never definitively established, I am using the "I" and the "self" here as parallel terms. See Ricoeur, *Oneself as Another*, 18.

[15] See Levinas, *Time and the Other*, 90. Levinas's insistence on the alterity of the Other stems in part from his critical observations of the treatment of the Other in Western philosophy, which he argues has been engaged in the systematic erasure of

the other is prior to the responsibility of the I to itself.[16] The anteriority of this responsibility to the other and its continued claim on the self *even in the absence of the other* constitute the ground of being for the I. I exist for the other, but in my existing, the other also exists for me. For Levinas it is this relationship that establishes not only the ground of being, but also the foundation for moral consciousness.[17]

In the sections that follow, I address the multi-levelled representations of the Self/Other relation in Sachs's and Ausländer's poetry, moving from the originary relationship to the other embodied in the mother/child bond to the processes and images of otherness that constitute national and ethnic identities, specifically those tensions between Germanness and Jewishness as well as between "Heimat" and exile that mark the lives, writings, and reception of both poets. Finally, using Buber's theory of the I-Thou relation as a point of departure, I explore the representations of the unspecified Self/Other constellation in Sachs's and Ausländer's post-Holocaust poetry and examine the implications these depictions have for an ethics of remembrance that reaches beyond the confines of collective memory to a generalizable and trans-temporal acknowledgment of responsibility for the other.

Mother and Child

Yea, a woman may forget the child of her womb, yet I will not forget thee.

— Isaiah, 49:15

The child. . . identifies with/as a subject-in-process, represented by the mother. Rather than fixing upon an object, (s)he identifies with the process of subjectivity, a mode of being, characterized by desire for otherness, ordered according to a logic of negativity: constant movement, change.

— Allison Weir[18]

---

alterity. In his essay, "The Trace of the Other," Levinas attributes this to a kind of xenophobia inherent in much of philosophical thought (346): "Western philosophy coincides with the disclosure of the other where the other, in manifesting itself as a being, loses its alterity. From its infancy philosophy has been struck with a horror of the other that remains other — with an insurmountable allergy."

[16] See Levinas, *Time and the Other*, 110.

[17] See Levinas, *Difficult Freedom*, 293.

[18] Allison Weir, "Identification with the Divided Mother: Kristeva's Ambivalence," in *Ethics, Politics and Difference in Julia Kristeva's Writing*, ed. Kelly Oliver, 89.

Our mother country is not where we find happiness at last. Our mother country, on the contrary, is with us, in us. Germany is alive in us, we represent it . . . in every country to which we go. . . . We are rooted in it from the beginning, and we can never emancipate ourselves from it.

— Leopold von Ranke[19]

It is well established in psychological theories of subject formation that the bond between the child and its primary caregiver is instrumental in the child's realization of an identity as a self in a differentiated environment. Nancy Chodorow's work in object relations theory investigates the mother/daughter constellation specifically and its relationship to the process of identity formation.[20] The ambivalence characterizing this mother/daughter bond stems from the conflict between the child's desire to return to a state of undifferentiated unity with the mother and the opposing wish to sever that connection and achieve independence and autonomy. Because of the oscillation in this relationship between identification and alienation, the transactions that define the child's self-formation are constantly being renegotiated.[21] The process of renegotiation in the encounter between the child and the mother posited by Chodorow's theory, although important for the theorization of the subject as "in-process"(i.e. the subject as continually defined and redefined through its relationships with the other[22]), leaves out an important aspect of the relationship of the self to the other: namely the recognition that the alterity of the other both mirrors and defines the otherness of the self. The realization of this otherness within the self is the prerequisite for the acceptance of the other exterior to the self [23]

---

[19] Excerpt from von Ranke's essay entitled "A Dialogue on Politics" quoted in Maier, *The Unmasterable Past*, 65.

[20] Cf. Chodorow, *The Reproduction of Mothering.*

[21] Cf. Nancy Chodorow, *Feminism and Psychoanalytic Theory* (New Haven, CT/London: Yale UP, 1989), 10.

[22] This concept of subject-in-process, already referred to in chapter 2, comes from Julia Kristeva, whose psychoanalytic semiotic theory combines the postulate that human subjectivity is grounded in language with a relational theory of subject formation. Cf. Julia Kristeva, *In the Beginning Was Love*, 9; quoted in note 126, page 120 of this book.

[23] The insistence that the self recognize its condition as always already other to itself is central to Julia Kristeva's theorization of the stranger and nationhood and the possibilities for a community of tolerance. Cf. Kristeva, *Strangers to Ourselves*, 182: "How could one tolerate a foreigner if one did not know one was a stranger to oneself?"; and *Nations without Nationalism.*

and represents a first step toward developing an environment supportive of heterogeneity and "unassimilated otherness."[24]

In Chapter Two I discussed the significance of the mother/
daughter relationship on several levels: as a central aspect in Sachs's and
Ausländer's biographies; as an alternative to monotheism through a
return to an older belief in the heterogeneity of an originary Mother in
response to the poets' crises of faith; and as a multi-levelled trope for
the primary relationship between the self and the other. In this section
I am again concerned with the mother/child bond as a paradigm for
the Self/Other relation, but also with the representations of childhood
and home as tropes for harmonious coexistence contingent upon the
presence of the mother. With the loss of the untroubled environments
of their youth as well as the motherland, both poets engage in compensatory strategies, re-creating the security of the childhood they had lost
via the surrogate maternal medium of the mother tongue. In these representations, Nelly Sachs emphasizes more the relationship of the child
to its mother: the intimacy and warmth of that connection are more
powerful for her than the mother's signification as "home." In contrast,
Rose Ausländer's poetic portrayals of childhood frequently focus on an
idealized version of the area where she grew up, the city of Czernowitz
and the Bukovina, locales often figured as female, maternal entities embracing the diversity of the population without insisting on assimilation
or conformity.[25]

The nostalgic power of these figurations of maternalized home
serves to counterbalance the numerous poems depicting the poetic persona as an orphan, often an orphan in exile, an image which underscores the extremity and extent of the loss of the maternal in its
multiple aspects: as mother, mother country, and mother tongue. The
loss of the mother represents therefore not only a loss of childhood as

---

[24] I am borrowing this term from Iris Marion Young's work on social relations
and the city. In her essay "The Ideal of Community and the Politics of Difference,"
Young argues that the conventional concept of community is exclusionary and privileges homogeneity via assimilation to the dominant group. What she opposes to this
restrictive model is what she terms the "unoppressive city" as an ideal social form
which she defines as "a 'being-together' of strangers" and "openness to unassimilated otherness."(318–19)

[25] Michaela Kessner, in her study of Rose Ausländer's work describes the city of
Czernowitz as an oasis of multicultural tolerance and coexistence. Cf. Kessner, 5–6.
While the spate of studies lauding the Bukovina region for its vibrant cultural diversity seem to tip in the direction of uncritical nostalgia, there is no question that the
atmosphere of multicultural exchange Ausländer experienced there exerted a lasting
influence on her writing.

sanctuary but also a loss of identity: the external conditions which constitute the individual's sense of self and being in the world. Yet this loss of identity is paradoxically also the catalyst for a process of maturation. The child/daughter is confronted with her solitude and must either reconcile herself to this condition of existential singularity or transcend it by working to fashion her own sense of community grounded in her relationships to others. In this pursuit, the daughter-as-poet contemplates several directions. She can turn inward and reflect upon her past as the foundation of her existence, whereby she remains in a condition of dependency on a maternal construct that exists only in memory. Or she can come to terms with her loss by connecting the past to the present, thereby preserving her memories without dissolving into them. Although Sachs and Ausländer do demonstrate moments of the first type and lapse into nostalgic aestheticizations of the mother/daughter relationship and home that bear little resemblance to lived experience, their figurations of the mother/child connection most often fall within the second category.

In the following discussion, I examine textual representations of this mother/child complex, beginning with those poems that demonstrate the child's longing for the maternal as a kind of all-encompassing unity, to the figurations of the poetic persona as a homeless orphan in a world characterized by alienation, estrangement, and perpetual exile,[26] to finally the imaging of the maternal as the hope for the future, whereby the poetic persona as child appropriates the generative capacity of the mother. In her idealized representation as the embodiment of peace and tolerance, the mother serves as a trope for the possibilities of viable pluralistic coexistence. The poetic persona's identification here with the mother as maternal fecundity is simultaneously a compensatory reduplication[27] of the mother she has lost and a transformation of the maternal into a form of agency for social change.

[26] The portrayal of the exile as an orphan apparent in Sachs's poems functions as a metaphor on the textual level and as a psychological strategy on the "real" level. This connection between the orphan and exile is echoed in Edward Said's assessment of the exile psyche in his essay "Reflections on Exile," *GRANTA* 13 (1984): 167. Said maintains that "exiles are always eccentrics who *feel* their difference (even as they frequently exploit it) as a kind of orphanhood. (. . .) Clutching difference like a weapon to be used with stiffened will, the exile jealously insists on his or her right to refuse to belong."

[27] This term comes from Allison Weir, whose discussion of the mother construct in Julia Kristeva's work in her essay "Identification with the Divided Mother" offers insights applicable to the representation of the maternal in Nelly Sachs's and Rose Ausländer's poems. Cf. Weir, *Ethics, Politics and Difference in Julia Kristeva's Writ-*

In Nelly Sachs's poem "Alles weißt du unendlich nun" (*FS* 232–33), the mother is figured as a cosmic entity, omniscient, mystical, and timeless in her relation to worldly existence and human history. The repetition of the phrase "Alles weißt du unendlich nun, / o meine Mutter" underscores the omniscient quality of the mother while the oceanic maternal metaphors emphasize her vastness. The mother, addressed as "Du" by the poetic persona, is a polyvalent figure, a maternal persona as well as a personification of the Earth Mother who has witnessed the progress of human history and thus possesses knowledge stretching back to Biblical times.

> ALLES WEISST DU unendlich nun,
> o meine Mutter —
> auch die Stelle, wo den Propheten
> das Ende des Weges
> flammend vom Leibe gerissen wurde.
>
> Auch des Esau
> ins Fell der Niederlage
> geweinte Träne.
>
> Auch die Nebelknospe
> der Schwermut im Blute.

The mother is endowed with a knowledge that transcends mortal and historical time. Hers is an awareness that spans human suffering and the apocalypse and it is the breadth of this maternal consciousness that the poetic persona praises and vicariously shares through her re-creation of the mother in the text. The omniscience and omnipresence of the maternal, as memory and as originary Mother, serves as a referent for the poetic persona's desire for continuity and reassurance in an environment that is maternally inscribed yet resistant to comprehension. The poem ends with an image of earth as a place bordered by water. The fluidity of the boundaries between fixed points implies a possibility for fluctuation, shifts, and changes which only the mother, in her connection to the forces of life and death, is privy to: "Und Ränder überall aus Meer— / du weißt."

The figuration of the maternal as simultaneously omnipresent and outside of time enables the poetic persona to identify with a force that precedes, exceeds, and succeeds her as the source, guardian, and executor of her existence. In Rose Ausländer's "Immer die Mutter" (V 66), the poetic persona's relation to the maternal is portrayed as one

---

ing, ed. Kelly Oliver, 86.

shifting between life and death, but always encompassed in an atmosphere of maternal infinitude:

> Mein Stern hängt
> an ihrer Nabelschnur
>
> Ich trinke ihre Milch
> bald
> werde ich geboren
>
> Hinter meinem Tod
> wächst sie mir zu

As in Sachs's "Alles weißt du unendlich nun," the mother in this poem
possesses a timeless, cosmic quality in her relation to the poetic persona's mortal existence. There is some comfort in this conceptualization in that the continuity and unbounded temporality of the maternal
lend the poetic persona both strength and life. Unlike Sach's poetic
persona, however, Ausländer's poetic I here does not identify with the
mother figure by engaging her dialogically as a "Thou." By referring to
the mother in the third person, the lyrical I emphasizes her distance
from the mother as her point of origin and thereby also asserts her
autonomy even as she acknowledges her subordination to the mother's
fertile ubiquity.

The representation of the maternal as an encompassing plenitude of
cosmic proportions is one strategy whereby the daugher-poet seeks to
recuperate the loss of the bond with the mother while simultaneously
appropriating maternal creative power. The figuration of the maternal
as a multivalent trope expands the intimate and private realm of the
mother/child connection into one that transcends the human finitude
of that relation. The appeal to the cosmic power of the Great Mother is
a redemptive gesture in an atmosphere otherwise marked by suffering
and catastrophe. The figuration of the maternal as timeless, encompassing presence contrasts with the nostalgic portrayals of childhood as
the point of origin of a vanished harmony. The idealization of childhood as the paradigm for an encouraging and supportive social atmosphere is at once an aestheticization of the past and a dream of a future
unaffected by the traumas of the present. The past as a past that never
was becomes the future that may never be but which the poetic persona
nevertheless strives to approximate in the realm of language.

In "Heimat I" (II 31), Rose Ausländer conflates mother and home
in a recollection of childhood as a time of security and intimacy. In the
first strophe, the lyrical I looks back at an irretrievable past from the
perspective of her present position as an exile:

> Dieser herbe Rausch der Fremde
> fremder Heimat ohne Ende
> hält mich immerfort in Atem

This condition of bitter intoxication with strangeness cannot displace the nurturing familiarity the displaced self longs for.[28] The end-rhyming trochaic tetrameter structure of the opening two lines creates an aura of expectancy that the rest of the poem will follow a similar pattern, but this expectation is immediately disappointed by the third line in which the absence of rhyme coincides with the semantic message of taut anticipation. This technique of disappointed, or better, deferred rhyme carries the poem through a succession of five strophes, to be broken then by the last where the poetic voice expresses longing for a bygone maternal refuge. The remembered comfort and harmony of the relation to the mother is echoed and tonally underscored by the rhyme in the poem's final two lines.

> Meine Sehnsucht kann nicht schlafen
> Träume wachen auf und haben
> meiner Mutter ewige Züge
> meiner Mutter sanfte Hände
> eigne Heimat ohne Ende

Unlike the rhyme scheme of the first strophe, the succession of lines in the concluding strophe demonstrates both a metric and a rhymed symmetry. The trochaic tetrameter structure is constant and the two rhymed pairs of lines flank the unpaired center line thus preserving a sense of symmetry. Here the desire for reassurance evoked but ungratified by the rhymed pair of lines at the beginning of the poem is realized in the poetic persona's recollection of her mother's image. The vastness of the foreign homeland, although provocative, parallels but cannot ever replace the encompassing sense of well-being the poetic persona associates with the remembered motherland.

In a later poem entitled "Mich trösten" (VII 304), however, Ausländer portrays the poetic persona's awareness of the childish and wistful nature of her recollections, while acknowledging that they serve to console her. In this text, the mother has assumed a different aspect. She is no longer the embodiment of a transtemporal force or the ex-

---

[28] Bernd Witte attributes the tendency toward nostalgia and longing for childhood in Ausländer's post-1945 poetry to her repeated experiences of forced emigration and persecution, but his conclusion that she then viewed the remainder of her life "als permanente Vertreibung aus dem Paradies der Kindheit" (cf. "Rose Ausländer," *KLG*, 9) ignores those works that question the figuration of childhood as an existential ideal.

panse of historical experience, and instead of admonishing the next
generation to remember the past, she encourages the child to forget:

> Mich trösten
> kindliche Träume
> und manchmal
> ein bißchen Musik
>
> das Walzerblut
> ist schon geronnen
>
> die Mutter sagt
> Liebling
> vergiß

The amnesia willed by the mother in "Mich trösten" is never
achieved. The memories of the lost and the pain of those experiences
persist, transformed and varied as themes and metaphors in accordance
with the poet's shifting focus on childhood, home, people, and language. In the poems discussed above, it was the mother's presence that
directed the poetic persona's reflections on the past and the future. In
the poems addressing the condition of exile, it is the absence of the
mother that informs the poetic persona's existence. Nelly Sachs's "Was
suchst du Waise" (FS 167–68) depicts the exile as an orphan, a stranger
without a mother(land), a survivor without a people:

> WAS SUCHST DU Waise
> in der Erde noch
> die Eiszeit deiner Toten fühlend —
> die blauen Monde
> erhellen schon die fremde Nacht.

Here the implied poetic persona is speaking to herself. The Thou
that had been directed at the conjured figure of the mother in the poems discussed above is now self-referential, there is neither mother nor
other in dialogue with the self, or rather this Other has been internalized in response to absence and loss. In the absence of an external
other with whom to identify, the poetic persona experiences a sense of
alienation — her surroundings are foreign and lifeless to her. The only
other being that thrives in this cold and alien atmosphere is the executioner whose appearance and presence in the fourth strophe further
emphasizes the alienating and antagonistic aura of the poem's opening
lines. The executioner represents the destructive forces that control the
world and determine the fate of the coming generation embodied in
the figure of the newborn child:

> Der Henker
> in der schuldbeladenen Finsternis
> hat seinen Finger tief im Haar
> des Neugeborenen versteckt
> das knospet Lichterjahre schon
> in ungeträumte Himmel fort.

The tone of resignation and the absence of any hope that the reign of the executioner might be broken contrasts sharply with the alternately redemptive and nostalgic tone of other poems in which the maternal is re-presented as memory, refuge, and all-encompassing power. The motherless poetic persona is presented in the final strophes as solitary, an orphan left to talk to herself and search in the sand for traces of that which she has lost. The ephemeral nature of experience and the lack of anchoring relationships marking the existential condition of the poetic Thou are literally punctuated by the dash that breaks off the poem's lament without ending it:

> Der Erde Nachtigallenzunge
> singt
> in deine Hände — Waise —
> die in des Sandes
> schwarzgewordnem Abschied suchen
>
> Geliebtes suchen
>
> das längst
> aus scharfgesägtem
> Sterngebiß
> entschwand —

Accompanied by the song of the synecdochical maternal nightingale-Earth-Mother, the themes of the trace and the irrevocably lost are melded in the image of the orphan's hands in the sand seeking to recuperate what can never be recovered.

Nelly Sachs again makes use of the orphan image to portray the condition of the exile in the concluding strophe of a later poem entitled "KOMMT EINER" (*FS* 300–301). This poem opens with a description of the potential strangeness of the foreigner stemming from the alien sounds of his language.

> KOMMT einer
> von ferne
> mit einer Sprache
> die vielleicht die Laute
> verschließt
> mit dem Wiehern der Stute

oder
dem Piepen
junger Schwarzamseln
oder
auch wie eine knirschende Säge
die alle Nähe zerschneidet —

The stranger is depicted as a wandering, homeless exile and like the poetic persona in "Was suchst du Waise" has retained the home he has lost in transmogrified form. Paradoxically, the loss of the homeland here becomes a physical presence, albeit an expired one that seems more a burden than a benefit to the wanderer:

Ein Fremder hat immer
seine Heimat im Arm
wie eine Waise
für die er vielleicht nichts
als ein Grab sucht.

In the absence of a place to call home, the orphan-exile retreats into language as the one maternal realm that remains. The mother tongue becomes the surrogate homeland and the locus of the poetic persona's projections for the future. In a poem entitled "Mutterland" (V 98) already discussed at length in Chapter Two, Rose Ausländer uses parental imagery to distinguish the geographical home she has lost from the figurative home she inhabits. The demise of the fatherland is compensated for by the enduring and nurturing familiarity of the mother tongue:

Mein Vaterland ist tot
sie haben es begraben
im Feuer
Ich lebe
in meinem Mutterland
Wort

The poetic persona's desire for hospice within the maternal space is transformed by collapsing the distinctions between the self as subject and the external world as object in Ausländer's "Erde" (III 254). Here the poetic persona sees herself as at one with her surroundings, she has become the all-encompassing maternal that contains and sustains, yet still retains a sense of self-identity:

Ich bin im Zimmer
es ist in mir

bin im Haus das
in mir wohnt

Die Erde auf der ich gehe
rollt in mir
durch den Weltraum

Ich trage das Haus auf den Schultern
zerlege mein Zimmer
in sechs Tafeln
und schreibe auf ihnen die Erde

The poetic persona's conceit as the generative and shaping force in the world indicates an appropriation of maternal and divine properties. The prevalence of the I in its permeation of an ever-broader spatiality is reminiscent of the pantheistic concept of deity presented by the seventeenth-century Jewish philosopher Benedict (Baruch) Spinoza,[29] whose work Ausländer had studied and admired.[30] Yet the images the poet chooses to portray the diffuse quality of the I are paradoxically images of containment: room, house, earth. In moving from the intimacy of domestic interiors as represented by the room and the house in the first two strophes to the more expansive yet still defined space of the earth, Ausländer connects the domestic and worldly aspects of the maternal trope with the divine act of creation in the final strophe. In a room of her own, the I recreates the world in an act of poetic genesis, whereby the choice of the number six for the tablets lends this poetic act a symbolic legitimacy in its parallel to the six days of creation. The poetic persona conflates both divine and maternal aspects and offers the potential for a regeneration and transformation of the world.

The representation of the poetic persona as the heir to the creative powers attributed to God and the Mother assumes a different form in Nelly Sachs's "ENGEL DER BITTENDEN" (FS 74–75). In this poem, children are portrayed as the locus of hope and change in an environment inscribed with devastation and death.

---

[29] In Proposition XV of *The Ethics*, Spinoza asserts the quality of God as that substance which pervades and contains all things: "*Whatsoever is, is in God, and without God nothing can be, or be conceived.*" Cf. *On the Improvement of the Understanding. The Ethics. Correspondence*, trans. R. H. M. Lewis (1883; New York: Dover, 1955), 55.

[30] Cf. Renate Wiggershaus, " 'Es war eine unendliche Sonnenfinsternis.' Ein Porträt der Dichterin Rose Ausländer," *Rose Ausländer: Materialien zu Leben und Werk*, ed. Helmut Braun, 94–95. Spinoza's teachings had a lasting effect on Rose Ausländer's spiritual self-understanding. In a letter to Peter Jokastra in 1965, she allies herself with Spinoza in her explanation of her religious views: "Ich bin im Spinozistischen Sinne nach *Atheistin*. Meine religiösen Themen sind anti-religiös oder mythisch zu verstehen." Quoted in Helfrich, 271.

ENGEL DER BITTENDEN,
nun, wo das Feuer wie ein reißendes Abendrot
alles Bewohnte verbrannte zu Nacht —
Mauern und Geräte, den Herd und die Wiege,
die alle abgefallenes Stückgut der Sehnsucht sind —
Sehnsucht, die fliegt im blauen Segel der Luft!

In this atmosphere of apocalyptic destruction, however, the children retain their innocence apparently unharmed by the catastrophe that destroyed the generation preceding them as the closing lines of the third strophe and their conclusive punctuation seem to indicate:

Aber immer noch spielen die Kinder im Sande,
formen übend ein Neues aus der Nacht heraus
denn warm sind sie noch von der Verwandlung.

In this depiction, Sachs appeals to the Jewish historical tradition of connecting destruction and regeneration in a contingent yet alternating relation in which catastrophe necessarily precedes renewal. The fires of destruction are the same fires that catalyze the metamorphosis that brings the next generation to life. In this context, the final strophe can be read as an attempt to find redemptive meaning in the apocalypse with which the poem opens:

Engel der Bittenden,
segne den Sand,
laß ihn die Sprache der Sehnsucht verstehn,
daraus ein Neues wachsen will aus Kinderhand,
immer ein Neues!

As in Ausländer's "Erde," this poem presents a conflation or fusion of divine and maternal aspects, a synthesis that enables the poetic persona to come to terms with the extremity of what has occurred. The facticity of the Holocaust inspired a crisis of faith that questioned the validity of a monotheistic conception of an omnipotent God. Here the omnipotent God is absent, displaced by an angel who, together with the maternal procreative power, is to aid the new generation in creating a new world. The poem ends with a longing for a world purged of the evil of the past where apocalyptic destruction has given rise to another world to be shaped and transformed by the coming generations. The poetic persona's allegiances to a paternal deity and a maternal force remain in a state of oscillation.[31] That this situation remains unresolved is a fur-

---

[31] To return to the relevance of object relations theory to the mother/child aspect of these constellations, the daughter-child in Chodorow's theory experiences a multi-layered oedipal situation in which she retains the pre-oedipal connection to the

ther reflection of how both Sachs and Ausländer persisted in their attempts to synthesize aspects of paternal and maternal representations in
a conception of faith that would enable them to remember the past
while remaining hopeful about the future.

While the poetic persona's mourning for the lost mother in some
sense parallels her mourning for the victims of the catastrophe, the implicit otherness of the maternal figure distinguishes it from the imposed
otherness of the victim. The loss of the mother is experienced as a loss of
multiplicity and mutuality whereas the loss of the victim/other is experienced as erasure. While the otherness of the mother as a trope supports
and embodies heterogeneity, the category of otherness applied to the
oppressed is a reduction of identity to an inventory of constructed characteristics designed to reify difference. In contrast to the fluid and mutable alterity of the maternal that points toward the multiplicity and
pervasiveness of difference, the otherness foisted upon the Jews under
Hitler represented both a denial and inscription of difference and an insistence on fixed identities. By figuring the Jew as the absolute Other,
the Nazis were able to establish a racial code of immutable differences
that justified first segregation and then dehumanization. The passage of
the Reich Citizenship Law in November 1935 denying Jews German
citizenship gave the already prevalent practice of othering the Jews a le-
gal framework and codified the racial division of Germany by disallowing
Jewish identification as Germans. With the deprivation of their status as
nationals, the Jews were rendered official strangers in opposition to the
mass of German citizenry who could produce recognized "volkisch"
pedigrees. The impact of this artificially constructed but rigidly enforced
opposition between German and Jew and its influence on the conceptions of Germanness and Jewishness both during the Third Reich and
into the post-war period is the subject of the next section.

---

mother and adds the oedipal attachment to the father. Although the bond with the
mother is the primal connection, the introduction of the father into the relation results in a situation where the maternal and the paternal bonds are in competition. Cf.
Nancy Chodorow, "Mothering, Object-Relations, and the Female Oedipal Configuration," *Feminist Studies* 4.1 (1978): 153. This psychological situation parallels the
oscillation between paternal and maternal representations of security and creative
power displayed by the poetic persona as daughter/child in the poems discussed
above. For a more detailed treatment of the poetic persona's oscillation between paternal and maternal imagos refer to Chapter Two.

German and Jew

The Holocaust has been the most momentous force to shape modern Jewish identity. Its force was felt not only among those Jews who directly experienced it but among all individuals who could even remotely perceive themselves as Jews.

(. . .) The treatment of a segment of society as Jews (whether Jewish or not) caused all those who had even the remotest sense of identification with the Jews to restructure their sense of self.

— Sander Gilman[32]

One cannot, in fact, be a Jew instinctively; one cannot be a Jew without knowing it. (. . .) Judaism is an extreme consciousness.

— Emmanuel Levinas[33]

All poets are Jews.

— Marina Zwetajewa[34]

The condition of homelessness that characterizes the orphan-stranger in Nelly Sachs's poetic figurations of exile represents the doubly motherless loneliness of the exile-survivor. The mourning for the lost motherland in these poems should not, however, be read as a reverence for the nation as the locus of identity. The violence of the Nazi assertion of a supremacist racial identity based on the subjugation and eradication of those peoples who did not fit into the ideal of the "Volk" grew out of its roots in a form of tribal nationalism with hegemonic pretensions. The National Socialists developed a detailed racial taxonomy cast in dichotomous and moralistic terms in which the German "Volk" and those peoples of the "Aryan race" were superior/good while non-Aryan peoples were inferior/evil. This system combined pseudo-scientific methods of determining race distinctions with a belief in the absolute supremacy of the Aryan race, which, once having regained a condition of racial purity, was the natural and rightful heir to the planet.[35] The insistence on an innate racial privilege served not only as a

---

[32] Gilman, *Jewish Self-Hatred*, 319.

[33] Levinas, *Difficult Freedom*, 6.

[34] Epigraph to Paul Celan's poem "Und mit dem Buch aus Tarussa," *Gesammelte Werke*, Vol. I (Frankfurt am Main: Suhrkamp, 1983), 287. English translation mine.

[35] For a discussion of the pseudo-scientific basis for the Nazi racial ideology and its use as justification for racial warfare, see Peter J. Haas, *Morality After Auschwitz: The Radical Challenge of the Nazi Ethic*, esp. 22–30. On the connections between

justification for German hegemonic pretensions but also as a legitima-
tion for genocide. The geographically bounded nation-state no longer
contained and defined the identity of a people and was displaced by a
racial conception of group identity. As a result of this redefinition of
peoples along racial lines, German-speaking Jews living in Germany and
in other countries under Nazi occupation were forced to reevaluate
their identities as Germans, Jews, and citizens of social communities
that had formerly accepted or at least tolerated them.[36] For Nelly Sachs
in exile in Sweden, this meant a clash between her childhood memories
of Germany and her experiences under the Third Reich, a conflict that
resulted in an ongoing reassessment of her concept of "Heimat" and
her relationship to the German language.

In a letter of September 1946, Sachs described her sense of loss in
terms that indicate a change in her sense of identity which she no
longer saw defined in terms of national and linguistic affiliations, but
rather in relation to a concept of world community: "Ich habe kein
Land und im Grunde auch keine Sprache. Nur die Inbrunst des Herzens, die über alle Grenzen hinwegeilen will."[37] This statement, quoted
in the preceding chapter in the context of language and "Heimat," not
only eloquently expresses the existential condition of the exile-poet, but
also points toward a theme that runs through much of Sachs's post-
Holocaust writing: the articulation of a shift from exclusionary codes
governing relationships and citizenship to a concept of human community transcending geographical, racial, cultural, and ethnic boundaries.

---

racism, expansionism, and world hegemony, see Hannah Arendt, *The Origins of Totalitarianism* (1951; New York: Meridian Books, 1958), esp. 170, 227–35.

[36] The much touted German-Jewish symbiosis attributed to the period from the
Enlightenment into the early twentieth-century has long been the subject of contes-
tation and debate. Although Gershom Scholem may have been one of the first to
dispute this alleged symbiosis, it was Dan Diner's essay "Negative Symbiose. Deutsche und Juden nach Auschwitz," *Babylon* 1 (1986): 9–20 that catalyzed a renewal of
the debate. The rash of commemorative events and an increasingly commodifying
politics of memory in reunified Germany have further fueled the discussion and
raised the stakes by connecting Germany's ostensibly enlightened past with the realization of a democratic state in the present. Since 1990 several book-length analyses
addressing the German-Jewish relationship across time have appeared, among them
Enzo Traverso's *The Jews & Germany: From the "Judeo-German Symbiosis" to the
Memory of Auschwitz* (Lincoln/London: U of Nebraska P, 1995); Steven Aschheim's
*Culture and Catastrophe: German and Jewish Confrontations with National Socialism
and Other Crises* (New York: New York UP, 1996); and Y. Michal Bodemann,
Gedächtnistheater: Die jüdische Gemeinschaft und ihre deutsche Erfindung (Berlin:
Rotbuch, 1996).

[37] Letter to Gudrun Dähnert, *Briefe*, 65.

Raised as the only child of assimilated Jewish parents in Berlin at the turn of the century, Sachs grew up in an environment in which the German cultural tradition, especially music and literature, played a central role. Although her parents were members of the Jewish community, they did not attend synagogue or celebrate traditional Jewish holidays. As a result of this minimal exposure to Jewish culture and tradition, Sachs had no developed sense of a Jewish identity in her youth and young adulthood. She regarded herself unselfconsciously as a German, in no way other or different from her peers. The degree to which Sachs's family had adopted a bourgeois, cosmopolitan concept of identity indifferent to ethnic or religious distinctions is revealed in an anecdote passed on by Bengt Holmqvist, a long-time friend of the poet during her life in Sweden. Holmqvist tells of an occasion where Sachs was completely bewildered at being labeled a Jew at the integrated school she attended as a girl in Berlin:

> Ein einziges Mal — und eigentlich ohne Bosheit — ist sie in der Schule als Jüdin bezeichnet worden. Die Eltern konnten ihr ruhig versichern, daß solche Distinktionen nunmehr vollkommen bedeutungsleer seien.[38]

As a young woman, Sachs was drawn to the works of the German Romantics, especially Novalis, as well as the works of Christian mystics such as Jakob Böhme, and these interests are reflected in the style and content of her early writings.[39] It was not until the 1930s and the advent of restrictive and segregational policies directed at the German-Jewish population that Sachs seriously began to explore Jewish traditions, immersing herself in works of and about Jewish mysticism by Martin Buber and Gershom Scholem. Nevertheless, her strong interest in these writings did not displace her earlier attraction to Christian traditions. Instead she combined and melded aspects from both Jewish and Christian sources in her subsequent works.

For Sachs, the division between her Jewishness and her Germanness would remain problematic. Her identification with both was a constant

---

[38] Bengt Holmqvist, "Die Sprache der Sehnsucht," *Das Buch der Nelly Sachs*, 25. This supports Claudia Koonz's observation from her interviews with German-Jewish women survivors that the social environment for school-age children was well integrated in Germany into the 1920s. Cf. Claudia Koonz, *Mothers in the Fatherland: Women, the Family, and Nazi Politics* (New York: St. Martin's Press, 1987), 351–52.

[39] For a discussion of the influence and evidence of Romanticism and Christian mysticism on Sachs's work, see Ruth Dinesen, *"Und Leben hat immer wie Abschied geschmeckt": Frühe Gedichte und Prosa der Nelly Sachs* (Stuttgart: Hans-Dieter Heinz Akademischer Verlag, 1987), and Claudia Beil, *Sprache als Heimat.*

source of tension in an atmosphere of oppression insistent that she assume a distinct and immutable identity.[40] The opposition between
Germans and Jews established under the Nazi regime would continue
to plague Sachs long after the end of the war, not only in her own self-
perception, but also in the reception of her work. The history of her reception in Germany indicates that the German media seemed intent on
upholding the dichotomous division of German and Jew and persisted
in classifying Sachs as a distinctly "Jewish" writer.[41] The tenacity of this
label is what Ehrhard Bahr sees as contributing to three phases or tendencies in the reception of Sachs's work in Germany. In his 1980
monograph, Bahr describes these three phases as follows:

> erstens die Vereinnahmung der Dichterin als Symbol deutsch-
> jüdischer Versöhnung, zweitens die Distanzierung von ihr als einer im
> Grunde fremden Dichterin und drittens eine pseudo-literar-kritische
> Haltung, die den falschen Kult, der um die Dichterin getrieben wur-
> de, zum Vorwand benutzte, um ihr Werk abzulehnen. . . . [42]

In the 1961 volume of *Nelly Sachs zu Ehren*, both Johannes Edfelt
and Hans Magnus Enzensberger praise Sachs as an ideal spokeswoman
for the suffering of the Jewish people and note with admiration that her
message is without a trace of hatred.[43] The apotheosis of Nelly Sachs
observable in the reviews in this collection led to a series of prestigious
literary prizes culminating in the Nobel prize award in 1966.[44] In her

---

[40] Dinesen discusses Nelly Sachs's relation to her dual identity as a unresolved crisis in which she remained suspended — split between two legacies which shaped her
and to which she felt divided loyalties. Cf. *Nelly Sachs: Eine Biographie*, 107. Dinesen
argues that it is this tension between her Germanness and Jewishness that serves as
the foundation of her poetry.

[41] Dinesen credits Kurt Pinthus as the first critic to label Sachs as a "Jewish" lyri-
cist in a 1936 collection of poetry he edited for a Berlin newspaper publication
(Dinesen, *Nelly Sachs*, 100). In the reception of Sachs's work after 1945, she was
consistently labelled as the poet of the Jewish fate (cf. Berendsohn) a restrictive categorization that her Swedish critic Olof Lagercrantz protested against as a continua-
tion of the tradition that had denied her Germanness during the Third Reich. Cf.
Lagercrantz, *Versuch über die Lyrik der Nelly Sachs*, 48–49.

[42] Ehrhard Bahr, *Nelly Sachs*, 18.

[43] Cf. Johannes Edfelt, "Die Dichterin Nelly Sachs," in *Nelly Sachs zu Ehren*
(Frankfurt am Main: Suhrkamp, 1961), esp. 58; Hans Magnus Enzensberger, "Die
Steine der Freiheit," in *Nelly Sachs zu Ehren*, esp. 47–50.

[44] It should be noted that Sachs was not seeking material profit from these literary prizes. In fact, she donated the entire sum of the Nobel prize award (300,000
Kronen) to the needy of the world. This is attested to by Michael Braun's introduction to *Nelly Sachs "an letzter Atemspitze des Lebens"*, 21.

monograph on Nelly Sachs, Gabriele Fritsch-Vivié claims that the consciously limited perception of Sachs as a specifically Jewish writer was
the basis for the Nobel committee's decision to award her the literature
prize, an argument which would seem to be supported by the fact that
the committee split the prize between Sachs and the Israeli poet Samuel
Joseph Agnon who wrote exclusively in Hebrew.[45] Ironically, the identification that had previously made her a target of persecution and oppression had been redefined as the justification for her worth as a poet.
Yet even this recognition was subject to the vicissitudes of a German
public still torn between remorse and resentment for its accountability
for the Holocaust. The status of her identity remained a problem for
this public, who, although briefly recognizing and grudgingly acknowledging Sachs as a Nobel laureate in 1966, still persisted in denying her
Germanness. This point is made all too clearly in the reactions of the
German press when Heinrich Böll was awarded the Nobel prize in
1972 and jubilantly lauded as "der erste Deutsche seit Hermann
Hesse!" Hesse had been awarded the Nobel prize in 1946.[46]

Questions of belonging, nationality, and individual identity raised
by the experiences of categorization and exile inform Sachs's work from
the 1940s onward and inspire transformations in her conceptions of
identity, selfhood, and "Heimat." In her poetic experimentations with
themes and images of tradition and community, Sachs appropriated aspects of Jewish tradition and Christian symbolism and synthesized a
construct of "home" resistant to conventional boundary distinctions.
Although the establishment of the state of Israel in 1948 triggered a series of poetic representations of a primordial Jewish "Heimat," the Israel Nelly Sachs envisioned in her poetry is a multi-layered trope,
shifting in its evocations of geographic place, historical tribe, suffering
body, and spiritual homeland. In an unpublished interview with Radio
Israel in 1966, Sachs describes the Jewish state in Palestine enthusiasti-
cally as

---

[45] Fritsch-Vivié, 134. This argument has a long history in Nelly Sachs scholarship, and Fritsch-Vivié here merely reiterates what has come to be a widely accepted
explanation for the Nobel committee's decision to award Sachs the prize for literature in 1966, where the fact that she received the prize together with the Hebrew
poet Samuel Joseph Agnon is used as the main defense of the argument that the
1966 award was largely a symbolic act of restitution for what the world had let happen to the Jews.

[46] In her article on Nelly Sachs, Ingrid Strobl condemns the reactions of the
German public and the persistent lack of recognition for Nelly Sachs's achievements
as a German poet in the German press. Cf. Ingrid Strobl, "Nelly Sachs," *Emma* 8
(1988): 31.

... eine Heimat für alle, die nach dem furchtbaren Weltgeschehen heimatlos geworden sind: Für die Gejagten und Gefolterten eine Zuflucht. Für die Jugend endlich das Glück, selbst die Fruchtbarmachung des eigenen Bodens zu erleben.[47]

Her attitude toward the state of Israel was not always so unequivocally positive, however. The founding of a specifically Jewish state also filled her with apprehension that the victims of yesterday would become the perpetrators of tomorrow. In a letter written in reaction to the assassination of UN ambassador Folke Bernadotte by Jewish terrorists in 1948 she wrote: "Wie soll man es nur ertragen das Einzige was wir besessen haben, die Reinheit der Verfolgten, verloren zu haben, nun selbst Verfolger zu werden."[48] A month later she expressed her concern in a more pleading tone: "Man kann nur bitten und flehen, daß die Verfolgten niemals Verfolger werden."[49]

In "AUF DASS DIE VERFOLGTEN NICHT VERFOLGER WERDEN" (*FS* 77–78), a poem that both suggests and decries the apparent interchangeability of persecutor and persecuted, Sachs depicts the continuity of persecution and violence culminating in the triumph of the executioners. Using the technique of repetition that recurs throughout her post-Holocaust writings, Sachs establishes a setting in which the victory of the "Henker" over the "Opfer" is predestined, inevitable, and unalterable.

> SCHRITTE —
> In welchen Grotten der Echos
> seid ihr bewahrt,
> die ihr den Ohren einst weissagtet
> kommenden Tod?
>
> Schritte —
> Nicht Vogelflug, noch Schau der Eingeweide,
> noch der blutschwitzende Mars
> gab des Orakels Todesauskunft mehr —
> nur Schritte —
>
> Schritte —
> Urzeitspiel von Henker und Opfer,
> Verfolger und Verfolgten,
> Jäger und Gejagt —

---

[47] Cited in Bahr, *Nelly Sachs*, 63.

[48] Berendsohn, 146.

[49] *Briefe*, 97.

Schritte
die die Zeit reißend machen
die Stunde mit Wölfen behängen,
dem Flüchtling die Flucht auslöschen
im Blute.

Schritte
die Zeit zählend mit Schreien, Seufzern,
Austritt des Blutes bis es gerinnt,
Todesschweiß zu Stunden häufen —

Schritte der Henker
über Schritten der Opfer,
Sekundenzeiger im Gang der Erde,
von welchem Schwarzmond schrecklich gezogen?

In der Musik der Sphären
wo schrillt euer Ton?

The scenarios represented here imply that the age-old conflict between the hunters and the hunted, paradigmatic of the "Us versus Them" opposition, is intrinsic to human nature and therefore unlikely to change. In fact, the conflict itself has come to serve a purpose in human history as a mechanism for marking time and the poetic persona notes with bitterness that the progress of mortal existence is measured according to this dependable cycle of oppression and conquest. In the sixth strophe, the steps of the persecutors drown out or walk over those of the victims, a superimposition that is transformed in the final lines of the poem into a conflation of the two in the plural You. This conflation of oppositions into a combined plural voice indicates their affinities and subsumes the apparent opposition between them. The association evoked by the repeated recurrence of the footsteps is that of an echo, here a representation of memory triggered by this trace of sound. The steps are both anticipatory and recollective, resonant with all that they suggest but do not name in the first strophe, they assume a prescient quality. No oracle foretells the deaths and destruction that follow, "nur Schritte —."

The motif of unrelenting footsteps that binds this poem together also serves as a central image in Sachs's only published prose account of her experiences in Germany under the Nazi regime. In this text entitled "Leben unter Bedrohung," the footsteps serve as an audible synecdoche for the oppressors and the advancing, inescapable quality of their power: "Es kamen Schritte. Starke Schritte. Schritte in denen das Recht sich häuslich niedergelassen hatte. Schritte stießen an die Tür. Sofort

sagten sie, die Zeit gehört uns!"[50] The ultimate triumph of the perpetrators foretold in "Schritte" comes across here in the active, aggressive,
and self-proclaimed assumption of control by the oppressors. While the
prose text is a recollection of the poet's victimization by the Nazis in
which the division between the persecuted and the persecutor is made
according to racial criteria, the poem transfigures this division of "Us
versus Them" by leaving the signifiers "Henker" and "Opfer" unin-
habited by specific characteristics that render them identifiable as members of this or that group. The ambiguity and openness of these
positions is precisely what represents the danger that they will be occupied in an endless chain of substitutions, as a fixed opposition dictating
human history.

In the context of this fear of an endless repetition and replication of
the hunter/hunted opposition, "AUF DASS DIE VERFOLGTEN
NICHT VERFOLGER WERDEN" marks a transition in Sachs's poetic
portrayal of Israel. After witnessing escalating Israeli-Arab violence and
unrest in the 1950s and 1960s, she increasingly distanced herself from
the state that was to have reestablished Zion as the historical and spiritual home of the Jews. Her own lyrical contribution toward the promotion of an atmosphere of spiritual community and harmony became
more important to her than the realization of a Jewish nation-state.

The recurring themes of flight and exile prevalent in Sachs's work
not only signify the sense of rootlessness and loss experienced by the
exile-survivor but also privilege this condition as a kind of existential
universal. The homelessness of the poetic persona is at once deplored
and presented as a positively valued potential for change. In losing the
bond to a geographically defined homeland, the exile assumes an open
and fluid relationship to the world enabling her to transcend the re-
strictions that bind and divide individuals and states. This privileged
condition of the exile is presented in the poem "IN DER FLUCHT"
(FS 262), which Sachs used as a closing for her Nobel acceptance
speech in Stockholm in 1966. In this poem the poetic persona's acknowledgment that the condition of flight and exile is permanent engenders an attitude not of despair but rather one open to change:

> IN DER FLUCHT
> welch großer Empfang
> unterwegs —
>
> Eingehüllt
> in der Winde Tuch

---

[50] Reprinted in Berendsohn, 10.

Füße im Gebet des Sandes
der niemals Amen sagen kann
denn er muß
von der Flosse in den Flügel
und weiter —

Der kranke Schmetterling
weiß bald wieder vom Meer —
Dieser Stein
mit der Inschrift der Fliege
hat sich mir in die Hand gegeben —

An Stelle von Heimat
halte ich die Verwandlungen der Welt —

The allusion to the hospitality of the place that gave refuge to the exile is both an acknowledgment of the reception Sachs met with in Sweden and an affirmation of a sense of community outside of national boundaries. Through the poetic persona's experience of exile, the former affinity with a specific "homeland" is displaced by a concern with the welfare of the world. In this, Sachs is also resisting the exclusivity of the orthodox view of the Jewish people as unique among nations and specially chosen by God.[51] Ruth Dinesen argues that the representation of exile in Sachs's work reflects both questions of her own position and identity as a German-Jewish poet writing in Sweden and a transformed concept of "Heimat" as community:

Der gefährliche Balanceakt zwischen dem Selbstverständnis der Dichterin als einer Deutschen und der aufgezwungenen jüdischen Identität hatte sie über die Grenzen der Nationalitäten zu einer Gemeinschaft von Menschen im Exil geführt, im Zustand des Fremdseins den Weg zu einer "eigentlichen" Heimat gewiesen. Ein weltumspannender Grundzustand, mit dem sie sich identifiziert, Begriffe wie Meridian, Äquator, Längen- und Breitengrade, Exil als Asyl, Flucht als Heimat sind in ihrer späten Dichtung Bilder für ein neues Identitätsganzes.[52]

The theme of homelessness Sachs addresses in many of her poems can be read as a consequence of attitudes toward identity that insist upon separation and autonomy and deny plurality and intermediary positions. Such identity politics are dependent upon categories that organize individuals into hierarchical groups, which for the racial taxonomy

---

[51] Cf. II Samuel 7: 23: "And what one nation in the earth is like thy people, even like Israel, whom God went to redeem for a people to himself, and to make him a name . . ."

[52] Dinesen, *Nelly Sachs*, 345.

practiced under Hitler meant that identity was grounded in blood and
not in language, birthplace, or belief. The connection between blood,
identity, and oppression is made clearly in the poem "EINEN
AKKORD spielen Ebbe und Flut" (*FS* 161) which also takes up the
theme of opposition between the hunter and the hunted as a cyclical
process akin to the ebb and flow of the tide.

> EINEN AKKORD spielen Ebbe und Flut,
> Jäger und Gejagtes.
> Mit vielen Händen
> wird Greifen und Befestigung versucht,
> Blut ist der Faden.
>
> Finger weisen Aufstellungen,
> Körperteile werden eingesetzt
> in sterbende Zeichnungen.
>
> Strategie,
> Geruch des Leiden —
>
> Glieder auf dem Wege zum Staub
> und die Gischt der Sehnsucht
> über den Wassern.

In the first strophe, the preoccupation with a system of categorization grounded in genetics is portrayed through the image of the many
hands grappling for a stable hold, i.e. the goal of distinguishing one
identity from another is a matter of mutual interest. Joined not only by
this common cause, the hunter and the hunted are also united in their
common mortality. Similar to the conclusion of "AUF DASS DIE
VERFOLGTEN NICHT VERFOLGER WERDEN" discussed above,
the opposition between the persecuted and the persecutor is represented as insignificant in the context of human mortality, evoked by the
image of disintegrating limbs in the last strophe: "Glieder auf dem
Wege zum Staub." What remains is a trace, transcient yet enduring, of
a unity that had never existed and a longing that spans the waters and
by association the world.

In the poem "Alle Länder haben unter meinem Fuß" from Sachs's
1965 collection *Glühende Rätsel* (*SL* 46), the poetic persona reflects
upon the experiences of aggressive and exclusionary nationalism that
have resulted in her uprooted condition:

> Alle Länder haben unter meinem Fuß
> ihre großen Schrecken angewurzelt
> die hängen schwer-uralte Ziehbrunnen
> immer überfüllend den Abend
> das tötende Wort —

So kann ich nicht sein
nur im Stürzen —

The roots associated with a sense of belonging to a country and an identification with the land here evoke unequivocally negative associations. Akin to Heine's image of hampered mobility due to the figurative accumulation of earth from the Fatherland on the soles of his shoes,[53] the traces of belonging are here painful stumbling blocks to a true escape into exile. In view of the resistance to categorization and the appeal to a universal humanity elsewhere in Sachs's writings, the horrors that ensnare the feet of the poetic persona in her travels across countries can be read as a recognition of the consequences of nationalism with its pretensions to hegemony and homogeneity which, when taken to the extreme, culminate in the eradication of all that is perceived as "other." The I is in flight from this legacy of violence and destruction, but still trails the metaphorical roots of those experiences that make tracks in her dreams and language. These tenacious roots that continue to impede her paradoxically lend her wandering a kind of anchoring fixity in what can be read as a bitter parody of rootedness-as-belonging.

The final two lines offer an ambiguous resolution to the poetic persona's dilemma. In one reading, the poetic I declares the unlivability of such an existence in which the root-like reminders of suffering and death weigh her down and trip her up. In this reading, the line "nur im Stürzen" refers to her present condition, always stumbling and falling, unable to maintain the balance requisite for being. Another reading of the closing lines reveals the act implied by "Stürzen" to be an alternative to the impeded and entangled wandering characterizing the poetic persona's path in the first strophe. Here the line "So kann ich nicht sein" emphasizes a break with the existential mode described in the preceding strophe and heralds a shift or a transformation in the poetic persona's condition. The uncertainty and ungroundedness of falling becomes a form of resistance to the fetters of bounded identity and to the encumbrance of roots associated with nationalism.

In a world environment that privileges nation and nationhood as the building blocks of sovereignty, the Jews were in an exceptional po-

---

[53] Heinrich Heine, *Briefe*. Vol. 2, ed. Friedrich Hirth (Mainz: Florian Kupferberg Verlag, 1950), 4–5: "Indessen: Fliehen wäre leicht, wenn man nicht das Vaterland an den Schuhsolen mit sich schleppte! (. . .) Es ist schmerzlich, im Luxemburg spaziren [*sic*] zu gehen und überall ein Stück Hamburg oder ein Stück Preußen oder Bayern an den Schuhsolen mit sich herumzuschleppen." I am grateful to Mareike Herrmann for alerting me to this passage in Heine's letters.

sition as simultaneous insiders and outsiders, with the result that they came to serve as paradigmatic figures of "ubiquitously supra-national, universal strangers."[54] The undecidability of the Jews' position as an internationally dispersed yet categorically united people posed a threat and a challenge to conventional notions of national identity. In the following passage from his study *Modernity and the Holocaust*, Zygmunt Bauman presents the nature of this challenge in the contemporary context:

> By the very fact of their territorial dispersion and ubiquity, the Jews were an international nation, a non-national nation. Everywhere, they served as a constant reminder of the relativity and limits of individual self-identity and communal interest, which the criterion of nationhood was meant to determine with absolute and final authority. (. . .) *The Jews were not just unlike any other nation; they were also unlike any other foreigners.* In short, they undermined the very difference between hosts and guests, the native and the foreign. And as nation-hood became the paramount basis of group self-constitution, they came to undermine the most basic of differences: the difference between "Us" and "Them."[55]

In the modern age of the nation-state, the Jews as a group were difficult to classify, a problem that has informed debates surrounding Jewish identity from the nineteenth-century to the present. Theodor Herzl's political Zionism with its insistence on the need for a Jewish state already in the late nineteenth-century spoke to a desire for recognition as a national people that was not to be officially realized until 1948. Ethnicity, religion, culture, and country all serve as criteria on which to base group identity and solidarity, but can also be manipulated to create an artificially homogeneous and exclusionary configuration of a people. In an essay entitled "Judaism" written in the early 1950s, Emmanuel Levinas contests the correlation of Judaism with religion and questions a definition of Jewish identity dependent on an inventory of attributes: "Is it a nationality or a religion, a fossilized civilization that somehow lives on, or the passionate desire for a better world?"[56] This question of what constitutes Judaism in the post-Holocaust context was of central concern for Nelly Sachs as well as Rose Ausländer both as German-speaking Jewish survivors in exile from

---

[54] Bauman, *Modernity and Ambivalence*, 195.

[55] Bauman, *Modernity and the Holocaust*, 52.

[56] Levinas, *Difficult Freedom*, 24.

the countries that had been homes to them and in their self-elected roles as guardians of memory.

Confronted with the extreme racial ideology that ordered their world during the Third Reich, European Jews came to an intensified self-understanding of their Jewishness, one that was for many externally coerced and then reinforced in reaction to persecution and segregation that far exceeded any previous levels of political anti-Semitism in modern Europe. For Nelly Sachs, this confrontation with her Jewishness and the pariah status associated with that identity would lead to an encounter with what she came to see as a universal condition of otherness in human society. In her poetic representations, she increasingly moved away from images of the Jewish people as an isolated collective identified through its alleged difference from the rest of the world toward portrayals of the Jews as representative of a universal humanity. This shift in emphasis to a shared humanity subverts a view of difference as absolute otherness and displaces fixed and stable categories of identification with a more relational and fluid paradigm.[57]

The tendency toward a global perspective of human community was to some extent enabled by Sachs's destabilized positions as survivor, witness, exile, and German-speaking Jew in suspension between multiple traditions and influences, cultural, religious, and historical. The outcome of her struggles to negotiate the complexity of these overlapping and conflicting positions in the anomie of the post-Holocaust world was an openness to transformation and a heightened sensitivity to the human similarities that perceptions of difference so often obscure. Her search for community was not one defined by geographical boundaries or group identities founded on exclusionary categories, i.e. criteria conventionally associated with cohering peoples into nations.[58] Like the poetic persona in Sachs's "Ich bin meinem Heimatrecht auf der Spur" (*SL* 92), the community she longed for was one based on acceptance:

[57] Iris Marion Young argues that a revaluation of difference as "specificity, variation, heterogeneity" is a prerequisite for achieving a condition of harmony in a pluralistic society. She argues that the logic of difference with its equation of difference and absolute otherness is central to the oppressive and exclusionary formulations of group identity. Cf. *Justice and the Politics of Difference*, 170–71.

[58] Here I disagree with Edward Alexander's assertion that Nelly Sachs's works after 1948 reflect a Zionist impulse. Alexander's argument rests on a constructed correlation between nationality and humanity, in which the establishment of an independent Jewish nation is the prerequisite for the Jews' recognition as human beings. This view, however, addresses one moment in Sachs's work and disregards the complexity of her shifting attitudes toward the concept of "homeland" and of community. Cf. Edward Alexander, *The Resonance of Dust*, 48–51.

Ich bin meinem Heimatrecht auf der Spur
dieser Geographie nächtlicher Länder
wo die zur Liebe geöffneten Arme
gekreuzigt an den Breitengraden hängen
bodenlos in Erwartung —

Rose Ausländer's turn to Jewish tradition, if it could be called that, was not as sudden or as marked as that of Nelly Sachs. Raised in a culturally vital Jewish environment in Czernowitz in the Bukovina, Rosalie Scherzer had a strong sense of her Jewish heritage as a child and as an adult was active in the Czernowitz Jewish community. Confronted with the uncertainties of living in an area of shifting national affiliation and appropriation, Ausländer's relationship to the German language and her Jewish heritage served as anchoring constants in an otherwise unstable environment. The destabilizing experience of living in a region subject to repeated annexations was further intensified by Rose Ausländer's emigrations, and these experiences combined to reinforce the split between residency and identity that informs Ausländer's biography and her poetry. [59]

Rose Ausländer emigrated to the United States for the first time in 1921 together with a university acquaintance, Ignaz Ausländer, whom she married in 1923. The relationship did not last and she divorced Ausländer in 1930, retaining her married name because it suited her self-understanding as a perpetual foreigner. In 1931 she returned to Rumania and lived alternately in Czernowitz and Budapest. After a brief return to New York in 1939, Ausländer remained in Czernowitz until her second emigration to the United States in 1946. After nearly twenty years in the country where she had twice been granted citizenship, Ausländer decided to return to Europe and settled permanently in West Germany in 1965. Influenced by her many travels and relocations, Rose Ausländer developed a concept of identity that transcended national and cultural boundaries. Yet perhaps because of her experiences as a multiple emigré, her articulation of this transgressive condition is

[59] The Bukovina as a region changed hands numerous times during Ausländer's residence there. Part of the Austro-Hungarian empire at the beginning of the twentieth-century, the Bukovina was then occupied by Russian troops during World War I. In 1918 it was incorporated into Rumania. During World War II, the Bukovina was occupied by the Nazi SS in 1941 and the Jews were targeted for liquidation, a massacre that only ten percent of the Jewish population survived. In 1944, Soviet troops took control of the Bukovina and the Soviet Union then annexed the territory at the end of the war. At that time, the resident population was given the choice of either naturalization as Soviet citizens or emigration. Ausländer and the surviving remnant of her family chose to emigrate.

more consciously autobiographical and less abstract than the terminology of universal human community Sachs adopts.

Ausländer's representations of the "self-in-process" are in part based on her own emigration experiences and in part on the ideals she developed for harmonious community and authentic human relationships. The poem "Selbstporträt" (V 203) from the 1979 collection *Ein Stück weiter* combines autobiographical references with the fantasy of a new self-constellation that bridges national boundaries.

> Jüdische Zigeunerin
> deutschsprachig
> unter schwarzgelber Fahne
> erzogen
>
> Grenzen schoben mich
> zu Lateinern Slaven
> Amerikanern Germanen
>
> Europa
> in deinem Schoß
> träume ich
> meine nächste Geburt

The poem opens with a heterogeneous image of the poetic persona's identity. The poetic persona's self-characterization as a German-speaking Jewish gypsy can be read as an attempt to address the multiplicity of positions she occupies. Cilly Helfrich argues for a different reading of the gypsy, namely as a metaphor for an interpreter of signs and fates, a kind of soothsayer whose calling is akin to that of the poet. The gypsy's art of interpreting signs from another system of meaning and putting them into language is yet another manifestation of the discursive foundation of the world.[60] The second strophe reveals the power national boundaries wield over the poetic persona: she is a pawn in the hands of anthropomorphized countries that move her around like a game piece. Neither her identity nor her residency are of her own choosing and it is only in the final strophe that she assumes a more active role in determining what constitutes her self, albeit only in the realm of a dream vision of an undivided Europe.

The aspect of choice absent in "Selbstporträt" is a central feature of Ausländer's later poem "Daheim" (VI 27) which is a thinly veiled portrayal of her decision to make Germany her adopted home:[61]

---

[60] See Helfrich, 62.

[61] Both Helmut Braun and Michaela Kessner read Ausländer's settlement in Germany in 1965 as a kind of return, "eine Rückkehr in den deutschen Sprachraum" (Kess-

> In der Fremde
> daheim
>
> Land meiner Muttersprache
> sündiges büßendes Land
> ich wählte dich
> als meine Wohnung
> Heimatfremde
>
> wo ich viele
> fremde Freunde
> liebe

Here the connections between language, identity, love, and community are made in a poetic idiom that renders a complex existential situation with deceptive simplicity. Each line both reveals and conceals a contradiction and conflict: between foreignness and belonging, language and nationality, guilt and atonement. Yet like the transgressive poetic persona in search of a community joined by acceptance rather than segregation in Sachs's "Ich bin meinem Heimatrecht auf der Spur," the poetic I in this poem finds that those conflicts can be overcome through friendships that have the power to transform the foreign into the familiar.[62]

The positive representations of exile presented in the works discussed above stand in contrast to the poetic depictions of return and homecoming in the following texts. Rose Ausländer's "Wandlung" (III 218) portrays the "homecoming" of the refugees not as a return to a society in which they are accepted as members, but as an ostracization that takes place in what had once been their home:

> Wir kamen heim
> ohne Rosen
> sie blieben im Ausland
>
> Unser Garten liegt
> begraben im Friedhof

---

ner, 15). In their readings of this return, they argue that for Ausländer the German language became fused with the concept of "home," which in this particular poem is somehow magically freed of the associations and implications of German history.

[62] In their comparative study of Rose Ausländer and Hilde Domin, Harald Vogel and Michael Gans offer an intriguing reading of the familiar and the foreign in this poem. They deconstruct the term "daheim" into its component parts, arguing that "da" signifies "die gegenwärtige Fremde" whereas "heim" evokes associations with home, "Heimat" and — in what seems to be an interpretive reach — also the convalescent home where Ausländer resided at the time. See *Rose Ausländer/Hilde Domin*, 157.

Es hat sich
vieles in vieles
verwandelt

Wir sind Dornen geworden
in fremden Augen

The roses of welcome are presented to the refugees ironically not by
their own country but by the countries where they found asylum. The
neglected offering of roses of homecoming in the first strophe is intensified by the image of the dead garden in the lines that follow. The garden that had belonged to the We has died, implying that this collective
has been displaced as a growing and living force, buried by the victors
who wish to erase the traces of the past. The contiguity of the images
of the roses and the vanquished garden evokes associations to the symbolic value of the rose as the essence or presentness of life.[63] Home is
no longer the life-infused environment it once was — and the roses
that were left behind in exile can be read as either the nostalgic long-
ings for now unrecuperable lives or the discarded petals of lives the We
no longer recognize as theirs. The transformation in the direction of
wider understanding and community that the refugees had hoped to
witness upon their return reveals itself to be a self-referential caricature
of change, a reversion to the hegemony of the They who had originally
cast them out as unwanted others.[64] In a bitter allusion to the absent
roses, the poetic voice notes that the We have themselves become par-
tial substitutes for the flowers, greeted, however, not with affection but
rather as unwelcome and thorny reminders of a past that the They
would rather deny.

The unshakeable opposition between the We and the They with its
resistance to the allegedly transformative processes of history and time
in Ausländer's "Wandlung" is presented in Sachs's "WELT, frage
nicht die Todentrissenen" (*FS* 114) as a conflict between the survivors

[63] This usage of the rose image as representative of life's essence can also be
found in several of Nelly Sachs's poems. I offer a brief treatment of the "rose" in
Sachs's poetry later in this chapter.

[64] In the portrayal of the problematic return of the Other as refugee, this poem
speaks to a phenomenon of displacement and repression that Eric Santner calls the
"denial of mourning" among the "German" population after the war. This denial
grew out of a refusal to recognize the subjectivity of the Other — the identity of the
Other was paradoxically erased once again in the process of denying its erasure, because "Germans had to mourn *as Germans* for those whom they had excluded and
exterminated in their mad efforts to produce their 'Germanness.'" Cf. Eric Santner,
Stranded Objects: Mourning, Memory, and Postwar Germany (Ithaca/London: Cornell UP, 1990), 6.

of the catastrophe and the rest of the world. In the first strophe, the survivors are portrayed as perpetual refugees, strangers who have been rendered permanently Other by the force of their experiences of persecution and destruction.

WELT, frage nicht die Todentrissenen
wohin sie gehen,
sie gehen immer ihrem Grabe zu.
Das Pflaster der fremden Stadt
war nicht für die Musik von Flüchtlingsschritten gelegt worden —
Die Fenster der Häuser, die eine Erdenzeit spiegeln
mit den wandernden Gabentischen der Bilderbuchhimmel —
wurden nicht für Augen geschliffen
die den Schrecken an seiner Quelle tranken.
Welt, die Falte ihres Lächelns hat ihnen ein starkes Eisen ausgebrannt;
sie möchten so gerne zu dir kommen
um deiner Schönheit wegen,
aber wer heimatlos ist, dem welken alle Wege
wie Schnittblumen hin —

The fatalism of the opening lines indicates the inescapability of death even for those who survived — paradoxically the survivors do not turn toward life after being spared, but instead remain focussed on the grave. This incapacity or incapacitation for a livable life is deepened by their sense of alienation in their present surroundings. Using a series of passive constructions to describe the refugees' strangeness and estrangement, Sachs emphasizes the victim status of the survivors and their lack of power as agents in their adopted environments. Their will, like their smiles, has been broken or extinguished by their oppressors, represented in the tenth line by the "starkes Eisen," an image that evokes associations to the martial strength and nationalistic ideology connected with the German "Blut und Eisen" tradition.

In their poetic representations of childhood, homeland, belief, and the Other, Sachs and Ausländer experimented with constructs of self and community that reflected their perceptions of the past, their understanding of the present, and their hopes for the future. The synthesis of these positions and identifications is manifest in their poems celebrating Israel as the primordial and redemptive home of the Jewish people while simultaneously mourning the loss of "Heimat" in the countries of their birth. It is further apparent in their identification with the victims of the Holocaust through poetic personæ who bear witness for the dead while simultaneously acknowledging the potential interchangeability of victim and oppressor. And it is demonstrated in their appropriation of both Jewish and Christian traditions bound together with their continued connection and loyalty to the German language.[65] The tensions between and combinations of Germanness and Jewishness in their writings are complicated by oppositions between "Heimat" and exile, an opposition that raises the question of relationship to a national homeland. Their disrupted relationships to a national identity result in a search for alternatives for identification and community that would transcend the narrow confines of conventional conceptions of nation with its exclusionary political and cultural boundaries.

The idea of "Heimat" as a kind of "'being-together' of strangers"[66] that Sachs and Ausländer attempted to construct through the medium of poetry is not grounded in land or language but in an ideal of mutual acceptance and respect that would transform human relationships and by extension the world. In part, this view of community could be read both as a response and a coping strategy in the condition of exile that necessitated a re-visioning of what constitutes belonging. The nation had proven itself untenable as a viable social form and another basis for belonging had to be found. The basis for this belonging in Nelly Sachs's vision was neither blood nor soil, but love and acceptance.[67]

From their writings, it is apparent that Sachs and Ausländer regarded the boundaries between their Jewishness and Germanness as at once exclusionary and permeable. Yet the tendency in their post-Holocaust works toward an extrapolation of Jewish experience to universal human experience testifies to their efforts to overcome the dichotomy between German and Jew, as well as that between the Jew as Other and the rest of the world. In their appeal to the universality of Jewish experience as a basis for ethical action, Sachs and Ausländer anticipate Levinas's post-war re-visioning of the idea of the Chosen People: "The idea of a chosen people must not be taken as a sign of pride. It does not involve being aware of exceptional rights, but of exceptional duties. It is the preroga-

---

[65] Cf. Claudia Beil for a detailed discussion of the synthesis of traditions and influences apparent in Sachs's and Ausländer's works. Beil focusses on the poets' affiliations and affinities with Jewish and Christian mysticism and Romanticism and argues that their works demonstrate a successful symbiosis of German and Jewish culture. Although Beil otherwise demonstrates critical acumen in examining her subject, she reveals a simplistic understanding of what constitutes culture in her argument that the poets' persistent use of the German language is the strongest evidence of their enduring bond to German culture (11).

[66] Young, "The Ideal of Community and the Politics of Difference," 318.

[67] Sachs's concept of community based on love and empathy rather than nationality or denomination parallels Simone Weil's ideal of being-at-home in the world even as an exile in *Gravity and Grace*, 86: "We must take the feeling of being at home into exile. We must be rooted in the absence of place."

tive of a moral consciousness itself."[68] It is this sense of duty and moral consciousness that pervades the works of both Sachs and Ausländer and compels them to continue writing. The atmosphere of acceptance they seek is one that has moved beyond restrictive systems of privilege based on citizenship and ethnicity to a global view of social relations grounded in recognition and responsibility.

Self and Other

We purchase identity at the price of estrangement. We know who we are only insofar as we know who we are not. We both crave and fear redemption because its reward and its price are the same: disappearance of the individual into the Source whence he came.

— Richard Rubenstein[69]

The disproportion between the Other and the self is precisely moral consciousness. Moral consciousness is not an experience of values, but an access to external being: external being is, par excellence, the Other.

— Emmanuel Levinas[70]

The mother/child bond discussed at the outset of this chapter serves as a paradigm for the originary Self/Other relation through which the process of identity formation takes place. The process of coming to identity as a coming to self-consciousness is, however, fraught with contradictory impulses that fragment the developing self. In the context of the Third Reich in which Self/Other distinctions were exclusionary and violently imposed rather than relational, the fundamental role of the Self-Other dyad in social relations was necessarily altered. Although the mother/child relation has been shown to contain points of conflict, these are imbedded in an implicit connection that can be resisted but not denied. The "othering" of the Jews in the opposition established and instrumentalized with genocidal purpose by the Nazis, however, demonstrates the total breakdown of the relational aspect of the Self-Other connection through the denial of the Other's humanity. The Jew as Other was not considered a reflection or even a foil to the self, but rather something absolutely Other, so alien and unassimilable as to justify calculated and systematic extermination. The recognition of

---

[68] Levinas, *Difficult Freedom*, 176.

[69] Rubenstein, *After Auschwitz*, 219.

[70] Levinas, *Difficult Freedom*, 293.

the Other as Thou, presented by Buber as the prerequisite for establishing a relationship founded on acceptance and respect, was thus forcibly erased by Nazi racial ideology.

It is the I-Thou relation with a human face, the interconnectedness of the other and the self, that Nelly Sachs and Rose Ausländer seek to reestablish in their poetry. The I represented in their poems is not an individual alone but obtains its sense of subjectivity through its identification and relation with a discursive other, recognized as a "Thou."[71] In the process of coming to self-realization through the other, however, the I experiences a moment of self-alienation, a recognition of itself as other to itself, as also and already a "Thou." This recognition precedes the final stage of self-realization in which the self becomes capable of entering into genuine relationships as an I encountering a "Thou."[72] The resulting I-Thou relation is based on mutual recognition and love, love not in the sense of an affection but rather as "an acceptance, a confirmation of the other as he [*sic*] is and even as he [*sic*] might become. (. . .) realized not in I nor in Thou as states of feeling. . . but between them."[73] In contrast to this ideal I-Thou relation, the reality of Self/Other encounters in an environment saturated with traditions of prejudice, ethnocentrism, and racism has a decidedly different quality. In a poem entitled "WAS IST DAS ANDERE" (*SL* 116), Nelly Sachs portrays the negative existential reality of the Other, here implicitly understood to be the Jew as paradigmatic pariah, within a social structure that denies this Other a human identity.

> WAS IST DAS ANDERE
> auf das ihr Steine werft?
> Das andere —
> Ist die salzige Rose
> die mein Volk in mein Blut geweint?
>
> Aber Sterbende
> werden nicht mehr
> von Menschenhand getroffen —

---

[71] Cf. Martin Buber's discussion of the dynamics of the I-Thou relation in *Werke I*, esp. 97: "Der Mensch wird am Du zum Ich."

[72] Buber, *Werke I*, 97: " . . . bis einmal die Bindung gesprengt ist und das Ich sich selbst, dem abgelösten, einen Augenblick lang wie einem Du gegenübersteht, um alsbald von sich Besitz zu ergreifen und fortan in seiner Bewußtheit in die Beziehungen zu treten."

[73] Cf. Alexander Kohanski's study *Martin Buber's Philosophy of Interhuman Relation* (East Brunswick, NJ: Associated UP, 1982) for a discussion of love as one of the four potencies in Buber's theory of communication, esp. 26–30.

The poetic persona in this text identifies herself with the Other, figured as an abstraction without human form. She contests this process
of abstracting and dehumanizing the Other, however, in her own specific definition of the Other in the second half of the opening strophe.
Here the poetic persona merges the iconography of Jewish tradition
with the racial terminology of Nazism in an attempt to repossess the
Other as the designation of a flesh-and-blood people whose history is
informed by suffering. The image of the rose in the fourth line, in its
association with the suffering people and the poetic persona's heritage,
draws on the symbolic figuration of Israel as a rose in the Hebrew Bible[74] and in traditional Jewish iconography.[75] The rose as a trope for the
tribe of Israel is reinforced by the next line in which the poetic I proclaims direct kinship with her people. Disturbed by her incomprehen-
sion as to what has inspired the hatred of the collective You she
addresses, the poetic persona seeks to reappropriate an embodied and
human identity for herself and her people through a manipulation of
racially tinged terminology. The attribution of the categories of "Volk"
and "Blut" to her people can be read as an illustration of the poetic
persona's attempt to assert the status of the Jews as a people and to reveal the injustice of their victimization as dehumanized "others."

In the second strophe, the singular and unspecific Other named in
the poem's opening lines has been multiplied and transformed into a
plural designation of the dying. This term has no direct referent in the
preceding strophe, yet its association with the Others' victimization is
clear. Those who die are necessarily removed from the sphere of human
influence. In the process, they enter into a condition of "otherness" in
which they are no longer vulnerable to the physical violence visited
upon them by their human tormentors, represented by the striking
hand in the final line.

"WAS IST DAS ANDERE" illustrates the failure to establish a relationship between an I and a Thou because of the constructed alienation
separating the Self from the Other. Through the "othering" of the
other, the I-Thou relation is obstructed. Yet this "othering" phenome-

---

[74] Cf. Song of Songs 2:1. The flower in this passage is variously translated as a
rose, a tulip, or a narcissus.

[75] In his discussion of Paul Celan's poem "Psalm" and the image of the "Nie-
mandsrose," Alvin Rosenfeld notes the significance of Celan's symbolism in connection with the tradition of Jewish religious imagery: "In the imagery of Jewish
religious thought, Israel is often portrayed as a rose growing with its heart toward
heaven, a symbol of the nation's repentance before God." Cf. Alvin Rosenfeld, *A
Double Dying: Reflections on Holocaust Literature* (Bloomington, IN: Indiana UP,
1980), 88.

non does not only occur in the perception of the stranger as radically different, but is infinitely adaptable, affecting even situations in which kinship customarily serves as a bond of relation. In a poem entitled "KAIN!" (*FS* 178–79) from the 1957 collection *Und niemand weiß weiter*, Sachs portrays the destructive violence of an "othering" between brothers, reinterpreting the Biblical story of Cain and Abel in light of contemporary history. In contrast to "WAS IST DAS ANDERE," the relationship of the poetic persona to the perpetrator is direct and immediate, conveyed through the use of "Du" in addressing Cain. Abel, as the corporeally absent Other/brother, is present only as an association and an accusation and otherwise remains unidentified and unnamed.

> KAIN! Um dich wälzen wir uns im Marterbett:
> Warum?
> Warum hast du am Ende der Liebe
> deinem Bruder die Rose[76] aufgerissen?
>
> Warum den unschuldigen Kindlein
> verfrühte Flügel angeheftet?
> Schnee der Flügel
> darauf deine dunklen Fingerabdrücke
> mitgenommen
> in die Wirklichkeit der Himmel schweben?
>
> Was ist das für eine schwarze Kunst
> Heilige zu machen?
> Wo sprach die Stimme
> die dich dazu berief?
>
> Welche pochende Ader
> hat dich ersehnt?
>
> Dich
> der das Grün der Erde
> zum Abladeplatz trägt
>
> Dich
> der das Amen der Welt
> mit einem Handmuskel spricht —
>
> Kain — Bruder — ohne Bruder —

---

[76] Cf. other references to the rose as a symbol of both sacrifice and life essence in Sachs's poems "Wurzeln schlagen" (*FS* 158: "denn mit Wolken schreibt der Schreiber: // *Rose* //schon an einen neuen Himmel / und die Antwort fiel in Asche.") and "Abraham der Engel" (*FS* 203: "Den Tod biegst du aus seiner gläsernen Haut, / bis er bluterschrocken an dir / zur Rose wird / Gott zu gefallen —").

The Biblical story of originary fratricide both anticipates the genocide of the Third Reich and provides it with a timeless foundation. In
the first strophe, the condition of brotherly love is finite and with its
disappearance murder becomes possible. The image of the rose here
again evokes a complex of associations: love, blood, and Israel. The
specificity of the biblical fratricide is expanded in the second strophe,
where the allusion to the premature deaths of innocent children connects the murder of the brother with mass murder and genocide. In the
following strophe, the poetic voice decries this wanton violence and the
senseless martyrdom it generates. Yet despite the direct address to Cain
as a "Du" and as the perpetrator of the murder(s), the poetic persona's
query about another voice of authority that had dictated Cain's actions
exonerates the "Du" from total responsibility. The reference to an outside authority ("Wo sprach die Stimme / die dich dazu berief?") as the
locus of the evil that has overtaken the world allows at least the potential for a reestablishment of a relationship with the "Du" on a human
level, implying the possibility that the I and the You could join in the
common mission of overcoming that evil.

The address to Cain as "Du" is also an illustration of the dialogic
process that Nelly Sachs repeatedly appropriates as a technique for representing the complexity of experience as a continual oscillation of past,
present, and future time in a realm that defies both temporal and spatial
fixity. By the end of the poem, however, the shimmer of hope for reconciliation offered by the potential of alliance against an external evil
appears dim. Cain is the brother, but a brotherless and hence Otherless
brother. The eradication of the brother is in a sense equivalent to Cain's
own erasure in that he defines and defined himself in relation to Abel.
In the end, Cain alone prevails as the spurious victor suspended before
a void of his own creation, a destructive act of eradication visually represented by the dash at the end of the closing line. But Abel's nameless
presence permeates the poem and evokes associations to the namelessness of the many victims of the oppressors for whom Cain figures as a
metaphor. The namelessness of the victim emphasizes the extremity of
his/her erasure as an identity, while the use of Cain's name as a multiple signifier for the originary and categorical murderer levels the particularity and individuality implied by the name. Cain is both himself
and other than himself, both individual and type.

For Rose Ausländer, the conflict between the two brothers is paradigmatic for a kind of primary divisiveness in the world. In a poem
tellingly entitled "Abel" (V 289), Ausländer moves from the familiarity
of a intimate domestic interior to a statement about the split condition
of relationships in the world:

ABEL

Bilder auf den Wänden
Bücher im Schrank

Verstohlen blüht
das kleine Zimmer

Worte Bilder
schenken mir die janusköpfige Welt

KAIN
sagt ein Gesicht

das andre sagt
ABEL

By giving the poem the title of the vanquished brother, Ausländer rein-
scribes Abel as a continuous presence, his murder in fact renders his
memory immortal as a testimony to the strife that separates peoples and
destroys allegiances. The references to pictures and books in the first
lines of the poem intimate a connection between word and image and
the primal conflict Cain and Abel represent. The message given by both
image and text is one of antagonism and ambivalence, characteristics of
the Janus-faced world but also reflected in representation itself. There is
an undecidability within representation, a contest of words and pictures
that remains without a clear victor — Cain may have killed Abel, but
Abel has, or is, both the first and last word in this poem.

The appeal to fraternal relationship as a paradigm for wider
Self/Other interaction is given a decidedly more optimistic portrayal in a
later poem by Rose Ausländer entitled "Bruder" (VI 186). Here the relationship between the poetic persona and the "brother" is one of mutual belonging that bridges the strangeness that separates them. In
contrast to the resigned and sorrowful tone of Sachs's "KAIN" poem,
Ausländer here conveys a hopeful attitude that a state of brotherhood,
exemplified by the I-Thou relation, can be achieved among all people:

Ich gehöre dir
Fremder
der mein Bruder ist
und mir gehört

The affinity the poetic I feels toward the stranger is simultaneously a
recognition of belonging and reciprocity that is not defined by any relationship outside of the encounter. This coincides with Buber's conception of the I-Thou relation as occurring in the "between," at the
place of encounter through which both the I and the Thou are realized: "Ich werde am Du; Ich werdend spreche ich Du. Alles wirkliche

Leben ist Begegnung."[77] The encounter with the Other as a Thou is an address, and the poem itself becomes an address to the Other and an attempt to create a dialogue. This conception of the poem as address to an Other reflects the influence of Buber's philosophy and also anticipates Paul Celan's celebrated description of poetry in "Der Meridian":

> Das Gedicht will zu einem Andern, es braucht dieses Andere, es braucht ein Gegenüber. Es sucht es auf, es spricht sich ihm zu.
> Jedes Ding, jeder Mensch ist dem Gedicht, das auf das Andere zuhält, eine Gestalt dieses Anderen.[78]

This dialogic quality of the poetic re-creation of the I-Thou relation is the theme of Ausländer's poem "Immer im Gespräch" (V 109). The existential condition of the I and the Thou is discursive and communicative:

> Ichworte Duworte
> die dich verwandeln
>
> Auf dem Weg
> zu Wasser Wäldern Bergen
> zu dir
>
> immer im Gespräch
> mit der Atemzeit

The transformative quality of the dialogic encounter with the other indicated in the first pair of lines engenders not only the realization of the You as a self, but also enables a connection with the wider world, signified by the water, forests, and mountains in the second strophe. The self-realization and perceptual enlightenment that grow out of the this dialogue are bounded by a temporal term that is at once the measure of the discursive exchange and the duration of human life: the "Atemzeit" as the time for breathing as well as the time when breathing ends.

In contrast to the implied finitude of the communicative situation in "Immer im Gespräch," the dialogic relation depicted in a somewhat later poem by Rose Ausländer fittingly entitled "Dialog" (VI 68) is explicitly endless, moving from the mortality of the individual to an infinite repetition of discursive encounters into perpetuity:

> Endlos
> der Dialog
>
> Du und die Blume
> du und der Stern

---

[77] Buber, *Werke I*, 85.

[78] Celan, *Gesammelte Werke III*, 198.

du und dein Mitmensch

Ununterbrochene
Zwiesprache
Funke an Funke

Der König in dir
der Bettler in dir

Deine Verzweiflung
deine Hoffnung

Endloser Dialog
mit dem Leben

The poem addresses three levels of dialogic interaction all of which are aspects of the "between" in which the dialogue with the Other takes place:[79] between the self (here self-addressed as "Du") and nature, the self and the cosmos, and the self and a human other.[80] The mutuality of the dialogue is not only discursive but also internalized, the Other is not only addressed and accepted, but is also recognized as an aspect of the self. Through the encounter with the Other, the I or the You as an I recognizes the other in itself, a realization that encourages both empathy and understanding and reveals the ethical quality of the relation.[81]

That the discursive quality of the human condition does not necessarily lead to communication and successful dialogue, however, is a patent fact undenied by the poetic persona even in the attempt to reconstruct the encounter with the Thou within the text. The poem, which in Celan's words is always in search of an Other with which to engage in dialogue, also contains within itself the possibility that this dialogue will not be achieved: "Das Gedicht wird . . . Gespräch — oft ist es verzweifeltes Gespräch."[82] As a dialogue of desperation the poem becomes self-referential, monologic, a plea or a cry against deafness and silence. The poetic I bids to be heard for it is only through the ac-

---

[79] Cf. Martin Buber, "Das Wort, das gesprochen wird," *Werke I*, 444–45.

[80] This parallels the divisions Alexander Kohanski ascribes to Buber's philosophy of communication: science (man/world), social technology (man/fellowman) and religion (man/God). Cf. Kohanski, 12–13.

[81] The recognition of the Other in the self through the medium of dialogue is central to Julia Kristeva's conception of the Self/Other encounter and ethics as "relational, dialogic *practice* in which one acknowledges both the otherness of the other and the otherness of the self to itself." Cf. Marilyn Edelstein's discussion of Kristeva's ethics, "Toward a Feminist Postmodern Poléthique: Kristeva on Ethics and Politics," in *Ethics, Politics, and Difference in Julia Kristeva's Writing*, ed. Kelly Oliver, 196.

[82] Celan, *Gesammelte Werke III*, 198.

knowledgment of the poem as communication that it will have any
resonance. This poetic communication is contingent upon an I-Thou
relation that necessarily involves mutual recognition, of the other, by
the other and as other, in order for dialogue to take place. Nelly Sachs's
"Sie stießen zusammen auf der Straße" (*SL* 73) illustrates a failure of
communication in an encounter between two individuals who are unable to bridge the otherness that both relates and separates them. Their
meeting does not lead to recognition and dialogue, but rather underscores their distance and difference from each other.

> Sie stießen zusammen auf der Straße
> Zwei Schicksale auf dieser Erde
> Zwei Blutkreisläufe in ihrem Adernetz
> Zwei Atmende auf ihrem Weg
> in diesem Sonnensystem
> Über ihre Gesichter zog eine Wolke fort
> die Zeit hatte einen Sprung bekommen
> Erinnern lugte herein
> Ferne und Nähe waren Eines geworden
> Von Vergangenheit und Zukunft
> funkelten zwei Schicksale
> und fielen auseinander —

The distinctiveness of the two individuals in this chance encounter is
emphasized even as those aspects that separate them (fate, blood, mortality) are also the ones that join them in a common humanity. This
separation is disrupted and momentarily overcome only once through a
flash of remembrance that conjoins the two in a shared history. During
this moment of recollection, spatial and temporal distinctions merge
into a potentiality for meeting and transformation in which the separation between the two individuals would be dissolved. But this conflation of time and space through memory is temporary and ultimately
does not serve to bridge the differences that prevent a genuine communicative exchange. It is this difficulty if not impossibility of truly
reaching the other without sacrificing the other's complexity or reifying
the relationship and the motility of the other's existence that Nelly
Sachs alludes to in a letter to Walter Berendsohn in July 1951: "Wie
soll man den Anschluß an das 'Andere' finden die Vieldeutigkeit auf-
weisen wollen ohne in ein Dogma zu geraten, ohne den Rahmen zu
durchbrechen, den runden Kreis? [*sic*]"[83]

---

[83] Unpublished letter, Nelly-Sachs-Archiv, Arch. 115, quoted in Dorothe Ostmeier, *Sprache des Dramas — Drama der Sprache. Zur Poetik der Nelly Sachs* (Tübingen: Niemeyer, 1997).

The unspecific otherness exemplified by the relationship between two isolated individuals in "Sie stießen zusammen auf der Straße" is given a more concrete cast in Ausländer's poem "Entfremdung" (III 41). Here it is the refugee who, after experiencing the otherness of exile, is unable to overcome feelings of alienation that inhibit communication and recognition of the Thou.

> Wir treffen uns
> hinter der Heimat
> im Haus mit
> gebrochenem Flügel
>
> schenken uns Fremde
> einer des andern
> Findling
>
> Staub auf den Lippen
> wortein wortaus
>
> wir tragen Meilensteine
> wohin
>
> Dein Atem weht
> in andre Richtung
> ich falle
> aus deinen Pupillen
> ins Dickicht
>
> Ich erkenne dich nicht

The separation from the "Heimat" indicated in the opening line serves as the catalyst for this sense of alienation and incapacity for being-together in a strange and broken environment. The second strophe initially offers hope for a connection, if only through the common strangeness of the two individuals who have found each other but who have no direction or destination. The We that conjoins them in a common fate is dismantled, however, in the last lines where the division into I and You does not signal mutual recognition but rather a divergence of paths and a triumph of strangeness.[84] The collective We that implies commonality and community cannot be maintained in view of the divisive forces of history that have broken the "Heimat" apart. The

---

[84] Christine Downing argues that it is this very failure of communication that underscores both the need for and the importance of dialogue with the other: "it is the relationship that is *not* established, the abyss between persons that is not overcome, which leads to insight, to the recognition of the overwhelming significance of conversation with the other." Cf. Downing, "Guilt and Responsibility in the Thought of Martin Buber," *Judaism* 18.1 (1969): 59.

ruined house in the first strophe, the symbolic "Heimat," has lost both
its wholeness and its ability to progress. With its broken wing it is incapable of providing viable support for reconciliation and recognition and
its former inhabitants disperse along the fault lines that divided it. No
longer conjoined in the wholeness of a shared community and distinguished by varying experiences, the I and the You separate. Once separated they are unable to communicate either with words or with
glances.

The breakdown of the We into the component voices of the I and
the You does not necessarily culminate in a kind of relational dispersion
in which commonality is lost, but instead can serve as a revelation of
the relationship between the subjects who constitute it.[85] The ideal We
implies a community of persons that both sustains and bridges the alterity and difference distinguishing the I and the You. The representation of the We as supportive of unity in diversity recalls the appeal to
the We as heterogeneity in the poetic persona's attempt to bear witness
to the multiple voices of memory discussed in the preceding chapter.
The idealization of the We as a community negotiating the tensions
between individuality and collectivity has affinities with Buber's conception of social relations and the realm of the "between." The
authentic encounter between the I and the Thou overcomes the false
dichotomy of individualism and collectivism through the realization of
dialogue and relationship. In "Das Problem des Menschen," Buber describes the "between" as the locus of the dialogic relationship that both
conjoins and transcends the individual and the collective:

> An den gewaltigsten Momenten der Dialogik wird es unverkennbar
> deutlich, daß hier weder des Individuellen, noch des Sozialen, sondern
> eines Dritten Stab den Kreis um das Geschehen zieht. Jenseits des
> Subjektiven, diesseits des Objektiven, auf dem schmalen Grat, darauf
> Ich und Du sich begegnen, ist das Reich des Zwischen.[86]

In Rose Ausländer's work, the search for the "between" as a bond
of relationship overriding all others is manifest in an increasing emphasis on shared humanity, peaceful coexistence, and tolerance. In a posthumously published poem entitled "Blutsverwandt" (VIII 19), Ausländer
consciously adopts the taxonomic terminology that usually serves to
categorize with exclusionary purpose but in her reinterpretation be-

---

[85] Cf. Buber, "Dem Gemeinschaftlichen folgen," *Werke I*, 471: "Das echte Wir
in seiner objektiven Existenz ist daran zu erkennen, daß, in welchem auch seiner
Teile es betrachtet wird, stets eine wesenhafte Beziehung zwischen Person und Person, zwischen Ich und Du sich als aktuell oder potentiell bestehend erweist."

[86] Buber, *Werke I*, 406.

comes merely descriptive, functioning simply as an inventory of unhier-
archical difference:

> Die Blauäugigen Schwarzhaarigen
> Dunkelhäutigen und Hellen
>
> Die Schwermütigen Fröhlichen
> Einsamen Verfolgten
>
> Die Schwärmer Rebellen
> und die paar Heiligen
>
> die ich nicht kenne
> die mich nicht kennen
> und doch wissen
> daß wir
> blutsverwandt sind

By using the image of blood as the commonality that unites all peoples, Ausländer deconstructs the association of blood as the mark of racial specificity and redefines it as the ground for universal human kinship.

As a response and a reaction to the aggressive nationalism that led to World War II, both Sachs and Ausländer strove to represent the Other as a potential Thou as an illustration of relationality rather than enmity. This emphasis on figuring the Thou represents a shift away from the oppositional and exclusionary view of identity implied in the "Jäger/Gejagt" constellation to an open and accepting relational view embodied in the I-Thou dyad. The addresses to the Other in their post-Holocaust poems are injunctions and not prescriptions; assays into ways of being that would encourage acceptance and coexistence based on mutual recognition, tolerance, and responsibility. The Thou as figured in their poetry assumes many forms, all in some relation to the I and all in some way representative gestures towards recovery and transformation. By recovery in this context I mean the project of recuperating the connection to the past and the lost, whether mother, homeland, or the memory of the Holocaust and its victims, through poetic dialogue. Transformation I am using here to signify the possibility of engendering or renewing relationships of responsibility by recognizing the Other as a "Thou." The Thou in its many manifestations as mother, stranger, victim, perpetrator, and Divine Other combines in a single term the multiplicity of associations, identities, and memories that the poets sought to represent and preserve in their writings.

The recognition of the Other as a Thou entails the assumption of responsibility for overcoming the oppositions between victim and perpetrator, citizen and foreigner, "Us and Them." The responsibility for the other, however, is contingent upon the acknowledgment of the in-

trinsic alterity of the self to itself as well as the recognition of the other
as necessary to the self not only on the microscale of interpersonal relations, but also and more importantly, on a global scale.[87] The *personal*
recognition of the Thou needs to be extrapolated to a *political* acceptance of responsibility for the Thou both as an individual and as a representative of the mass of humanity. The I-Thou dyad then becomes
the building block for a relational model of human community counter
to restrictive and exclusionary constructs of group identity and offers
instead a dynamic, flexible, and adaptive ground for social relations responsive to the diverse needs of its members.[88]

[87] This responsibility for and to the other is at the center of Levinas's ethics. In
Time and the Other, he clearly presents this responsibility as limitless (109–10): "The
alterity of the Other is the extreme point of the 'thou shalt not kill' and, in me, the
fear of all the violence and usurpation that my existing, despite the innocence of its
intentions, risks committing. Here is the risk of occupying — from the *Da* of my
Dasein — the place of an Other and, thus, in the concrete, of exiling him, dooming
him to a miserable condition in some 'third' or 'fourth' world, bringing him death.
Thus an unlimited responsibility would emerge in this fear for the other person, a responsibility with which one is never done, which does not cease with the neighbor's
utmost extremity. . . ."

[88] This ideal of community evidences parallels to Buber's concept of 'Gemeinschaft' in "Pfade in Utopia," *Werke I*, 999, where he advocates a form of community
that is not static, but dynamic and capable of adapting to changing situations: "Auch
Gemeinschaft darf nicht zum Dogma werden; auch sie soll, wenn sie auftritt, nicht
einem Begriff, sondern einer Situation Genüge tun."

Conclusion: Towards an Ethics of Remembrance

Das Vergessenwollen verlängert das Exil, und das Geheimnis der Erlösung heißt Erinnerung.

— Ernst Benda[1]

Whence will renewal come to us — to us who have defiled and emptied the whole earthly globe? From the past alone, if we love it.

— Simone Weil[2]

Das Gedicht ist einsam. Es ist einsam und unterwegs. Wer es schreibt, bleibt ihm mitgegeben. Aber steht das Gedicht nicht gerade dadurch, also schon hier, in der Begegnung — im Geheimnis der Begegnung?

— Paul Celan[3]

THROUGHOUT THEIR WRITINGS AFTER THE HOLOCAUST, Nelly Sachs and Rose Ausländer struggled to do justice to the memories of genocide and address the effects which the events of the past had on their faith and their hopes for the future of human society. In the process, they experimented with representations of catastrophe and crisis, oscillating between historical and realistic figurations of the genocide as well as wishful and despairing images of transcendence. Their poems offer a perception of human history as an interpolation of myth and reality, good and evil, empathy and hatred. By giving voice to memory as a multi-layered, multi-dimensional construct, they sought to demonstrate the interdependence and simultaneity of forces that conjoin and divide individuals. Through conscious and active engagement with memory, the subject comes to recognize the particularities and com-

---

[1] Cited in Jürgen Wallmann, "Israels 'Feuerweg'," *Rheinische Post*, 25 August 1984. This is in fact a variation on the quotation from the Baal Shem Tov that graces a plaque at the exit to the historical museum at Yad Vashem Holocaust Memorial in Jerusalem: "Forgetfulness leads to exile. While remembrance is the secret of redemption." Richard von Weizsäcker later used the same phrase ("das Geheimnis der Erlösung heißt Erinnerung") to emphasize the need for remembrance in his speech of 8 May 1985 commemorating the fortieth anniversary of the end of World War II.

[2] Weil, 229.

[3] "Der Meridian," *Gesammelte Werke III*, 198.

monalities inherent in history and the ideologies that inform them. An awareness of history as a composite of parallel and conflicting narratives of experience is then the prerequisite for interpreting memory and assessing its "truth" value. By juxtaposing and interweaving the voices of victims, survivors, exiles, bystanders, and perpetrators, Sachs and Ausländer not only give expression to the multiplicity of testimonies and memories which constitute historical understanding but also to the magnitude of the task and responsibility of remembrance.

Their efforts to demonstrate the common humanity of the victims and the oppressors and the mortality that conjoins the dead and the living are tinged with guilt and responsibility:[4] guilt for the evil that humanity has conceived and implemented and responsibility to fight against the spread and triumph of evil. This evil can be understood as the failure to recognize the common humanity of the other, whether unconscious or willed this lack of recognition leads to the dehumanization or de-subjectification of the other that precedes and legitimates extermination. Despite the negativity of their experiences, both poets expressed hopes for the future, combining messianism (as a desire for both a return to a *time before* and the arrival in a *never before*) with a belief in humanity's potential to realize harmonious coexistence in a world community where agonistic conceptions of identity would no longer determine the fates of individuals and peoples. In Rose Ausländer's "Jenes Land" (VII 41) the poetic persona offers the wishful image of such an environment of the future where the tensions and distinctions between friend and foe have been dissolved:

> Aus Blumen
> Schnee und Gefahr
> jenes Land
>
> Feinde die auch
> Freunde sind
>
> Kein Unterschied
> zwischen dir und mir
>
> in jenem Land

To retain hope for community and reconciliation in the face of the negativity and complexity of human history requires a strength of faith

---

[4] In her discussion of guilt and responsibility in the work of Martin Buber in *Judaism* 18.1 (1969): 60, Christine Downing defines guilt as "not being there for the other; it is the failure to enter into relation, to respond as we are able." This definition, however, is not clear enough in stressing that it is namely the recognition of a relation combined with a failure to act on that relation that constitutes guilt.

that balances a confrontation with the past with anticipatory possibilities for a redemptive future. Ausländer's "Alt und neu" (IV 198) figures this confrontation as a balance between memory and transformation that reveals itself to be the prerequisite for living:

> Mit alten und neuen
> Landschaften
> neuen und alten Worten
> verlorenen und wiedergefundenen Freunden
> leben
>
> Blicke deuten
>
> Vor dem Abgrund
> die Augen nicht schließen
>
> Sich mit Altem zufriedengeben
> protestieren
>
> Endlos
> von neuem anfangen

The retention of the old in the shaping of the new is part of the process of transformation. Transformation and regeneration do not grow out of the artificial ground of selective memory, but rather must be achieved through a conscious, open, and continuous encounter with the past.

The social project of beginning anew, in actuality a call for transformation and change, is predicated by a conscientious consideration of the past through a dynamic process of recollection that both preserves and questions the legacies of history. Any program for social relations designed to promote tolerance of difference and heterogeneity must therefore include a concern with memory. Both Martin Buber's and Emmanuel Levinas's relational models of social interaction based on the I-Thou dyad present a paradigm for an ethics which has the recognition of, responsibility toward, and respect for the other as its central tenets. Nelly Sachs and Rose Ausländer appropriate this relational model of ethics but transform it by emphasizing the aspect of love[5] and integrating the component of remembrance.

It is important to once again underscore the difference between the kind of remembrance represented in Sachs's and Ausländer's poetry and the commemorative practice characterizing public rituals in "official" memorializations of the Holocaust, particularly in Germany. German

---

[5] I am using "love" here in Buber's sense as he defines it in "Ich und Du" (*Werke I*, 88): "Liebe ist Verantwortung eines Ich für ein Du."

public commemoration has to a large extent become institutionalized and with it, the diverse voices of victims, survivors, perpetrators, and bystanders have been melded together into a unified narrative focussed on the questions of guilt and atonement.[6] The memories of which Sachs and Ausländer speak are simultaneously representations of the past and of the relational nature of human existence, a relationality that is determined by where and how the boundaries are drawn between the self and the other. In their attempts to break down these boundaries by revealing them to be shifting and arbitrary, Sachs and Ausländer sought to reconcile identity and difference.

Their appeals to individual and shared responsibility for a common humanity were and are protests against the selective and exclusionary morality characterizing tribalism and racism that divides the world into insiders (good) and outsiders (evil). In *The Origins of Totalitarianism* Hannah Arendt argues that tribalism and racism are expressions of an attempt to transform universal responsibility for humankind into a more manageable task. Privileging the select group over against other groups ultimately legitimizes an exclusionary concept of responsibility restricted to the welfare of the select group.[7] As bearers of witness, survivors, exiles, and German-speaking Jewish women, these poets demonstrated profound strength and integrity in their confrontations with memory and otherness, otherness as a condition they had witnessed and experienced and as a fundamental characteristic of human interaction that they sought not only to illuminate but also to overcome through their works.

The polysemous quality of the poetic word and the mutability embedded in the poetic form are well-suited to a project intent upon an exploration of the multivalence of memory, the alterity of experience, and the mediation of difference. The tension in the poetic word between its singularity and density as a signifier mirrors the tension in the poem itself and in turn enables it to represent a simultaneity of per-

---

[6] Dan Diner argues that Holocaust commemoration is an essential part of the self-understanding and identity formation of the German state. The repeated revisitations of the question of German guilt, he continues, seems to imply that the today's German state cannot allow itself to forget the conditions under which it came into being. See Diner, "On Guilt Discourse and Other Narratives: Epistemological Observations Regarding the Holocaust," trans. Joel Golb, *History & Memory* 9, nos. 1/2 (Fall 1997): 301–2.

[7] Cf. Arendt, *The Origins of Totalitarianism*, 236: "Tribalism and racism are the very realistic, if very destructive, ways of escaping this predicament of common responsibility."

spectives that would otherwise break apart.[8] Through their poetry Nelly Sachs and Rose Ausländer sought to integrate moral responsibility with an acceptance of difference into an ethics in which remembrance as an ongoing transformative process is a central feature in the establishment and preservation of heterogeneous community.

Sachs's and Ausländer's Holocaust testimonials are informed by the disturbing proximity of "Jäger" and "Gejagt," "Henker" and "Opfer," oppressor and oppressed, a proximity that is both spatial and existential. By placing these oppositions in relation to one another within the intensified space of the poem and within the construct of the poetic persona reveals an awareness of what Julia Kristeva terms "the potentialities of *victim/executioner* which characterize each identity, each subject, each sex."[9] Assuming responsibility for this relationship not just as a potential but as a practice is a move in the direction of peace, which, as a practice, is by definition relational and contingent upon mutuality.[10]

The ethics of remembrance I am invoking in relation to Sachs's and Ausländer's poetry refers to the intersection of the temporal understanding and historical positioning of the Self in relation to the presence and presentness of the Other, i.e. the interdependence of action, identification, and remembrance in the relation of the Self and Other. This relation is thus not only grounded in time, but also in a particular mode of processing that time, or the passage of time, as remembrance and as a component in the structuring of presentness or being in the present. The Other of this presentness is not only the "face of the other" exterior to oneself, but also the "others" contained and sustained within the Self.

In response to the moral challenge presented by the Holocaust, the concept of what constitutes "ethics" and "morality" has been subjected to scrutiny. The diversity of opinions on this subject can be illustrated by a comparison of two selected positions. In *Morality after Auschwitz*, Peter J. Haas argues for a definition of "ethic" as

---

[8] Cf. Kelly Oliver's discussion of poetic language in Julia Kristeva's theory in *Reading Kristeva: Unraveling the Double-bind* (Bloomington: Indiana UP, 1993), 12: "In poetic language, identity is infused with alterity without completely breaking down." Oliver also attributes an intrinsic otherness to poetic language, which is both language and not language, but rather "points to the heterogeneity of language" (182).

[9] Julia Kristeva, "Women's Time," trans. Alice Jardine and Harry Blake, *Signs* 7.1 (1981): 34.

[10] Cf. Weil, 137: "We should strive to become such that we are able to be non-violent. This depends also on the adversary."

a complete and coherent system of convictions, values, and ideas that provides a grid within which some sorts of actions can be classified as evil, and so to be avoided, while other sorts of actions can be classified as good, and so to be tolerated or even pursued.[11]

While Haas's definition appears to be conflating ethics and morality, Paul Ricoeur in *Oneself as Another* distinguishes the two, defining ethics as motivational and morality as normative.[12] For Ricoeur, ethics is based on choice and agency while morality is based on rules and control. In Ricoeur's paradigm, ethics is seen as parallel to self-esteem as that quality of being that relates to personal agency, efficacy, and growth, while morality is parallel to self-respect as that quality affiliated with an adherence to the norms that determine "rightness" and justice.

The disparity between the theoretical if not hypothetical ethical ideal and the harsh reality of social interaction is made explicit in Nelly Sachs's poem "EIN FAUSTSCHLAG" from the cycle *Teile dich Nacht* (*SL* 154). This poem, depicting the indifference to violence and the suffering of others in the world, conveys a tone of resignation that attitudes of social responsibility and care will ever be realized in and as social practice.

EIN FAUSTSCHLAG hinter der Hecke
Da liegt einer
Nichts Schlimmeres als Vorübergehen
Keiner bleibt stehn
Nichts zu sagen
Der Jasmin hat nicht seinen Duft gewechselt —

In this realistic but bitter depiction of brutality and indifference, Sachs reveals the tenacity and imbeddedness of the violence and destruction that continue to characterize social relations and which, as forces in society, in part stem from a widespread, conscious disregard for the shared humanity of the Other. The representation of these forces at work in this poem evokes associations to a historical continuum of violence that reached a peak in the unprecedented and systematic cruelty of the oppressors towards their victims in the Holocaust.

Toward the end of her life, Nelly Sachs retreated more and more into a remembered past, looking backwards with sorrow and longing, but with a diminished hope in the potential for transformation through poetic language alone. Particularly in her last poems where she is suffering from cancer and anticipating her own death, the future is no en-

---

[11] Haas, 3.

[12] See Ricoeur, *Oneself as Another*, 170.

ticement and the poetic voices she speaks through are moving ever closer to silence, the silence of death that follows aging. Rose Ausländer, although she too is plagued by the infirmities of age and the anticipation of death, dwells in her memories in a much different way. Instead of focussing on suffering and darkness, she returns to those moments of beauty, love, and inspiration, recreating through poetic remembrance the aspects of her life that she found most stimulating.

Despite these differences in the mood of their late poetry, both Sachs and Ausländer (to a more limited extent) persisted in demonstrating the relationship between oppressor and victim. The potential for either of these aspects to flourish within the Self taken together with the Self's internalization of the Other undermined the already destabilized opposition between good and evil, once again revealing this dichotomy to be completely inadequate as a means of addressing the complexities of history and morality after the Holocaust.[13] In their representations of catastrophe and oppression, Sachs and Ausländer moved away from a Manichaean view of history and morality toward one that addressed the complexity of events and actions as syntheses of good and evil, responsibility and power, care and indifference. In reaction to the complexity and simultaneity of ostensibly opposing forces informing their historical and subjective experiences, they devised a system of ethics based on remembrance and responsibility in an effort to bridge the gap between identity and difference, negotiating the forces that conjoin and divide human experiences while remaining responsive to the realities and potentialities of social interaction in the past, present, and future.

In contrast to approaches to Holocaust memory that segregate and divide succeeding generations into different collectives according to their perceived affiliation with the victims or the perpetrators, Sachs's and Ausländer's poems testify to their struggle to deconstruct such binary oppositions, and by association the boundaries between good and evil and guilt and innocence. There can be no dialogue if Holocaust remembrance is instrumentalized to reinscribe a line of demarcation between the collective memories of "the Jews" and "the Germans" with varying

---

[13] Cf. Shoshana Felman's discussion of morality after the Holocaust which has forever destabilized easy distinctions between good and evil. Felman and Laub, 122: "We blind ourselves to the historical reality . . . by reducing its obscurity to a paradigm of readability — an easily intelligible and safely remote Manichaean allegory of good and evil. . . (. . .) . . . 'we,' as opposed to 'they,' are on the right side of history — a side untouched, untainted by the evil of the Holocaust. But the very nature of the Holocaust was precisely to belie this opposition between 'We' and 'they'."

degrees of moral superiority or moral culpability assigned to each.[14] Here again, Levinas's ideas on the responsibility to the other and how this relationship with the other determines time, are invaluable in breaking free of this opposition.[15] As Rachel Brenner has perceptively pointed out, Levinas's thinking on ethical relations is particularly relevant here because it came into being after the Holocaust. In order to develop a theory of ethics and morality in the wake of this catastrophe, Levinas had to find a basis for morality and ethical interaction independent of history.[16] Levinas's conception of time as the time of "being for the other" that is not contingent upon the other's presence collapses conventional temporal distinctions in a fashion similar to the mystical time figured in much of Sachs's and Ausländer's poetry.

This conception of time as unrestricted by a linearity of past, present, and future, is also echoed in Gary Saul Morson's discussion of "open time" and life as a process rather than an inevitable result of a deterministic system in his insightful book on time and representation, *Narrative and Freedom*. Morson's idea of "open time" renders the relationship between the past and the present, the present and the future, resonant in many directions. In contrast to "closed" conceptions of time that eliminate the possibility for creativity and choice, "open time" allows for both dialogue and change and enables ethical action.[17] This openness of time and the concomitant understanding of being as "in-process" is reflected in the practice of reworking themes and motifs that Sachs and Ausländer appropriate across the breadth of their writings.[18]

---

[14] In her study *Jews in Germany after the Holocaust: Memory, Identity and Jewish-German Relations* (Cambridge/New York: Cambridge UP, 1997), Lynn Rapaport reports finding precisely this tendency toward a moral consciousness and self-understanding grounded in the categorical view of Germans as perpetrators and Jews as victims among younger generation Jews in Germany. While her study is marred by moments of unreflected language and frequent lack of nuance, Rapaport's book does provide some valuable insights into the use and abuse of Holocaust memory in the contemporary German-Jewish context.

[15] See Levinas, *Time and the Other*, 79: "Relationship with the future, the presence of the future in the present, seems all the same accomplished in the face-to-face with the Other. The situation of the face-to-face would be the very accomplishment of time; the encroachment of the present on the future is not the feat of the subject alone, but the intersubjective relationship."

[16] See Rachel Brenner, *Writing as Resistance*, 176.

[17] See Gary Saul Morson, *Narrative and Freedom*, 21, 28–29.

[18] In their discussion of Rose Ausländer's poetry, Harald Vogel and Michael Gans describe this practice of variations on a theme in Ausländer's writing as: "die sukzessive Entwicklung der Verarbeitung eines Inhaltes" by which they mean that

This kind of poetic activity represents an on-going dialogue with the ideas that propel and motivate their writings as well as an embrace of the realization, even if painful, that there is no definitive answer to the questions that concern them. In the process, dialogue becomes a necessity both because of its possibility and its potential as a mediator between the temporal, existential, and spiritual aspects of the relationship with remembrance.

The ethics of remembrance that grows out of Sachs's and Ausländer's poetry should not be read as one geared toward atonement or reconciliation, but rather toward a recognition and responsibility for the past as well as for the future of the Other. This ethics acknowledges the difference in memory between groups, but enables a dialogue by virtue of this difference.[19] The ethical relation as one grounded in the essential difference between the Self and the Other is central to Levinas's thought, which attempts to come to terms with the destruction of morality in the Holocaust by making the Other absolutely anterior to the I and subjectivity. The anteriority of the Other in Levinas's conception can be seen as parallel to the anteriority of language for Sachs and Ausländer, both of whom become caretakers of the mother tongue that serves as the continuous partner in their dialogue with event, place, and time. Whereas the mother had served as originary Other, language and the dialogue made possible through the representation of remembrance within language function as the Other of the present while anticipating the Other of the future. Here the Other of the present can be equated with the poem, while the Other of the future is parallel to the reader. The reader as anticipated futurity can be viewed in a parallel sense to Levinas's conception of the Other as future presence and present absence.[20] The relationship to the Other within the context of time does

the intent of this process is to somehow realize the idea or theme to its full potential. See *Rose Ausländer/Hilde Domin*, 144.

[19] See Dan Diner's discussion of German versus Jewish memory of the Holocaust in his article "On Guilt Discourse and Other Narratives," 309. Diner argues that while "German" memory of the Holocaust tends to focus on *circumstances*, "Jewish" memory of the same event focuses on *motives*.

[20] Cf. Levinas, *Time and the Other*, 90.

not demand the Other's presence, but only the sense of obligation to communicate with the Other. Similarly, it is the represented past, not the past itself, that is the substance of remembrance and subsequently the stuff of the dialogue with the past. In Sachs's and Ausländer's poetry there is a clear awareness of divided and multiple memory, and they each turn to the poem itself in an attempt to negotiate the divide, to appeal to the otherness of experience and thereby enter into a relation that simultaneously engages and seeks to overcome history.

Works Cited

Works by Nelly Sachs

Briefe aus der Nacht. Unpublished manuscript. Nelly-Sachs-Archiv, Arch. 238. Stadt- und Landesbibliothek Dortmund, Germany.

Briefe der Nelly Sachs. Edited by Ruth Dinesen and Helmut Müssener. Frankfurt am Main: Suhrkamp, 1984. [= *Briefe*]

Fahrt ins Staublose. Frankfurt am Main: Suhrkamp, 1988. [= *FS*]

Legenden und Erzählungen. Berlin: F. W. Mayer, 1921.

Suche nach Lebenden. Edited by Margaretha and Bengt Holmqvist. Frankfurt am Main: Suhrkamp, 1971. [= *SL*]

Verzauberung: Späte szenische Dichtungen. Frankfurt am Main: Suhrkamp, 1970.

Zeichen im Sand: Die szenischen Dichtungen der Nelly Sachs. Frankfurt am Main: Suhrkamp, 1962.

Nelly-Sachs-Archiv. Stadt- und Landesbibliothek Dortmund, Germany.

Works by Rose Ausländer

Gesammelte Gedichte. Edited by Hugo Käufer and Berndt Mosblech. Cologne: Braun, 1978.

Gesammelte Werke in acht Bänden. Edited by Helmut Braun. Frankfurt am Main: Fischer, 1984–1990. [=I-VIII]

Ausländer, Rose. Papers. Rose-Ausländer-Dokumentationszentrum, Cologne, Germany.

Secondary Works

Adorno, Theodor W. "Kulturkritik und Gesellschaft." In *Prismen: Kulturkritik und Gesellschaft.* Frankfurt am Main: Suhrkamp, 1955.

———. "Engagement." In *Noten zur Literatur III.* 109–135. Frankfurt am Main: Suhrkamp, 1965.

———. *Negative Dialektik: Jargon der Eigentlichkeit*. Frankfurt am Main: Suhrkamp, 1973.

Alexander, Edward. *The Resonance of Dust. Essays on Holocaust Literature and Jewish Fate*. Columbus, OH: Ohio State UP, 1979.

Allen, Jeffner, and Iris Marion Young, eds. *The Thinking Muse: Feminism and Modern French Philosophy*. Bloomington/ Indianapolis: Indiana UP, 1989.

Améry, Jean. "Wieviel Heimat braucht der Mensch?" In *Jenseits von Schuld und Sühne: Bewältigungsversuche eines Überwältigten*. Munich: Szczesny Verlag, 1966.

Angel, Klaus. "On Symbiosis and Pseudosymbiosis." *Journal of the APA* 15.2 (1967): 294–316.

apropos Nelly Sachs. Frankfurt am Main: Verlag Neue Kritik, 1997.

Arendt, Hannah. *The Origins of Totalitarianism*. 1951. New York: Meridian Books, 1958.

———. "We Refugees." In *The Jew as Pariah: Jewish Identity and Politics in the Modern Age*, edited by Ron Feldman. 55–66. New York: Grove Press, 1978.

Aschheim, Steven. *Brothers and Strangers: The East European Jew in German and German Jewish Consciousness, 1800–1923*. Madison, WI/London: U of Wisconsin P, 1982.

———. *Culture and Catastrophe: German and Jewish Confrontations with National Socialism and Other Crises*. New York: New York UP, 1996.

Assmann, Aleida, and Dietrich Harth, eds. *Mnemosyne: Formen und Funktionen der kulturellen Erinnerung*. Frankfurt am Main: Fischer, 1991.

Bachmann, Ingeborg. *Werke*. 1978. Munich: Piper, 1984.

Bahr, Ehrhard. *Nelly Sachs*. Munich: C. H. Beck, 1980.

———. "Flight and Metamorphosis: Nelly Sachs as a Poet in Exile." In *Exile: The Writer's Experience*, edited by John M. Spalek and Robert F. Bell. 267–77. Chapel Hill: U of North Carolina P, 1982.

———. "Paul Celan und Nelly Sachs: Ein Dialog in Gedichten." *Datum und Zitat bei Paul Celan*, edited by Chaim Shoham and Bernd Witte. 183–94. Bern: Peter Lang, 1986.

———. "'My Metaphors Are My Wounds': Nelly Sachs and the Limits of Poetic Metaphor." In *Jewish Writers, German Literature: The Uneasy Examples of Nelly Sachs and Walter Benjamin*, edited by Timothy Bahti and Marilyn Sibley Fries. 43–58. Ann Arbor: U of Michigan P, 1995.

Bahti, Timothy, and Marilyn Sibley Fries, eds. *Jewish Writers, German Literature: The Uneasy Examples of Nelly Sachs and Walter Benjamin*. Ann Arbor: U of Michigan P, 1995.

Baleanu, Avram Andrei. "Das Rätsel Rose Ausländer." *Menora. Jahrbuch für deutsch-jüdische Geschichte* (1990): 327–56.

Bartkowski, Fran. "Travelers vs. Ethnics: Discourses of Displacement." *Discourse* 15.3 (1993): 158–76.

Bartmann, Franz-Josef. ".‌.‌. *denn nicht dürfen Freigelassene mit Schlingen der Sehnsucht eingefangen   werden .‌.‌..*" *Nelly Sachs (1891–1970) — eine deutsche Dichterin.* Dortmund: Zimmermann-Engelke Verlag, 1991.

Bassin, Donna, Margaret Honey, and Meryle Mahrer Kaplan, eds. *Representations of Motherhood.* New Haven/London: Yale UP, 1994.

Bauer, Yahuda. *A History of the Holocaust.* New York: Franklin Watts, 1982.

Bauman, Zygmunt. *Modernity and the Holocaust.* Cambridge: Polity Press, 1989.

———. *Modernity and Ambivalence.* Ithaca, NY: Cornell UP, 1991.

Baumann, Gerhart. "Rose Ausländer — Aufbruch in das 'Land Anfang'." *Neue Rundschau* 92.4 (1981): 45–60.

Beauvoir, Simone de. *The Second Sex.* 1952. New York: Vintage Books, 1974.

Beil, Claudia. *Sprache als Heimat: Jüdische Tradition und Exilerfahrung in der Lyrik von Nelly Sachs und Rose Ausländer.* Munich: tuduv, 1991.

Beitchman, Philip. *Alchemy of the Word: Cabala and the Renaissance.* Albany: State U of New York P, 1998.

Ben-Chorin, Schalom, ed. *Zwischen neuen und verlornen Orten: Beiträge zum Verhältnis von Deutschen und Juden.* Munich: dtv, 1988.

Benhabib, Seyla. *Situating the Self: Gender, Community and Postmodernism in Contemporary Ethics.* New York: Routledge, 1992.

Benjamin, Walter. *Illuminations.* Ed. by Hannah Arendt. 1955. New York: Schocken, 1969.

Bennholdt-Thomsen, Anke, and Alfredo Guzzoni. "Melusine: Herkunft und Bedeutung bei Nelly Sachs." *Euphorion* 81.2 (1987): 156–70.

Benstock, Shari, Robert Con Davis, Ronald Schleifer, eds. *Textualizing the Feminine: On the Limits of Genre.* Norman, OK: U of Oklahoma P, 1991.

Benyoëtz, Elazar. *Treffpunkt Scheideweg.* Munich: Carl Hanser, 1990.

Benz, Wolfgang, ed. *Die Juden in Deutschland 1933–1945: Leben unter national-sozialistischer Herrschaft.* Munich: C. H. Beck, 1989.

Berendsohn, Walter. *Nelly Sachs: Einführung in das Werk der Dichterin jüdischen Schicksals.* Darmstadt: Agora Verlag, 1974.

Berkovits, Eliezer. *Faith after the Holocaust.* New York: Ktav, 1973.

Berman, Russell. "'Der begrabenen Blitze Wohnstatt': Trennung, Heimkehr und Sehnsucht in der Lyrik von Nelly Sachs." In *Im Zeichen Hiobs*, edited by Gunter Grimm and Hans-Peter Bayerdörfer. 280–92. Königstein/Taunus: Athenäum, 1985.

Bernasconi, Robert, and David Wood, eds. *The Provocation of Levinas: Rethinking the Other*. London/New York: Routledge, 1988.

Bernstein, Michael André. *Foregone Conclusions: Against Apocalyptic History*. Berkeley/Los Angeles/London: U of California P, 1994.

Blanchot, Maurice. *The Writing of the Disaster*. Trans. Ann Smock. Lincoln, NB/London: U of Nebraska P, 1986.

Blomster, W. V. "A Theosophy of the Creative Word: The *Sohar*-Cycle of Nelly Sachs." *The Germanic Review* 44.3 (1969): 211–27.

Bloom, Harold. *Kabbalah and Criticism*. New York: The Seabury Press, 1975.

———. *Poetry and Repression*. New Haven, CT: Yale UP, 1976.

———. *Ruin the Sacred Truths: Poetry and Belief from the Bible to the Present*. Cambridge, MA/London: Harvard UP, 1989.

Bock, Gisela. "Ordinary Women in Nazi Germany: Perpetrators, Victims, Followers, and Bystanders." In *Women in the Holocaust*, edited by Dalia Ofer and Lenore J. Weitzman. 85–100. New Haven/London: Yale UP, 1998.

Bodemann, Y. Michal. *Gedächtnistheater. Die jüdische Gemeinschaft und ihre deutsche Erfindung*. Berlin: Rotbuch, 1996.

Bonner, Frances, et. al, eds. *Imagining Women: Cultural Representations and Gender*. Cambridge, UK: The Open University, 1992.

Boose, Lynda E., and Betty S. Flowers, eds. *Daughters and Fathers*. Baltimore: The Johns Hopkins UP, 1989.

Bosmajian, Hamida. *Metaphors of Evil: Contemporary German Literature and the Shadow of Nazism*. Iowa City: U of Iowa P, 1979.

———. "German Literature about the Holocaust — A Literature of Limitations." *Modern Language Studies* 16 (1986): 51–61.

Bossinade, Johanna. "Fürstinnen der Trauer. Die Gedichte von Nelly Sachs." *Jahrbuch für Internationale Germanistik* 16.1 (1984): 133–57.

Boyarin, Jonathan. "The Other Within and the Other Without." In *The Other in Jewish Thought and History*, edited by Laurence J. Silberstein and Robert L. Cohn. 424–52. New York/London: New York UP, 1994.

Boym, Svetlana. *Death in Quotation Marks: Cultural Myths of the Modern Poet*. Cambridge, MA/London: Harvard UP, 1991.

Braham, Randolph L., ed. *Reflections of the Holocaust in Art and Literature*. New York: Columbia UP, 1990.

Braun, Helmut, ed. *Rose Ausländer: Materialien zu Leben und Werk.* Frankfurt am Main: Fischer, 1991.

Brenner, Rachel Feldhay. *Writing as Resistance: Four Women Confronting the Holocaust.* University Park, PA: Pennsylvania State UP, 1997.

Bridenthal, Renate, Atina Grossmann, and Marion Kaplan, eds. *When Biology Became Destiny: Women in Weimar and Nazi Germany.* New York: Monthly Review Press, 1984.

Brinker-Gabler, Gisela. "Mit wechselndem Schlüssel: Annäherungen an Nelly Sachs' Gedicht 'Bin in der Fremde'." *The German Quarterly* 65.1 (1992): 35–41.

Brügmann, Margret. "Weiblichkeit im Spiel der Sprache. Über das Verhältnis von Psychoanalyse und 'écriture féminine'." *Frauen-Literatur-Geschichte: Schreibende Frauen vom Mittelalter bis zur Gegenwart,* edited by Hiltrud Gnüg and Renate Möhrmann. 395–415. Frankfurt am Main: Suhrkamp, 1989.

Brunner, Constantin. *Science, Spirit, Superstition: A New Enquiry Into Human Thought.* Trans. Abraham Suhl. Toronto: U of Toronto P, 1968.

Buber, Martin. *Die Legende des Baalschem.* Zürich: Manesse Verlag, 1955.

———. *Werke I. Schriften zur Philosophie.* Munich: Kösel, 1962.

———. *Der Jude und sein Judentum.* Cologne: Joseph Melzer Verlag, 1963.

———. *Werke III. Schriften zum Chassidismus.* Munich: Kösel, 1963.

———. *Werke II. Schriften zur Bibel.* Munich: Kösel, 1964.

———. *Der utopische Sozialismus.* Cologne: Jakob Hegner, 1967.

———, ed. *Ten Rungs: Hasidic Sayings.* New York: Schocken Books, 1947.

Buchka, Peter. *Die Schreibweise des Schweigens.* Munich: Carl Hanser Verlag, 1974.

Burgauer, Erica. *Zwischen Erinnerung und Verdrängung — Juden in Deutschland nach 1945.* Reinbek bei Hamburg: Rowohlt, 1993.

Butler, Judith. *Gender Trouble: Feminism and the Subversion of Identity.* New York: Routledge, 1990.

Cain, Seymour. "The Question and the Answers after Auschwitz." *Judaism* 20.3 (1971): 263–78.

Carlson, Kathie. *In Her Image: The Unhealed Daughter's Search for Her Mother.* Boston/Shaftesbury: Shambhala, 1989.

Carmely, Klara P. *Das Identitätsproblem jüdischer Autoren im deutschen Sprachraum: Von der Jahrhundertwende bis zu Hitler.* Königstein/Taunus: Scriptor, 1981.

Celan, Paul. *Gesammelte Werke.* Frankfurt am Main: Fischer, 1983.

———. *Gedichte*. Vol. 1. 1975. Frankfurt am Main: Suhrkamp, 1991.

Cervantes, Eleonore. *Struktur-Bezüge in der Lyrik von Nelly Sachs*. Bern/ Frankfurt am Main: Peter Lang, 1982.

———. "A Woman's View of the Holocaust: The Poetry of Nelly Sachs." *Rendezvous: Journal of Arts and Letters* 22.2 (1986): 47–50.

Chanter, Tina. "Feminism and the Other." In *The Provocation of Levinas: Rethinking the Other*, edited by Robert Bernasconi and David Wood. 32–56. London/New York: Routledge, 1988.

Chase, Cynthia. "Desire and Identification in Lacan and Kristeva." In *Feminism and Psychoanalysis*, edited by Richard Feldstein and Judith Roof. 65–83. Ithaca, NY: Cornell UP, 1989.

Chicago, Judy. *Holocaust Project: From Darkness into Light*. New York: Penguin, 1993.

Chodorow, Nancy. "Mothering, Object-Relations and the Female Oedipal Configuration." *FS. Feminist Studies* 4.1 (1978): 137–58.

———. *The Reproduction of Mothering: Psychoanalysis and the Sociology of Gender*. Berkeley: U of California P, 1978.

———. *Feminism and Psychoanalytic Theory*. New Haven, CT/ London: Yale UP, 1989.

Cixous, Hélène. "The Laugh of the Medusa." Trans. Keith and Paula Cohen. *Signs* 1.4 (1976): 875–93.

Cocks, Joan Elizabeth. *The Oppositional Imagination: Feminism, Critique and Political Theory*. New York: Routledge, 1989.

Cohen, Richard. "The Face of Truth in Rosenzweig, Levinas, and Jewish Mysticism." In *Phenomenology of the Truth Proper to Religion*, ed. Daniel Guerrière. 175–201. Albany: State U of New York P, 1990.

Colin, Amy. *Paul Celan: Holograms of Darkness*. Bloomington/ Indianapolis: Indiana UP, 1991.

———. "A Tragic Love for German. Holocaust Poetry from the Bukovina." *Cross Currents: A Yearbook of Central European Culture* 10 (1991): 73–84.

Conway, Jill, Susan Bourque, and Joan Scott, eds. *Learning About Women: Gender, Politics, and Power*. Ann Arbor, MI: U of Michigan P, 1989.

Cortese, Anthony. *Ethnic Ethics: The Restructuring of Moral Theory*. Albany: State U of New York P, 1990.

Crowder, Diane Griffin. "Amazons and Mothers: Monique Wittig, Hélène Cixous, and Theories of Women's Writing." *Contemporary Literature* 24 (1983): 114–43.

Crownfield, David, ed. *Body/Text in Julia Kristeva*. Albany: State U of New York P, 1992.

Cernyak-Spatz, Susan E. *German Holocaust Literature*. New York/ Berne/Frankfurt am Main: Peter Lang, 1985.

Dallery, Arleen, and Charles E. Scott, eds. *The Question of the Other: Essays in Contemporary Continental Philosophy*. Albany: State U of New York P, 1989.

Davidson, Cathy N., and E. M. Broner, eds. *The Lost Tradition: Mothers and Daughters in Literature*. New York: Frederick Ungar, 1980.

DeKoven, Marianne. "Gendered Doubleness and the 'Origins' of Modernist Form." *Tulsa Studies in Women's Literature* 8.1 (1989): 19–42.

Demetz, Peter. *After the Fires: Recent Writing in the Germanies, Austria and Switzerland*. San Diego/New York/London: Harcourt, Brace, Jovano-vich, Inc., 1986.

Derrida, Jacques. *Writing and Difference*. Trans. Alan Bass. Chicago: U of Chicago P, 1978.

———. *Cinders*. Trans. Ned Lukacher. Lincoln: U of Nebraska P, 1991.

Deutscher, Isaac. *The Non-Jewish Jew and Other Essays*. Ed. Tamara Deutscher. London/New York/Toronto: Oxford UP, 1968.

Diner, Dan. "Negative Symbiose. Deutsche und Juden nach Auschwitz." *Babylon* 1 (1986): 9–20.

———. "On Guilt Discourse and Other Narratives: Epistemological Obser-vations regarding the Holocaust." Trans. Joel Golb. *History & Memory* 9, nos. 1/2 (Fall 1997): 301–20.

Dinesen, Ruth. "Das Ziel des Kosmos: Zum Element 'Fisch' in der Lyrik von Nelly Sachs." *Jahrbuch der Deutschen Schiller-Gesellschaft* 26 (1982): 445–66.

———. "Verehrung und Verwerfung. Nelly Sachs — Kontroverse um eine Dichterin." In *VII. Kongress der Internationalen Vereinigung für Germa-nische Sprach- und Literaturwissenschaft*. Vol. 10, ed. Karl Pestalozzi. 130–37. Göttingen: Niemeyer, 1985.

———. "Paul Celan und Nelly Sachs." In *Datum und Zitat bei Paul Celan*, edited by Chaim Shoham and Bernd Witte. 195–210. Bern: Peter Lang, 1986.

———. *"Und Leben hat immer wie Abschied geschmeckt": Frühe Gedichte und Prosa der Nelly Sachs*. Stuttgart: Hans-Dieter Heinz Akademischer Verlag, 1987.

———. *Nelly Sachs: Eine Biographie*. Trans. Gabriele Gerecke. 1991. Frank-furt am Main: Suhrkamp, 1992.

Dischner, Gisela. *Poetik des modernen Gedichts: Zur Lyrik von Nelly Sachs*. Bad Homburg/Berlin/Zürich: Verlag Gehlen, 1970.

———. "Zu den Gedichten von Nelly Sachs." In *Das Buch der Nelly Sachs*, ed. Bengt Holmqvist. 309–54. 1968. Frankfurt am Main: Suhrkamp, 1977.

———. "Die Lyrik von Nelly Sachs und ihr Bezug zur Bibel, zur Kabbala und zum Chassidismus." In *Nelly Sachs*, edited by Heinz Ludwig Arnold. 25–40. Munich: text + kritik, 1979.

———. "Noch feiert der Tod das Leben. . . ." In *apropos Nelly Sachs*. 7–50. Frankfurt am Main: Verlag Neue Kritik, 1997.

Domin, Hilde. "Nachwort" to *Gedichte*, by Nelly Sachs. Frankfurt am Main: Suhrkamp, 1977.

———. *Aber die Hoffnung: Autobiographisches aus und über Deutschland*. Munich: Piper, 1982.

———. *Wozu Lyrik heute*. Munich: Piper, 1988.

Downing, Christine. "Guilt and Responsibility in the Thought of Martin Buber." *Judaism* 18.1 (1969): 53–63.

———. *The Goddess: Mythological Images of the Feminine*. New York: Crossroad, 1981.

Drewitz, Ingeborg. "Die Leichtigkeit der Schwere. Rose Ausländer: 'Mein Atem heißt jetzt'." *Die Horen* 32.1 (1987): 157–60.

Du Plessis, Rachel Blau. *Writing beyond the Ending*. Bloomington: Indiana UP, 1985.

Easthope, Antony. *Poetry as Discourse*. New York: Methuen, 1983.

Edfelt, Johannes. "Die Dichterin Nelly Sachs." In *Nelly Sachs zu Ehren*. 58–63. Frankfurt am Main: Suhrkamp, 1961.

Elias-Button, Karen. "The Muse as Medusa." In *The Lost Tradition: Mothers and Daughters in Literature*, edited by Cathy Davidson and E. M. Broner. 193–206. New York: Frederick Ungar, 1980.

Elshtain, Jean Bethke. *Women and War*. New York: Basic Books, 1987.

Enzensberger, Hans Magnus. "Die Steine der Freiheit." In *Nelly Sachs zu Ehren*. 45–51. Frankfurt am Main: Suhrkamp, 1961.

Ezrahi, Sidra DeKoven. *By Words Alone*. Chicago/London: U of Chicago P, 1980.

Fackenheim, Emil L. *The Jewish Return into History*. New York: Schocken Books, 1978.

———. *To Mend the World*. New York: Schocken Books, 1982.

Falkenstein, Henning. *Nelly Sachs*. Berlin: Colloquium Verlag, 1984.

Feldstein, Richard and Judith Roof, eds. *Feminism and Psychoanalysis*. Ithaca, NY: Cornell UP, 1989.

Felman, Shoshana, and Dori Laub, M.D. *Testimony: Crises of Witnessing in Literature, Psychoanalysis, and History.* New York: Routledge, 1992.

Felski, Rita. *Beyond Feminist Aesthetics: Feminist Literature and Social Change.* Cambridge, MA: Harvard UP, 1989.

Fine, Ellen S. "Women Writers and the Holocaust: Strategies for Survival." In *Reflections of the Holocaust in Art and Literature,* ed. Randolph L. Braham. 79–95. New York: Columbia UP, 1990.

Flax, Jane. "The Conflict between Nurturance and Autonomy in Mother-Daughter Relationships and within Feminism." *FS. Feminist Studies* 4.2 (1978): 171–89.

Fletcher, John and Andrew Benjamin, eds. *Abjection, Melancholia and Love: The Work of Julia Kristeva.* London: Routledge, 1990.

Flynn, Elizabeth and Patrocino Schweikart, eds. *Gender and Reading: Essays on Readers, Texts and Contexts.* Baltimore: The Johns Hopkins UP, 1986.

Foot, Robert. *The Phenomenon of Speechlessness in the Poetry of Marie Luise Kaschnitz, Günter Eich, Nelly Sachs and Paul Celan.* Bonn: Bouvier, 1982.

Forman, Frieda Johles, and Caoran Sowton, eds. *Taking Our Time: Feminist Perspectives on Temporality.* Oxford: Pergamon Press, 1989.

Freud, Sigmund. *The Standard Edition of the Complete Psychological Works of Sigmund Freud,* Vol. XII. Translated and edited by James Strachey. 1958. London: The Hogarth Press, 1971.

Freund, Winfried. "Die Wahrheit des Mythos. Gedanken zu Rose Ausländers Gedicht 'Abendstern'." *Neue deutsche Hefte* 35.2 (1988): 440–43.

Friedländer, Saul. *Memory, History, and the Extermination of the Jews of Europe.* Bloomington/Indianapolis: Indiana UP, 1993.

———. *Nazi Germany and the Jews.* Vol. 1, *The Years of Persecution, 1933–1939.* New York: HarperCollins, 1997.

———, et. al., eds. *Visions of the Apocalypse: End or Rebirth?* New York/London: Holmes + Meier, 1985.

———, ed. *Probing the Limits of Representation: Nazism and the 'Final Solution'.* Cambridge, MA: Harvard UP, 1992.

Friedrich, Hugo. *Die Struktur der modernen Lyrik.* 1956. Reinbek bei Hamburg: Rowohlt, 1985.

Fritsch-Vivié, Gabriele. *Nelly Sachs.* Reinbek bei Hamburg: Rowohlt, 1993.

Füglister, Notker. "Die Wirkgeschichte biblischer Motive in den Dichtungen von Nelly Sachs." In *Die Bibel im Verständnis der Gegenwartsliteratur,* edited by Johann Holzner and Udo Zeilinger. 47–60. St. Polten: Niederösterreichisches Pressehaus, 1988.

Funkenstein, Amos. *Perceptions of Jewish History.* Berkeley/Los Angeles/ Oxford: U of California P, 1993.

Gallop, Jane. "Reading the Mother Tongue: Psychoanalytic Feminist Criticism." *Critical Inquiry* 13 (Winter 1987): 314–29.

Gardiner, Judith Kegan. "On Female Identity and Writing by Women." *Critical Inquiry* 8.2 (1981): 347–61.

Garner, Shirley Nelson, et. al., ed. *The (M)other Tongue: Essays in Feminist Psychoanalytic Interpretation.* Ithaca, NY: Cornell UP, 1985.

Gilligan, Carol. *In a Different Voice: Psychological Theory and Women's Development.* Cambridge, MA: Harvard UP, 1982.

Gilman, Sander. *Jewish Self-Hatred. Anti-Semitism and the Hidden Language of the Jews.* Baltimore/London: The Johns Hopkins UP, 1986.

———. *Inscribing the Other.* Lincoln, NB/London: U of Nebraska P, 1991.

———. "The Visibility of the Jew in the Diaspora: Body Imagery and Its Cultural Context." B. G. Rudolph Lecture in Judaic Studies. Syracuse University, 10 Oct. 1991.

Glenn, Jerry. "Blumenworte/Kriegsgestammel: The Poetry of Rose Ausländer." *Modern Austrian Literature* 12, nos. 3/4 (1979): 127–46.

Goldberg, Arnold M. *Untersuchungen über die Vorstellung von der Schekhinah in der frühen rabbinischen Literatur: Talmud und Midrasch.* Berlin: de Gruyter, 1969.

Goltschnigg, Dietmar and Anton Schwab, eds. *Die Bukowina: Studien zu einer versunkenen Literaturlandschaft.* Tübingen: Francke Verlag, 1990.

Greenberg, Irving, and Alvin Rosenfeld, eds. *Confronting the Holocaust: The Impact of Elie Wiesel.* Bloomington: Indiana UP, 1978.

Greenberg, Jay R., and Stephen A. Mitchell. *Object Relations in Psychoanalytic Theory.* Cambridge, MA: Harvard UP, 1983.

Gross, Elisabeth. "The Body of Signification." In *Abjection, Melancholia, and Love. The Work of Julia Kristeva*, edited by John Fletcher and Andrew Benjamin. 80–103. London/New York: Routledge, 1990.

Haas, Peter J. *Morality after Auschwitz: The Radical Challenge of the Nazi Ethic.* Philadelphia: Fortress Press, 1988.

Habermas, Jürgen. *Moral Consciousness and Communicative Action.* Trans. Christian Lenhardt and Shierry Nicholsen. 1983. Frankfurt am Main: Suhrkamp. Cambridge, MA: MIT Press, 1990.

Halbwachs, Maurice. *On Collective Memory.* Ed. and Trans. Lewis A. Coser. Chicago/London: U of Chicago P, 1992.

Hamburger, Michael. *The Truth of Poetry: Tensions in Modern Poetry from Baudelaire to the 1960's.* New York: Harcourt, Brace & World, 1969.

Hamm, Peter. "Unser Gestirn ist vergraben im Staub. Zum 100. Geburtstag der Dichterin Nelly Sachs am 10. Dezember." *Die Zeit*, 6 December 1991, 76.

Hand, Sean, ed. *The Levinas Reader*. New York: Basil Blackwell, 1989.

Handelman, Susan A. *Fragments of Redemption: Jewish Thought and Literary Theory in Benjamin, Scholem, and Levinas*. Bloomington/Indianapolis: Indiana UP, 1991.

Hardegger, Luzia. *Nelly Sachs und die Verwandlungen der Welt*. Frankfurt am Main: Peter Lang, 1975.

Harries, Karsten. "Metaphor and Transcendence." In *On Metaphor*, ed. Sheldon Sacks. 71–88. Chicago/London: U of Chicago P, 1979.

Hartberger, Birgit. *Das biblische Ruth-Motiv in deutschen lyrischen Gedichten des 20. Jahrhunderts*. Altenberge: Oros Verlag, 1992.

Hartman, Geoffrey H., ed. *Holocaust Remembrance: The Shapes of Memory*. Cambridge, MA: Basil Blackwell, 1994.

Hayes, Peter, ed. *Lessons and Legacies: The Meaning of the Holocaust in a Changing World*. Evanston, IL: Northwestern UP, 1991.

Heine, Heinrich. *Briefe*. Vol. 2. Edited by Friedrich Hirth. Mainz: Florian Kupferberg Verlag, 1950.

Heinemann, Marlene E. *Gender and Destiny: Women Writers and the Holocaust*. Westport, CT: Greenwood Press, 1986.

Helfrich, Cilly. *Rose Ausländer. Biographie*. 1995. Zürich: Pendo Verlag, 1998.

Herder-Lexikon Symbole. Freiburg/Basel/Vienna: Herder, 1978.

Heschel, Susannah. "From the Bible to Nazism: German Feminists on the Jewish Origins of Patriarchy." *Tel Aviver Jahrbuch für deutsche Geschichte* (1992): 319–33.

Heuer, Renate, ed. *Lexikon deutsch-jüdischer Autoren*. Vol. 1. Munich/London/New York/Paris: K. G. Saur, 1992.

Higonnet, Margaret, Jane Jenson, et. al, eds. *Behind the Lines: Gender and the Two World Wars*. New Haven/London: Yale UP, 1987.

Hirsch, Marianne. *The Mother/Daughter Plot*. Bloomington/Indianapolis: Indiana UP, 1989.

Hirschmann, Nancy J. *Rethinking Obligation: A Feminist Method for Political Theory*. Ithaca/London: Cornell UP, 1992.

Hirsh, Elizabeth A. "Modernism Revised: Formalism and the Feminine (Irigaray, H. D., Barnes)." Ph.D. diss., University of Wisconsin-Madison, 1989.

Hofer, Walther, ed. *Der Nationalsozialismus: Dokumente 1933–1945*. Frankfurt am Main: Fischer, 1957.

Hoffman, Charles. *Gray Dawn: The Jews of Eastern Europe in the Post-Communist Era.* New York: HarperCollins, 1992.

Hoghe, Raimund. "Sie hält fest an ihren Träumen." In *Ich zähl die Sterne meiner Worte,* by Rose Ausländer. Frankfurt am Main: Fischer, 1985.

Hölderlin, Friedrich. *Sämtliche Werke.* Vol. 2.1. Stuttgart: Cotta, 1951.

Holmqvist, Bengt, ed. *Das Buch der Nelly Sachs.* Frankfurt am Main: Suhrkamp, 1977.

Holschuh, Albrecht. "Lyrische Mythologeme. Das Exilwerk von Nelly Sachs." In *Die deutsche Exilliteratur 1933–1945,* ed. Manfred Durzak. 343–57. Stuttgart: Reclam, 1973.

Homans, Margaret. *Women Writers and Poetic Identity.* Princeton: Princeton UP, 1980.

———. *Bearing the Word: Language and Female Experience in Nineteenth-Century Women's Writing.* Chicago/London: U of Chicago P, 1986.

Huder, Walther. "Über Nelly Sachs." *Die Diagonale* 3/4 (1967): 17–24.

Humphries, Jefferson. "Troping the Body: Literature and Feminism." *diacritics* (Spring 1988): 18–28.

Jabès, Edmond. *Das Buch der Fragen.* Trans. Henriette Beese. Berlin: Alphëus Verlag, 1979.

———. *From the Book to the Book: An Edmond Jabès Reader.* Trans. Rosmarie Waldrop. Hanover, NH: Wesleyan UP, 1991.

———. *A Foreigner Carrying in the Crook of His Arm a Tiny Book.* Trans. Rosmarie Waldrop. Hanover, NH: Wesleyan UP, 1993.

———. *The Book of Margins.* Trans. Rosmarie Waldrop. Chicago: U of Chicago P, 1993.

Jardine, Alice. *Gynesis: Configurations of Woman and Modernity.* Ithaca/London: Cornell UP, 1985.

Jendreiek, Helmut, ed. *Nelly Sachs zur Freude: Nelly-Sachs Schülerinnen interpretieren Nelly Sachs.* Neuss: n.p., 1968.

"Jewish Values in the Post-Holocaust Future: A Symposium with Emil Fackenheim, Richard Popkin, George Steiner and Elie Wiesel." *Judaism* 16.3 (1967): 266–99.

Jones, Ann Rosalind. "Writing the Body: Towards an Understanding of L'Ecriture Féminine." *FS - Feminist Studies* 7 (Summer 1981): 247–63.

Joseph, Norma Baumel. "Zakhor: Memory, Ritual, and Gender." *Canadian Women's Studies Journal* 16.4 (1996): 28–35.

Juhasz, Suzanne. *Naked and Fiery Forms.* New York: Harper & Row, 1976.

Jung, C. G. "Die psychologischen Aspekte des Mutterarchetypus." *Gesammelte Werke.* Vol. 9. Olten: Walter-Verlag, 1976.

Kahane, Claire. "Questioning the Maternal Voice." *Genders* 3 (1988): 82–91.

Kahn, Lothar. *Between Two Worlds: A Cultural History of German-Jewish Writers.* Ames, IA: Iowa State UP, 1993.

Kahn, Robbie Pfeufer. "Women and Time in Childbirth and During Lactation." In *Taking Our Time: Feminist Perspectives on Temporality,* edited by Frieda Johles Forman and Caoran Sowton. 20–36. Oxford/New York: Pergamon Press, 1989.

Kaplan, Marion A. "Women's Strategies in the Jewish Community in Germany." *New German Critique* 14 (1978): 109–18.

Katz, Steven T. *Post-Holocaust Dialogues.* New York: New York UP, 1985.

———. *Historicism, the Holocaust, and Zionism: Critical Studies in Modern Jewish Thought and History.* New York: New York UP, 1992.

Keller, Lynn. *Re-making It New: Contemporary American Poetry and the Modernist Tradition.* Cambridge/New York: Cambridge UP, 1987.

Kellner, Menachem, ed. *The Pursuit of the Ideal: Jewish Writings of Steven Schwarzschild.* Albany: State U of New York P, 1990.

Kersten, Paul. "'Und Schweigen ist ein neues Land —'." In *Nelly Sachs,* ed. Paul Kersten. 5–38. Hamburg: Christians Verlag, 1969.

———. *Die Metaphorik in der Lyrik von Nelly Sachs.* Hamburg: Hartmut Lüdke Verlag, 1970.

Kessler, Michael and Jürgen Wertheimer, eds. *Nelly Sachs: Neue Interpretationen.* Tübingen: Stauffenburg, 1994.

Kessner, Michaela. "Die Lyrik Rose Ausländers." Master's thesis, Ludwig-Maximilian-Universität München, 1990.

Kiedaisch, Petra, ed. *Lyrik nach Auschwitz? Adorno und die Dichter.* Stuttgart: Reclam, 1995.

Klein, Melanie. *Envy and Gratitude and Other Works 1946–1963.* London: Virago, 1988.

Klepfisz, Irena. *A Few Words in the Mother Tongue: Poems Selected and New (1971–1990).* Portland, OR: Eighth Mountain Press, 1990.

Klingmann, Ulrich. *Religion und Religiösität in der Lyrik von Nelly Sachs.* Frankfurt am Main: Peter Lang, 1980.

Kloepfer, Deborah Kelly. *The Unspeakable Mother: Forbidden Discourse in Jean Rhys and H. D.* Ithaca, NY/London: Cornell UP, 1989.

Köhl, Gabriele. "Heimat und Exil in Leben und Werk Rose Ausländers." *Südostdeutsche Vierteljahresblätter* 37.1 (1988): 25–29.

———. *Die Bedeutung der Sprache in der Lyrik Rose Ausländers.* Pfaffenweiler: Centaurus-Verlagsgesellschaft, 1993.

Köppen, Manuel, Ed. *Kunst und Literatur nach Auschwitz*. Berlin: Erich Schmidt, 1993.

Kohanski, Alexander. *Martin Buber's Philosophy of Interhuman Relation*. East Brunswick, NJ/London/Toronto: Associated UP, 1982.

Kohlberg, Lawrence. *The Psychology of Moral Development*. Vol. 2. *Essays on Moral Development*. New York: Harper & Row, 1984.

Kohlhammer, Siegfried. "Anathema. Der Holocaust und das Bilderverbot." *Merkur* 48.6 (1994): 501–9.

Koonz, Claudia. *Mothers in the Fatherland: Women, the Family and Nazi Politics*. New York: St. Martin's Press, 1987.

Korte, Hermann. *Geschichte der deutschen Lyrik seit 1945*. Stuttgart: J. B. Metzler, 1989.

Krieg, Matthias. *Schmetterlingsweisheit: Die Todesbilder der Nelly Sachs*. Berlin: Selbstverlag Institut Kirche und Judentum, 1983.

Kristeva, Julia. *Desire in Language*. Trans. Thomas Gora, Alice Jardine, and Leon S. Roudiez. New York: Columbia UP, 1980.

———. "Women's Time." Trans. Alice Jardine and Harry Blake. *Signs* 7.1 (1981): 13–35.

———. *Revolution in Poetic Language*. Trans. Leon S. Roudiez. New York: Columbia UP, 1984.

———. *In the Beginning Was Love: Psychoanalysis and Faith*. Trans. Arthur Goldhammer. New York: Columbia UP, 1987.

———. *Tales of Love*. Trans. Leon S. Roudiez. New York: Columbia UP, 1987.

———. *Strangers to Ourselves*. Trans. Leon S. Roudiez. New York: Columbia UP, 1991.

———. *Nations without Nationalism*. Trans. Leon Roudiez. New York: Columbia UP, 1993.

Kurz, Paul Konrad. *Über moderne Literatur*. Frankfurt am Main: Josef Knecht, 1967.

———. "Ortlos — im Wort: Rose Ausländers Gedichtband 'Mein Atem heißt jetzt'." *Süddeutsche Zeitung*, 25–27 December 1981, 68.

LaCapra, Dominick. *Representing the Holocaust: History, Theory, Trauma*. Ithaca/London: Cornell UP, 1994.

———. *History and Memory after Auschwitz*. Ithaca/London: Cornell UP, 1998.

Lagercrantz, Olof. Trans. Helene Ritzerfeld. *Versuch über die Lyrik der Nelly Sachs*. Frankfurt am Main: Suhrkamp, 1967.

Lang, Berel. *Act and Idea in the Nazi Genocide.* Chicago: U of Chicago P, 1990.

———, ed. *Writing and the Holocaust.* New York/London: Holmes & Meier, 1988.

Langer, Lawrence L. *The Holocaust and the Literary Imagination.* London/New Haven: Yale UP, 1975.

———. "Nelly Sachs." *Colloquia Germanica* 10 (1976/77): 316–25.

———. *Versions of Survival: The Holocaust and the Human Spirit.* Albany, NY: State U of New York P, 1982.

———. *Holocaust Testimonies.* New Haven: Yale UP, 1991.

Lasker-Schüler, Else. *Sämtliche Gedichte.* Munich: Kösel Verlag, 1984. [All rights held by Suhrkamp Verlag, Frankfurt/M.]

de Lauretis, Teresa. *Technologies of Gender.* Bloomington/Indianapolis: Indiana UP, 1987.

Lermen, Birgit and Michael Braun. *Nelly Sachs 'an letzter Atemspitze des Lebens.'* Bonn: Bouvier Verlag, 1998.

Levi, Primo. *The Drowned and the Saved.* Trans. Raymond Rosenthal. London: Abacus, 1989.

Levinas, Emmanuel. *Totality and Infinity.* Trans. Alphonso Lingis. Pittsburgh: Duquesne UP, 1969.

———. "The Trace of the Other." In *Deconstruction in Context,* ed. Mark C. Taylor. 345–59. Chicago: U of Chicago P, 1986.

———. *Time and the Other.* Trans. Richard A. Cohen. Pittsburgh: Duquesne UP, 1987.

———. *Difficult Freedom: Essays in Judaism.* Baltimore: The Johns Hopkins UP, 1990.

Lorenz, Dagmar C. G. *Verfolgung bis zum Massenmord: Holocaust Diskurse in deutscher Sprache.* New York: Peter Lang, 1992.

———. *Keepers of the Motherland: German Texts by Jewish Women Writers.* Lincoln, NE/London: U of Nebraska P, 1997.

Lurker, Manfred, ed. *Wörterbuch der Symbolik.* Stuttgart: Kröner Verlag, 1988.

Macciocchi, Maria-Antonietta. "Female Sexuality in Fascist Ideology." *Feminist Review* 1 (1979): 67–82.

Maier, Charles S. *The Unmasterable Past: History, Holocaust, and German National Identity.* Cambridge, MA: Harvard UP, 1988.

———. "A Surfeit of Memory? Reflections on History, Melancholy and Denial." *History & Memory* 5.2 (1993): 136–52.

Man, Paul de. *Blindness and Insight*. Minneapolis: U of Minnesota P, 1983.

Margetts, John. "Nelly Sachs and 'Die haargenaue Aufgabe'. Observations on the Poem Cycle *Fahrt ins Staublose*." *Modern Language Review* 73 (1978): 550–62.

Martin, Biddy and Chandra Mohanty. "Feminist Politics: What's Home Got to Do with It?" In *Feminist Studies / Critical Studies*, ed. Teresa de Lauretis. 191–212. Bloomington: Indiana UP, 1986.

Martin, Elaine, ed. *Gender, Patriarchy and Fascism in the Third Reich*. Detroit: Wayne State UP, 1993.

McClain, William. "The Imaging of Transformation in Nelly Sachs's Holocaust Poems." *The Hebrew University Studies in Literature* 8.2 (1980): 281–300.

Mendes-Flohr, Paul R. *From Mysticism to Dialogue: Martin Buber's Transformation of German Social Thought*. Detroit: Wayne State UP, 1989.

Michel, Peter. "Mystische und literarische Quellen in der Dichtung von Nelly Sachs." Ph.D. diss., Freiburg im Breisgau, 1981.

Michnik, Adam. Interview with Jürgen Habermas, *Die Zeit*, Overseas Ed. 24 December 1993: 8.

Miller, Judith. *One, by One, by One: Facing the Holocaust*. New York: Simon & Schuster, 1990.

Miller, Nancy, ed. *The Poetics of Gender*. New York: Columbia UP, 1986.

Mintz, Alan. *Hurban: Responses to Catastrophe in Hebrew Literature*. New York: Columbia UP, 1984.

Mitscherlich, Alexander and Margarete Mitscherlich. *Die Unfähigkeit zu trauern*. Munich: Piper, 1967.

Mitscherlich, Margarete. *Erinnerungsarbeit: Zur Psychoanalyse der Unfähigkeit zu trauern*. Frankfurt am Main: Fischer, 1987.

Moi, Toril, ed. *The Kristeva Reader*. New York: Columbia UP, 1986.

Monaghan, Patricia. *The Book of Goddesses & Heroines*. St. Paul, MN: Llewellyn Publications, 1990.

Montefiore, Jan. *Feminism and Poetry*. New York: Pandora, 1987.

Morgan, Michael L. "Overcoming the Remoteness of the Past: Memory and Historiography in Modern Jewish Thought," *Judaism* 38.2 (1989): 160–73.

Morson, Gary Saul. *Narrative and Freedom: The Shadows of Time*. New Haven/London: Yale UP, 1994.

Mosler, Peter, ed. *Schreiben nach Auschwitz*. Cologne: Bund-Verlag, 1989.

Murdoch, Brian. "Transformations of the Holocaust: Auschwitz in Modern Lyric Poetry." *Comparative Literature Studies* 11.2 (1974): 123–50.

Neher, André. *The Exile of the Word: From the Silence of the Bible to the Silence of Auschwitz*. Trans. David Maisel. Philadelphia: Jewish Publication Society of America, 1981.

———. *They Made Their Souls Anew*. Trans. David Maisel. Albany: State U of New York P, 1990.

Nelly Sachs zu Ehren. Frankfurt am Main: Suhrkamp, 1961.

Nelly Sachs zu Ehren: Zum 75. Geburtstag am 10. Dezember 1966. Frankfurt am Main: Suhrkamp, 1966.

Nelson, Cary. *Repression and Recovery: Modern American Poetry and the Politics of Cultural Memory. 1910–1945*. Madison: U of Wisconsin P, 1989.

Neumann, Erich. *Die Große Mutter: Der Archetyp des großen Weiblichen*. 1956. Olten/ Freiburg im Breisgau: Walter-Verlag, 1989.

Nietzsche, Friedrich. *Zur Genealogie der Moral*. In *Sämtliche Werke. Kritische Studienausgabe*, vol. 5, edited by Giorgio Colli and Mazzino Montinari. 245–412. Munich: Deutsche Taschenbuch Verlag; Berlin/New York: Walter de Gruyter, 1980.

Nora, Pierre. *Zwischen Geschichte und Gedächtnis*. Trans. Wolfgang Kaiser. Berlin: Klaus Wagenbach, 1990.

O'Brien, Mary. "Periods." In *Taking Our Time: Feminist Perspectives on Temporality*, edited by Frieda J. Forman and Caoran Sowton. 11–18. Oxford/New York: Pergamon Press, 1989.

Oliver, Kelly. *Reading Kristeva: Unraveling the Double-bind*. Bloomington: Indiana UP, 1993.

———, ed. *Ethics, Politics, and Difference in Julia Kristeva's Writing*. New York/London: Routledge, 1993.

Olschner, Leonard. "Der mühsame Weg von Nelly Sachs' Poesie ins literarische Bewußtsein." In *Die Resonanz des Exils: Gelungene und mißlungene Rezeption deutschsprachiger Exilautoren*, edited by Dieter Sevin. 267–85. Amsterdam/ Atlanta, GA: Rodopi, 1992.

Ofer, Dalia and Lenore J. Weitzman, eds. *Women in the Holocaust*. New Haven, CT/London: Yale UP, 1998.

Olden, Christine. "Notes on the Development of Empathy." *Psychoanalytic Study of the Child* 13 (1958): 505–18.

Ostmeier, Dorothee. *Sprache des Dramas — Drama der Sprache. Zur Poetik der Nelly Sachs*. Tübingen: Niemeyer, 1997.

Ostriker, Alicia. *Stealing the Language: The Emergence of Women's Poetry in America*. Boston: Beacon Press, 1986.

———. *Feminist Revision and the Bible*. Cambridge, MA: Blackwell, 1993.

Owings, Alison. *Frauen: German Women Recall the Third Reich*. Rutgers, NJ: Rutgers UP, 1993.

Ozick, Cynthia. *Metaphor and Memory: Essays*. New York: Knopf, 1989.

Patai, Raphael. *The Hebrew Goddess*. Detroit: Wayne State UP, 1990.

Patterson, David. *The Shriek of Silence: A Phenomenology of the Holocaust Novel*. Lexington, KY: UP of Kentucky, 1992.

Peperzak, Adriaan. *To the Other: An Introduction to the Philosophy of Emmanuel Levinas*. West Lafayette, IN: Purdue UP, 1993.

Perloff, Marjorie. *Poetic License: Essays on Modernist and Postmodernist Lyric*. Evanston, IL: Northwestern UP, 1990.

Plaskow, Judith. *Standing again at Sinai: Judaism from a Feminist Perspective*. San Francisco/New York: Harper & Row, 1990.

Raddatz, Fritz. "Welt als biblische Saat: Nelly Sachs." In *Verwerfungen: Sechs literarische Essays*. Frankfurt am Main: Suhrkamp, 1972.

Rapaport, Lynn. *Jews in Germany after the Holocaust: Memory, Identity and Jewish-German Relations*. Cambridge/New York: Cambridge UP, 1997.

Rey, William. "'. . . welch großer Empfang. . . .' Zum Tode der Dichterin Nelly Sachs." *The Germanic Review* 45 (1970): 273–88.

———. *Poesie der Antipoesie: Moderne deutsche Lyrik*. Heidelberg: Stiehm, 1978.

Rich, Adrienne. *Of Woman Born: Motherhood as Experience and Institution*. New York/London: W. W. Norton & Co., 1986.

———. "Defy the Space That Separates." *The Nation*, 7 October 1996, 30–34.

Richter-Schröder, Karin. *Frauenliteratur und weibliche Identität: Theoretische Ansätze zu einer weiblichen Ästhetik und zur Entwicklung der neuen deutschen Frauenliteratur*. Frankfurt am Main: Athenäum, 1986.

Ricoeur, Paul. *Oneself as Another*. Trans. Kathleen Blamey. Chicago/London: U of Chicago P, 1992.

Riley, Denise. *"Am I That Name?" Feminism and the Category of "Women" in History*. Minneapolis: U of Minnesota P, 1988.

Rittner, Carol and John K. Roth, eds. *Different Voices: Women and the Holocaust*. New York: Paragon House, 1993.

Roiphe, Anne. *A Season for Healing: Reflections on the Holocaust*. New York/London: Summit Books, 1988.

Rosen, Norma. *Accidents of Influence: Writing as a Woman and a Jew in America*. Albany: State U of New York P, 1992.

Rosenbaum, Irving. *The Holocaust and the Halakhah*. New York: Ktav, 1976.

Rosenfeld, Alvin. "The Poetry of Nelly Sachs." *Judaism* 20.3 (1971): 356–64.

———. "Poetics of Expiration: Reflections on Holocaust Poetry." *The American Poetry Review* 7.6 (1978): 39–42.

———. *A Double Dying: Reflections on Holocaust Literature.* Bloomington, IN: Indiana UP, 1980.

Rosenthal, Bianca. "'Der unsichtbare Chor.' Entwurf eines Grundrisses des deutschen Schrifttums in der Bukowina." *Germanic Notes* 22, nos. 1/2 (1991): 16–20.

Rosenzweig, Franz. *The Star of Redemption.* Trans. William W. Hallo. 1964. Boston: Beacon Press, 1972.

Roskies, David G. *Against the Apocalypse: Responses to Catastrophe in Modern Jewish Culture.* Cambridge, MA /London: Harvard UP, 1984.

Rubenstein, Richard. *After Auschwitz: Radical Theology and Contemporary Judaism.* Indianapolis/New York/Kansas City: Bobbs-Merrill, 1966.

Rudnick, Ursula. *Post-Shoa Religious Metaphors: The Image of God in the Poetry of Nelly Sachs.* Frankfurt am Main: Peter Lang, 1995.

Ryan, Judith. "Nelly Sachs." In *Die Deutsche Lyrik 1945–1975: Zwischen Botschaft und Spiel,* ed. Klaus Weissenberger. 110–18. Düsseldorf: August Bagel Verlag, 1981.

Sager, Peter. "Die Lyrikerin Nelly Sachs." *Neue deutsche Hefte* 17.4 (1970): 26–45.

Said, Edward. "Reflections on Exile." *GRANTA* 13 (1984): 157–172.

Santner, Eric L. *Stranded Objects: Mourning, Memory, and Postwar Germany.* Ithaca/London: Cornell UP, 1990.

Schallück, Paul. "Nelly Sachs." *Emuna* 2.1 (1967): 36–43.

Schlenstedt, Silvia. "Bilder neuer Welten." In *Frauen-Literatur-Geschichte,* edited by Hiltrud Gnüg and Renate Möhrmann. 300–317. 1985. Stuttgart: Suhrkamp, 1989.

Schlösser, Manfred. "Deutsch-jüdische Dichtung des Exils." *Emuna* 3.4 (1968): 250–65.

Scholem, Gershom. "Zur Entwicklungsgeschichte der kabbalistischen Konzeption der Schechinah." *Eranos-Jahrbuch* 21 (1952): 45–107.

———. *Major Trends in Jewish Mysticism.* 1941. New York: Schocken Books, 1954.

———. *On the Kabbalah and Its Symbolism.* Trans. Ralph Manheim. 1965. New York: Schocken Books, 1969.

———. "Juden und Deutsche." In *Judaica II,* ed. Gershom Scholem. 20–46. Frankfurt am Main: Suhrkamp, 1970.

————. *The Messianic Idea in Judaism and Other Essays on Jewish Spirituality.* New York: Schocken Books, 1971.

————. *Kabbalah.* Jerusalem: Keter, 1974.

————. "Alchemie und Kabbala." In *Judaica IV*, ed. Rolf Tiedemann. 19–128. Frankfurt am Main: Suhrkamp, 1984.

————. *Origins of the Kabbalah.* Princeton: Princeton UP, 1987.

————, ed. *Zohar: The Book of Splendor.* New York: Schocken Books, 1949.

Schwartz, Regina M. *The Curse of Cain: The Violent Legacy of Monotheism.* Chicago/London: U of Chicago P, 1997.

Schwedhelm, Karl. "Nelly Sachs." In *Der Friede und die Unruhestifter*, ed. Hans Jürgen Schultz. 166–180. Frankfurt am Main: Suhrkamp, 1973.

————. "Auschwitz und Kanaan: Die Dichtung der Nelly Sachs." In *Figur und Zeichen: Essays aus dem Nachlass.* 75–103. Aachen: Rimbaud, 1993.

Schweik, Susan. *A Gulf So Deeply Cut: American Women Poets and the Second World War.* Madison/London: U of Wisconsin P, 1991.

Shreiber, Maeera. "The End of Exile: Jewish Identity and Its Diasporic Poetics," *PMLA* 113.2 (1998): 273–87.

Silbermann, Edith. "Rose Ausländer — die Sappho der östlicher Landschaft. Zum Tode der Dichterin." *Südostdeutsche Vierteljahresblätter* 37.1 (1988): 9–25.

Silverman, Kaja. *The Subject of Semiotics.* New York: Oxford UP, 1983.

Simon, Lili. "Nelly Sachs." *Deutsche Dichter der Gegenwart: Ihr Leben und Werk*, ed. Benno von Wiese. 33–45. Berlin: Erich Schmidt Verlag, 1973.

————. "Nelly Sachs: Dichterin der großen Trauer." *Neue deutsche Hefte* 35.4 (1988): 687–704.

Sowa-Bettecken, Beate. *Sprache der Hinterlassenschaft: Jüdisch-christliche Überlieferung in der Lyrik von Nelly Sachs und Paul Celan.* Frankfurt am Main: Peter Lang, 1992.

Spinoza, Benedict de. *On the Improvement of the Understanding. The Ethics. Correspondence.* Trans. R. H. M. Lewis. 1883. New York: Dover, 1955.

Staiger, Emil. *Basic Concepts of Poetics.* Trans. Janette Hudson and Luanne T. Frank. 1946. University Park: The Pennsylvania State UP, 1991.

Stanton, Domna. "Difference on Trial: A Critique of the Maternal Metaphor in Cixous, Irigaray, and Kristeva." In *The Poetics of Gender*, ed. Nancy K. Miller. 157–82. New York: Columbia UP, 1986.

Steiner, George. *Language and Silence.* New York: Atheneum, 1967.

Stiehm, Jamie. "Only Academic? Community and Communitarians." *The Nation*, 18 July 1994, 87–89.

Strauss, Herbert, W. Bergmann, and C. Hoffmann, eds. *Der Anti-Semitismus der Gegenwart*. Frankfurt/New York: Campus, 1990.

Strobl, Ingrid. "Nelly Sachs." *Emma* 8 (1988): 27–31.

Suleiman, Susan. *Subversive Intent: Gender, Politics and the Avant-Garde.* Cambridge, MA/London: Harvard UP, 1990.

Syrkin, Marie. "Nelly Sachs — Poet of the Holocaust." *Midstream* 13.3 (1967): 13–23.

Tager, Michael. "Primo Levi and the Language of Witness." *Criticism* 35.2 (1993): 265–88.

Taylor, Mark, ed. *Deconstruction in Context*. Chicago: U of Chicago P, 1986.

Terdiman, Richard. *Present Past: Modernity and the Memory Crisis.* Ithaca/London: Cornell UP, 1993.

Thuswaldner, Anton. "Nelly Sachs." *Kritisches Lexikon zur deutschsprachigen Gegenwartsliteratur*. Munich: text + kritik, 1984. 1–9.

Todd, Janet. *Feminist Literary History: A Defense*. Cambridge: Polity Press, 1988.

Traverso, Enzo. *The Jews & Germany: From the 'Judeo-German Symbiosis' to the Memory of Auschwitz*. Lincoln/London: U of Nebraska P, 1995.

Tröger, Annemarie. "German Women's Memories of World War II." *Behind the Lines: Gender and the Two World Wars*, edited by Margaret Higonnet, et. al. 285–99. New Haven: Yale UP, 1987.

Tronto, Joan C. *Moral Boundaries: A Political Argument for an Ethic of Care*. New York/London: Routledge, 1993.

Turczynski, Emanuel. *Geschichte der Bukowina in der Neuzeit: Zur Sozial- und Kulturgeschichte einer mitteleuropäisch geprägten Landschaft*. Wiesbaden: Harrassowitz, 1993.

Unterman, Alan. *Dictionary of Jewish Lore and Legend*. London: Thames and Hudson, 1991.

Vaerst, Christa. *Dichtung- und Sprachreflexion im Werk von Nelly Sachs*. Frankfurt am Main: Peter Lang, 1977.

Vidal-Naquet, Pierre. *Assassins of Memory: Essays on the Denial of the Holocaust*. Trans. Jeffrey Mehlmann. New York: Columbia UP, 1992.

Vogel, Harald and Michael Gans. *Rose Ausländer, Hilde Domin. Gedichtinterpretationen*. Baltmannsweiler: Schneider Verlag, 1997.

Vries, S. Ph de. *Jüdische Riten und Symbole*. 1981. Reinbek bei Hamburg: Rowohlt, 1990.

Wallmann, Jürgen. "Deutsche Lyrik unter jüdischem Dreigestirn." *Merkur* 12.225 (1966): 1191–94.

————. "'Ein denkendes Herz, das singt.' Materialien zu Leben und Werk Rose Ausländers." In *Gesammelte Gedichte*, by Rose Ausländer, edited by Hugo Käufer and Berndt Mosblech. 519–47. Cologne: Braun, 1978.

————. "Ich will wohnen im Menschenwort. Die Lyrik von Rose Ausländer." *Literatur und Kritik* 142 (1980): 73–78.

————. "Rose Ausländer." In *Neue Literatur der Frauen*, ed. Heinz Puknus. 25–28. Munich: C. H. Beck, 1980.

————. "The Poetess Rose Ausländer: Her Work and Significance." *Universitas* 22.3 (1980): 195–202.

————. "Mein Atem heißt jetzt. Ein Gespräch mit Rose Ausländer." *Literatur und Kritik* 157/158 (1981): 474–76.

Waugh, Patricia. *Feminine Fictions: Revisiting the Modern*. New York: Routledge, 1989.

Weil, Simone. *Gravity and Grace*. Trans. Arthur Wills. 1952. Lincoln: U of Nebraska P, 1997.

Weissenberger, Klaus. *Zwischen Stein und Stern: Mystische Formgebung in der Dichtung von Else Lasker-Schüler, Nelly Sachs und Paul Celan*. Bern/Munich: Francke Verlag, 1976.

Wenzel, Wolfgang. "Jüdische Tradition in Rose Ausländers lyrischem Werk." Abschlussarbeit für das Lehramt, Universität des Saarlandes, 1986. Unpublished manuscript, Rose-Ausländer-Dokumentationszentrum, Cologne, Germany.

Werner-Birkenbach, Sabine. "'Durch Zeitgeräusch wandern von Stimme zu Stimme. . . .': Die Lyrikerin Rose Ausländer." *German Life and Letters* 45.4 (1992): 345–57.

West, William. "The Poetics of Inadequacy: Nelly Sachs and the Resurrection of the Dead." In *Jewish Writers, German Literature: The Uneasy Examples of Nelly Sachs and Walter Benjamin*, edited by Timothy Bahti and Marilyn Sibley Fries. 77–104. Ann Arbor: U of Michigan P, 1995.

Weyrather, Irmgard. *Muttertag und Mutterkreuz: Der Kult um die 'deutsche Mutter' im Nationalsozialismus*. Frankfurt am Main: Fischer, 1993.

Wiggershaus, Renate. "'Es war eine unendliche Sonnenfinsternis.' Ein Porträt der Dichterin Rose Ausländer." In *Rose Ausländer: Materialien zu Leben und Werk*, ed. Helmut Braun. 93–105. Frankfurt am Main: Fischer, 1991.

Witte, Bernd. "Rose Ausländer." *Kritisches Lexikon zur deutschsprachigen Gegenwartsliteratur*. Munich: text + kritik, 1984. 1–13.

Wolf, Christa. *Kindheitsmuster*. 1976. Darmstadt: Luchterhand, 1986.

Yaeger, Patricia, and Beth Kowaleski-Wallace, eds. *Refiguring the Father: New Feminist Readings of Patriarchy*. Carbondale: U of Southern Illinois P, 1989.

Yerushalmi, Yosef Hayim. *Zakhor: Jewish History and Jewish Memory*. 1982. New York: Schocken, 1989.

Young, Gloria L. "The Moral Functioning of Remembering: American Holocaust Poetry." *Studies in American Jewish Literature* 9.1 (1990): 61–72.

Young, Iris Marion. "Impartiality and the Civic Public: Some Implications of Feminist Critiques of Moral and Political Theory." In *Feminism as Critique*, edited by Seyla Benhabib and Drucilla Cornell. 57–76. Minneapolis: U of Minnesota P, 1987.

———. *Justice and the Politics of Difference*. Princeton: Princeton UP, 1990.

———. "The Ideal of Community and the Politics of Difference." In *Feminism/Postmodernism*, ed. Linda Nicholson. 300–323. New York/London: Routledge, 1990.

Young, James E. "Versions of the Holocaust." *Modern Judaism* 3 (1983): 339–46.

———. *Writing and Rewriting the Holocaust: Narrative and the Consequences of Interpretation*. Bloomington/Indianapolis: Indiana UP, 1988.

———. *The Texture of Memory: Holocaust Memorials and Meaning*. New Haven: Yale UP, 1993.

———. "Germany's Vanishing Holocaust Monuments." *Judaism* 43.4 (1994): 412–17.

———. "Between History and Memory: The Uncanny Voices of Historian and Survivor." *Passing into History: Nazism and the Holocaust beyond Memory*, ed. Gulie Ne'eman Arad. *History & Memory* 9, nos. 1/2 (Fall 1997): 47–58.

Yuter, Alan J. *The Holocaust in Hebrew Literature*. Port Washington, N.Y.: Associated Faculty Press, 1983.

Ziarek, Ewa. "Kristeva and Levinas: Mourning, Ethics, and the Feminine." In *Ethics, Politics, and Difference in Julia Kristeva's Writing*, ed. Kelly Oliver. 62–78. New York/ London: Routledge, 1993.

Index

I.
Poems by Nelly Sachs and Rose Ausländer

(Pages on which poems are quoted in full or in substantial part are indicated in boldface type.)

II. General Index

OHIO UNIVERSITY LIBRARY

Please return this book as soon as you have finished with it. In order to avoid a fine it must be returned by the latest date stamped below. All books are subject to recall after two weeks or immediately if needed for reserve.

DEC 14

CF